Nebraska
Symposium on
Motivation
1976

*Nebraska Symposium on
Motivation, 1976,* is Volume 24
in the series on
CURRENT THEORY AND
RESEARCH IN MOTIVATION

University of Nebraska Press
Lincoln/London 1977

Nebraska Symposium on Motivation 1976

Personal Construct Psychology

James K. Cole	*Series Editor*
Alvin W. Landfield	*Volume Editor*
Theodore R. Sarbin	*Professor of Psychology and Criminology University of California, Santa Cruz*
James C. Mancuso	*Professor of Psychology State University of New York at Albany*
Don Bannister	*External Research Staff British Medical Research Council Bexley Hospital, England*
Joyce Agnew	*Principal Psychologist Stratheden Hospital, Scotland*
Alvin W. Landfield	*Professor of Psychology University of Nebraska – Lincoln*
Seymour Rosenberg	*Professor of Psychology Rutgers University*
Miller Mair	*Director of Psychological Services and Research Crichton Royal Hospital Dumfries, Scotland*
Han Bonarius	*Professor of Psychology University of Utrecht, The Netherlands*

Science recognizes eternal questions, but spurns eternal answers. Its challenge is not in the discovery of truth that is as dead as a known fact. The scientist is inspired by an idea of truth that is elusive, forever changing while warming his heart in affording him the conviction that his reach is coming closer and closer to his ideal, even though he knows he will never hold it fully in his grasp.

Henry Morgenau, "The New Style of Science"

Contents

Introduction

*P*rofessor George A. Kelly, an American psychologist, expressed the hope that his philosophy of constructive alternativism and his invention, the personal construct, would provide useful and creative ways of viewing the psychological natures of man. Although Kelly developed his ideas while on the faculty of the Ohio State University, they first gained acceptance in Great Britain and Europe, where numerous books and articles appeared carrying titles related to the psychology of personal constructs. Those readers who are unacquainted with Kelly's writing should read his "Brief Introduction to Personal Construct Theory," in *Perspectives in Personal Construct Theory*, edited by Don Bannister (London: Academic Press, 1970).[1]

In the United States, where behaviorism and trait psychology were solidly entrenched in the universities, interest in personal constructs grew more slowly. Nevertheless, Kelly's ideas have attracted sufficient attention in this country as well as abroad to justify an intensive consideration of the theory. Using the Nebraska Symposium on Motivation as a vehicle for this analysis, seven speakers read papers and participated, with nine invited discussion leaders, in small group sessions following each lecture. Although the seven lectures fill most of the pages of this volume, a brief Addendum encompasses several interesting themes and questions which emerged from the discussion groups.

In his opening lecture, Dr. Theodore Sarbin provided a keynote for the symposium with his discussion of the academic ecology of personal construct theory and of contextualism as a world view for modern psychology. Dr. James Mancuso continued the emphasis on contextualism and provided insights into personal construct themes which appear in research by authors who do not reference Kelly. Dr. Don Bannister, in collaboration with Joyce Agnew, shared research

1. Professor Kelly's basic works are *The Psychology of Personal Constructs* (New York: Norton, 1955), 2 vols., and *Clinical Psychology and Personality: The Selected Papers of George Kelly*, edited by Brendan Maher (New York: Wiley, 1969). A paperback entitled *A Theory of Personality* (New York: Norton, 1963) encompasses the first three chapters of his initial publication.

on the child's conception of selfhood. His observation that self may be articulated by experiences of isolation struck an empathic chord with his audience. Dr. Alvin Landfield first introduced Mrs. George A. Kelly and then discussed his research with the Interpersonal Transaction Group with Rotating Dyads. He also took a step beyond cognitive complexity by presenting a new measurement of construct ordination. Dr. Seymour Rosenberg presented his latest work on implicit personality theory and related it to personal constructs. His work highlighted both structural and content aspects of individual subjects. Dr. Miller Mair stressed the pervasiveness of the metaphor in science and in everyday life. In this context, he clearly described the metaphoric quality of Kelly's "man-the-scientist" and pointed to the central importance of Kelly's philosophy of constructive alternativism. In the final lecture, Dr. Han Bonarius reviewed his studies of meaningfulness and provided insights into how one might approach human beings within his Interaction Model.

The small group discussions which followed these lectures were chaired by the speakers and group leaders. Group leaders included: Dr. Fay Fransella, University of London; Dr. Franz Epting, University of Florida; Dr. Joseph Doster, University of Georgia; Dr. Finn Tschudi, University of Oslo; Dr. Duane Varble, University of Nevada; Dr. Carlton Paine, Lincoln-Lancaster Mental Health Center; Dr. Walter Danforth, University of Arkansas; Dr. John Carr, University of Washington; and Dr. Michaela Lifshitz, University of Haifa.

Although the formal structure for the conference was the Nebraska Symposium on Motivation, the consensus of the participants suggests an equally important designation for this meeting: the First International Conference of Personal Construct Theorists and Researchers.

On behalf of the Department of Psychology, I wish to express appreciation to the administration of the University of Nebraska and to the National Institute of Mental Health for supporting this symposium. Also, on behalf of the many visitors to the symposium, I wish to thank the faculty members and students of our department who so graciously extended their hospitality.

ALVIN W. LANDFIELD
Professor of Psychology

Contextualism: A World View for Modern Psychology[1]

Theodore R. Sarbin

University of California
Santa Cruz

*T*he core of this symposium is the late George Kelly's theory of personality as represented in *The Psychology of Personal Constructs* (1955). In my preparation for the symposium, I entertained and subsequently rejected the suggestion that I provide an exegesis of personal constructs. I rejected the idea mainly because the other participants are better qualified for this task. I was also influenced by the lesson of the story entitled *All About Penguins*.

> An English gentleman called his bookseller and asked him if he had any books about penguins. The bookseller had no such books in stock and offered to obtain one. In due course the gentleman received in the post a book of 1231 pages entitled *All About Penguins* and he set out to learn about penguins. At a chance meeting a couple of months later, the bookseller asked the gentleman if the book had been satisfactory. He replied: "Yes it was satisfactory—but frankly, it was more than I wanted to know about penguins."

My paper is addressed, instead, to an analysis of Kelly's contribution in the light of the recent history and present status of the psychology of personality.

INTRODUCTION: THE ROOT-METAPHOR METHOD

The focus of interest is in that subdiscipline of psychology that is subsumed under the label personality, sometimes rendered as personology. I shall review the status of the psychology of

1. The notes for this paper were originally prepared during my tenure as a visiting fellow of the Center for the Humanities, Wesleyan University, Spring, 1975.

personality at the time that George Kelly was developing the ideas that ultimately found their way into his magnum opus.

To make the review more than a sterile compilation of names and dates, I shall attempt to fit the concurrent conceptions of personality into a conceptual framework. I shall employ the root-metaphor theory of Stephen Pepper (1942). This framework will be helpful in illuminating the prevailing theoretical landscape at the time of Kelly's thinking and writing. Then I shall offer some cautious speculations on the probable origins of Kelly's constructions. (To anticipate somewhat, I shall propose that Kelly made a valiant but not entirely successful attempt to break away from the implications of the root metaphor of the machine by adopting a model that emphasized context.) I hope to demonstrate that contextualism is a more fruitful world view for students of the human condition, including personality psychologists. The final sections of the paper will explicate the contextualist world view with illustrative analyses from selected areas of study.

The framework is drawn from a contribution to the history of metaphysics, the late Stephen Pepper's seminal work, *World Hypotheses*. Published in 1942, it has gone through many printings and has already achieved the status of a classic. Pepper employed a method of analysis called the root-metaphor method. In brief, he allocated the world views of philosophers to one of six classes: animism, mysticism, formism, mechanism, contextualism, and organicism. (The first two, animism and mysticism, he rejected as not having sufficient scope or communicable categories.) Each of the classes of world hypotheses is derived from a basic or root metaphor. The root metaphor operates to provide a frame for the analysis and understanding of occurrences in the natural and man-made worlds. The frame constrains the kinds of philosophical or scientific models to be applied either to the task of observation and experiment or to the hermeneutic task. The categories of analysis and the kinds of questions to be asked are similarly constrained by the choice of root metaphor.

Root metaphors reflect a common achievement of human beings: metaphor making. When a person is faced with an occurrence for which he has no ready-made category or class, the occurrence remains uninstantiated (unclassified, unassimilated, unidentified) until a class, category, or dimension is located. The recognition of similarity on some dimension (construct) provides the basis for analogy, and if linguistic translation is necessary, the partial similarity is expressed as metaphor. To say that the ruler of a state is a puppet of one of the superpowers communicates the analogy of political power. Once the metaphor is expressed by a speaker and decoded by a listener, the world of puppetry provides auxiliary metaphors, such as pulling strings, manipulating characters, the puppet stage, the script writer, and so on. Freud, as we all know, was a prolific metaphor maker. One of his analogies, that the human mind is like a hydraulic system, has enriched our vocabulary with such terms as *repression* and *tension-discharge* and has given a kind of scientific legitimacy to many of the presenting complaints recorded in psychological clinic files, such as "I feel like I'm about to burst with overwhelming anxiety," "If I don't get relief from this tension, I'll blow my stack," "My repressed anger is discharged in migraine headaches."

One feature of our facility in metaphor making needs special emphasis. As long as the metaphor is marked by clear context, emphasis, or the use of auxiliary modifiers, such as in the sentence "it is *as if* the psyche is a municipal water system," the interpreter of the human condition is free to create and use other metaphors. He may notice similarities between the occurrence of interest and familiar events other than those that supplied the vehicle for the initial metaphor. For example, the psyche (itself a metaphor-turned-myth) is a many-layered geological system; a tree with roots, trunk, and branches; a multistranded rope; a glazed pot; a computer; and so on.

For reasons that can be identified (Chun & Sarbin, 1971; Sarbin, 1968a), once a metaphor has done its job of making sense of an occurrence, the metaphoric quality tends to become submerged. In time, the metaphor takes on the characteristics of an entity, it becomes literalized, reified. One description of the reification of metaphor is provided by C. S. Lewis (1939):

> On the one hand, there is the metaphor we invent to teach by, on the other, the metaphor from which we learn. They might be called the 'master's metaphor' and the 'pupil's metaphor.' The first is freely chosen. It is one among many possible modes of expression, it does not at all hinder, and slightly helps, the thought of its maker. The second is not chosen at all; it is the unique expression of a meaning that we cannot have on any

other terms; it dominates completely the thought of the recipient; his truth cannot rise above the truth of the original metaphor.

When a curious man or woman turns attention to cosmological questions, such as What is the substance of the world? or What is the essence of creation? or What is humankind? he has no choice but to construct or invent a metaphor. In so doing he employs a master's metaphor and at the same time is on the way to a cosmological theory.

Anthropological and historical sources make clear that human beings create problems for themselves by asking cosmological questions. Pepper tells the story of Thales, the Milesian philosopher of the sixth century B.C., who puzzled about the nature of the world. He was not satisfied with current mythological explanations. He made note of a "common-sense fact," water. As a resident of a maritime city, he was bombarded with the importance of water and entertained the hypothesis that water was the key to unlocking the secrets of all objects and events. After all, water covers large areas of the known world, it has multiple forms such as mist, clouds, fog, and rain. It evaporates and condenses. Water is necessary to sustain life and its absence is equivalent to death.

Thales provided the master's metaphor. It was picked up and further developed by a series of pupils—water remaining the core of the pupillary metaphor. Pepper (1942) points out that the successor to Thales, Anaximander, regarded as incomplete the postulate "All things are water." "The substance of all things, metaphysical water, was not after all common water" (p. 92). The substance of all things was not only water, as usually perceived, but also all the phases, qualities, and *forms* of water.

The master's metaphor "The world is water" becomes the basis for a world view, a world hypothesis, a metaphysical system. Pepper employed *root metaphor* as a term to mark the master's metaphors for world views. Pepper summarizes the root-metaphor method as follows:

A man desiring to understand the world looks about for a clue to its comprehension. He pitches upon some area of common sense fact and tries to understand other areas in terms of this one. This original area becomes his basic analogy or root metaphor. He describes as best he can the characteristics of this area, or, if you will, discriminates its structure. A list of its structural characteristics [categories] becomes his basic concepts of explanation and description. . . . In terms of these categories he proceeds to study all other areas of fact. . . . He undertakes to interpret all facts in terms of these categories. As a result of the impact of these other facts upon his categories, he may qualify and readjust . . . them so that a set of categories commonly changes and develops [over time]. [P. 91]

The following is a brief abstract of the four root metaphors identified as relatively adequate by Pepper.

Formism is the term applied to views that stress the organization of the world on the basis of similarities and differences among entities. The formist concentrates on describing events by classifying. This world view is associated with Plato, Aristotle, and the Scholastics, among others.

The common-sense root metaphor of formism is derived from two sources: the activities of the artisan in fashioning different things on the same plan, such as a baker baking loaves of bread or a chandler making candles, and the observation of natural objects whose appearance follows the same plan, such as redwood trees, poodle dogs, ears of corn. Take a dozen loaves of bread. The baker has an ideal form or plan for the loaves. The plan is the implicit norm which the baker employs to shape each loaf. The norm may never be precisely fulfilled—but the loaves come out recognizably similar. The similarity is accounted for by the identity of plan. It is important to note that the norm is not fully revealed in the loaves, but transcends them. Norms exist in nature.

Exemplars of psychological theories flowing from the formist root metaphor are the turn-of-the-century structuralists and contemporary personality trait theorists. The first posited structures or dimensions of the mind; the second, structures or dimensions of the personality. I am indebted to White (1972) for pointing out the connection of the formist root metaphor to the underlying structure of the *idiographic* method. Gordon Allport (1937) gave currency to the term in his argument that the idiographic method provided a more valid portrait of the individual than the nomothetic method. Allport leaned on the historiographer Windelband (1921), who argued that the nomothetic, or rule-seeking, method was the appropriate method for *Naturwissenschaften*, the idiographic, or descriptive, method for *Geisteswissenschaften*, such as history and biography. In the following pages, I use formism and idiography interchangeably.

Mechanism is the dominant world view in modern western civilization. The root metaphor is the machine. The kind of machine used as the underlying image may be a simple lever, a clock, a dynamo, a computer. Mechanism is the name given by some to a world view associated with such figures as Democritus, Lucretius, Galileo, Descartes, Berkeley, and Hume. The mechanist world view regards events in nature in terms of the transmittal of forces; modern science has been dominated by this world view, a view that supports the scientist's endless quest for causes. Cause and effect, sometimes rendered as antecedent and consequent or efficient causality, is the stock in trade of the scientist working one or another paradigm within the world view of mechanism. Behaviorism in its many forms exemplifies the commitment to the mechanistic world view.

Contextualism, according to Pepper, might as easily be termed pragmatism. The world view is connected to the writings of C. S. Pierce, William James, John Dewey, and G. H. Mead. While formism and mechanism are analytic types of theories, contextualism is a synthetic type. The root metaphor for contextualism is the historical event. Not necessarily an event in the past, the event is alive and in the present. In this sense, history is an attempt to re-present events, to bring them to life again. The historic event, the event in actuality, is the dynamic dramatic act.

One would run the least risk of being misunderstood if one spoke only with present participles to illustrate the root metaphor of contextualism. Reference may be made to incidents in the plot of a drama or a novel—*persuading* a crowd, *solving* a mystery, *performing* a role, or *diagnosing* a disease.

Contextualism at first appears chaotic to those who have been schooled to use the idiographic or the mechanist world views. The categorical statements of contextualism assert *change* and *novelty*. Events are in constant flux; the very integration of the conditions of an event will alter the context of a future event which appears to have a similarity to a preceding event. The texture of an event, argues the contextualist, can be understood by noting the integration of the conditions of the event within the context of the event.

Piaget's theories of psychological functioning illustrate the use of a contextualist paradigm. Piaget (1954) has constructed category statements which attempt to define the cognitive activity of the person. These statements embody a conception of persistent change. In describing a psychological event, Piaget expounds a basic principle that any incorporation of the stimulus situation into a person's cognitive structures implies adjustments (accommodations). These adjustments alter the conditions that enter the context of seemingly similar future events.

Organicism is often referred to as absolute or objective idealism. It is associated with Hegel, Bradley, and Royce, among other philosophers. Organicism views the world as an organism rather than a machine. The philosopher or psychologist committed to organicism is concerned with understanding parts within wholes. The familiar cliché "The whole is greater than the sum of its parts" is an organistic notion. To the organicist, every actual event is a more or less concealed organic process. Organicism directs us to engage in careful examination of an event in order to determine its organic structure—that is, in noting step-by-step growth and in recognizing the ultimately achieved organic structure. There is an ideal structure to be attained somewhere at the end of the progressive steps or stages.

Exemplars of this view among recent and contemporary psychologists would include Maslow (self-actualization), Rogers (personal growth), K. Goldstein (the organism), and developmental psychologists who depend on the notion of stages of maturation.

Clearly, this has been a very rough sketch. In the analysis to follow, I shall make little use of the last-named world view. Although the root metaphor of the organism has not been completely neglected, its categories have been less widely used by personality psychologists than the categories of the other three world views.[2]

GEORGE A. KELLY AND THE PSYCHOLOGY OF PERSONALITY AT MID-CENTURY

With this sketch as a background, let us look at George Kelly's personal construct theory. My original intention was to write an analysis of the ideological premises underlying Kelly's theory of

2. J. D. Laird and M. Bethel (1974) of Clark University have constructed a personality assessment scale based on Pepper's four relatively adequate metaphysical systems. Individuals are given scores in terms of their preferences for explanations of everyday events. Preliminary data suggest that such metaphysical preferences are relatively firm. Laird and Bethel are presently investigating demographic and other correlates of world hypotheses preferences.

personality called constructive alternativism. Because he did not document the sources of his ideas, one must speculate on the basis of biographical materials. The published obituary is not very informative. I communicated with a number of Kelly's former colleagues and students and acquired not a little useful information about this very interesting man.

One informant suggested that Kelly's not identifying the source of his ideas was certainly in keeping with his own construction of personal construct theory. Every construing is de novo, as it were. If one construing is similar to another, so be it. Construals need not be sterile repetitions of past construals, one's own or others'. But Kelly did not live in a world of solipsistic cognizing. He interacted frequently with graduate students, with clients, with colleagues. The academic setting—even at Ohio State University at mid-century —was not a place where one could be quarantined from the ideas of others. Graduate students, no less than colleagues, talk about theory and research. I suggest that Kelly was influenced not only by his dissatisfaction with the state of theory in clinical and personality psychology but by the byproducts of intensive interaction with mature, industrious, bright, thoughtful graduate students, some of whom have since become leaders in contemporary psychology. The available theories of personality were either heavily weighted with psychoanalysis or with other forms of mentalism, as reflected in G. W. Allport's volume (1937) that had set out to define the field of personality.

The problems of concern for Kelly's theorizing, let us remember, fell into that area identified as *personality*. By exclusion, personality is not sensory physiology, not learning theory, not psychophysics (although these disciplines may contribute to ultimate understanding). Various terms have been used to identify the subject matter of personality, for example, the study of the whole person, the psychology of the *person* as contrasted to the *organism*, even "higher mental processes." G. W. Allport attempted to define the field as the psychology of individuality, a definition that fit ideological premises flowing from the impact of social Darwinism (Hofstadter, 1944). The contributions of Freud and others had been assimilated to the prevailing individualistic psychology of personality.

Consider Allport's influential views in terms of the root-metaphor approach. His category, neuropsychic disposition, also rendered as *trait*, under careful scrutiny, can be nothing other than a platonic form. Allport's emphasis on the idiographic method lends credibility to this conclusion. The outcomes of idiographic studies are descriptions of events in terms of a priori categories. Prediction, a category more usually contained within the world view of mechanism, is not a category derived from Plato's ideal forms. The forms are the *givens* for a theory. The trait concept in the sense employed by G. W. Allport is a formistic notion.

The psychology of personality at mid-century made no claim to analyze the mind in terms of mentalistic dimensions, say, in the manner of the turn-of-the-century introspectionists. If one had to point to a central organizing concept of personality psychologists, it was the self, represented earlier by Mead as the "I and the me" and by Freud as *"das Ich,"* unhappily translated as "the ego." The atmosphere in the 1950s was redolent with theories about the self, a category closely related to individuality.

In the final years of the 1940s, papers had begun to appear bearing what was then called the "new look" in perception. Hardly a laboratory was not involved in performing experiments that demonstrated how perception (a concept belonging to laboratory and experimental psychology, derived from mentalism and developed by the Gestalt psychologists) was influenced by more than the primary qualities of the stimulus object; the perceptual report reflected such person variables as wishes, needs, habits, emotional constraints, defensive maneuvers, and "motives." The call was loud and clear: return to person to perception and to cognition and to all psychological processes. I submit that George Kelly's thinking took place in an atmosphere that included not only the residuals of Allport's individualistic psychology, not only Freudian psychoanalysis, but reports of the new-look experiments and thoughtful theoretical analyses of such experiments by writers such as Jerome Bruner, Hadley Cantril, Muzafir Sherif, and Floyd Allport, among others.

Another possible influence was the work of G. H. Mead (1934). By the mid-1940s, when Kelly was called to Ohio State, Mead's *Mind, Self, and Society* had had wide circulation. At first, Mead's work interested only sociologists and philosophers. But the emphasis on sociality, the concept of role-taking—in fact, the whole dramaturgical perspective—was picked up by many social psychologists, among them, T. M. Newcomb, and even by the leader of the "interpersonal" theory of psychiatry, Harry Stack Sullivan. I submit that Mead's role-taking ideas, at least some of them, made their way directly or indirectly into Kelly's cognitive matrix. (I might mention parenthetically that at an earlier time, Kelly had taught dramatics.) I do not suggest unintentional plagiarism from Mead. I am committed to the belief that theories and models do not arise sui generis but have remote origins and concurrent influences.

In view of Kelly's more or less conventional training one might have anticipated a more tradition-bound approach to the problems of clinical psychology. As an undergraduate Kelly studied physics and mathematics. He worked for a year with Godfrey Thomson in England on statistical methods, and took his PhD at University of Iowa. His doctoral dissertation was a factor-analytic approach to reading and spelling disorders in children. It would be interesting to speculate why Kelly did not develop further the self psychology of Carl Rogers (Kelly had been called to Ohio State to take the position vacated by Rogers when the latter moved to the University of Chicago); or why he did not continue in the psychometric tradition employing the skills acquired under Thomson in England. Or why he rejected the models that at that time drew so much attention in the journals: the learning theories of Hull and Tolman.

Biographical material supplied by my informants, my own reading of Kelly's work, and my experience as a clinical psychologist during the same years converge to suggest that the prevailing doctrines in psychology were feebly inadequate for the practicing nonmedical clinician. Kelly had his clinical baptism in a traveling clinic in Kansas. Psychodynamic theories were hardly appropriate to an overworked and understaffed traveling clinic in rural communities. It was common sense that served such clinicians, faced with the garden varieties of clinical problems. Psychoanalytic doctrine was too demanding of time and credibility; trait theory offered no efficient method for assessing traits nor for using such assessments in the clinical intervention.

As a direct result of the funneling of tax dollars by the Veteran's Administration and the National Institutes of Health into the training of mental health professionals, universities—eager to share in the government's largesse and to serve the need of the country for trained clinicians—opened new clinical training programs or enlarged old ones. This was true for Ohio State University as well as for Harvard.

When Kelly was offered the job of professor in the prestigious clinical training program at Ohio State, he was unique in that he was an academic who had had 13 years of practical experience as a clinical psychologist. He now had the setting to refine his common-sense observations made in the course of providing services in the traveling clinic and demonstrate that clients were in principle like himself and other scientists—they tried to make sense out of their imperfect worlds by anticipating events. This simplified restatement of Kelly's basic postulate belongs in the same family of conceptions as Mead's taking-the-role-of-the-other and the distillation of the then newly developing cognitive psychology arising from the work of the "new look" people. Allport's central formistic concept, "trait," was not helpful to Kelly. The insistence on individuality, as expounded by Allport, continued as a tacit premise.

Prior to the publication of his major work, Kelly had published little. He commenced his writing in order to catalog and organize his clinical experience. But a catalog of techniques was not likely to be seen as a contribution to the intellectual and scholarly life of a prestigious department of psychology. Clearly, at a time when clinicians were eagerly seeking theories to give form to their efforts, a new theory of personality was called for, one that would reflect dissatisfaction with psychometric trait theories and with the explicit mechanistic models advanced by psychologists committed to stimulus-response and reinforcement notions.

The basic postulate and eleven corollaries of Kelly's system represent a departure from trait theory, from psychodynamic theories, and certainly from S-R theories. Kelly's operative metaphor was the scientist. Everyman is a scientist, employing prediction to test his cognitions. He makes inferences from incomplete data and these inferences are the raw material for scientific guessings. The scientist, whether clinician or client, is also enjoined to take into account the context of silent or expressed inferences of other actors. That is, contexts make a difference.[3]

3. The present author was also engaged in efforts to make a scientific enterprise out of clinical psychology (Sarbin, Taft, & Bailey, 1960). From my present perspective, I would apply many of the same judgments to my earlier work as to the work of Kelly. In the 1950s, we were both budding contextualists, although neither of us could break completely with the mechanistic world view. My interest in role theory (and in the historic event as root metaphor) is reflected in the earlier work, probably as a result of exposure to Mead's symbolic interactionist point of view.

Kelly's contextualism did not go far enough. When we distill the imagery in Kelly's writings, we still see the clinician and the client in a professional relationship constructing hypotheses about the cognitive activities of the client. Personal construct theory has been called a cognitive theory of personality. Such labeling is appropriate if the intended reference for personality follows from one of the usages identified by Allport (1937) as "the player himself, an assemblage of personal properties."

Kelly did not follow the implications of his apparent departure from prevailing mechanistically oriented theories. To do so would have meant a radical shift from concern about antecedent-consequent relations and, even more, a departure from his self-image as a clinician-cum-scientist. I want to stress from personal knowledge that to be a professor in a department of psychology at mid-century meant striving to meet the requirements of a scientific ethos. Kelly broke out of the mechanistic constraints when he declared that cognitive activity was a *doing*, and that *construals* were not mere happenings of inert beings. But his range of convenience foreshortened his perspective. To have formed a model consistent with the contextualist root metaphor would have meant the adoption of an image of man, not as an individual, but as an active part of an ongoing social context. This move would have brought about a shift in metaphors from the person as scientist to the person as actor. The image of the actor is not incongruent with the *doings* aspect of Kelly's scientist but is *not* congruent with Kelly's emphasis on the individual as knower. Man as actor implies a social context and directs the psychologist to a consideration of, for example, political structures, ideology, cultural forms, and the symbolic world (Lukes, 1973).

In taking into account the larger social context, and employing the metaphor of man as actor, one moves quickly into the arena of social identity. A social psychological theory of identity is a belated development when one recognizes the fact that 19th-century social critics were concerned with such problems as the effects of industrialization and urbanization on personal adjustment. Marx and Durkheim, among others, grappled with problems of social identity in their attempts to illuminate such conditions as anomie and alienation. It is interesting to comment on the lack of interest shown by personality theorists (including Kelly) in problems associated with the personal and social effects of the transvaluation of social identity. It is not that conceptual tools were not available. William James, James Mark Baldwin, and George Herbert Mead, for example, had earlier written detailed accounts of the development of the self, including discussions of the development of a social self. They saw how personality was formed in interaction with others. Mead, especially, accented the interaction of self and society. But these writers were constrained to stay close to discussions of mental acts, cognitive processes, and the complexities of dyadic communication. For all their liberality and breadth, they remained close to the individual. This was, of course, consistent with their ideological commitment to the genteel tradition. Such a commitment was alien to a search for the not-so-genteel antecedents of selfhood in economic determinism, political forces, bureaucracy, and class structure. The search for self, like the search for an elusive mind, was centered on the individual. It was not that James and Mead and, later, Kelly turned their backs on the broad proposition that the social self was a product of antecedent happenings and doings. Rather they adopted a narrow focus: the individual and his immediate surround.

Kelly's conceptual boundaries appeared to be in the individual and in his efforts at construing his interpersonal world. After reading Kelly's two volumes, one student remarked: "He is the ultimate scientist of the internal workings of the individual human mind." This student shared my judgment that Kelly was indeed operating as a scientist, looking for causality in a person's psychological processes.

In Ward's paper on the philosophy of individualism (1972), there appears a paragraph that could be paraphrased to illuminate the occasion of the development of theories of personality that isolated the individual from his social context.

> The ideal of individualism [an ideological development of recent times] had in view the millenium of a simple society of equal self-governing individuals, and it served to smooth the way for the passage into a complex world of social power where increasing interdependence left the individual less and less in control of his own fortunes. Americans wanted that world, too, the world of wealth and power, but they did not foresee that in it the meaning of the individual would shift from his self to his *role in society*. [P. 22]

The concentration on the individual as a way of construing the self is especially clear in Kelly's corollaries. All eleven of the corollaries turn the readers' attention to the construing process, although the commonality and sociality corollaries make contact with the social world. For Kelly, the self does not emerge from the person's *actions* as a social role-taker, but from his knowings, his reflexive construals, and his construals of others.

THE DRAMATURGICAL MODEL AND EMPLOTMENT

The historical event as the root metaphor of contextualism requires some further explication. The imagery called out by the historical event metaphor is that of an ongoing texture of multiply elaborated episodes, each leading to others, each being influenced by collateral episodes, and by the efforts of multiple actors who perform actions in order to satisfy their needs and meet their obligations. Contained in the metaphor is the idea of constant change in the structure of situations and in the positions occupied by the actors. Linearity is not intended.

In social psychology, at least two models have been constructed which can be cited as exemplars of the contextualist root metaphor: the field theory of Kurt Lewin (1935) and the dramaturgical model attributed to G. H. Mead (1934), and elaborated by Goffman (1959), among others.

Lewin's field theory influenced the development of one wing of modern social psychology. The language of physics—valences, forces, barriers, permeability—however, gave the model a mechanistic cast, especially with its quasi-mathematical equations. However, Lewin did bring into the purview of psychology the proposition that contexts such as group membership had to be included in the texture of an event. The group dynamics movement is one outgrowth of Lewin's field theory, a movement whose practitioners dropped the language of physics and willingly sacrificed precision for scope. The incongruity of the language of physics for describing ongoing social events no doubt contributed to the loss of interest in field theory. The physical science metaphors, providing mechanistic overtones to the theory, probably helped to influence some social psychologists of the 1940s and 1950s to seek general laws by taking their problems to the laboratory. As we know

now from bitter experience, the yield from laboratory studies has been disappointing. The laboratory warranty of objectivity—of making experimental subjects into manipulable objects—could not be ratified. Only recently have social psychologists recognized that the meanings attributed to the laboratory situation are an important part of the context of the subject's performances. (See, for example, Orne, 1962.)

The dramaturgical model has acquired a large circle of adherents in the sociological wing of social psychology. George Herbert Mead, especially during the 1920s, influenced the prestigious University of Chicago social scientists. Large numbers of scholars employed the concepts of the drama as vehicles for understanding social behavior. Mead's concept of role-taking as the central unit of his system has continued to win adherents. The drama as a model of human action has face validity, at least, especially when we recognize that the drama is a vehicle for illuminating the recurring problems of human beings trying to make their way in imperfectly organized and changing social worlds. Central to Mead's system is the concept "taking the role of the other." This concept is patently contextual. Not only must the person take into account the role of the other in formulating his own actions; the role performances and the judgments made about such performances serve as building blocks for construing the self.[4]

4. Lyman and Scott, in *The Drama of Social Reality* (1975), compare Freud, Mead, and Goffman, all of whom employed dramatistic metaphors. They point out that Freud's dramas are peopled by such allegorical characters as id, ego, and superego, and the actions are carried out on a psychic stage. In short, an individual is de-composed into psychic components, and these become the dramatis personae for a "monodrama." Freud's use of dramatistic metaphors is compared with Mead's and Goffman's. In comparing Freud to Mead, Lyman and Scott hold that Mead conceived of psychological acts in a more complex way: "generalized *monodrama* and specific *naturalistic* dramas." The monodrama has but two actors, the well-known "I" and "me." The naturalistic dramas are essentially rehearsals and recollections of actual performances in social life. Lyman and Scott comment on these rehearsals, "they stand in relation to an actual performance as a pre-text stands to a text. They are models of and for action" (p. 103). This interpretation of Mead is not unlike my interpretation of Kelly's view of "psychological processes." Both Mead and Kelly thought of "mind" or "psychological processes" as a pre-text for role performance, as one of the conditions for action.

Goffman's dramaturgy is different in that the performances are not in people's heads but in public places. His analysis (1959) suggests that people,

The principal characteristics of the dramaturgical model may be listed as follows:

1. The dramaturgical model guides the study of "meaningful" conduct. The meaning arises through interaction among participants; meaning is therefore social.

2. The self, self-identity, the self of continuity, the recognition of individuality and of separateness of others, etc., does not arise sui generis but is constructed in social interactions.

3. The dramaturgical perspective regards the participants in social interaction as actors. It is important to note that actors not only respond to situations but also mold and create them. In this respect the model is *clearly not* a mechanistically determined one—its propositions have a future reference (reminiscent of Kelly's anticipation notion).

4. The operations of a hypothesized Cartesian mind have no place in the definition of the situation. The interactions of participants define the situation. The units are not individuals, not organisms, not assemblages of traits, but interacting persons.

5. As episodes begin and end, human beings continually construct and reconstruct meanings to make sense of their observations of the performances of others and of self (Turner, 1974).

This is not the place to present a detailed account of one form of dramaturgical model: role theory (see Sarbin & Allen, 1968). Suffice it to say that the observation of central interest is *role enactment*. It is appropriate to look for the strands that contribute to a particular role enactment. Among these strands are the actions of various reciprocal role players and of audiences. We are reminded that Kelly made use of the concept of role. His usage reflected the essential difference between personal construct theory and role theory, namely, *the locus of concern*. Personal construct theory is concerned with the contemporary version of what goes on in the interval between the presentation of a stimulus and the verbal or motoric acts. Role theory is concerned with *actions* of persons in social situations. Personal construct theory, in common with other cognitive theories of the 1950s and '60s, tried to explicate the

_____

not mental objects, entertain the dramaturgical perspective in their efforts to solve everyday problems arising from the demands of social life.

A complete psychology, of course, would find all three dramatistic perspectives useful in uncovering the plot structure of an episode.

conditions of *knowing*. It evolved from the central concerns of mentalist philosophers and psychologists. Role theory has tried to explicate the conditions for action. Kelly's prototype is the scientist, role theory's prototype is the actor.

In any drama a particular action of one actor can influence the actions of other actors. The influence is of course mediated by a plot, the features of which are constantly reconstructed as the result of the changing social identity of each actor. Rather than look for the causal connections between antecedent and concurrent events as demanded by mechanistic models, or for immanent causality as in formistic models, the contextualist looks for the method of emplotment. This conception is something like Kelly's construals, but the construal is about entire episodes, acts, scenes, and not isolated individuals. (Kelly apparently failed to develop the argument that construals develop in the context of action.)

In employing the metaphor of emplotment (the construction and elaboration of dramatistic plots) we are reminded of the *as if* quality of the drama. The theater-goer, as well as the participant in any social interaction, must be able to place an arbitrary frame around a given episode or scene to separate it from other episodes or scenes (Goffman, 1974; Bateson, 1972). (It was Kurt Lewin who popularized the expression "frame of reference" for psychologists.) In the theater, the framing is carried out by artifacts such as curtains, programs, costumes, makeup, seating, lights, and bells, and by conventions acquired by both actors and audiences. The construction of the frame supports the stage actor's role-taking, "It is as if I am King Lear," and the audience's complementary role-taking, acting toward the staged drama *as if* it were as credible as events in the commonplace world. In everyday behavior, frames have to be constructed, also for purposes of emplotment, in order to make sense of the complex of happenings of nature and the doings of persons. A clear-cut example of constructing a frame for social behavior is the shift from serious goal-directed activity to play. The message "This is play," no matter how delivered, whether by word, gesture, facial expression, or contextual marker, frames one scene from another. The communication "This is play" signals a particular context, the condition for special kinds of role enactment (Miller, 1973; Bateson, 1972).

How can we describe complex role enactments and the implied context in ways that would make sense to social scientists? So accustomed are we to thinking in terms of cause and effect that the mere suggestion of an alternate form of description invokes puzzlement, if not incredulity. The psychologist's image of a world bereft of causality is, to say the least, upsetting. Consider that the science of psychology was born into a world molded by the Newtonian laws of motion, weaned on Cartesian dualism, schooled in the transferral of forces implicit in motivational concepts, and confirmed by advocates of stimulus-response mechanics.

It would serve our purposes briefly to inquire into the concept of causality. In everyday speech and in the lexicon of science, causality is a taken-for-granted category. In dealing with the relatively stable world of objects, we have become accustomed to describing happenings in terms of antecedent happenings. Our familiar clockwork universe is a metaphoric description employing levers, wheels, screws, inclined planes, forces, and so on. Observations are replicable, and causal (functional) relations are discovered and confirmed. The utility of the root metaphor of the machine has given a broad warrant to the concept of causality. That the efforts of scientific psychology have been addressed to the uncovering of causality needs no documentation here. Since Helmholtz and Fechner, and probably before, scientific psychologists have sought to emulate the physical sciences in providing functional relations of the form: given stimulus condition A, response B is the inevitable consequent. Save in trivial situations, such functional relations in psychology have not been firmly established. An error term, usually large, remains. The error is assumed to be a reflection of the crudity of mensuration devices or sampling, and that with more attention to refinement of the variables under study the error terms would decrease, ultimately to zero.

Error is only one way of looking at discrepancies from prediction. There is another way of looking upon such events: *situations* are variable. Stimulus A is a condition for response B if conditions 1, 2, . . . *n* obtain. Although multivariate design can in principle take into account such interactions, the fact of novelty and change induced by the interaction of the components in a behavioral formula renders such efforts futile.

Must we despair? Is there no alternate way of describing human actions? Perhaps we are at a historical junction not unlike the period when idiographic descriptions were challenged by the apparently more powerful mechanistic descriptions. I have already alluded to an alternate approach to describing human events, an approach that follows from the root metaphor of contextualism: *the historical event*. Human beings carry on their commerce with each other and with the natural and man-made worlds episodically. The episode, or to be more dramaturgical, the scene, is, to be sure, a multivariate scene, but in addition, a *changing* scene. The root metaphor of science—the machine—is feebly inappropriate as a trope to convey the complexity of human episodes and the effect of a constantly changing milieu. But episodes, scenes, acts—even lives—are describable without recourse to the immanent causality of forms or the transferral-of-force causality of the machine. I have already suggested that contextual description requires attention to actors engaged in reciprocal actions and that their developing actions can be epitomized as plots. In place of causality as the ultimate description of human action, let us look at emplotment. It is an alternate way of attaining a systematic description of episodes or scenes that has the warrant of long usage, if not the seal of science. The notion of emplotment provides us with at least minimal assurance that we can explore other possibilities before we surrender to chaos.

Is it possible to classify plots? Yes, if we work from the premise that the classification has limited purposes, such as understanding a relatively circumscribed event involving a limited number of actors. Such a modest aim will obviate one scholar establishing a presumably exhaustive list of plots and another scholar compiling a different list. With our modest aim, we are not likely to repeat the futile history of the hormic psychologists, each of whom advocated a different list of instincts as the *ultimate* explicanda of human action.

I have no firm catalog of plots to offer. The dramaturgic literature contains a suggestion for studying emplotment. Polti (1916) made a claim that there are no more than 36 dramatic plots. He supported his claim by analyzing the dramatic situation in 1,200 literary works, 1,000 from dramatic literature, 200 from other literary genres. The sample includes works from the Orient and the Occident, from the classical period, the Middle Ages, the Renaissance, the romantic revival, and modern times. Polti believed that the classification was useful beyond literature; "this investigation can and should be pursued in human nature, in courts of justice, and in daily life" (p. 11).

The metaphor employed by Polti is that of "emotions."

> There are in life but 36 emotions. . . . there we have the
> unceasing ebb and flow which fills human history like tides of
> the sea; which is, indeed the very substance of history, since it
> is the substance of humanity itself. . . . 36 situations, 36
> emotions, and no more.
>   It is then comprehensible that in viewing on the stage the
> ceaseless mingling of these 36 emotions, a race or nation arrives
> at the beginning of its definite self-consciousness; the Greeks,
> indeed, began their towns by laying the foundations of a
> theater. [P. 9]

To illustrate Polti's method, I list a few of the plots.

    I. Supplication (dramatis personae: a persecutor, a supplicant,
a power in authority whose decision is doubtful).

    II. Deliverance (dramatis personae: an unfortunate, a threatener,
and a rescuer).

    IX. Daring enterprise (dramatis personae: a bold leader and an
adversary, and a desired object).

    XX. Self-sacrificing for an ideal (dramatis personae: the hero and
the "creditor" or the person or thing sacrificed, and the ideal).

    XXII. All sacrificed for a passion (dramatis personae: the lover, the
object of the fatal passion, and the person [or thing]
sacrificed).

To be sure, another cataloger of dramatic situations could compile
a different list, one suggested by a metaphor other than emotion. My
present objective is only to show that plots are, in principle, subject
to taxonomic sorting.

Besides dramatistic literature, the classifier of plots may get some
help from the folklorists. For well over a century, scholars of the folk
tale have been engaged in taxonomic efforts. Aarne and Thompson
(1964) and Thompson (1946) are the most frequently cited sources.
Their efforts at classifying the world's folktales have been fruitful—at least, folklorists can communicate with each other through
the use of a well-developed classification. If we assume that folk tales
are not casual, capricious, or meaningless, but rather reflect episodes
in the lives of human beings, then the modern psychologist's study
of emplotment might be illuminated by the efforts of the folklorists.
After all, we are interested in answering the same questions about
the human condition as the folklorist: our raw materials are drawn
from the actions of men and women trying to make their way in
imperfectly organized and changing worlds; the folklorist's raw
materials are the folk tales about men and women (or their symbolic

equivalents) trying to accommodate to the same kinds of worlds. Shared by the actions of actors in folk tales and actors in contemporary real-life drama is the notion of plot.

Thompson (1946), in considering the numerous forms of oral narrative, such as fairy tales, legends, *Märchen*, novellas, household tales, sagas, and the like, remarks:

> We shall find these forms not so rigid as the theoretician might wish, for they will be blending into each other with amazing facility. Fairy tales become myths, or animal tales, or local legends. As stories transcend differences of age or of place and move from the ancient world to ours, or from ours to a primitive society, they often undergo protean transformations in style and narrative purpose. For the plot structure of the tale is much more stable and more persistent than its form. [P. 10]

In his systematic classification, Thompson employs *type* and *motif*. The type is a traditional narrative that "has an independent existence" (p. 415). That is, it requires no support from other tales in order to understand its plot. A motif is the smallest element in a story, an element that provides the conditions for persistence of the tale. The motif, in order to provide the conditions for persistence, must have something unique, striking, and unusual. Thompson says that most motifs can be sorted with a threefold classification: (a) actors, such as gods, witches, ogres, and conventionalized human social types like the cruel stepmother, the firstborn son, the favorite youngest child; (b) background items, such as magic objects, strange beliefs, and unusual customs; (c) single incidents. The third class of motifs can, of course, have an independent existence and become coterminous with a type.

Reference to the work on folk tales is only for the purpose of illustrating my claim that complex material, not unlike the accounts of everyday dramatic episodes, has been subject to systematic analysis. It remains to be seen whether we are creative enough to describe, for example, the functions of dramatis personae in everyday episodes as usefully as Propp's (1968) analysis of the functions of the dramatis personae in fairy tales.[5]

5. Colby (1970) has enlisted the aid of computers to investigate regularities in narrative patterns. By identifying frequencies of occurrences of selected classes of words, he was able to point to cultural differences in narrative patterns. Contributions of this type may suggest additional approaches to the study of emplotment.

I point to another effort that may be helpful in constructing a taxonomy of plots. The late Eric Berne (1964), operating from a contextualist stance, identified a number of "games people play" in their efforts to solve their problems. His choice of the language of games reflects the dramatistic, performing, acting features of human social conduct rather than the "exchange" features often associated with mathematical game theories.

The context for Berne's sorting was the psychotherapeutic transaction—but his descriptions of plots go beyond traditional psychopathological formulations. That Berne recognized "change and novelty," the central features of the historic-event root metaphor, is noted in the following quotation:

> The collection [of games] is complete to date (1962), but new games are continually being discovered. Sometimes what appears to be another example of a known game turns out, on more careful study, to be an entirely new one. . . . The individual items of the analyses are also subject to change as new knowledge accumulates, for example, where there are several possible choices in describing dynamics, the statement given may turn out later not to have been the most cogent one. [P. 69]

He systematically employed a set of analytical categories, among them title, thesis, aim, roles, dynamics, examples, paradigm, moves, and advantages. His plot analyses drew their main descriptors from the run of attention of the actors, rather than from remote psychological or psychiatric theories. He coined colloquialisms to identify games, a word or a phrase that identified the plot structure. His classification includes life games, such as "Alcoholic," "Kick me," "See what you made me do"; marital games, such as "If it weren't for you," "Look how hard I've tried"; Party games; sexual games; underworld games; consulting room games; good games. Each game is described in terms of the analytical categories, the composite description carrying most of the meaning of emplotment. Linear causality is eschewed in favor of looking upon human social actions as embedded in historical contexts.

SELECTED ILLUSTRATIONS OF THE USE OF CONTEXTUALIST MODELS

At this juncture, I shall consider selected subject-matter areas to show how models developed from idiographic, mechanistic, and contextual root metaphors account for observations. Studies of schizophrenia, hypnosis, and imagination lend themselves to comparative formulations.

Before embarking on a discussion of these substantive areas, a word is in order about the propriety of comparing research models constructed from different world views. Pepper has argued that it is inappropriate to use the categories of one root metaphor to evaluate the adequacy of another. Since the four world views are all reasonably adequate in terms of such criteria as scope and precision, the metaphysician need not concern himself with making comparisons, save to reject world views that have inadequate scope or precision. However, one may be interested in comparing the effectiveness of different models in accounting for processed data. Pepper would have been the first to point out that "data," that is, that which is given, may be differentially construed by the users of different models. Most of us, recognizably influenced by the materialist-mechanistic paradigm, can in principle agree on the criteria for establishing what are data. In this connection, Pepper's position calls for "rational clarity in theory and reasonable eclecticism in practice." For intellectual clarity, he goes on, "we want our theories pure and not eclectic."

Schizophrenia

In a short time, James Mancuso and I will have completed our book, tentatively entitled *Schizophrenia: Verdict or Diagnosis.* A preview of our study will show the usefulness of the root-metaphor method in understanding the monumental failure of the schizophrenia theory as employed by practitioners of the normal science.

With a few notable exceptions, most of the work done on schizophrenia takes its point of departure from the root metaphor of the machine. In its simplest form, the disease "schizophrenia" is the consequent; the antecedent is biochemical abnormalities, neurological defects, genetic lacks, perceptual disorders, cognitive slippage, schizophrenogenic mothers, the double bind, inability to respond to censure, inability to hold a segmental set, or loss of the abstract attitude. If schizophrenia could be diagnosed in the same way as, say, pneumonia, then the carefully executed research of the past 60 years would have identified at least one causal agent. But—and this may surprise you—*not one dependent measure* has been identified that would allow a professional diagnostician to make a reliable diagnosis, in the ordinary sense of the term.

Mancuso and I reviewed 300 research articles on schizophrenia published in the *Journal of Abnormal Psychology* and its predecessor, the *Journal of Abnormal and Social Psychology* (1958–1974). We selected this publication outlet because of its high standards. The usual experiment followed a simple model. The experimenter (usually a Ph.D. candidate) selected 30 to 50 schizophrenics residing in a mental hospital (usually a Veterans Administration hospital). The diagnosis was made by "two psychiatrists," "a psychiatrist and a psychologist," "diagnostic staff consensus," etc. For control subjects, he would enlist 30 to 50 hospital staff members, relatives, nonschizophrenic patients, and sometimes college students. Sometimes, but not always, he would try to match on demographic variables.

Then, drawing upon a theory derived from an apparently mechanistic metaphor, he would propose a hypothesis: the schizophrenics will do poorly on my experimental task when compared with the normals. The experimental task can be anything from guessing colors to solving syllogisms to operating a pursuit-rotor. Making use of his skills in experimental inference, the experimenter analyzes the data and, more often than not, discovers that the means of the schizophrenics represent poorer performance when compared with the means of the controls. In general, the mean differences are small. The experimenter concludes that schizophrenia is caused by whatever it is that is assessed by his experimental task. The purpose of all this work is to find an objective means of diagnosing schizophrenia; therefore, the experimental task should in principle be substitutable for the subjective judgments of the psychiatrists. But this is not what happens!

The overlap in distributions is so great that the use of the experimental variable produces an inordinate member of false positives and false negatives. A review of the distributions leads to the conclusion that most schizophrenics are like most nonschizophrenics.

The failure of the schizophrenia model is not difficult to locate, given the root-metaphor method. The experimenters begin at the wrong place, selecting subjects who have been through various bureaucratic, legal, medical, and nursing routines. The subjects have been removed from their communities for the alleged violation of propriety norms. The prepatient conduct may lead significant and powerful others to invoke the formistic concept "badness." A person who engages in "bad" conduct (residual deviance) finds his way to a mental hospital, where the moralistic label "bad" is illicitly converted to the scientific-sounding label "schizophrenic." As mentioned before, eclecticism, combining the categories of formism and mechanism, leads to confusion. All the scientific apparatus of neurology, psychology, genetics, and the like cannot identify the implied immanent causality of forms, in this case the form of "badness."

Is it any wonder that, to date, not one hard scientific fact can be uttered about schizophrenia? The independent variable schizophrenia-nonschizophrenia is a *moral* judgment, and the dependent variable is a performance; the moral judgment requires the actions of another person. To focus only on the object of moral judgment, and not on the person making the judgment, speciously reduces the data for analysis.

Because we argue that schizophrenia is a myth, we are not ignoring the fact that human beings—all of us—sometimes violate propriety norms. We have become accustomed to speaking of deviant conduct. But the underlying metaphor is the historical event: the target person's actions and the moral judgments of relevant (usually powerful) others are both regarded as strands in the texture of the event. The case of the dissident Soviet scientist who is incarcerated in a psychiatric hospital makes our own "diagnostic" procedures more clear.

The contextualist takes as his unit, not schizophrenia, not improper conduct, not the rules of society, but as much of the total context as he can assimilate. His minimal unit of study would be the man who acted as if he believed he could travel unaided through space *and* the person or persons who passed judgment on such claims. Elsewhere I have spoken of the power of the ideological premises held by jurists and physicians who have the legitimate power to assign labels such as madness, psychosis, insanity, and schizophrenia (Sarbin, 1974).

In sum, the traditional mechanistic science of deviance has failed because its practitioners overlooked the fact that they were participating in a moral, not a scientific, enterprise (Sarbin & Mancuso, 1970).

Hypnosis

The history of attempts to understand the conduct subsumed under the label *hypnosis* lends itself nicely to a discussion of the place of root metaphors. Since the scientific study of hypnotism goes back about 200 years, we would expect to find theories predicated on the root metaphor of the machine. Mesmer, for example, made use of animal magnetism, borrowing from the known properties of mineral magnetism. He posited the transmittal of forces via a subtle fluid to account for the counterexpectational conduct of his patients. Like many other theorists who followed, he made an eclectic slip by admitting formist categories. The "magnetic force" was a form, a natural gift, that was given to him and perhaps a few others. The "magnetic force" could not be accounted for by mechanical principles.

Theorists in the 18th and 19th centuries employed various eclectic combinations of formist categories and mechanical transmission. The claims of the 19th-century Nancy School were primarily concerned with antecedent-consequent causality and employed "suggestions" as the mechanical force. Their pronouncements made no claims for esoteric forms, preferring naturalistic common-sense explanations. Suggestibility, however, was not clearly defined. Not subject to categorization as a scientific, mechanical concept, suggestibility took on the character of a form.

At the same time, Charcot, in Paris, developed a theory of hypnosis using neuropathology as a model. Although working during a period of rapidly expanding neurological knowledge, knowledge that made the nervous system a medium for the mechanical transmittal of force, Charcot's theory of hypnosis was primarily formist. For him, it was in the nature of neuropathological patients to exhibit unusual behavior, and hypnosis was an artificially induced neuropathology.

Most contemporary theories of hypnosis continue the metaphysical eclecticism. Because of individual differences in response to hypnotic induction, a form, a trait, "hypnotizability," was posited. The record shows that the 50-year search for a psychometric test for hypnotizability has been futile. However, the methods of psychological science—the control experiment, sampling of subject populations, and so on—have been widely employed. The older mechanistic notion that "the hypnotic induction" was a prerequisite to the counterexpectational conduct is no longer viable. The same kinds of conduct can be produced by subjects who are "motivated," asked to imagine, or asked to simulate. Barber (1969), among others, has shown the influence of settings on role performance.

Until recently, the underlying notion of the hypnotic subject was that of a passive organism, a biological machine, so to speak. Contributing to the belief was the apparent automaticity of the subject's actions. Today, we know that the automaticity is apparent only—that the subject performs in ways that meet the expectations of the role. The older descriptions made use either of immanent causality or of mechanical causality: this practice was implied as a consequence of regarding the behavior of the subject or client as a *happening*. Popular literature depicting mechanical puppetlike responses in passive women, the strings manipulated by a sinister Svengali, helped to fix the belief of hypnosis as a happening.

I invoked the dramaturgical model in the early 1940s and emphasized hypnosis as a *doing* rather than a *happening*. The conduct of the hypnotic subject can be seen as the enactment of a role. Anyone who has witnessed a clinical or experimental demonstration is aware of the dramaturgical possibilities. The most recent work takes into account not only the actions of the role-performer, but also the actions of the audience, including the hypnotist. It came as a surprise to some "scientists" that the conduct of a person reflects the subtle characteristics of his audiences (see Rotenberg & Sarbin, 1971).

In the limited space, I can not do justice to the details of the dramaturgical approach to the hypnotic performance (see Sarbin, 1950; Sarbin & Coe, 1972). Let me point to one feature that came to light only because a contextualist metaphysic was at work. The depth of hypnosis has long been a subject of interest. Various psychometric devices have attempted to assess degrees of depth. The recognition that depth is a metaphor was late in coming. Once recognized as a metaphor, the question could be asked, What actions of Subject A allows the experimenter to say, "He is deeply hypnotized," and of Subject B, "He is not deeply hypnotized"?

When a subject agrees to enact the role of hypnotic subject, he assists the experimenter by engaging in actions that enhance his credibility. The actions associated with the hypnotic role are counterexpectational. If the subject performs according to the usual expectations, then he would have no credibility as a hypnotic subject. If I say to you, "You cannot raise your arm," the normal expectation is that such benign talk will have no effect on your arm-raising. The contrary expectation is that the subject will not raise his arm. If he appears to put forth effort in the apparent attempt not to raise his arm, then his credibility is enhanced. But motoric actions, such as arm rigidity, catalepsy, and the like, are easily simulated. For this reason, contemporary hypnosis experimenters are investigating phenomenal report.

Phenomenal reports of hypnotic subjects may be of many kinds. Here are three:

Subject A: My feet hurt because I'm wearing new shoes.

Subject B: I am reminded of my first day at the university.

Subject C: I am floating through the air.

The statements of Subjects A and B would have little interest for the hypnotist, they place no strain on the hypnotist's everyday perspective. The statement of Subject C would be taken as an indicator of "depth." Why? The hypnotist's own belief system becomes a strand in the texture of explanation. If the hypnotist cannot share the fictive perspective held by Subject C, he might conclude, "The subject is hallucinating, he is deeply hypnotized." Elsewhere I have argued at length that the experimenter, no less than the subject, operates from a fictive construct system (Sarbin & Juhasz, 1975).

The depth of hypnosis becomes a contextual variable. If the subject and the hypnotist share the same fictive perspective, then the subject's response would not be taken as counterexpectational, but if the two participants operate from widely disparate perspectives, then "depth" is likely to be the metaphor of choice. In a more detailed analysis, Subject C's report would be located within a context where the experimenter had encouraged the subject to engage in imaginings and had given sanction to descriptions of such imaginings without the use of metaphoric markers, such as "it seems," or "it is as if."

Current research underscores the worth of the dramaturgical perspective. For example, the dramatistic possibilities of the laboratory, of the clinic, and of the nightclub are quite different one from the other. The performances of all the actors—subjects, hypnotists, and audiences—are influenced by the differential contexts. Hearkening back to my discussion of emplotment, it becomes apparent that different plot structures are represented when the dramatis personae interact with stage settings designed for ostensibly different purposes: scientific experiments, healing, and entertainment.

Imagination

In a series of papers (Sarbin 1967a, 1972; Sarbin & Juhasz, 1966, 1967, 1970, 1975; Sarbin, Juhasz, & Todd, 1971) I laid the groundwork for an understanding of "hallucination." Historical-linguistic analysis, laboratory experiments, and clinical observation all converged on the conclusion that no determinate logical or psychological tests could differentiate one imagining from another so that one might be labeled hallucination.

The traditional views, based on formist and mechanist notions, was that hallucination was a product of a disordered mind, or the end result of biochemical, neurological, or psychic forces. Our research led us to the conclusion: hallucination is a term the definition for which is not content-free. The problem for the student of imaginings is not, What are the causes of a person's imaginings? but rather, What are the contexts that (a) encourage a person to report his imaginings, and (b) influence another person to regard a particular imagining as pejorative, hence, hallucination?

In order for an imagining to be assigned the label hallucination, a number of events must occur: the imaginer must be brought to the attention of a diagnostician who is empowered to employ the loaded term "hallucination," and the diagnostician's values about imaginings must be different from the imaginer's. If the imaginer can be shown to be a poet or novelist, then the diagnostician might not employ the hallucination label. The seed of a contextual model was planted.

In our early studies, we treated imagining as a primitive term, a term that all could agree upon. However, we learned that imagining, like many other psychological concepts, was not marked by universality. The concept "pictures in the mind" is a residue of mentalism—a model propelled by idiographic metaphysics. The mind is a form, one of its actions is to produce "pictures." Clearly, the phrase is a metaphor, since no postmortem of brain or undressing of mind has revealed anything resembling a picture. It is interesting to note that the serious study of imagination stopped about 1910, when introspective methods were found unsuitable to the newly developing mechanistic science of psychology.

In the late 1930s and 1940s several attempts were made to apply stimulus-response models to the study of imagining. This was a blind alley. The claim that an "image" is a conditioned response has received no empirical or logical support.

It was not until imagining was treated as actions, as doings, of actors that we could write a psychology of imagination. Here the dramaturgical perspective proved helpful. The actor can engage in conduct at various levels or "hypotheticalness." He can pretend, can engage in *as if* behavior, can play one part and then its reciprocal part, and so on. Not only can he engage in *as if* conduct overtly, but he can play his parts covertly. He can mute his actions. His hypothetical conduct can be enacted against a backdrop of hypothetical persons and stage props. The skill to operate at different levels of hypotheticalness frees the person from domination by the immediate environment and allows for action at a distance, not only in space but in time.

The dramaturgical view of imagining has led to some interesting demonstrations. For example, subjects can imagine the taste of salt in distilled water when appropriate contexts are arranged. Complex tests of imagery and of imagining reveal that a simple stimulus-response causality does not hold. The actor has the power, within limits, to construct imaginings that in no way are explicable as transmittal of forces.

In order to illustrate the formist, mechanist, and contextualist approaches to imaginings, I cite several reference cases that would be called instances of imagining by most psychologists.

1. A three-year-old child engages in animated play with a fictitious rabbit. She is said to have an imaginary playmate.

2. A novelist describes his work habits as having conversations with imaginary characters. This is often called creative activity.

3. A Plains Indian, after suitable preparation, ventures into the unknown and returns with tales of the supernatural. He is said to have had a vision.

Descriptions drawn from a mentalist (formist) model would approximate the following: the three-year-old plays with a rabbit, a replica of which is in her mind; the novelist listens to the conversation of his characters with his mind's ear (parallel to his mind's eye); the Plains Indian is hallucinating, is having an unreal or absurd or distorted image in his mind.

Descriptions drawn from a mechanistic model would be something like the following: the three-year-old has been conditioned to have a sensation of seeing a rabbit under precisely these circumstances, and to say that she is seeing it; the novelist has been conditioned to hear voices of his characters under precisely these conditions, and to say that he hears them; the Plains Indian has been conditioned to say under precisely these circumstances, "The Spirit of the Mountain spoke to me and said . . . "

Descriptions drawn from a contextual-dramaturgical model would approximate the following: the three-year-old child entertains the hypothesis that she is playing with a rabbit (the casual observer, on the contrary, might say she is playing with nothing); the novelist constructs hypothetical occurrences about his fictional characters; the Plains Indian solves an existential problem by forming the hypothesis that the Spirit of the Mountain is present, that he "sees," "hears," and "speaks to" the Spirit.

The serial descriptions of the reference cases contain the basis for continued dissatisfaction with the formist-mentalist and the mechanistic formulations of imagining. The descriptions in the language of hypotheticals appear to be most continuous with the data as seen from a common-sense point of view.

I have sketchily presented three areas of study with which I have been intimately involved. Like most of my contemporaries, I began long ago from a mechanistic metaphysic. I have discovered, sometimes unhappily, that the search for knowledge about people and their actions is unsatisfying when the starting premise is that man is a machine, subject to study the same as other objects that fit the machine metaphor.

Mine is not a lonely voice crying in the wilderness. I have plenty of company. More and more, contemporary psychologists are recognizing that the causal models of 18th- and 19th-century science are not fruitful. To illustrate, I point to papers by Jenkins (1974), Cronbach (1975), and Gergen (1973).

Under the unforgettable title "Remember That Old Theory of

Memory? Well, Forget It!," Jenkins (1974) has demonstrated how associationism, the principal category of the mechanistic world view, guided the work of experimental psychologists. In relation to learning and memory, the findings of numerous experiments are found wanting because of a failure to take into account the context. In fact, Jenkins reviews the data collected under the guidance of the associationist doctrine and concludes that the contextual view better accounts for the data than traditional associationism. This is not the place to review Jenkins's exciting paper—one sentence will communicate the thrust of his review: *"what memory is depends on context"* (p. 786). His contrast of associationism with contextualism is worth repeating. "Association [mechanism] asserts that there is one correct and final analysis of any psychological event in terms of a set of basic units and their basic relations. When you have reduced an event to these terms, you are through. . . . The contextualist takes the much less comfortable position that a "complete" or "final" analysis is a myth, that analyses mean something only in terms of their utilities for some purposes. This means that being a psychologist is going to be much more difficult than we used to think it to be" (p. 789).

Cronbach (1974), for example, in updating his influential paper (1957) that identified "the two disciplines of psychology," had argued that research in psychology had been held back because of a historical schism between experimental psychology and the study of individual differences. The experimentalists manipulated variables, the observers of individual differences correlated variables. He recommended a crossbreeding, the issue of which would be a science of "Aptitude x Treatment Interactions" (ATIs). In his more recent essay, addressing inconsistencies in instructional research, he says: "Important as ATIs are proving to be, the line of investigation I advocated in 1957 no longer seems sufficient. Interactions are not confined to the first order; the dimensions of the situation and of the person enter into complex interactions. This complexity forces us to ask once again, should social science aspire to reduce behavior to laws?" (p. 116).

He documents the fact that, all too often, inconsistency is evidence of unidentified interactions. "Once we attend to interactions, we enter a hall of mirrors that extends to infinity. However far we carry our analysis—to third order or fifth order or any other—untested interactions of a still higher order can be envisioned" (p. 119).

Although his diagnosis of the plight of contemporary psychology is abundantly documented, he only hints at a solution. He recognizes that an untenable premise has served as the foundation of our research strategy: that psychological processes are perduring and can be isolated one from the other. From this premise, formal questions can be raised, to be answered by scientific experiments and/or by systematic observation to fill the cells of a correlation matrix. "Intensive local observation," Cronbach asserts, "goes beyond discipline to an open-eyed, open-minded appreciation of the surprises nature deposits in the investigative net. *This kind of interpretation is historical rather than scientific. I suspect that if the psychologist were to read more widely in history, ethnology, and the centuries of humanistic writings on man and society, he would be better prepared for this part of his work*" (p. 125, italics added).

In a concisely written article, "Social Psychology as History," Gergen (1973) arrives at a conclusion that would be congenial to Cronbach's position, quoted above. The thrust of Gergen's argument is that theories of social behavior that guide the search for antecedent-consequent causality are primarily reflections of contemporary history. The scientific search for the authoritarian personality, for example, was a response to a historically engendered interest in the personal attributes of fascists. Gergen points to the interaction of historically generated research and actions taken by people in response to that research. People who are "psychologically enlightened" may react to promulgated scientific findings by intentionally engaging in conduct that would contradict, ignore, or conform to such findings. Making public the results of scientific research introduces "change and novelty," a condition with which mechanistic science cannot cope.

Gergen concludes that social scientists are essentially engaged in a systematic account of contemporary affairs, not in the search for the ultimate dimensions for a social science. He offers a prescription for a historical science of social behavior in the form of five alterations to present practice. When examined and distilled, the contents of the paragraphs that describe these alterations—in the language of the present paper—are critical of those operations that flow from the mechanistic world view. Gergen's arguments fit nicely into the proposition: the root metaphor of the historical event is likely to engender models for a more complete understanding of concrete contemporary human and social problems.[6]

RECAPITULATION

I have introduced you to my interpretation of the root-metaphor method and especially the root metaphor of the historic event. My point of departure was George Kelly's efforts to attempt a systematic approach to the problem of knowledge. His personal construct metaphor appeared to flow from a metaphysical position that leaned on contextualism. To recognize that he was unable to break away completely from the effects of deeply entrenched mechanistic models is not to find fault. In practice, as Pepper noted, eclecticism is to be expected. In any case, the clients who brought their problems to Kelly, the students who shared his seminars, and the men and women who undertook discipleship were introduced to a contextualist set of metaphors that were reasonably independent of other root metaphors, especially formistic and mechanistic.

My analysis has suggested that Kelly was more eclectic than was necessary, given the status of psychology in the mid-'50s. Had he not perserverated on the metaphor of man as scientist he could have gone on to employ a metaphor superordinate to scientist, namely, actor. With this metaphor, he could have adopted a more complete contextualist theory, one that made use of dramaturgical conceptions, incorporating a theory of action as well as a theory of cognition.

The latter sections of my paper described selected psychological topics that have been subject to analysis by means of dramaturgical metaphors. I have tried to show that, given the values as expressed in the documents of contemporary humanism, at least in a pragmatic sense, the contextualist root metaphor is more productive. That is to say, it is more satisfying to those who value scope over minutiae and whose goals are more modest than those of, say, Galileo, Newton,

6. Among other voices who have joined the chorus are the Braginskys (1974), Rommetveit (1974), and Olson (1970). Working in rather disparate areas, they, too, have concluded that models arising from formistic and mechanistic metaphysics fail to provide satisfactory explanations, given such diverse criteria as pragmatic utility, intersubjectivity, and meaning.

Einstein. If I may be allowed a minimal bit of rhetorical license: for the problems considered, formist metaphors have proven futile, mechanist metaphors have proven sterile.

Coda

Being asked to deliver a keynote address imposes a special burden on the speaker. He is expected to set the stage (to use one of my dramatistic metaphors) and also to utter some prophetic remarks.

I have had little experience in the art of prophecy, in spite of the years spent in the study of prediction, but I have lived through the heyday of a number of approaches to the study of the person. At times I have even declared truth value on the implications of some of these theories.

I agree with Gergen (1973) that theories of personality, like theories of astronomy, theories of illness, or theories of moral development, do not emerge from a vacuum. New theories are posited to answer persisting questions the traditional answers to which have become aesthetically unsatisfying, if not pragmatically false. Models drawn from the prevailing root metaphors guide the selection of analogues from commonplace experience and, of course, from the language of other disciplines.

I would like to submit for your examination the following proposition: that theories of personality are constructed to provide a systematic framework for answering the following questions: What is man? Who is man? This is awkward grammatically and I believe mental philosophers and psychologists would usually personalize the questions to: What am I? and Who am I?

The *What am I* question has several forms. The person who asks, What am I in relation to the world of nature? will seek answers from concurrent construals (theories) of man-nature relations. If he is in control of technologically sophisticated instruments for taming the forces of nature, the answer might be "I am master." If technologically primitive, the answer might be "I am a pawn."

The person who asks, What am I in relation to the moral order? (i.e., the normative ecology) will seek answers by comparing his conduct with concurrent moral rules. In this connection, theories of personality generated by Christian moralists have tended to focus on the formistic categories of good and evil.

The person who asks, What am I in relation to the transcendental ecology? will seek answers that guide his location of self in the world of symbols and abstractions: What am I in relation to, for example, justice, liberty, virtue, and fairness? Ethical philosophers have constructed theories to help account for the conduct of persons who are guided by abstractions that transcend conventions rather than rules that support conventions.

Finally, the person seeking answers to the *Who am I* question will seek answers in the world of social organizations, in the role ecology. The failure to find satisfying answers to the *Who am I* question is currently represented by such metaphors as alienation, estrangement, depersonalization, loss of identity, and so on.

The technological, political, bureaucratic, and economic contexts of alienation have been repeatedly exploited, and I shall not repeat the persuasive arguments of such authorities as Marx, Durkheim, Muller, Ellul, and Mumford. Which of these questions are the nagging ones? Which compel answers? I suggest that contemporary scholars of personality will focus on the construction of theories that attempt to illuminate the problems of the formation of identity, to make sense of answers to the *Who am I* question. A common concern today is addressed to problems created by transvaluations of social identity (Sarbin, 1967b, 1968b; Sarbin & Scheibe, 1970).

Which root metaphor is likely to generate models that help make sense of such transvaluations? Though my conclusion may reflect a blind spot, I cannot see how formistic, mechanistic, or organistic metaphors are especially helpful. Unlike the individualistic epiphenomenal self, purportedly construed without reference to social organization, identity is a product of group life. One's identity is construed from actions, that is, from role enactments, and from the values placed on such actions by self and by vital and significant others. For this reason, dramaturgical metaphors are more likely to lead to credible propositions.

One subliminal implication of this declaration is the shift in materials for study. For example, the works of Freud will be only of historical interest. Freud's theories can be used by historians to reveal the incongruity in linking moral forms to mechanistic causality. Freud's attempt to bring together categories from formism and mechanism failed as a general theory of human conduct. Adler (1934) may be restored to an eminent position—his notion of the guiding fiction is continuous with notions of role rehearsal and (to a lesser degree) continuous with the conceptual framework for solving problems of location in the symbolic world. Rather than construe the work of scholars in neighboring disciplines as outside the range of convenience, as Kelly did, the new theorist of personality will welcome the models advanced by writers such as Erving Goffman, Ernest Becker, Kenneth Burke, and others in the dramaturgical tradition.

I anticipate another change. The new scholars of personality will engage in a radical shift. Instead of looking upon 19th- and 20th-century natural sciences as models, they will explore the structure of identity and the means of identity transvaluation where these occurrences are most clearly presented—where the importance of contexts is continually affirmed—the world of literature, especially dramatistic literature. Shakespeare, Goethe, Thomas Mann, Kafka, Dostoevsky, O'Neill, Shaw, and Pirandello come immediately to mind as writers who could be perceived as authorities on identity shaping and on the contextual features that support the imputation or withdrawal of respect and esteem for role enactments.

I am painfully aware that this prediction has an antiscientific coloring. I say "painfully" because I have construed myself as scientist for almost 40 years. When I look at the achievements of science (rooted in mechanism) in such areas as deviance, hypnosis, and imaginings, already alluded to, and also language, moral development, teaching, and learning, I must admit that science may justifiably be called the false messiah—at least for the problems that we identify as psychological.

Models that flow from the root metaphor of contextualism may appear to reflect chaos—especially to the mechanistically inclined. The latter tries to avoid chaos by simplifying the object of study, by fragmentation, by ecological impoverishment, and by striving for replicability. But chaos is a relative term. Episodes in a drama might appear chaotic to a scientist who looks at the blurred actors through an out-of-focus high-powered microscope. But the human condition must be lived in episodes that are not arbitrarily simplified, fragmented, ecologically impoverished, or replicable.

As I said before, continual change and novelty are fundamental aspects of the dramaturgical model. From my perspective, continual change and novelty are fundamental to the set of facts that need to be ordered into descriptions of human conduct.

Are we compelled to adopt the historical event as the root

metaphor for making sense of the world? Are we ready to heed the contextualist's overriding emphasis on novelty and change? William James once argued that "each step [that persons or collectivities] make brings unforeseen chances into sight, and shuts out older vistas, and the specifications of the general purpose have to be daily changed." Here is a nicely phrased statement that points to the "novelty and change" feature of the contextualist world view. No documentation is required to support the fact that the success of a purposive action only churns up new sources of strain, new conflicts to be dissolved.[7]

In their very efforts to construct actions to serve their values, men and women alter their contexts and find themselves in worlds that are ever renewing. Earlier dramatists invoked the formistic concept of *fate* to explain the observation that the intentions of human beings result in unforeseen and unwanted outcomes, in unintended consequences. Although useful to the Greek playwrights, fate is not likely to be restored as a model of causality in the contemporary world. More recently developed psychological models based on the root metaphor of the machine are not designed to deal with novelty and change. It is my belief that no aesthetically satisfying account of the human condition can be constructed without taking into account the continually changing texture of events. Our job now is to find a way of satisfying our need to describe how people live their lives. Since neither fate nor mechanical causality are convincing descriptions, we are directed to seeking other ways of describing contexts. As a start I suggest we seek enlightenment from the efforts of dramatists, novelists, and other observers who view life as theater. Their success as portrayers of the human condition lies in their ability to construct plots, narratives that hang together. The magnitude of the task may be greater than our resources: but I see no

7. At another time, I hope to amplify this proposition, incorporating additional arguments based on dialectical theory. Burke (1945) and Riegel (1975), among others, offer penetrating dialectical analyses. Another helpful source is Turner (1974), who sees social dramas as arising in conflict situations. He identifies four phases of public action in such social dramas: (a) breach of norm-regulated social relations; (b) crisis; (c) redressive action; and (d) reintegration. The fact of reintegration does not imply stasis, nor even a value judgment about societal equilibrium. Borrowing from W. H. Auden, Turner advises us "to learn to think of societies as continually 'flowing' as a 'dangerous tide . . . that never stops or dies . . . And held one moment burns the hand'" (p. 37).

place for psychology in the modern world unless we turn our attention and our creative talents to the study of emplotment. Our goals should be modest. The gigantic scientific feats of Newton, Linnaeus, and Mendeleev should be put aside as models to be emulated. Instead, let us deal with the human condition as we find it: in ever changing, ever renewing drama.

REFERENCES

Aarne, A., & Thompson, S. *The types of the folktale* (2nd ed., rev.). Helsinki: Suomalainen Tiedeakatemia, 1964.

Adler, A. *Practice and theory of individual psychology.* New York: Harcourt, Brace, 1924.

Allport, G. W. *Personality: A psychological interpretation.* New York: Holt, 1937.

Barber, T. X. *Hypnosis: A scientific approach.* Princeton, N.J.: Van Nostrand, 1969.

Bateson, G. *Steps to an ecology of mind.* New York: Ballantine Books, 1972.

Berne, E. *Games people play: The psychology of human relationships.* New York: Random House, 1964.

Braginsky, B. M., & Braginsky, D. D. *Mainstream psychology: A critique.* New York: Holt, Rinehart & Winston, 1974.

Burke, K. *A grammar of motives.* Englewood Cliffs, N.J.: Prentice-Hall, 1945.

Chun, K., & Sarbin, T. R. An empirical demonstration of the metaphor-to-myth transformation. *Philosophical Psychology,* 1970, **4**, 16–21.

Colby, B. N. Cultural patterns in narrative. In J. C. Mancuso (Ed.), *Readings for a cognitive theory of personality.* New York: Holt, Rinehart & Winston, 1970. Pp. 557–571.

Cronbach, L. J. The two disciplines of scientific psychology. *American Psychologist,* 1957, **12**, 671–684.

Cronbach, L. J. Beyond the two disciplines of scientific psychology. *American Psychologist,* 1975, **30**, 116–127.

Gergen, K. J. Social psychology as history. *Journal of Personality and Social Psychology,* 1973, **26**, 309–320.

Goffman, E. *The presentation of self in everyday life.* Garden City, N.Y.: Doubleday, 1959.

Goffman, E. *Frame analysis.* New York: Harper & Row, 1974.

Hofstadter, R. *Social darwinism in american thought.* Philadelphia: University of Pennsylvania Press, 1944.

Jenkins, J. J. Remember that old theory of memory? Well, forget it! *American Psychologist*, 1974, **29**, 785–795.

Kelly, G. A. *The psychology of personal constructs* (2 vols.). New York: W. W. Norton, 1955.

Laird, J. D., & Bethel, M. *World hypotheses as psychological variables*. Unpublished manuscript, 1974.

Lewin, K. *A dynamic theory of personality*. New York: McGraw-Hill, 1935.

Lewis, C. S. Bluspels and flalansferes. In *Rehabilitations and other essays*. New York: Oxford University Press, 1939. Pp. 135–158.

Lukes, S. *Individualism*. New York: Harper & Row, 1973.

Lyman, S. M., & Scott, M. B. *The drama of social reality*. New York: Oxford, 1975.

Mead, G. H. *Mind, self, and society* (C. M. Morris, Ed.). Chicago: University of Chicago Press, 1934.

Miller, S. N. Ends, means, and galumphing: Some leitmotifs of play. *American Anthropologist*, 1973, **75**, 89–99.

Olson, D. R. Language and thought: Aspects of a cognitive theory of semantics. *Psychological Review*, 1970, **77**, 257–270.

Orne, M. T. On the social psychology of the psychological experiment: With particular reference to demand characteristics and their implications. *American Psychologist*, 1962, **17**, 776–783.

Pepper, S. C. *World hypotheses*. Berkeley: University of California Press, 1942.

Piaget, J. *The construction of reality in the child* (M. Cook, Trans.). New York: Basic Books, 1954.

Polti, G. *The thirty-six dramatic situations* (L. Ray, Trans.). Boston: Writer, Inc., 1916.

Propp, V. *Morphology of the folktale* (2nd ed.). Austin: University of Texas Press, 1968.

Riegel, K. F. (Ed.). *The development of dialectical operations*. Basel: Karger, 1975.

Rommetveit, R. *On message structure*. New York: Wiley, 1974.

Rotenberg, M., & Sarbin, T. R. Impact of differentially significant others on role involvement: An experiment with prison social types. *Journal of Abnormal Psychology*, 1971, **77**, 97–107.

Sarbin, T. R. Contributions to role-taking theory: I. Hypnotic behavior. *Psychological Review*, 1950, **57**, 255–270.

Sarbin, T. R. The concept of hallucination. *Journal of Personality* 1967, **35**, 359–380. (a)

Sarbin, T. R. The dangerous individual: An outcome of social identity transformations. *British Journal of Criminology*, 1967, **7**, 285–295. (b)

Sarbin, T. R. Ontology recapitulates philology: The mythic nature of anxiety. *American Psychologist*, 1968, **23**, 411–418. (a)

Sarbin, T. R. The transformation of social identity: A new metaphor for the helping professions. In L. Roberts, N. Greenfield, & M. Miller, *Comprehensive mental health programs: The challenge of evaluation.* Madison: University of Wisconsin Press, 1968. Pp. 97–124. (b)

Sarbin, T. R. Imagining as muted role-taking: A historico-linguistic analysis. In P. Sheehan (Ed.), *The function and nature of imagery.* New York: Academic Press, 1972. Pp. 333–354.

Sarbin, T. R. *Ideological constraints on the science of deviant conduct.* Keynote address, Fifth Annual Meeting of the American Association for the Abolition of Involuntary Mental Hospitalization, New York, April 14, 1974.

Sarbin, T. R., & Allen, V. L. Role theory. In G. Lindzey & E. Aronson (Eds.), *Handbook of social psychology* (Vol. 1). Reading, Mass.: Addison-Wesley, 1968. Pp. 488–567.

Sarbin, T. R., & Coe, W. C., *Hypnosis: The social psychology of influence communication.* New York: Holt, Rinehart & Winston, 1972.

Sarbin, T. R., & Juhasz, J. B. On the "false alarm" metaphor in psychophysics. *Psychological Record,* 1966, **16**, 323–327.

Sarbin, T. R., & Juhasz, J. B. The historical background of the concept of hallucination. *Journal of the History of the Behavioral Sciences,* 1967, **3**, 339–358.

Sarbin, T. R., & Juhasz, J. B. Toward a theory of imagination. *Journal of Personality,* 1970, **38**, 52–76.

Sarbin, T. R., & Juhasz, J. B. The social context of hallucinations. In R. K. Siegel & L. J. West, *Hallucinations: Behavior, experience, and theory.* New York: Wiley-Biomedical, 1975. Pp. 241–256.

Sarbin, T. R., Juhasz, J. B., & Todd, P. The social psychology of "hallucinations." *Psychological Record,* 1971, **21**, 87–93.

Sarbin, T. R., & Mancuso, J. C. Failure of a moral enterprise: Attitudes of the public toward mental illness. *Journal of Consulting and Clinical Psychology,* 1970, **35**, 159–173.

Sarbin, T. R., & Scheibe, K. E. *The transvaluation of social identity.* Unpublished manuscript, 1970.

Sarbin, T. R., Taft, R., & Bailey, D. E. *Clinical inference and cognitive theory.* New York: Holt, Rinehart & Winston, 1960.

Thompson, S. *The folktale.* New York: Holt, Rinehart & Winston, 1946.

Turner, V. *Dramas, fields, and metaphors.* Ithaca, N.Y.: Cornell University Press, 1974.

Ward, J. W. Individualism: Ideology or utopia. *Hastings Center Studies,* 1974, **2**, 11–22.

White, H. Interpretation in history. *New Literary History,* 1972–1973, **4**, 281–314.

Windelband, W. *An introduction to philosophy.* London: T. Fisher-Unwin, 1921.

Current Motivational Models in the Elaboration of Personal Construct Theory

James C. Mancuso
State University of New York at Albany

*W*hen George Kelly published his theory of personal constructs in 1955, he advanced a position shaped on the paradigm that has deeply infiltrated current psychological science. Kelly spoke of nothing so dramatic as a paradigm revolution. Instead, he presented his work unpretentiously, almost casually spinning out a wisdom accumulated through his lively personal contact with people, events, and his academic discipline. But Kuhn (1970), speaking of paradigm pioneers, seems to have Kelly in mind: "The man who embraces a new paradigm at an early stage must often do so in defiance of evidence provided by problem solving. . . . A decision of that kind can only be made on faith" (p. 158). Reading Kelly's work, considering the status of the mechanist[1] paradigm which dominated psychology

1. The terms *contextualist* and *mechanist,* as used in this paper, originated in the belatedly honored magnum opus of Stephen Pepper (1942). In this work Pepper describes and fully discusses four workable and intellectually viable metaphysical positions—world hypotheses—each of which embodies an epistemological position which is compatible to itself. Pepper labels the positions so that his labels convey the essence of the "root metaphor" which guides each position. For example, the root metaphor of mechanism is the machine. A psychologist following this root metaphor would shape his "true statements" so that he would describe energy transformations and transmissions. He might speak of "response strength," or "bonding," and devises principles describing reinforcement. A psychologist following the root metaphor of contextualism, which is the historical act, might speak of persons-in-situations. He would go on, as does Kelly, to stress the utility of principles that give the person's constructions of the event a status equal to any other "strand" in the event. Other features of these world hypotheses will get attention as we proceed.

Pepper's remaining categories of world hypotheses—formism and organicism—also appear as the guiding frames in psychological science. These two important classes of paradigms, however, are of little concern to this essay.

25 years ago, and considering the current advance of contextualism in psychology, one might better view Kelly as a visionary who has pronounced his faith in a paradigm that would rapidly take a commanding position in psychology.

Psychology in 1955, we recall, reveled in its mechanist world view. Graduate students in psychology were mastering the ins and outs of personality theory by reading Dollard and Miller (1950), and were learning all about learning by plowing through the appropriate chapters of Stevens's (1951) *Handbook of Experimental Psychology*. There they learned that reinforcement drives the psychic machine. Numerous psychologists whose professional aspirations prompted their avid efforts to integrate a meaningful personality theory—the ones aspiring to assess and to alter persons—were trying to discover the meaning of the little blue streaks in the corner of Rorschach's Card X. These secrets, they knew, would be theirs just as soon as they had mastered Klopfer and Kelley's (1942) version of psychoanalytic dynamic flow in persons.

Considering the immense power of the mechanistic world view which then dominated psychology in the United States, one can only be puzzled by origins of a theory that chose to explain persons by building from a contextualist perspective. Perhaps we must accord some credibility to Kuhn's hypothesis that paradigm pioneers operate on faith.

This essay shall assert that a contextualist world view now permeates important segments of psychology. We would hesitate to claim that the revolution has overrun the province called personality theory. At times, in fact, we are advised that personality theory, like Rorschach's test and God, has died. We reject such advice, however, knowing that such false counsel intends to tell us that the mechanist and formist world views, which have dominated personality theory, have proved to be quite worthless as a scientific guide. Thus, we find, personality theory does not lie dead. That part of personality theory which operated from formist and mechanist principles has become lifeless, and easily deceived counselors believe that when they witness the morbidity of mechanism and formism they witness the death of personality theory. We can return to our faith—contextualism as expressed in constructivism—knowing that we are still watching a very vital part of personality theory endeavor.

Our faith, however, does not produce sustained comfort. Reading several lines onward from the above passage taken from Kuhn's (1970) treatise, one finds this statement:

This is not to suggest that new paradigms triumph ultimately through some mystical aesthetic. On the contrary, very few men desert a tradition for these reasons alone. Often those who do turn out to have been misled. But if a paradigm is ever to triumph it must gain some first supporters, men who will develop it to the point where hardheaded arguments can be produced and multiplied. [P. 158]

Contextualism has swept through much of experimental psychology, pushing mechanism into a sideline position. Personality theory has become a shambles as formist-oriented investigators struggle to describe persons as bodies which live out immanent and observable traits, while mechanist metaphors fail to describe persons as machines through which external controlling agents shunt energies. Can one turn to Kelly's personal construct theory, which is built on a contextualist world view, to find a perspective from which "hard-headed arguments can be produced and multiplied?"

One would best avoid a direct answer to this last question. Recall, we are talking about personal construct theory as *an examplar* of a revolutionary paradigm. We advise against restricting discussion to the fine points in Kelly's theory, to argue each grain of the matter as if the whole theory would stand or fall over the placement of a comma. Instead of engaging in this task, we might better ask, Has *contextualism* developed to the point where hardheaded arguments can be produced and multiplied? The answer to this question is unequivocal. Contextualism has taken a key position in psychological science.

Can we show also that a theory like personal construct theory, which has developed from the precepts of a contextualist world view, holds a legitimate place among theories of persons? Will personality theorists follow close behind as experimental psychologists move rapidly to take up a contextualist position? Those of us who have already deserted tradition now have the small task of showing that contextualist precepts have legitimate scientific status, and that a "complete person" can be described within categories that blend into the contextualist world view.

The remainder of this essay will illustrate the exciting possibilities which follow from joining personal construct theory, as a contextualist theory, to the contextualist revolution taking place in other areas of psychology. We first present some elucidation of the concept *contextualism*, emphasizing some ideas that already have been developed in Professor Sarbin's paper. Thereafter, we offer some evidence for the claim that contextualism has infused psychology.

THE CONTEXTUALIST PARADIGM
REPLACING MECHANISM

Pepper (1942), in his masterful analysis of major world hypotheses, spelled out the distinguishing features of those epistemological systems that can be classed as contextualist world views. The small space here devoted to Pepper's treatise cannot properly describe the explanatory power of his superb work. The testimony to this book's value comes from the ever increasing attention now being given to it by scholars in every discipline. To describe contextualism, we cite a long quotation from the recent work of a contextualist who has converted from mechanism. Jenkins's (1974) statement on contextualism follows the candid admission that as he had tried to cast the work of his long and productive scientific career into a mechanistic metatheory, he had been "caught in a metatheoretical trap, a trap that I had built for myself without ever realizing it" (p. 785).

> Contextualism holds that experience consists of *events*. Events have a *quality* as a whole. By quality is meant the total meaning of the event. The quality of the event is the resultant of the interaction of the experiencer and the world, that is, the interaction of the organism and the physical relations that provide support for the experience. The relations can be thought of and analyzed into *textures*. A texture in turn consists of *strands* lying in a *context*. Consider as an example of an event a listener hearing a sentence. The total meaning of the sentence in that context is the quality of the event. We might note that the event persists in time over some period but that all of it at once forms a single, unified psychological moment. This is the "specious present" of William James—the span of dimensionalized time is psychologically unified in experiencing the quality of the event. The textures that support the quality of the event are those of the hearer and those of the world. If our concern is with the qualities of the utterance, we can turn our

attention to its texture, which consists of the words and grammatical relations between them in that context. Within that texture we can easily make out strands that make up the phrases. We can also see that some of the strands extend across the context of the phrases, that a word in one phrase depends on or determines a word elsewhere. We can become aware of the choices and presuppositions that the analyzed strands refer to. Some words and phrases can be shown to acquire their exact meaning *in that event* from their relations to more far-flung aspects of the context: a gesture, a reference, a topic previously spoken of, an event known to both the speaker and the hearer to be in the future, presumed common knowledge, and so on.

In this fashion, the analysis of the utterance will proceed far beyond the immediate physical context of the sentence and far beyond the physical stimuli immediately present. For the contextualist, no analysis is "the complete analysis." *All* analyses eventually "sheer away" from the event into more extensive contexts. This argues that there is no one analysis, no final set of units, no one set of relations, no claim to reducibility, in short, no single and unified account of anything. What makes an analysis good or bad for us is its appropriateness for our research and science and its utility in our pursuit of understanding and application. [Pp. 786–787]

By openly advocating contextualism Jenkins has joined other investigators whose works have been guided by a contextualist perspective. For example, Posner's studies (see Posner, 1973, for an extended review of cognitive studies based on a contextualist position) representatively illustrate the current scholarly work of building models for understanding cognitive functioning. In the passage to follow we find Posner reflecting Jenkins's observation that from a contextualist position "the quality of the event is the resultant of the interaction of the organism and the physical relations that provide support for the experience." Posner uses a contextualist stand to talk about memory.

This study suggests that a classification system imposed upon material at input limits the ways in which the material can be used at retrieval. If subjects are allowed to use their input categories, recall can be relatively effortless and effective. Otherwise, recall is slow and less accurate. The organization of information during learning has consequences for the ease with which it can be used later. [P. 33]

Posner's review of work in cognitive psychology, in many ways, updated Neisser's (1967) outstanding treatise. Neisser's text, one of the major position papers of the contextualist revolution, does not specifically identify the underlying contextualist metaphysic on which the discussion had been based. Neisser does use the term *constructivism*, however, which serves as an index term to identify contextualism in current psychological science. Neisser, by inextricably uniting the perceiver's construct system and the object, writes as a contextualist by averring that

Under normal conditions, then, visual perception itself is a constructive act. The perceiver "makes" stable objects, using information from a number of "snapshots" together. Such a process requires a kind of memory, but not one which preserves pictorial copies of earlier patterns. Instead there is a continuously developing schematic model, to which each new fixation adds new information. The individual "snapshots" are remembered only in the way that the words of a sentence are remembered when you can recollect nothing but its meaning: they have contributed to something which endures. Every successive glance helps to flesh out a skeleton which the first already begins to establish. [P. 140]

Similarly, Cofer (1973), taking his stand relative to the cognitive revolution, uses a contextualist perspective to discuss the way in which meanings, not individual words in a sentence, are remembered. He argues, essentially, that a psychologist is compelled to include a person's abstracting constructs, and not simply some sort of "bonded memory trace," in the context that shall be called "a memory."

If memory is constructive and if "storage" is in terms of schemata, as we have argued from our data, then the kind of representation it probably has in the brain is very difficult to characterize. It cannot be in the form of Bartlett's (1932) "innumerable, fixed, lifeless traces" specifically related to words, syntactic forms, and the like. The representation must in some sense be abstract, since it can be manifested in paraphrase and other kinds of productive forms. [Pp. 542–543]

The quotation to follow further illustrates the extent of the contextualist revolution, and also focuses on an important issue which Cofer raised: How may a theorist characterize the kind of representation which is "stored" to provide a strand of the context within which new information becomes individualized and constructed? Paivio (1974) discusses two broad positions on this issue, one of which proves to be familiar to those acquainted with personal construct theory.

> I shall discuss two contrasting views of the form and structure of knowledge. According to one view, information is stored mentally, much as in a richly illustrated encyclopedia or an audiovisual film library, with knowledge of the world represented as perceptual images of concrete things and events accompanied by relevant verbal descriptions and commentaries. According to the other view, the perceptual and verbal forms are only superficial expresssions of an abstract information base. . . . [P. 5]
>
> The trend [the first view] is characterized by the idea that we think at least partly in terms of perceptual analogs of the appearance of things and spatial groupings of things. A notable early exception to the imagery tradition was the view set forth in the 16th century by the French philosopher, Peter Ramus. Ramus explicitly rejected the old imagistic art of memory and substituted a method called "dialectical order." A subject was set out in schematic verbal form descending from general to more specific aspects in a series of dichotomized classifications. [P. 5]

One must restrain the inclination to explore further the context—the state of the sociology of knowledge—in which these contextualist models have crowded mechanism out of its leading position in this branch of psychological scholarship. This introduction, however, must be restricted. The ease with which one could lift the restriction demonstrates our point. Contextualism has become the guiding epistemological position for a large group of very active and convincing investigators.

The remainder of this essay is aimed toward demonstrating the ease with which personal construct theory can accommodate and assimilate the conceptualizations and schemata which develop out of the paradigm revolution being carried out in the experimental psychologic journals. To do this we shall trace through some of the thinking on the topic of "motivation." Personal construct theorists and the current contextualists share similar perspectives as they seek to discuss the directional changes in the flow of human conduct. When we read articles written by the revolutionaries, we see many concepts and terms which are familiar to personal construct theorists. In the end, the arguments in this essay will prove most useful if they show that a theorist holds an effective position when he uses the contextualist paradigm exemplified by personal construct theory. To further our claim for the utility of contextualism, as a finale, we will later turn to some empirical work applying contextualism to the study of motive to follow rules.

MOTIVATIONAL CONCEPTS IN A CONTEXTUALIST PARADIGM

In our search for a motivational statement that would satisfy a contextualist, we can profitably look at George Kelly's (1958, 1962) efforts to dissociate prevailing mechanistic motivational concepts from his overall contextualist position. Kelly's discussions of conduct stability and change follow from his Fundamental Postulate and his Choice Corollary.

> Fundamental Postulate: A person's processes are psychologically channelized by the ways in which he anticipates events. [1955, p. 46]

> Choice Corollary: A person chooses for himself that alternative in a dichotomized construct through which he anticipates the greater possibility for extension and definition of his system. [P. 64]

We note that both these statements use the term *anticipate*. Bannister and Fransella (1971), in their discussion of Kelly's Fundamental Postulate, stress the importance of using the term *anticipate*.

> . . . it implies that a man checks how much sense he has made of the world by seeing how well his "sense" enables him to anticipate it; and it implies that a particular man is the kind of sense he makes of the world. The word "anticipates" is nicely

chosen because it links the idea of prediction with the idea of reaching out and beating the world to the punch. [P. 20]

Here we see some key notions which placed Kelly's contextualist theory of persons quite at odds with the dominant mechanist paradigms of his era. To explain conduct channelization or change, personal construct theory places stress on the ways in which one anticipates events, the person's "system" or "the kind of sense he makes of the world." The vectors in the theory relate to the idea of anticipation, rather than being discussed as a push from behind.

A mechanist explaining the instigation and the direction of conduct favors concepts which describe prior attachments of energies to observable responses. Concepts like *drive reduction, inhibition, reinforcement, stimulus-response bonding or strengthening*; that is, concepts that explain response direction in the terms of previous attachment or diminution of energies, find favor in mechanistic systems. Concepts that portray a person as "reaching out and beating the world to the punch" would not mesh into mechanistic world views. Mechanism, following a 400-year tradition of scientific practice, eschews causality statements that cannot be specified as antecedent-consequent relationships. Rychlak (1968, 1973) already has analyzed carefully the mechanist's demands that a "scientific law" be stated in terms of *efficient* causality. Something causes another event, within a mechanistic system, only if the consequent occurs as a time-bound sequel to the instigating event. It is this kind of statement which efficiently allows tests by prediction, and such tests of deterministic sequences are the sine qua non for establishing mechanistic scientific truth.

Following contextualism, on the other hand, one avoids imposing a linear time scheme on an event. Temporal relationships are not separated out of the event. In fact, the spread of the event can extend through what might be called "infinite time." Pepper (1942) puts it this way: "For the contextualist, the dimensional 'time' of mechanism is a conceptual scheme useful for the control and ordering of events, but not categorical or, in that sense, real" (p. 240). Jenkins (see above), in clarifying a contextualist's view of time, aptly refers to "the specious present of William James." A contextualist, like Cronbach's (1957) correlational psychologist, can be satisfied when describing the strands which flow through a context; and he feels no great arousal over an inability to specify antecedent and consequent relations, which Cronbach's experimental psychologist would describe as independent and dependent variables. With these assumptions the contextualist, as scientist, may admit a concept of anticipation which is not locked into dimensional time. He is not constrained to consider sequence when he asks questions such as: What instigates and alters the flow of a person's conduct? A contextualist simply can have more fun! He speaks of a person's anticipations.

THE CONCEPT OF ANTICIPATION: ITS TROUBLES AND UTILITY

One sees obvious origins of the scientific sanctity of efficient causal statements. Consider a situation as follows: We observe Joey breaking a vase. He apologizes profusely to his mother, and then offers to use his allowance to pay for the vase. Further, he loses a baseball belonging to one of his friends. He replaces it. Someone asks, Why is such conduct maintained? Or, what motivates his repeating those apparently similar behaviors? A behavior scientist might try to explain as follows: "He's trying to be a good boy."

Such an explanation—speaking of having adopted behaviors in order to fulfill a goal that previously had not been defined—would fall very quickly before the arguments of an empirically oriented critic. "How does Joey *know* what one needs to do in order to be a good boy?" "How will Joey's definition of goodness define his conduct when he enters a situation where a child smaller than himself strikes out at him?" "Will his action still be seen as being consistent with his striving to become a good boy?" A serious scholar couldn't accept a motivational principle which defines cause as a future, final goal that "pulls" a person's conduct. That "future, final goal" can, however, become a strand in the context of the specious present!

Another metatheoretical trap lies waiting in the illustration given above. The statement "He's trying to be a good boy" may, indeed, be classed as a telic kind of statement, illustrative of those kinds of causal statements which Aristotle would call *final causes*. We also see that the statement contains an implicit use of· a formist, or idiographic, world view (see White, 1972–73, p. 299, for a cogent argument that Pepper's term *formism* be replaced with the term *idiography*). Formism, a variety of metaphysic exemplified in

psychology by the kind of trait which specified "in-born dispositions," cannot easily be excluded from psychological explanation.
Crude formism appears at those points where behavior scientists
speak of releaser mechanisms for aggression, as if aggression can be
depicted graphically by an observer who has developed the intricate
skill of recognizing or knowing the "true" or "proper" form of the
"thing" released. From this perspective an investigator tries to
develop measures of the "true forms." A good test of *aggressiveness*,
or of *honesty*, will provide a valid measure of these traits in that they
measure the amount of the trait—the amount of the true form—that
the person harbors.

In speaking of Joey, the transgressor in our example, the
idiographer might try to give a graphic representation of the level of
goodness (morality, superego strength?) the boy has developed. This
procedure would follow from the implicit assumption that "good-
boyness" is an identifiable essence, which can be discovered by a
diligent scholar (through factor analysis?), and that behaviors
exemplifying this trait are readily associated with this extant entity.
Indeed, behavior scientists have assumed that one can identify
"good-boyness," and that investigators will be able to demonstrate
the association between this trait—this existing, out-there entity—and particular behaviors. We recognize that Hartshorne,
May, and Maller (1928) were led into this kind of idiographic
assumption, and they had verbalized an allegiance to strict
mechanistic principles. Their hypotheses inadvertently followed
from the assumption that all the world "knows" all the behaviors
that a *good boy* will enact. Character training based on mechanistic,
reward-punishment principles would lead children to develop the
behaviors that were subsets of the overall idiograph for goodness;
and children would thenceforth be honest, trustworthy, and generally not deceitful. When their tests failed to confirm their hypotheses
they might have recognized their metatheoretical error regarding
their own construct, deceit, and they might have turned their
attention to the ways in which children construe deceit. That is, they
might have replaced their formist with contextualist assumptions.
Instead, they were dragged off by their own metaphors and suggested that the children had not been taught to recognize that
specific situations are instances of the more inclusive form, *deceit*.
But the times were not right for talking about moral conduct from a
contextualist perspective. Few psychologists understood the revolutionary character of William James's approach, and Bartlett's (1932)

constructivist treatise was four years from publication. Happily, as beneficiaries of an added half century of psychological work, we can talk about morality in terms of our subject's constructions.

The Everyday Appeal of Anticipation as Motivation

What then is the value of saying that Joey's moral conduct represents an *anticipation* of goodness? First, in that we would not accept the position that goodness is extant in the world, we cannot declare that Joey's basic humanness allows him to recognize and to aspire to achieve that positive state known as goodness. But, if he doesn't automatically grasp the quality of goodness—if he must be taught goodness—we must explain how he acquired that recognition. The mechanists have told us that such recognition has been determined by the past. He recognizes goodness because he has been properly reinforced for categorizing certain behaviors as good. He also reenacts "good" behaviors because he has been properly reinforced for reenacting those behaviors. If he anticipates anything, he anticipates a positive reinforcement for his good conduct! Why talk about anticipations when mechanistic principles can put the determinations into the observable past?

School-aged children are creative in their moral judgments. They can be presented with outlandish situations, in which they are asked to imagine acquiring immense reward for having done a completely unfamiliar act (for example, delivering a secret potion to a disguised witch who lives in the neighborhood). Large segments of the children who consider this situation will creatively invent a line of conduct that ignores the reward, and they will state that the conduct they have advised would be the "right" thing—the behavior that one would choose were he trying to be a good boy.

Consider the following: A 10-year-old child observes Joey as he tries to fill his mother's vase with water. The vase slips through Joey's hands and crashes to the floor. The average 10-year-old, as would most adults, says that Joey need not be held responsible to restitute for the broken vase.[2] "He didn't mean to do it. He was trying to help." The "common sense," then, readily resorts to

2. D. Allen & J. C. Mancuso, Children's perceptions of a transgressor as a function of intentionality and type of chastisement. Manuscript submitted for publication, 1976.

behavior explanation referring to the actor's anticipations. People invent behaviors which match some kind of "inner template" for goodness, and they simply assume that they can judge that others have such templates which are used as guides for directing their own behaviors.

There are promising signs that psychologists will recognize the benefits of clarifying the principles underlying this everyday, naive, implicit personality theory. Within the more demanding realm of empirical psychological study one finds numerous significant data collections to show that few predictor variables serve more effectively than does the simple expedient of asking a person what he will try to do—that is, what he expects (Scott & Johnson, 1972; O'Hara, 1966). People are able to predict their own conduct, and they regulate their conduct to confirm the accuracy of their self-predictions.

The Need to Prespecify Anticipations

The modern behavior scientist must meet the challenge that he give demonstrative experimental bases to formulations which describe the direction of a person's psychological processes in terms of anticipations. Let us take Joey into an experimental setting and then ask him, "What would you do if a boy much smaller than yourself were to hit you?" Under what conditions shall Joey's verbal response be used as a prediction of what he will do in an in-life situation? To prove the utility of a motivational principle which stresses anticipation, a behavior scientist must, among other demands, solve the problem: How does an investigator determine a person's anticipation? Further, such determination must be complete before the person is placed into the behavior-inducing situation. Expedient, after-the-fact explanations do not earn scientific respectability.

ANTICIPATION AS COGNITIVE STRUCTURE MAINTENANCE

We want to argue, nevertheless, that an explicit embracing of a contextualist position can allow one to formulate motivational statements that focus on anticipation. In the process, there might be some alteration in what is meant by anticipation, but one should expect nothing else.

To set our stage, let's retrieve that earlier question about the motivation for Joey's repetitions of "good boy" conduct. Rather than considering the response, "He's trying to be a good boy," let's consider the explanatory response, "He's trying to maintain his self-image as a good boy." This latter response reflects a prior acceptance of a broad assumptive base—a base which derives from adopting a more general contextualist world view to describe behavior. This explanatory statement reflects a contextualist orientation in that it places the person's existing organizational system—his cognitive system—squarely into the unit of study. In fact, an investigator could brashly proclaim that the situation has no meaning whatever without considering the person's imposed structures.

There is yet work to do. How does one speak of structures? How does one describe the origins of structures? By what processes do structures change? What principles describe the application of structures? There is a long distance between saying that Joey is trying to maintain his image as a good boy and accepting that statement as an instance of the general motivation statement, a person's processes are psychologically channelized by the ways in which he anticipates events.

The Centrality of Implicit Personality Theory

As a start, a contemporary psychologist may try to analyze Joey's conceptualization of "good boy." Such an analysis will proceed from a context that includes (a) Joey's understandings of "good" in interpersonal relationships; (b) the interrelationships of his understandings of "goodness" and his conceptions of his observer's understandings of "goodness"; (c) Joey's locations of his own person within these person-perceiving structures—that is, his self-construction; and (d) what happens when Joey's hypotheses about himself are or are not validated. In other terms, the analysis of the event must consider Joey's *implicit personality theory*. The concept of *implicit personality theory*, which is obviously very important to what shall be said as we proceed, has been getting the excellent treatment that it deserves—as we see in another contribution to this symposium—from Seymour Rosenberg (Rosenberg & Jones, 1972; Rosenberg & Sedlak, 1972) and others (Livesley & Bromley, 1973; Schneider, 1973; Warr & Knapper, 1968). We will pass by further discussion of this important concept, reiterating the need for assuming that the person's implicit personality theory must be regarded as an exceedingly important strand in the situation being analyzed.

Self-image Maintenance, Implicit Personality Theory Maintenance, and Cognitive Structure Maintenance

With this broad assumption clearly fixed, we return to the statement that Joey's conduct is channelized by a process of maintaining his self-image as a good boy. Note that these statements focus on *maintaining* self-image, whereas the fourth point, above, alerts us to the high probability that persons do not attain that happy state where all information input validates their construct systems. Invalidation, we can eventually argue, is good for the system. Invalidation encourages elaboration. To proceed smoothly, the discussion centers on maintenance of the system, implying that the person's processes maintain *the utility* of his system.

The last subsection offered the argument that self-construction represents a subspecies of person perception. As such, one argues that the utility of self-constructions is interrelated with the utility of overall implicit personality theory. To state that Joey's conduct involves a process of maintaining the utility of his self-image as a good boy implies that self-image maintenance accompanies maintenance of the utility of his implicit personality theory. Thus, when one brings out a motivational statement which says that a person's psychological processes maintain his self-image, he might just as well immediately expand the statement to say a person's processes maintain his person-cognizing structures. Then, why not go all the way: People's psychological processes maintain the utility of their cognizing structures. The conduct of a person reflects the functioning of an information-processing system which is channelized by anticipatory orderings, by which the system's utility attains validation.

Well, we just can't get any broader than that. But accepting this major premise only intensifies the problem of assessing a person's anticipations. And, in the end, what value will derive from accepting this very broad contextualist statement? Obviously the thrust of this essay is to argue that these questions should be answered positively. We'll try to say that this view helps to assess what a person anticipates, and we'll promote the general point that a behavior scientist is in good shape if he takes a broad contextualist view.

Talking about a Person's Specific Anticipations

At the outset, to answer broadly the question of what a person anticipates, we had said that persons anticipate that their organizing structures will successfully integrate events; that is, persons anticipate that the hypotheses deriving from their organizing structures will gain validation. This should be a familiar statement to those familiar with Kelly's view that every act is an experiment and that every man is a scientist (Kelly, 1969).

Large gaps still exist in the model. An investigator cannot present convincing demonstrations of the model by saying, very broadly, "This person anticipates confirmation of hypotheses." To produce a strong validation of a motive statement based on anticipation, an investigator needs to produce experimental evidence that a person walks about his life carrying a specific set of personal constructs; that from these constructs he builds the specific hypotheses he tries to test; and that the flow of his behavior is directed and altered by the successes and failures of his in-life experiments.

Researchers explicitly committed to personal construct theory have studied and have produced methods of directly assessing an individual's person-perceiving construct repertoire. Other investigators who have been working the field generally known as person perception also have invented ingenious approaches to assessing the structural and process aspects of individual systems for locating persons with whom they interact. Much of this work, in addition, has pushed into understandings of what takes place as a person draws inferences and builds person-explaining hypotheses within his implicit personality theory. Such work has given extended credibility to the premise that persons do try to anticipate the confirmation of specific hypotheses about the conduct of themselves and of other persons.

Outside of this broad, but still somewhat restricted, area of psychological study, there also has developed an immense reserve of support (to which we shall turn shortly) for the motivational principle which states that a person's behavior is guided by his efforts to anticipate events. In addition, this same reserve shows us a useful means by which to assess a person's cognizing structures and the hypotheses which emerge from an individual's specific structures. The steady infusion of contextualism, which we observe in general psychology, has produced a stream of studies which can be used to show the utility of speaking about anticipation.

In actuality, the investigations to which we refer illuminate the processes that follow when a person "tries out" his constructions in situations where he meets *failure* to anticipate. One can now find innumerable studies which show the motivational effects of *"novelty"*; and these studies are particularly useful in that they show that the stream of conduct is channelized by discrepant information—that is, that *attention* is regulated by discrepancies between input and existing structure. These studies also alert us to strands which help to explain how systems are elaborated through the process of accommodation—that is, "bending the system to fit" the novel information. We turn to some of the studies of discrepancy and attention to show the cogency of the general assumption that behavior is guided by a person's anticipations.

NOVELTY, ATTENTION, AND ANTICIPATION

Mechanistically inclined theorists haven't had an easy time as they have tried to construe the kinds of energy that would push a person into novelty seeking (see Mancuso, 1970, pp. 3–26; Fowler, 1965). Kelly, in his usual style, located and offered his resolution to their dilemma.

> Our position regarding spontaneous activity permits us to formulate a rational explanation of why children, and adults too, appear to seek danger and discomfort. Neither self-preservation theory nor hedonistic theory has been able to handle this problem satisfactorily. Psychoanalytic theory, a double-ended version of hedonistic theory, handles it by postulating the instincts of Eros and Todestrieb, thus

bracketing all kinds of behavior while defining none. The explanation of danger-seeking and discomfort-seeking behavior, which the psychology of personal constructs offers, is that it is an elaboration of one's psychological systems in an area where the regnant constructs are permeable enough to permit such elaboration. In simpler, though somewhat looser language, spontaneous activity, even though it involves danger and discomfort indicates where a person's areas of richest experience lie. . . .

. . . one tends to choose what events he will elaborate because they appear to be amenable to treatment. Thus, the man who spends his leisure hours listening to a sports broadcast sees that as a closely interrelated series of happenings which he can anticipate without utter bafflement, but which is not so monotonously repetitive that it does not invite any extension or definition of his predictive system. [P. 735]

In this way Kelly laid out a constructivist perspective on the processes of *attention* in relation to *personalized novelty*. Attention, in this formulation, appears in those contexts where information input represents a moderate discrepancy from existing construction capabilities. And one readily identifies this same conceptualization in current studies of cognitive operations, where *attention* has become the index word for discussion of channelization of conduct. In the language growing out of Broadbent's (1958, 1971) influence in this area of psychology, investigators have tried to devise descriptions of how information gains access to the "central processor."

In a favorite model used to study the matter of access to the central processor, a subject is placed into a situation where several varieties, or "channels," of controlled information can simultaneously affect the person's receptor mechanisms. He is then given instructions which direct him to make overt responses based on the information arriving through one particular channel. Concurrently or later, nevertheless, he must report an aspect of the information that had been directed to other channels. The findings show that the other channels have somehow "been registered." Subjects can repeat, under certain conditions, important segments of the material that had not occupied the central processor. Furthermore, while subjects engage the material in the central processor, there are means of regulating and manipulating stimuli so that material entering the ancillary channels will take over the central processor.

Inevitably, *novelty* appears to be implicated as the salient variation that describes the material from the ancillary channels which enter the central processor. A key figure in the research on reaction to novelty, we all know, has been E. N. Sokolov, whose work has made the term *orienting reflex* a household word among students of attention. Perhaps Sokolov's work has gained its special status because he has painstakingly associated response to novelty to physiological functioning, and has thus given this area of study the kind of "substance constructs" (Rychlak, 1973, p. 4) to which many scholars willingly offer scientific status.

> Orientation reflexes are characterized by wide-spread excitation (ocular and head movement, peripheral vasoconstriction, galvanic skin reactions), and arising with the participation of either cortical or subcortical centres. The orientation reflex is the first response of the body to any new stimulus. [Sokolov, 1963, p. 23]

> . . . any new stimulus gives rise to peripheral vasoconstriction which becomes weaker and ceases with repetitive stimulation. Painful stimuli, and the application of cold, give rise to similar reactions which do not disappear with repetition. [P. 36]

> Any alteration affecting the stimulus leads to an increased level of excitability in the orientation apparatus, and inhibition of the connexions between the impulses produced by the start of stimulation and the specific reaction apparatus. Consequently, at the start of its action a stimulus gives rise to the orientation reaction. [P. 69]

Yet, without any attempt to denigrate the fine contributions which Sokolov has made, "psychology is not something 'to do until the biochemist comes'" (Neisser, 1967, p. 6). Attention may be discussed within other metaphors. Morey (1970) does so:

> *Assumption 1.* At any moment a listener is sampling only one message. All others are totally rejected. . . .
> *Assumption 2.* A running average of the level of activity in each "channel" is kept (i.e., some kind of "adaptation level" is monitored). . . .
> *Assumption 3.* A sudden departure from the current running average state of a locus will result in the switch being called to that locus for at least a short time (with the option of staying

there longer once it is there) or after current processing on the accepted channel has reached a decision providing the accepted channel is then silent. If it is active the call will become effective at the next silent period, or when voluntarily switched.

Assumption 4. Sampling may be continued on one channel indefinitely until the switch is "called" by another channel. There is probably no quantal effect or upper limit on the sample duration. [Pp. 190–191]

However another theorist puts it, we will step in and say that *attention is regulated by deviation from anticipations.* It would be easy to say simply that attention is regulated by novelty.

This latter formulation immediately puts us into difficulty. If one implicates novelty without taking into account the person's cognizing structures, he faces the cogent criticisms leveled by Thompson and Bettinger (1970):

A photograph of the moon is in some sense completely novel to a cat; it is also completely uninteresting. While definitions of novelty (as it is used in much current research) commonly invoke stimulus parameters such as intensity, suddenness, irregularity, and absence of prior presentation, in the last analysis, degree of stimulus novelty is defined by the organism's response to it. A novel stimulus is one to which the organism attends. It is distinguished from certain other categories of stimuli (e.g., reinforcing stimuli) by the fact that response to a novel stimulus habituates. This reflects back to the definition of attention in terms of orienting. The response an organism makes to a novel stimulus is an orienting response and it habituates with stimulus repetition. This in turn suggests that response habituation is the necessary condition to define attention. [P. 392]

To avoid the circularity of defining novelty in terms of the person's after-the-fact response to the presented information, one must previously specify the structures which apply as a person monitors the stimulus input. To do this, one speaks rather of *incongruity* or *discrepancy* than of novelty. Thus, to show that incongruity shares the context with attention one must first settle on a method of assessing and/or prespecifying the cognitive structures which a person has available and which he will apply as he monitors the input. Experimental demonstrations of the efficacy of describing motivation by speaking of anticipations must begin with an a priori statement of what the person as subject will anticipate, and thereby includes specifications of how the stimulus input will disrupt the person's anticipations. In short, the experimental hypotheses must speak of the novelty, or lack of novelty, in terms of the person's existing construct systems. This, we see, revives the perennial problem of prespecifying the person's existing conceptualizations.

Another major point tempts a digression. Note that Sokolov, as well as Thompson and Bettinger, indicate that orienting responses diminish rapidly as the person habituates to the incongruent stimulus. If we are building a theory to explain behavior by using a principle which states that anticipation regulates the flow of conduct, we can profit from offering an extended answer to the question, How does one account for habituation? Our answer would be: Either the person's structures are altered so that the stimulus can be integrated, or the stimulus situation can, after all, be incorporated in terms of existing structures. In short, at this point a contextualist describes learning.

Another point also needs our attention. Thus far the argument has focused largely on the effects of failure to anticipate—on incongruity. If one accepts the principle that attention is regulated by deviation from anticipation, he must take care that he does not assume implicitly that persons continually seek to avoid failure to anticipate. There are two sides to the coin. One side of this coin is studied under the rubric of "novelty seeking."

Kelly, as we saw earlier in this section, related novelty seeking to elaborations of the more permeable of a person's constructions. Granting that Berlyne (1971) clings rather tenaciously to his mechanistic constructs, a constructivist hears a familiar theme when Berlyne speaks about a person's seeking out of situations which might temporarily produce perceptual disorientation and uncertainty.

> There are grounds for suspecting that an essential difference in function [of exploratory behavior and aesthetic behavior] underlies the distinction that we have felt compelled to draw between specific and diversive exploration. Specific exploration is a response to conflict and uncertainty resulting from incomplete perception. Since the selection of an adaptive or optimal course of action depends on information about conditions in the external environment and conditions inside the organism, it is

easy to see that uncertainty (lack of information) and conflict among competing courses of action, none of which is strong enough to prevail over the others, threatens adaptation. Consequently, it is useful for an animal to find uncertainty aversive, so that it takes steps to gather the missing information, and for relief of certainty to be rewarding. Because of the considerable hedonic value with which satisfaction of curiosity is invested, an organism that is equipped to do so (as the human organism is) can be expected to seek out situations productive of perceptual disorientation, uncertainty, and curiosity when they hold out prospects of orientation and clarification without too much cost or delay. Art affords such opportunities, as does the behavior of the rat that enters novel, changing portions of a maze in preference to others. So do other human intellectual activities, such as philosophy, mathematics, and science, as well as crossword puzzles and games of chess.

Through diversive exploration, animals seek out stimulation from any source that has the right collative properties. This presumably means stimulation that yields an arousal increment within the rewarding range. Such behavior is particularly strong when the arousal potential of the environment has been inordinately sparse for some time. Diversive exploration must surely be connected with the fact that the human nervous system is made to cope with a certain influx of information or rate of stimulus change. [Pp. 289–290]

Connecting the Basic Postulate to Attention Studies

These points regarding attention can now be gathered to support the position that a person's conduct is regulated by his anticipations. To reach this premise, one accepts the corollary that a person's existing structures must be taken into the account. Under these assumptions the meaning of *anticipate* deviates from the meaning frequently assigned to the term, in that anticipation does not necessarily imply a deliberate, future test of the applicability of the person's constructions. In short, we forestall the risk that we will transfer the energies of mechanism from the back end to the front end. Here, the idea subsumed by the term *anticipation* relates to the "current running average state" which Moray postulates as part of his theory of attention. The current average running state would be defined by the person's existing construction systems. As the person goes through his life, he is perpetually engaged in a monitoring process whereby *all* stimulus input is checked against existing structure. Where there occurs a discrepancy between input and existing structure—"expectations"—the input to the disrupted channel is shifted to the central processor. This stimulus occupies "attention" until the incongruity is resolved—either through a recheck that shows that there can be, indeed, as stimulus/construction match, or through a change in structure. These periods of "problem solving" are accompanied by physiological arousal, and when the incongruity has been resolved, there is "habituation," marked by a diminution of the physiological activation. On the other hand, where there is a long period of stimulus redundancy, the central processor is usurped by stimuli that have less impact (see Fiske & Maddi, 1961, for a highly relevant and illuminating discussion of impact). That is, the central processor is usurped by stimuli which are less incongruent relative to the incongruent stimuli that ordinarily would take over the central processor.

ANTICIPATION, MOTIVATION, AND PERSONALITY THEORY

These samples of work in a very active area of current psychological science bear witness to the utility of using a contextualist approach to understanding behavior. One must agree that the thought that has guided these works has been as hardheaded as any in psychology. Further, these samples illustrate the utility of a contextualist approach in defining a substantive area of theory—namely, the definition of a principle that explains the channelization of conduct. Working from the assumptions constructed from this work on attention, one readily accepts the large utility of Kelly's Fundamental Postulate and Choice Corollary.

A person's processes—his conduct—are directed toward those events which are incongruent with the internalized structures against which information has been monitored. Resolution of discrepancy occupies the major part of a person's life activity. At the same time, prolonged immersion in a state approaching absolute absence of discrepancy also "motivates," in that attention is diverted toward low-discrepancy material following periods of high redundancy.

The Limits on Structural Change in Resolving Incongruity

Incongruity can be resolved by a revision of the internalized structures. In personal construct theory this kind of variation is known as learning. And a construct theorist would willingly agree that most persons resolve most of their incongruity encounters by learning—that is, by revising structure. However, "to be effective, the construction system must have some regularity" (Kelly, 1955, p. 76). Thus, while trying to explain motive to change, the theory also must account for limits to change. Here one needs the Choice Corollary. One would not be left with a theory of *persons* if he were to hypothesize that every incongruity will lead to a rapid and effective change of structure. This would mean that with every novel stimulus a person would apply a novel structure. Any structure would do, and there simply would be no regularity of structure. Obviously, a contextualist approach collapses without a proposition that asserts the continuity of structure. A contextualist assumes that personal constructs will be a part of every event. Structure is categorical in the metatheory. The centrality of this assumption leads a contextualist, like Kelly, to make structure—one's way of anticipating events—a part of the Fundamental Postulate. If the person's structure is taken to be a part of the flow of conduct, then one does not expect structure to change abruptly from one segment of the flow to the next. Change is implied when one speaks of flow and channelization, but the change is epigenetic—the new represents a development out of the old. In any specific event discrepancy signifies an invalidated hypothesis. The same system that produced the invalidated hypothesis must produce another. Not any hypothesis will do. The choice of new hypotheses will be limited to those that allow for "the greater possibility for extension and definition of [the person's] system" (Kelly, 1955, p. 64).

Correspondingly, Pepper (1942) noted that a contextualist perspective does not focus on static categories. "The ineradicable contextualist categories may thus be said to be *change* and *novelty*" (p. 235). Recall that Kelly rejected the "cognitive psychology" of his era, hedging at the possibility that the focus of theory would become the fixed "cognitive dispositions." He proposed a theory that would at once speak of some regularity as well as *extending* and *defining*. The focus was not to be the fixed construct system, but the focus was to be the process of *maintaining* the utility of the system. As Pepper (1942) explained the root metaphor—the basic model—of contextualism, which he identifies as the historical act, he emphatically tells us,

> the contextualist does not mean primarily a past event, one that is, so to speak, dead and has to be exhumed. . . . To give instances of this root metaphor (the historical act) in our language with the minimum of risk of misunderstanding, we should use only verbs. It is doing, and enduring, and enjoying. . . . These acts are continuously complex, composed of interconnected activities with continuously changing patterns. They are like incidents in the plot of a novel or drama. They are literally the incidents of life. [Pp. 232–233]

Similarly the contextualist, acting as a personality theorist, will not describe a person as a fixed being held together with traits or constructs. A person's regularities need to be described, but the description must be that of a *regularity in a process*. From this perspective emerges the principle describing the limits of change of the existing structure. The limits on change within a system, that is, the range of choices that can be applied to an event, are set by the system itself.

SO, WHAT ELSE IS NEW?

The preceding sections contain many repetitions of the claim that important segments of psychology have been undergoing a paradigm revolution, and that the replacement paradigm is built around conceptualizations which allow it to be classed as a contextualist paradigm. This claim bears such repetition, for we are attempting to show that personal construct theory, as personality theory, has been a contributor and a beneficiary of this revolution. Our essay aims at showing that the development of personal construct theory, as propounded by Kelly (1955) and as it has been elaborated by numerous active investigators and interpreters (see, for example, Bannister & Fransella, 1971; Bieri, Atkins, Briar, Leaman, Miller & Tripodi, 1966; Bonarius, 1970; Jaspers, 1966; Landfield, 1971; Mancuso, 1970), has shared in the revolution.

There must be some claim, however, for Kelly's originality and daring. He did, after all, stage a rather bold foray when he offered a contextualist theory as a complete theory of personality. One must also agree that the boldness and originality of this move has not yet been fully appreciated. This claim finds verification through a review of the most recently published introductory psychology textbooks. One of these ideally illustrates our point. The first author of this textbook (Haber & Fried, 1975) has been a major participant in the progress toward establishing cognitive modes of discussing human conduct. In fact, one of Haber's (1958) early entries into contextualism proves to be a very suitable demonstration of the utility of a motivation principle built on the concept of discrepancy from expectations. As one expects in a textbook reflecting Haber's background in experimental psychology, the sections of the book which treat learning, motivation, information processing, language, and so forth reflect the vigor of the contextualist revolution. But the hapless beginning student of psychology who takes seriously an effort to relate the work of experimental psychology to general explanations of behavior must flounder when he tries to study the chapter in which the authors discuss personality theory. This chapter differs little from chapters which appeared in introductory textbooks written in 1945. Personal construct theory apparently has not been reviewed by the authors of this text, and Haber and Fried leave the critical student to conclude that the contextualist revolution has managed to reach only to the frontiers of Haber's area of specialization.

Kelly's originality, then, must be acclaimed on the score that he did presage the possibilities of a complete personality theory built on a complete contextualist paradigm. Something seems to restrain other psychologists from pushing to this point. Consider the recent appearance of an exciting book by Levine (1975). In this book one finds the chronicle of 40 years of building a contextualist view of "learning theory." Levine traces out the radical changes in theories of learning which followed Kretch's (see Krechevsky, 1932) serious application of the perspective that even the lowly rat was guided by his anticipations—his "hypotheses." What restrains other psychologists from recognizing that these radical changes can be articulated to personality theory? Somewhere in this set of events one should discover a valuable principle applying to the sociology of knowledge!

Kelly (1955) has stated explicitly, using the most direct language, that a learner is a hypothesis tester. The following passage, though somewhat more poetic than that which one finds in Levine's (1975) text on learning, would not be out of place in that book.

> The subject in a learning experiment is no exception to our psychological rule. He too directs his psychological processes by seeking the recurrent theme in the experiment. If he segments the experience into separate "trials," and then further separates the "trials" into "reinforced trials" and "unreinforced trials," he may hear the same repetitive theme which the experimenter hears. On the other hand, he may not be so conventional. He may listen for other kinds of themes he has heard before. He may not even segment his experience into the kinds of trials or events the experimenter expects. In the language of music, he may employ another way of phrasing. Viewed in this manner, the problem of learning is not merely one of determining how many or what kinds of reinforcements fix a response, or how many nonreinforcements extinguish it, but rather, how does the subject phrase the experience, what recurrent themes does he hear, what movements does he define, and what validations of his predictions does he reap? [Kelly, 1955, pp. 75–76]

One cannot miss the very strong resemblance between Kelly's personality theory and the kinds of concepts used by the theorists discussed by Levine (1975). Yet, while theorists now willingly analyze learning as a venture in hypothesis testing—giving positive status to the contextualist revolution in the discussion of learning—personal construct theory has not fully entered the range of convenience of the category labeled *personality theory*. How is this to be explained? What allowed Kelly and his co-theorists to think of a contextualist approach to learning as personality theory, while specialists who have worked to develop contextualist concepts persist in believing that one must use mechanistic metaphors to talk about personality theory?

Consider this bold proposition. Psychologists and laymen construe personality theory and mechanistic motivational principles as largely overlapping constructions. Thus, they cannot reconceptualize basic functions of behavior in terms other than *push, pull,* and *shove.* Personal construct theory can't be personality theory, in that it simply doesn't tell us about how the machine is powered! Personality theory always has told us about the powerhouse of the machine! Thus, the largest barrier to general acceptance of personal construct theory as a general theory of behavior has been the barrier that arises when the thoughtful scholar asks questions like, "But what motivates the person to concentrate on discrepancy resolution? How does the 'need' to anticipate become so salient that it would lead a person to alter his self-construction?" Such plaintive questions evolve from the deep entrenchment of the view that a person would stay glued to dead nothingness were he not pushed or dragged through life. Entrapped in mechanism, scholars cannot believe that a bit of flesh known as a baby could become the complex psychological entity known as a person. Adam Smith, believe it or not, dictates the prevalent views of personality.

Kelly's special contribution, then, derived from his ability to throw off mechanism and to declare that persons are in business to anticipate—and that's their only business. Persons aren't trying to collect goody points. Obversely, persons aren't trying to avoid getting kicked. Kelly could not be lured into trying to show that a person's previous reinforcement history determines his commitment to the business of anticipations. In Kelly's view of the person, anticipatory activity does not live on energy borrowed from, or imported from, other "real" drives and motives.

A continuation of the discussion of current studies on attention highlights the utility of Kelly's propositions. Infants attend. What is the context in which infants show signs of activity associated with failure to anticipate? Do infants attend only after having been rewarded for attending behavior? If attending, or information seeking, can be seen in infants exposed to a wide variety of stimuli, what common features occur in the context associated with such information seeking?

Infant Attention and Discrepancy

Shortly after Kelly published his theory of personality, Solley and Murphy (1960) published their conceptualization of attention. Children attend on borrowed energy!

During physical and psychological development the individual learns to attend or . . . to respond maximally to a large but finite number of things. . . . We believe that most acts of attending are conditioned along the lines of operant conditioning . . . , although classical conditioning is conceivable. That is, if an individual makes receptor adjustments, or some search behavior, and is immediately given a reinforcement stimulus, then the probability of his repeating that attentive response will increase. Let us go a step further and examine the factors that control or direct attending, because attending rarely arises spontaneously. One of the major factors, at least in the early stages of development, is motivation. [Pp. 187–188]

Solley and Murphy then discuss a study which they regard as a prototype of the conditioning of attention—that is, the importing of energy from one motive force to be used as an energizer for search behavior. Nine- and ten-year-old children looked at and named four figurines, representing various animals, that appeared in one of four windows. Each time that the child named one particular figurine, during the course of his naming all the figurines in the display, the experimenter "rewarded" the child with a verbalization that reflected approval. As predicted, after having engaged in this procedure, the child would more frequently look toward the "rewarded" figurine.

This kind of demonstration is hard to beat. To criticize the apparent conclusions one must first meet the standard mechanist's challenge—"It works, doesn't it?" Of course it works—as do these conditioning demonstrations. And, of course, it would be very useful to know the hypothesis that guides the child's search behavior. One might also want to consider the possibility that the children had hypothesized that by keeping an eye on the "rewarded" figurine they could get out of the rather silly situation in which they were trapped. In other words, the "conditioning procedure" worked, but its working might have more to do with the coercive conditions of the study than with the postulated importation of the energy generated by the experimenter's "rewards." Attention, in this situation, might yet be explained in terms of the child's efforts to remove himself from the situation which was incongruent with its overall self-definition—specifically, in this case, a situation in which two adults had asked him to engage in a rather mysterious problem.

In that one cannot be sure what hypothesis guided the behavior of these older children, the demonstration reported by Solley and

Murphy does not convincingly frame attention and motivation. More recent work on attention, using very young infants, offers a sounder basis for relating attention to an overall contextualist theory on person development.

Infant Attention

The work of Lewis and his many collaborators (see Lewis, 1971) best illustrates the investigations of infant attention. These investigators follow a line of experiment and thought which consistently describes infant attention within a contextualist model which emphasizes the principle that infant attention is guided by its anticpations.

Characteristically, Lewis and his collaborators have presented young infants (as young as 3 months) with repeated signals. The signals might be simple, to an adult. A blinking light, for example, might be repeatedly presented. Fixation time and cardiac rate deceleration provide measures of attention. The findings of this kind of demonstration are direct. Very young infants remain "aroused" for relatively long periods of time; that is, they fixate for a longer period of time, and their heart rate remains lowered for a relatively longer period of time. Older children, by comparison, show a more rapid decrement of attentional responding.

Lewis concludes that the processes should be discussed in terms of the infant's building internal representations, that is, "models." The older child, already having available the elements—we would call them constructs—out of which to build a short-term model, would quickly find the repeating stimulus to be redundant. The younger child, having yet to develop the constructs out of which to build a model to which the repeated stimulus may be assimilated, cannot rapidly accommodate the information, and the very young infant will continue to show a "novelty reaction" for a relatively greater number of stimulus repetitions.

In a demonstration like that described above, the infant's models, or cognitive structures, are developed in the experimental situation; and in that way these models are not analogues to the long-term models that adults would use in their anticipating processes. It seems profitable to think of one's model of himself, for example, as a long-term model, which is carried from situation to situation. One then thinks of these models as the guide to the anticipatory activity of a person. The analogue to this process of using long-term models also appears in very young children.

Figural representations of the human face and the human form evoke varied responses from young children at various points during their first year of life. A 4-month-old child will show markedly longer attention to a "regulation," achromatic representation of a face, while it will show relatively less attention to an abstract, geometrically varied form (McCall & Kagan, 1967). At the same time, children of this same age show greater attention to a "face-like" face than they show to spatially arranged stimuli that are very discrepant from "faceness" (Haaf & Bell, 1967; Finley, Kagan, & Layne, 1972). By the end of the eighteenth month of age, the infant gives equal attention to photographic representations of faces and to the presence of a person. Photographic representations appear to become complete schemata unto themselves, and they no longer represent discrepancy from the "real face" schemata.

To conduct a more stringent test of the discrepancy/attention hypothesis, Finley, Kagan, and Layne (1972) designed a series of faces and a series of representations of a whole person. Within each series, the individual representations were judged to deviate, in stepwise fashion, from the relevant schema that the child would have developed in daily living. Four representations, for example, portrayed the complete human form and three discrepant representations: (a) the complete, normal form; (b) the torso and head with no limbs, normally represented; (c) a scrambled figure, in which appendages were attached rather randomly; and (d) a free-art form that occupied the same general area as occupied by the other representations. Fixation time was taken as the measure of attention. The results of the study confirmed the hypotheses in every way. Further, the patterns of fixation were identical in children from two widely different cultural situations. Children in Cambridge, Massachusetts, responded very much as did the children of rural Mayan families in the Yucatan Peninsula.

The youngest children (1 year old) attended longest to the most facelike or bodylike representation and gave less and less attention to the representations as they became less and less facelike. On the whole, 2- and 3-year-old children gave longer times to integrating the scrambled figures. Finley et al. conclude:

One way to interpret these developmental changes is to posit the activation of hypotheses as outlined by Kagan (1970a,

1970b). Kagan has suggested that toward the end of the first year, duration of attention comes under the partial control of a process called activation of hypotheses. The essential notion is that the child attempts to transform a discrepant stimulus into the form with which he is familiar, the latter being labelled a schema. [P. 292]

As studies reach publication, the model takes on more and more credibility. As another example, Berg (1972) has completed a thorough study which shows that 4-month-old infants habituate to sound patterns of varied frequency and temporal sequencing. Heart-rate deceleration measures provided the data for analysis. Within five or six repetitions of the stimulus the infants showed very rapid recovery of heart-rate deceleration following the onset or offset of the stimulus pattern. When the quality of the stimulus pattern was changed from the original habituating pattern, the heart-rate deceleration again required a lengthy recovery time. Here, again, the expectancy was created in the experimental situation, and the accommodating of the infant's schemata can be seen to be associated with a diminution of heart-rate changes.

One could persist in arguing that these infants had been conditioned earlier to respond to novelty. The argument, however, is nonproductive and unnecessary. In the first place, knowing what we do about classifying behavior in youngsters (Inhelder & Piaget, 1964; Kendler & Kendler, 1962, 1969), it becomes difficult to believe that an infant can build a class "novel events" to which it can then generalize a conditioned fear response. The puzzles within the mechanistic paradigm will be best solved by adopting the contextualist paradigm and its motivational principle: A person is—right off—in business to anticipate.

The Loving Mother as Novelty Regulator

Developmental psychologists show particular affinity for the proposition that moderate discrepancy guides the psychological processes of the developing person. Ginsburg and Opper (1969), in discussing Piaget's transparently contextualist theory, say about Piaget's concept of disequilibration, as reflected by infant search behavior:

But the infant does not simply look at more and more things.

His visual preferences become selective. The infant's attention is directed at events which are *moderately novel*: " . . . one observes that the subject looks neither at what is too familiar, because he is in a way surfeited with it, nor at what is too new because this does not correspond to anything in his [schemes] . . . " (Piaget, 1952, p. 68). This motivational principle may appear deceptively simple and trite. In reality, however, it represents a point of view which is radically different from previous (and some current) theories and is only now receiving the attention it deserves. First, like the principle of assimilation, the moderate novelty principle is strongly at odds with theories which stress avoidance of stimulation as the only kind of motivation. On the contrary, according to Piaget's view, the child actively seeks out new stimulation—he is not forced to look at novel objects. Second, the moderate novelty principle is different from other motivational theories in that it is a relativistic concept. That which catches an individual's curiosity is not entirely the physical nature of the event. It is not the object *per se* that attracts attention; instead curiosity is a function of the *relation* between the new object and the individual's previous experience. . . . In sum, the novelty principle asserts that what determines curiosity is not the physical nature of the object, but rather the degree to which the object is discrepant from what the individual is familiar with, which, of course, depends entirely on the individual's experience. [P. 39]

The strength and importance of this principle are well illustrated by the fact that the principle now becomes fully integrated into first-level developmental psychology textbooks. In a recent edition of a widely used child development textbook (Mussen, Conger, & Kagan, 1974) we find an important chapter on social factors in development which contains the following statement:

We shall use the term attachment to refer to the infant's tendency during the first 24 months to approach particular people, to be maximally receptive to being cared for by these people, and to be least afraid with these people. The primary objects of the child's attachment have the greatest power to placate him and to protect him from fear when he experiences a strange event or is in an unfamiliar situation. [Pp. 204–205]

In this chapter, the writer dismisses the old mechanistic view that a mother achieves her "loved-one status" through her acquisition of the positive energies that were originally attached to "hunger reduction" or other need gratification. Instead, the mother becomes a focus of the child's attachment as a function of the mother having properly enacted the role of *novelty moderator*. In turn, the infant develops a well-articulated schema of the specific persons who regularly care for him. Thereafter, the child's processes, including the external behaviors associated with them, will flow in directions that maintain optimum discrepancy between input and his well-articulated schemata of the novelty moderator. For example, those "fear behaviors" he emits when the novelty moderator would leave him alone in a novel situation represent behaviors that can bring the moderator back into the situation. When the moderator's conduct confirms the child's expectation—for example, by his accompanying the child in the novel situation—the child will carry out the arousing exploration of his new surroundings. Similarly, in a learning situation a child will more carefully follow the leads of a well-articulated novelty moderator. By definition, the child cannot construe a successful moderator as *arousal-producing*. Thus, when in the moderator's presence, the child functions from an anticipation that he will achieve success in working with new, construct-expanding information.

The writers of this textbook have not chosen to abandon totally those mechanistic motivational concepts that have traditionally filled developmental literature. They have, nevertheless, given thorough treatment to the important concept that the "love" which is so very important to infant development can be discussed in terms of discrepancy regulation. We want to make much more of this principle, as it relates to person development.

MORAL JUDGMENTS AND DISCREPANCY RESOLUTION

One can clearly see the differences among contextualist, mechanist, and idiographic motivational principles when he looks at theories applied to explaining rule-following or rule-violating behavior. Idiographic or formist paradigms are currently not favored as approaches to the explanation of rule-oriented behaviors. Concepts such as "moral degenercy" or "constitutionally criminal" have scant place in modern developmental studies of crime. A student would be surprised to find a contemporary academic scholar who would speak, as did Lombroso, of inborn, fixed character which finds expression in conduct that "has the form of" immorality. On occasion a concept implicating a genetic disposition toward criminality does appear in the literature, but most authors would not maintain a serious idiographic perspective in their discussion of rule orientations. Thus, we pass quickly to a discussion of mechanistic and contextualist views of a person's responses to rules.

It is useful to begin with Bannister and Fransella's (1971) treatment of aggression and hostility. Following Kelly, they take the position that "a person is being aggressive when he actively experiments to check the validity of his construing; when he extends the range of his constructions (and thereby his activities) in new directions; when he is exploring" (pp. 37–38). Used this way the concept of aggression loses a special meaning. Bannister and Fransella describe aggression as the process that we would call discrepancy resolution. In this sense, all active learning efforts would be construed as aggression. Perhaps this loss of the special meaning of *aggression* is useful. Always a rather unsatisfactory concept in the psychological literature, it could be dropped from discussion.

When they discuss *hostility*, however, Bannister and Fransella are talking about a special category of discrepancy resolution. When a person cannot abandon the constructions from which he derived his expectations he can try to "extort evidence, to bully people into behaving in ways which confirm his predictions" (p. 35). From this notion of "bullying" we move forward to building a way of construing our loving mother as novelty moderator and so-cializer—the teacher of rules.

At those points in a mother-child interaction at which the mother attempts to lay down a rule, an investigator can identify an instance of two people applying alternative constructions to the same event. For example, a child who breaks a vase which he had been trying to fill with water might construe the situation as "an *accident, inad-vertently* resulting from his efforts to be *helpful*." His mother might see the scene as "*carelessness*, an *avoidable* event, had the child been more *thoughtful*." The mother gives verbal expression to her construction of the event. (Note that this immediately introduces discrepancy into the child's short-term schema of the event. Following assumptions laid down earlier, we may say that the event takes over the central processor, and the discrepancy must be resolved.) Suppose that the child gives verbal expression to his construction of the event. (The child's statement introduces further discrepancy into the mother's system of explanation.) It would not be difficult to imagine the mother's response to be as follows: "Don't argue with me. You must learn to be careful. You get right to your room, and you stay there until I tell you that you may come down for supper." The mother now has shown hostility, in Bannister and Fransella's terms. To avoid confusion of terms, let us use the term *coercion*.

We will also add a refinement to the definition of coercion. We will say: Coercion refers to behavior that diverts attention from a socially produced rule-relevant discrepancy to another, nonrelated discrepancy. By sending a child to his room, the mother expresses a prediction that the child will face a disconfirmation of its self-schemata, relative to its constructions of *freedom-constraint*. Confinement to one's room, like a swat to the backside, is not relevant to the immediate problem of how to construe the breaking of the vase. If the child construes the situation as constraint, this discrepant information, which can be described as a coercive measure, has no direct relationship either to the child's construct *careful-careless* or to his location of his own actions along that construct. In fact, following the theory of attention which we have tried to develop, coercion diverts the child's attention from a currently central construction process to the process of construing the new discrepant stimulation that is produced by the coercive behavior. The theory tells us that if he learns anything in this situation—and here we speak of Kelly's concept of learning, which is the altering of constructions—he will learn about how to respond to coercion.

If this analysis is correct, one must ask: Why do coercive techniques retain their perennial appeal? Our answer to this rhetorical question must please any constructivist. People coerce because coercion repeatedly appears as a part of the context of behavioral reform. Coercion *appears* to work! A contextualist cannot be satisfied, however, to allow the implication that coercion "works" by attaching negative energies to the unwanted conduct. That formulation we leave to the mechanistic "behavior modifier" who speaks of his technique "working." A contextualist would not claim that coercion produces negative vectors to the unwanted conduct by some kind of energy transfer. Rather, the contextualist might say that *coercion works because a person finds submitting to coercion to be incongruent with those schemata which define his self.*

Essentially, we are saying that a person builds a construct which he identifies as *coercion-persuasion.* Concommitantly, he comes to recognize that *coercion-persuasion* is subordinate to the construct *good-bad,* with the polarity *coercion* being aligned with the polarity *bad.* If he were able to respond to Osgood's (1973) conjunctive sentences he would write *and,* not *but,* into the blank in the following sentence: The child was bad —— his mother was provoked to coercion. Thus, whenever he is exposed to coercion he knows that he is being asked to accept the view that his conduct marks him as *bad.*   At this point we again see the clarifying utility of Kelly's Choice Corollary. To predict a person's response to coercion, and its inferred signal that the actor is *bad,* we would need to know that person's constructions of the coercer. It is proposed that the subject of the coercion will work out for himself that construction which, in that context, will most probably enhance and elaborate his total existing system. He might even, for example, submit to very harsh coercive measures without indicating that he has altered his constructions (and his conduct) relative to the rule to be followed. In this way, the child who places strong negative value on the coercer can maintain his self-role definition as an "anti-authority cat who can't be pushed around." If he regularly relies on the coercer to provide him with valid ways of construing himself and events, he will accept the construction of his act as *bad,* and by doing that he enhances his total system.

We have argued that parental reprimand represents a mismatch between schema and input. Reprimand can take the form of either direct disconfirmation or coercion, but both forms represent a kind of descrepancy to be resolved. We could use the language of Dienstbier, Hillman, Lehnoff, Hillman and Valkenaar (1975). We could ask about the child's understandings of the "causal origins of the emotional response" (p. 300) that accompanies the discrepancy. Both the direct and the indirect forms of discrepancy, we assume, can be arousing. Dienstbier et al. suggest that

> In order for that emotional arousal to serve an inhibitory function, the individual must identify his emotional discomfort as due to a relevant cause, such as the transgression per se (and

the implications of the transgression for self-image, etc.), rather than as due to irrelevant cause, such as fear of punishment. [P. 300]

Where the mother has previously helped the child to locate successfully the sources of discrepancy and has helped him to bring about resolutions that elaborate and enhance his existing system, we expect that the mother's view of the situation will prevail. She will focus upon the transgression per se and will not resort to coercion—the irrelevant discrepancy producer. The child, having built his schema of his mother, will follow her leads toward discrepancy resolutions. He will focus on the problem represented by the mismatch between his construction and her construction, and will move toward incorporating her construction.

Thus far, our discussion of moral judgment has promoted these points: (a) any effort to promulgate a particular rule involves a situation in which a person gets a message to construe his own conduct, or another event, in terms which match the construction system of the rule-giver; (b) a rule-giver, like any other person who might attempt to extort confirmation of his construction system, can take recourse to coercion; (c) coercion is defined as the production of information input resulting in a discrepancy which diverts attention from the discrepancy under consideration; (d) coercion, in that it associates with the *bad* pole of the superordinate *bad-good* construct, instigates the target person's considerations of how his total self-system is affected by maintaining that judgment of himself ("You're bad"); (e) a person's psychological processes in the presence of coercion and a particular coercer will be directed toward deriving a resolution which best enhances and maintains the person's existing construction system; (f) the mother who has become established as a successful moderator of novelty will focus on the relevant incongruities and will avoid coercion, thus promoting greater acceptance of rules.

The Values of Thinking about Coercion Rather Than about Punishment.

So far we have successfully avoided the term *punishment*. It would have been easy to use it, and in doing so we could have edged into a type of mechanism. Why not say that *punishment* induces behavior change? After all, *punishment* is an ancient and venerated term. Legal systems throughout the world rely on the concept of punishment. So do large numbers of mothers, fathers, educators, and employers.

The fact that the concept is old and venerable prompts us to avoid its use. To talk of punishment immediately encourages people to think of negative valences, with an assurance that such valences automatically develop as a result of one or another environmental reaction toward a person. This essay would become far too long were we to digress into showing that the concept has been very unsatisfactory. If we were to indulge in that digression we would argue that punishment, as a concept for discussing behavior regulation, has no utility until it is subsumed under the general concept of coercion—the application of an incongruity which diverts attention from the discrepancy under consideration. The mother who has "punished" her child has regulated the introduction of novelty into the child's construction system. Her "punishment" shifts attention from the conceptualization under discussion—the rule—to the tangential stimulation coming from the "punishment." The punishment will serve to regulate acceptance of the rule only insofar as the "punishment stimulus" is viewed as a signal that the person's conduct must be altered before the coercer—the punisher—will again judge the transgressor as *good*. If the punishment does not signal this information, or if the transgressor can otherwise maintain the integrity of his self-concept by dismissing the evaluation of that particular punisher, the punishment cannot be effective in regulating behavior. Because we do not want to think of negative forces and valences, but instead want to focus on the construction system which the person brings into the context, we will avoid the term *punishment* just as assiduously as we will avoid the term *reward*.

In effect, we will best understand rule-related behavior when we think of rule promulgation as a matter of encouraging agreed-upon constructions of events. (All this would take us into Kelly's Commonality and Sociality corollaries, of course. And, if we wished, we could venture into the social psychology of influence processes. We would see that investigators like Kelman, 1961, have analyzed these issues from a more mechanistic perspective.) If rule following is to be regarded as agreed-upon constructions of events, we had best focus on the processes by which a person builds his constructions and his self-systems, within which his violation of a rule would produce discrepancy. And, if this becomes our focus, we certainly would want to avoid using diverting techniques at those times when we are trying to have people understand that accepting an agreed-upon construction would enhance and elaborate their self-systems. (Dienstbier et al., 1975, effectively elaborate the point in this last sentence.) In other terms, if we're trying to get a person to see the wisdom of a rule, let's stick to the subject. Let's not divert attention to the issue of who can deliver the most effective diversion. Besides, if coercion does regulate behavior, then it would be most democratic if we allow everyone access to the effective diverters. To each his own atom bomb!

Empirical Study of Reprimand as Incongruity Introduction

Using this kind of approach to the study of moral judgment, can we honor our earlier declaration that a paradigm should be evaluated in terms of whether or not it produces hardheaded validating evidence? Can we empirically show the utility of looking at moral judgment as a matter of anticipating from within one's construction system? Nothing grand can be promised; but we can, at least, begin thinking in these terms. Something interesting is bound to happen. Something like the following has happened.

Our position on coercion has been presented above. In certain circumstances one may conclude that coercion effectively produces an adopting of the rule whose transgression produced the punishment. Our interpretation of personal construct theory does not encourage that conclusion. Instead, we conclude that coercion distracts the transgressor from reorganizing his constructions relative to the event under consideration.

From a different perspective, Dienstbier et al. (1975) reach a similar conclusion.

> On the other hand, responses by socializing agents that threaten the child or that become salient through pain draw sufficient attention away from the transgression so that the child is likely to attribute his emotional discomfort exclusively to confrontation with the socializing agent. When later facing a similar temptation situation, a child treated in the latter manner might experience a high level of emotional arousal, but by attributing his arousal to fear of detection and punishment he could tend to

resist temptation only if he believes detection was likely.
[P. 303]

In language that we tried to establish in the earlier part of this essay, we would say that coercion does not change the "average running state" on which depends the child's actions relevant to the transgression situation. In the absence of such change, the child's participation in the transgressive behavior would continue to remain congruent with his self-constructions, and ensuing participation in that behavior would not produce cognitive strain.

The progression of our argument may be summarized as follows: In the first place, the person enacts a behavior that will be classed as a transgression of propriety. Consistency with the constructivist system induces us to say that he enacted this behavior as a part of his constant propensity to anticipate the greatest elaboration of his existing system. Note carefully that we would not say that the transgressor (a) has yielded to temptation, (b) has acted out an impulse, (c) has performed a response that has been sufficiently rewarded in the past, or (d) has followed the human propensity to do evil. Our formulation explicitly rejects eclecticism. In fact, we disdain eclecticism, taking it as a sign of a sloppy examination of the paradigm's assumptive structure.

Second, when the person is reprimanded he faces an effort by the moral arbiter to declare an alternative construction to the transgressive event. Third, coercion can be one means by which the arbiter may approach the transgressor's "incorrect" construction. Fourth, coercion is regarded as a distracter from the event under consideration. Coercion induces a focus on resolving the existing cognitive strain introduced by the arbiter's having set a nonrelevant condition—namely, that if the transgressor does not accept the arbiter's construction, the transgressor will be presented with a stream of hard-to-integrate stimuli. (The application of such stimuli commonly has been regarded as "punishment.") Fifth, it would follow that the transgressor who is subjected to coercion would attend to the coercion and would engage in the task of resolving the incongruous input deriving from that source. Thus, coercion would divert from the task of developing a reconstruction of the transgressive event. Sixth, if achieving an alternative view of the transgressive situation is the moral arbiter's goal, he might best strive to keep the focus on that task.

A most puzzling aspect of this view of moral training is that the approach has not earned extensive adherence. As we said earlier, the currently popular counter view, that persons develop their notions of propriety through infusions of goodies or through exposure to pain, constantly looks like "it works." Furthermore, my own informal data gathering allows me to believe that the majority of our population believe they should view themselves from a mechanist perspective. When psychologists ask, people believe they should tell us that they accept propriety as a means of achieving gain and avoiding pain. We will only partially resist the temptation to digress, and offer our explanation of why people so readily introspect in terms of this mechanistic motivational position regarding their own behavior. Consider the now infamous Milgram (1963) study. Why didn't the subjects turn to the experimenter and say, "Listen, mister, this is nonsense. Hurting that guy, as you're asking me to do, won't help him to learn one bit better." The subjects, after all, know the niceties of social interaction. They undoubtedly anticipated that had they expressed such a view, they would have disconfirmed all of that avid experimenter's "knowledge" about the mechanistic laws of learning. And, further, the experimenter had the coercive power to announce that the subject was an idiot in the matter of human behavior.

As a part of our effort to work out an overall contextualist view of behavior in situations usually called moral judgment situations, we have set up a series of studies which investigate children's understandings of parental efforts to alter children's constructions of events. We hope to illuminate children's views of parents' pronouncements of rectitude; their views of parental methods of extracting the child's compliance; and their views of other children as they respond directly to parental reprimand. We have used a person-perception approach, in which we ask how children—at various stages of their development—perceive transgressors under different conditions of transgression, reprimand, response to reprimand, and so forth.

Our efforts to work this model are facilitated by the fact that the contextualist paradigm has been the guide to much study of children's views of persons in moral judgment situations. Piaget's (1932, first published in French in 1928) work on the child's developing moral judgment systems has been a fruitful stardard guide to an impressive research and theoretical literature (see Lickona, 1976). On the basis of that work one can draw some rather firm and convincing conclusions about the average child's moral judgment processes.

Piaget showed, among many other things, that a young child judges a transgressor to be bad on the basis of whether a parental proscription has been violated, regardless of how a more experienced person might judge the act itself. In all, Piaget's formulations about moral judgments solidify the view that one best studies this area by following the assumption that conduct is "good" or "bad" only within the context of the judging person's general construction systems.

In the series of studies we have conducted we have explored the matter of moral judgment as a person-perception process, seeking to delimit the kinds of constructs that developing children can bring to the judging situation. Like Piaget (1932) and many other investigators (Buchanan & Thompson, 1973; Costanzo, Coie, Grumet, & Farnill, 1973; Gutkin, 1973) we have explored how children develop the use of the construct *intentional-inadvertent* as applicable to their moral judgments. In our latest study we looked at how children judge a transgressor who has or has not been reprimanded by his mother. This study explores how children think of the effects of coercion and direct cognitive reorganization.

In these studies youngsters watch a videotaped sequence of a boy character (Joey) as he performs a putative transgression. Through use of videotape, we can systematically vary any number of the strands of the context. In this case, we are particularly interested in the variations of the mother's response to the transgression. In one sequence, no parental response is shown. In the second sequence, the mother exacted expiation for the transgression by telling the child that he was to be restricted to his room. In a third sequence, the mother asks that Joey recognize the inappropriateness of his behavior and that he sees the need for more careful conduct.

Two measures provided the data for our analysis. One measure was a straightforward rating scale, the Global Rating Scale (GRS) which was developed for use in Morrison's (1973, 1975) study of moral judgment processes. The GRS enables subjects to rate the filmed transgressor in varying degrees of bad (ratings 1, 2, 3), varying degrees of good (ratings 5, 6, 7), or as neither good nor bad (the rating of 4). To help young children make their judgments, the scale not only has words (very, very good; very good, etc.), it also shows seven smiling or frowning faces, corresponding to each of the seven verbally labeled divisions of the *good-bad* dimension.

The second device, the Moral Behaviors Prediction Test (MBPT),

Table 1

Mean Scores on the Global Rating Scale and Moral Behavior Pre-

Grade	Acc-no rep		Int-no rep		Acc-coerc	
	GRS[b]	MBPT	GRS	MBPT	GRS	MBPT
Kindergarten	3.58	7.17	1.33	3.08	2.42	3.58
Third	4.58	7.75	2.00	1.50	3.58	5.08
Sixth	4.67	8.58	2.33	1.50	4.75	8.92

(table header continued) Conditions[a]

[a]Abbreviations for conditions are as follows:

Acc-no rep = Accidental damage—no reprimand
Int-no rep = Intentional damage—no reprimand
Acc-coerc = Accidental damage—cocercion

presents subjects ten pairs of pictures showing a boy's responses in a variety of situations. As they respond to the test the pictures are verbally described. One of the options depicts "bad" behavior, whereas the other depicts "good" behavior. Subjects indicate their predictions of the filmed transgressor's behaviors in the ten depicted situations. As an example, subjects indicated whether the transgressor (Joey) would leave the playroom in disarray or whether he would carefully put the room into order before leaving. This technique derives from the propositions that persons categorize other persons, and that it is the use of these categories which generates anticipations regarding the perceived persons. If the subject had attributed badness to the actor, after having viewed the transgression and its associated parental reaction, then the subject would maintain constructive congruity by predicting the transgressor to conduct himself badly in the situations depicted on the MBPT.

The GRS responses were given numerical values ranging from 1 (very, very bad) to 7 (very, very good). A child could respond to the MBPT so that he would produce a score of 0 to 10, one point being assigned to each of the "good" alternatives chosen as a prediction of Joey's behavior.

diction Test by Grade Level and Condition

Acc-explan		Int-coerc		Int-explan	
GRS	MBPT	GRS	MBPT	GRS	MBPT
2.25	5.50	1.25	1.58	1.42	2.25
4.17	8.25	1.75	2.08	3.42	3.92
5.08	9.42	3.33	3.83	3.50	3.42

Acc-explan = Accidental damage–explanation
Int-coerc = Intentional damage–cocercion
Int-explan = Intentional damage–explanation

[b]GRS = Global Rating Scale; MBPT = Moral Behavior Prediction Test.

Results of the Study

Table 1 shows the mean scores that were yielded by the responses of the different-aged children who had been subjects in each of the six conditions of transgression and reprimand portrayed in the filmed sequences. Two separate analyses of variance, one of GRS data and one of MBPT data, provided comparisons of ratings made after viewing the variations in intention of the transgressor (trying to help, intentional kicking of the vase), coupled with the varied reprimand conditions (no reprimand, expiation, explanation).

Other analyses had been conducted to explore a variety of familiar issues that have been studied by other investigators who have worked in this area. For example, as the means in Table 1 suggest, we were able to show again that kindergarten-aged children generally will rate an accidental transgressor as "bad," whereas sixth-grade children rate him as "good."

Our main concern, however, leads to a focus on how the children's constructions of the transgressor relate to the varied contexts associated with the variations in the mother's response to the transgression. Figure 1 summarizes the reactions that relate to variations in the mother's reprimand technique. The points plotted represent the means obtained by collapsing across the *intentional-accidental* dimension for the expiation, or coercive, and the explanation conditions. This collapse is logically allowed, in that the grades by intentional-accidental interaction produces no significant variations in rating trends. That is, children at all grades judged the intentional transgressor to be more "bad" than is the accidental transgressor. This relationship holds at all grade levels, on both measures, even though the youngest children reflected their belief that both kinds of transgressors (the accidental and the intentional) are quite bad.

The intuitive analysis of the curves in Figure 1 are generally supported by the significance tests from the analysis of variance. The variations in the mother's approach to reprimand were significantly

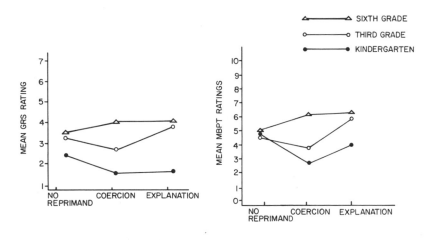

FIG. 1. Mean scores on Global Rating Scale and on Moral Behaviors Prediction Test, for each grade level in each reprimand condition.

related to the variations in the scores on the GRS: F $(2,198) = 3.62$, $p < .05$. The variations on the MBPT scores, though parallel to those on the GRS scores, did not reach a level that would have allowed them to be ascribed convincingly to the variations in the shown reprimand conditions. On the whole, the child who was administered an expiative treatment was judged to be more negative than was the child who was given no parental reprimand, whereas the child who was given an explanatory treatment was judged to be more positive than was the child who was not given a parental reprimand. This overall effect was derived, in large part, from the judgment patterns of the third-graders. The children at this level clearly differentiated the two kinds of reprimand, and they made strongly dissimilar judgments of the differently treated children. Kindergartners, as we would expect from the work of Piaget (1932), judged the reprimanded transgressor, whatever the form of the reprimand, to be more "bad" than was the transgressor who received no parental reaction. Both types of parental response influenced the sixth-graders to perceive the transgressor to be more positive. This last result, then, shows sixth-graders to respond so that their judgments about reprimand are reverse to those developed by the kindergartners.

Some Interpretations

As we see it, the main point of all this is as follows: Children of different ages do not see the same thing when they look at a specific event which an authority would define as reprimand. Obviously we need to do a great deal more exploration before we can crawl out on a long explanatory limb, but we are willing to follow our theory. To begin, we are willing to assume that a child uses the same constructions to integrate all the reprimand situations he experiences, whether the reprimand is administered to himself or is administered to others. We can't adduce strong evidence for this assumption, but we are not willing to assume that persons build one construction system for self-categorization and another system for categorizing others. Yet, one must agree with Bem (1972) that it is too early to offer a conclusive statement on the similarities and differences between self- and other-perception.

Following this, we first note that sixth-graders and kindergartners don't indicate, on these measures, that they see a difference between a person who has been treated by coercion and a person who has experienced straightforward explanations. Yet, these two age groups do differ in their views of transgressors. Kindergartners conclude that children subjected to either treatment are equally bad, while sixth-graders seem to judge that either treatment is associated with adopting proper conduct. We expected this result from the kindergartners. In that they depend on adults for definition of *good-bad*, an adult's signal—no matter how it is given—must be accepted as a sign that the transgressor is bad! Sixth-graders, on the other hand, see a general acceptance of propriety to be associated with either parental treatment.

Third-graders, by comparison, construe a person who has been coerced to be relatively negative, while a person who has been given an explanation is construed as more positive. Third-graders and sixth-graders, then, show a belief that straightforward explanation is associated with a person's accepting of positively valued behavior, but third-graders react as if a person on whom coercion has been used is a bad person.

Of course we can't say, on the basis of our small investigatory effort, why the children in this study indicated a positive view of the film character who had been exposed to explanation. We willingly offer our fondest hunch: These children had concluded that persons who have been treated as if they can understand the basis of rules are likely to be persons who would accept rules. In other terms, our older subjects concluded that if a person is treated as if he were rational, he will behave rationally—he will try to understand the morality of reciprocity that guides sound rule formation. Third-graders, on the other hand, appear to infer that people who are treated coercively are generally bad. By their responses they appear to indicate that coercion does not change a person toward goodness. They seem to be saying that the coercion they saw serves as a means of evoking retribution, and apparently they do not ascribe corrective properties to expiative measures. To third-graders, then, coercion simply signifies a judgment of badness, as it does to kindergartners. Sixth-graders do not seem to assume that a person who has been treated coercively is to be construed (and to construe himself) as being generally bad. Why has this shift occurred?

To keep things within our theory, we would say that sixth-graders have built a person-construing system within which coercion signals the fact that "badness" has been attributed to the transgressor. They know that the transgressor can hypothesize that this informational input will be removed after he has altered the constructions and self-conduct that produced the attribution. In this way, the sixth-graders know, coercion can effectively produce an alteration of behavior.

Of course, the responses of these sixth-graders might also show that they have built mechanism into their implicit personality theories. They, like many of the authorities that they model and like many of the behavioral scientists who provide the public with their behavior-explaining systems, might attribute direct energic character to a class of events that are called punishment. Also, like their mentors, our older subjects might be unable to articulate the contextualist principles that explain their rule-following behavior—namely, that "punishment" represents a variant of incongruity-producing stimuli, and that elimination of this incongruity is contingent on giving credence to the constructions of the reprimander.

If these sixth-grade subjects do accept the mechanism of their mentors, however, they are left with the same kinds of problems that afflict the theory of other mechanists. How has a boy like Joey become *generally good* through having had counter-energy (punishment) attached to *one* particular behavior? What implicit personality theory could have led them to believe, after having watched Joey being coerced in but one situation, that Joey generally conducts himself properly? Using a mechanistic paradigm pushes a theorist into a corner when he tries to work over the problem of congruity or consistency (see Mischel, 1973, for an effort to reach a workable position on this issue. Bem and Allen, 1974, sagely recognize that a personal construct point of view proves most efficient in treating this matter.) Our sixth-graders, as would the most sophisticated theorists, did *infer* a great deal from observing but one small piece of the transgressor's behavior. By what process did this observation lead them to attribute goodness to Joey?

Our sixth-graders, we again propose, used a constructivist, contextualist implicit personality theory to conclude that Joey is a good boy. The overall context in which the coercion took place led them to believe that Joey would engage in conduct that would maintain his concept as a good boy. Our subjects predicted, therefore, that in other choice situations the boy whom they had watched would enact the proper behaviors. They had concluded, in other words, that Joey would use his mother's behavior as a signal that his own conduct was judged incongruous with his overall "good boy" self-image.

In any event, we feel that this little investigation amply demonstrates that efforts to induce rule-following behavior cannot be treated as entities which have a special, extant character which functions outside of the context of the construct system of the person to whom these efforts are directed. "Punishment" means different things to different persons, particularly when these persons are of different ages. To understand the effects of what we would call coercion we will need to understand what coercion means to the person to whom it is administered.

RECAPITULATION

This essay promotes the position that contextualism, as a general metaphysic, has infused the normal science of psychology. Personal construct theory, as an exemplar of a contextualist theory, readily adapts as a contextualist theory of persons. As such, it can amalgamate much of the exciting progress that has come from the application of a contextualist position to those branches of study that generally have been called experimental psychology.

As an example, the multitude of studies which have been designed to explain *attention* fit neatly with the contextualist motivational principles which are stated in George Kelly's Fundamental Postulate and Choice Corollary. The theorist who proposes that attention is guided by deviations from a "running average state" clarifies the Fundamental Postulate, which states that a person's psychological processses are channelized by the ways in which he anticipates events. The ways in which a person anticipates events reflect the running average state of his internalized coding systems. When information input cannot be fit into the internally coded running average state, the person is mobilized to resolve an existing incongruity.

Finally, we wish to show that this kind of thinking can usefully guide empirical demonstration. Our example and its theoretical support come from developmental psychology. We attempt to show the relationships of arousal moderation and the development of understandings of rule-following behavior. The study we discussed explores children's concepts of reprimand. The findings of the study lead us to affirm the premise that alteration of constructions relative to propriety of behavior are basically induced by producing incongruous information input. We have tried to advance and to clarify the position that reprimand for transgression can invoke two classes of incongruity. Reprimand can produce incongruity that we construe as *coercion*—that is, incongruity which is irrelevant to the construction of the event under consideration. Another form of incongruity is classed as event-relevant, in that the reprimander aims directly at reorganization of the constructs associated with the transgression.

By the time that an average child completes sixth grade, he believes that exposure to either form of incongruity is associated with adopting "proper" behaviors. An average third-grade child does not predict positive conduct from a person who has been exposed to coercion, whereas he does predict positive behaviors from a person who received explanation of transgression. We propose that the developmental transitions we observed show the progression toward an understanding of how self-attributions work in guiding personal behavior.

Our example represents a small beginning toward understanding rule-following behavior in terms of a contextualist position. We are trying to say that a person following rules represents a specific instance of a person moving to anticipate himself in relation to the social world about him. Rule following and rule rejection, like any other personal conduct, reveals a person "reaching out and beating the world to the punch." Rule following and rule rejection represent specific instances of a person designing experiments in living which will answer his perpetual question: "Who am I in relation to you?"

REFERENCES

Bannister, D., & Fransella, K. *Inquiring man.* Baltimore: Penguin, 1971.

Bartlett, F. C. *Remembering.* Cambridge: Cambridge University Press, 1932.

Bem, D. J. Self-perception theory. In L. Berkowitz (Ed.), *Advances in experimental social psychology.* New York: Academic Press, 1972. Pp. 1–62.

Bem, D. J., & Allen, A. On predicting some of the people some of the time: The search for cross situational consistencies in behavior. *Psychological Review,* 1974, **81**, 506–520.

Berg, W. K. Habituation and dishabituation of cardiac responses in 4-month-old, alert infants. *Journal of Experimental Child Psychology,* 1972, **14**, 92–107.

Berlyne, D. E. *Aesthetics and psychobiology.* New York: Appleton-Century-Crofts, 1971.

Bieri, J., Atkins, A. L., Briar, S., Leaman, R. L., Miller, H., & Tripodi, T. *Clinical and social judgment.* New York: Wiley, 1966.

Bonarius, J. C. J. Fixed role therapy: A double paradox. *British Journal of Medical Psychology,* 1970, **43**, 213–219.

Broadbent, D. E. *Perception and communication.* London: Pergamon Press, 1958.

Broadbent, D. E. *Decision and stress.* New York: Academic Press, 1971.

Buchanan, J. P., & Thompson, S. K. A quantitative methodology to examine the development of moral judgment. *Child Development,* 1973, **44,** 186–189.

Cofer, C. Constructive processes in memory. *American Scientist,* 1973, **61,** 537–543.

Costanzo, P. R., Coie, J. D., Grumet, J. F., & Farnill, D. A reexamination of the effects of intent and consequence of children's moral judgments. *Child Development,* 1973, **44,** 154–161.

Cronbach, L. J. The two disciplines of scientific psychology. *American Psychologist,* 1957, **12,** 671–684.

Dienstbier, R. A., Hillman, D., Lehnhoff, J., Hillman, J., & Valkenaar, M. C. An emotion-attribution approach to moral behavior: Interfacing congnitive and avoidance theories of moral development. *Psychological Review,* 1975, **82,** 299–315.

Dollard, J., & Miller, N. *Personality and psychotherapy.* New York: McGraw-Hill, 1950.

Finley, G. E., Kagan, J., & Layne, O. Development of young children's attention to normal and distorted stimuli. *Developmental Psychology,* 1972, **6,** 288–292.

Fiske, D. W., & Maddi, S. R. *Functions of varied experience.* Homewood, Ill.: Dorsey, 1961.

Fowler, H. *Curiosity and exploratory behavior.* New York: Macmillan, 1965.

Ginsburg, H., & Opper, S. *Piaget's theory of intellectual development.* Englewood Cliffs, N.J.: Prentice-Hall, 1969.

Gutkin, D. C. The effects of systematic story changes on intentionality in children's moral judgments. *Child Development,* 1972, **43,** 187–195.

Haaf, R. A., & Bell, R. Q. A facial dimension in visual discrimination by human infants. *Child Development,* 1967, **38,** 893–899.

Haber, R. N. Discrepancy from AL as a source of affect. *Journal of Experimental Psychology,* 1958, **56,** 370–375.

Haber, R. N., & Fried, A. H. *An introduction to psychology.* New York: Holt, Rinehart & Winston, 1975.

Hartshorne, H., May, M. A., & Maller, J. B. *Studies in the nature of character. Vol. 1. Studies in deceit.* New York: Macmillan, 1928.

Inhelder, B., & Piaget, J. The early growth of logic in the child. London: Routledge & Kegan Paul, 1964. Paperback edition, New York: W. W. Norton, 1969.

Jaspers, J. M. F. *On social perception.* Leiden, The Netherlands: Drukkerij Lectura, 1966.

Jenkins, J. J. Remember that old theory of memory? Well, forget it. *American Psychologist*, 1974, **29**, 785–795.

Kagan, J. Attention and psychological change in the young. *Science*, 1970, **170**, 826–832. (a)

Kagan, J. The determinants of attention in the infant. *American Scientist*, 1970, **58**, 298–306. (b)

Kelly, G. A. *The psychology of personal constructs.* New York: W. W. Norton, 1955.

Kelly, G. A. Man's construction of his alternatives. In G. Lindzey (Ed.), *The assessment of human motives.* New York: Holt, Rinehart & Winston, 1958. Pp. 33–64.

Kelly, G. A. Europe's matrix of decision. In M. R. Jones (Ed.), *Nebraska Symposium on Motivation, 1962.* Lincoln: University of Nebraska Press, 1962. Pp. 83–125.

Kelly, G. A. The language of hypothesis: Man's psychological instrument. In B. Maher (Ed.), *Clinical psychology and personality.* New York: Academic Press, 1969. Pp. 147–162.

Kelman, H. C. Three processes of social influence. *Public Opinion Quarterly*, 1961, **25**, 57–78.

Kendler, H. H., & Kendler, T. S. Vertical and horizontal processes in problem solving. *Psychological Review*, 1962, **69**, 1–16.

Kendler, H. H. & Kendler, T. S. Reversal-shift behavior: Some basic issues. *Psychological Bulletin*, 1969, **72**, 229–232.

Klopfer, B., & Kelley, D. M. *The Rorschach technique.* Yonkers-on-Hudson, N.Y.: World Book, 1942.

Krechevsky, I. "Hypotheses" in rats. *Psychological Review*, 1932, **39** 516 536.

Kuhn, T. S. *The structure of scientific revolutions.* Chicago: University of Chicago Press, 1970.

Landfield, A. W. *Personal construct systems in psychotherapy.* Chicago: Rand McNally, 1971.

Levine, M. *A cognitive theory of learning: Research on hypothesis testing.* Hillsdale, N.J.: Lawrence Erlbaum Associates, 1975.

Lewis, M. Individual differences in the measurement of early cognitive growth. In J. Hellmuth (Ed.), *Exceptional infant: Studies in abnormalities.* New York: Brunner/Mazel, 1971.

Lickona, T. (Ed.). *Moral development and behavior: Theory, research and social issues.* New York: Holt, Rinehart & Winston, 1976.

Livesley, W. J., & Bromley, D. B. *Person perception in childhood and adolescence.* New York: Wiley, 1973.

Mancuso, J. C., (Ed.). *Readings for a cognitive theory of personality.* New York: Holt, Rinehart & Winston, 1970.

McCall, R., & Kagan, J. Stimulus-schema discrepancy and attention in the infant. *Journal of Experimental Child Psychology*, 1967, 5, 381–390.

Milgram, S. Behavioral study of obedience. *Journal of Abnormal and Social Psychology*, 1963, 67, 371–378.

Mischel, W. Toward a cognitive social learning reconceptualization of personality. *Psychological Review*, 1973, 80, 252–283.

Moray, N. *Attention: Selective processes in vision and learning.* New York: Academic Press, 1970.

Morrison, J. K. A developmental study of moral judgment as person perception. Unpublished doctoral dissertation, State University of New York at Albany, 1973.

Morrison, J. K. Developmental study of person perception of young children. In H. C. Lindgren (Ed.), *Children's behavior: An introduction to research studies.* Palo Alto, Calif.: Mayfield, 1975. Pp. 15–22.

Mussen, P. H., Conger, J. J., & Kagan, J. *Child development and personality.* New York: Harper & Row, 1974.

Neisser, V. *Cognitive psychology.* New York: Appleton-Century-Crofts, 1967.

O'Hara, R. P. Vocational self concepts and high school achievement. *Vocational Guidance Quarterly*, 1966, 15, 106–112.

Osgood, C. C., & Richards, M. M. From Yang and Yin to and or but. Language, 1973, 49, 380–412.

Paivio, A. Language and knowledge of the world. *Educational Researcher*, 1974, 3, 5–12.

Pepper, S. *World hypotheses.* Berkeley: University of California Press, 1942.

Piaget, J. *The moral judgment of the child.* London: Kegan Paul, 1932. Paperback edition, New York: Free Press, 1966.

Posner, M. J. *Cognition: An introduction.* Glenview, Ill.: Scott, Foresman, 1973.

Rosenberg, S., & Jones, R. A method for investigating and representing a person's implicit theory of personality: Theodore Dreiser's view of people. *Journal of Personality and Social Psychology*, 1972, 22, 372–386.

Rosenberg, S., & Sedlak, A. Structural representatives of implicit personality theory. In L. Berkowitz (Ed.), *Advances in experimental social psychology.* New York: Academic Press, 1972.

Rychlak, J. F. *A philosophy of science for personality theory.* Boston: Houghton Mifflin, 1968.

Rychlak, J. F. *An introduction to personality and psychotherapy.* Boston: Houghton Mifflin, 1973.

Schneider, D. J. Implicit personality theory: A review. *Psychological Bulletin*, 1973, 79, 294–317.

Scott, W. A., & Johnson, R. C. Comparative validities of direct and indirect personality tests. *Journal of Consulting and Clinical Psychology*, 1972, **38**, 301–318.

Sokolov, E. N. *Perception and the conditioned reflex.* New York: Macmillan, 1963.

Solley, C. M., & Murphy, G. *Development of the perceptual world.* New York: Basic Books, 1960.

Stevens, S. S. *Handbook of experimental psychology.* New York: Wiley, 1951.

Thompson, R. F., & Bettinger, L. A. Neural substrates of attention. In D. I. Mostofsky (Ed.), *Attention: Contemporary theory and analysis.* New York: Appleton-Century-Crofts, 1970. Pp. 367–401.

Warr, P. P., & Knapper, C. *The perception of people and events.* New York: Wiley, 1968.

White, H. Interpretation in history. *New Literary History*, 1972–73, **4**, 281–314.

The Child's Construing of Self

Don Bannister
Bexley Hospital, England[1]

Joyce Agnew
Stratheden Hospital, Scotland

*I*f we reject theory in favor of the eclectic style, then life becomes a rainbow of special cases, a lucky dip of freshly minted and disposable mini-explanations. We are free, for example, to coin many psychologies out of the idea of *self*. We can formulate and reformulate "the self-concept" and speculate on the identity crisis. We can call upon the notion of self in any form needed—say, the "distorted self"—to explain the plight of the schizophrenic. We can expand it to a respectable area, as in ego psychology, or contract it to any one of its hyphenated forms, ranging from self-abasement to self-salience. We can use it as touchstone and battle flag in the ideological conflict between behaviorists and phenomenologists.

To ask what is *self* within personal construct theory deprives us of the opportunity to compose any singular or self-contained formulation, but it offers us the compensating possibility of resolving our views of self in such a way that we have equally resolved our views of, or raised problems in relation to, the nature of man. Construing of self will have to be seen as an act of construing like any other. The ways in which we elaborate our construing of self must be essentially those ways in which we elaborate our construing of others, for we have not a concept of self but a bipolar construct of *self–not self* or *self–others*. The ways in which we respond to validation or invalidation of core role constructs and the strategies by which we test out the implications of self are part of our repertoire for construing our world as a whole. If "a person's processes are psychologically channelized by the ways in which he anticipates events," then events can be anticipated by being seen as *relating to–not relating to, destroying–creating, flowing to–flowing from, constituting–being no part of*, SELF.

Equally, within construct theory, there is no separate psychology for the child. We may speculate about and investigate how the child elaborates his construing of self, but that elaboration will be seen in the same terms as the elaboration which continues for the whole of a person's life. We cannot have the delights or even the chapter-heading usefulness of a "developmental psychology" because, in construct theory terms, it is impossible to make sense of the contrast pole. What would a nondevelopmental psychology be about?

Kelly (1955, p. 131) talks of self as a construction in the following terms:

> the self is, when considered in the appropriate context, a proper concept or construct. It refers to a group of events which are alike in a certain way and, in that same way, necessarily different from other events. The way in which the events are alike is the self. That also makes the self an individual, differentiated from other individuals. The self, having been thus conceptualized, can now be used as a thing, a datum, or an item in the context of a superordinate construct. The self can become one of the three or more things—or persons—at least two of which are alike and are different from at least one of the others.
>
> When the person begins to use himself as a datum in forming constructs, exciting things begin to happen. He finds that the constructs he forms operate as rigorous controls upon his behavior. His behavior in relation to other people is particularly affected. Perhaps it would be better to say that his behavior in comparison with other people is particularly affected. It is, of course, the comparison he sees or construes which affects his behavior. Thus, much of his social life is controlled by the comparisons he has come to see between himself and others.

Construct theory does give a special status to a person's constructs about self. They are termed *core constructs*—those constructs which govern a person's maintenance processes, as contrasted with *peripheral constructs*, which can be altered without serious modification of the core structure. This distinction stresses the function of core construing in maintaining the person *as a person*. They suggest that to see a "person" is to acknowledge another "self," to speak as a "self" is to claim the status of "person." The term "processes" underlines the argument that in each of us our notion of self is constructed and elaborated over time, as is our notion of anything else.

We can begin an inquiry into ways in which self is construed by speculating about the kinds of discrimination which might evolve into a total subsystem of constructs about self. In an attempt to describe the essence of *person*—which it is argued is the same venture as defining the essence of *self*—Bannister and Fransella (1971) set out what they saw as the kinds of construction which contribute to a total notion of self.

Each of us entertains a notion of our own separateness from others derived from the privacy of our own consciousness. It could be that we become aware of a contrast in the ways in which we need to go about communicating. To communicate with others necessarily involves relatively cumbersome signaling, arm waving, shouting, hinting, swearing, supplicating, bearing gifts: to communicate with ourselves in more instantaneous, less effortful, has the feel of recognition rather than transmission. There are further distinctions stemming from this which we might come to make. Thus to communicate with specific others is to run the risk of being overheard, spied upon, having your messages intercepted; to communicate with ourselves seems to involve no such risk. Moreover, we can experience our communications with ourselves as overriding in the sense that it is *out of them* that we construct our communications with others. An act as simple as telling a lie demonstrates to us our capacity to remake our communication with ourselves into other forms before we communicate it to others.

What we are trying to do here is not to define *self* in some generalized and abstract way but to point to constructions which may be involved in building up a subsystem about self and to point to the *kinds of experience* (i.e., construed events) which validate, and through which are elaborated, these constructions. Thus, the three particular constructions pointed to here are discriminations of *self* from others in terms of communication being instantaneous and easy versus communication being relatively laboured; communication which can be overheard versus that which cannot be overheard; and primary communication versus derived communication. We are alleging that these constructs are commonly erected by persons and contribute towards their eventual subsystem of self. An immediate and most relevant test of whether they are commonly erected by people and whether they have the kind of implications that we are suggesting can be made by your checking them directly against your experience.

We entertain a notion of the integrity and completeness of our own experience in that we believe all parts of it to be relatable because we are, in some vital sense, the experience. This is to argue that we will always discriminate broadly between events which concern us and have significance for us as against irrelevant events. We attempt to see relationships between those events which concern us more actively and needfully, and from them we constitute our notion of "our situation," "our world." The boundaries of "our world" are not easily defined, just as the events we see as significant are not necessarily those most immediate in time and space. Yet it may be that we define ourselves, for ourselves, in part by our "possession" of an interpreted world. Clearly, there is a danger of tautology in this kind of argument, but again, the best test of its meaningfulness is for the reader to examine it against his own experience and to dispute it if it fails thus to make sense.

We entertain the notion of our own continuity over time, we possess our biography and live in relation to it. The separate arguments being advanced here are, like all such catalogues, relatively arbitrary, and the notion of "biography" can be seen as a kissing cousin to the argument about "a personal world" already noted. One of the relationships which may emerge between all events which concern us is that "we were involved," they were part of our biography, and they are proof of our continuity over time. Most of us insist that we are "the same person" as we were five minutes ago or five years ago, or at least a modified version of that person. The desperation with which we struggle to maintain our sense of continuity when it is threatened is itself an acknowledgment of its importance. Our sense of history, of past, carries its contrast pole, a sense of present and future, a sense of what we have become, may yet become.

Again, we are here trying to identify the superordinate construction ("my life") which may be elaborated out of many subordinate constructions of particular past deeds done by and to. Nor are these superordinates equally central for different persons—some of us may use our past very elaborately as defining self while others may make little of their history and much of their here and now.

We entertain a notion of ourselves as causes, we have purposes, we intend, we accept a partial responsibility for the effects of what we do. The construing of ourselves as agent is clearly a superordinate contribution towards a total construction of a self. Again, the notion of self as purposive (and being defined by purpose) is alleged to be a superordinate built up gradually to cover the multitude of occasions on which we have discriminated between events for which we hold ourselves responsible and events for which we do not hold ourselves responsible. This kind of discrimination begins with, or even before, our first cry of "I didn't do it" or "it was me" or "that is mine," on to our most elaborate arguments about determination and free will.

We work towards a notion of other persons by analogy with ourselves, we assume a comparability of subjective experience. This could be argued to be a two-stage affair. We can construe ourselves as distinct from others without assuming that others resemble us in terms of their experience. We may initially see and treat others as moving objects or mechanisms. Yet it seems, in practice, that we elaborate by collecting evidence for the proposition that what moves us does, in a broad sense, move others. The "broad sense" here points to the idea, central in personal construct theory, that to see an element as *contrasted* with another is yet to see it *in the same terms*, along the axis of the same bipolar construct. Thus to argue that you are *kind* whereas another is *cruel* is essentially to admit comparability, and it may be that our notion of ourselves as individuals develops very much in terms of such comparisons.

COMMON CONCLUSIONS

To derive these arguments from personal construct theory is not to imply that similar ideas could not be and have not been derived from other sources. Some of the points made above are clearly included, for example, in Allport's (1955) "Attributes of the Proprium": awareness of bodily self; sense of continuity over time; ego enhancement, or a need for self-esteem; ego extension, or the identification of self beyond the borders of the body; rational process, or the synthesis of inner needs with outer reality; self-image, or the person's perception and evaluation of himself as an object of knowledge; the self as knower or as executive agent; and propriate striving (motivation to increase rather than decrease tension and to expand the awareness and seek out challenges). However, it can be shown (as with any theoretical framework) that the further we pursue the argument the more particularly we take our direction, if not the whole of our starting position, from construct theory.

Another proponent of the argument as set out so far is Epstein (1973, p. 407); in a paper which specifically refers to Kelly's views, he argued as follows:

> What is it that consists of concepts that are hierarchically organized and internally consistent; that assimilates knowledge, yet, itself, is an object of knowledge; that is dynamic, but must maintain a degree of stability; that is unified and differentiated at the same time; that is necessary for solving problems in the real world; and that is subject to sudden collapse, producing total disorganization when this occurs? The answer, by now, should be evident. In case it is not, I submit that *the self-concept is a self-theory*. It is a theory that the individual has unwittingly constructed about himself as an experiencing, functioning individual, and it is part of a broader theory which he holds with respect to his entire range of significant experience. Accordingly, there are major postulate systems for the *nature of the world, for the nature of self, and for their interaction.* Like most theories, the self-theory is a conceptual tool for accomplishing a purpose. The most fundamental purpose of the self-theory is to *optimize the pleasure/pain balance of the individual over the course of a lifetime.* Two other basic functions, not unrelated to the first, are to *facilitate the maintenance of self esteem*, and to *organize the data of experience in a manner that can be coped with effectively.*

Much of what has been argued is contained in Epstein's discourse. The idea of an elaborated self-theory rather than simply a self-concept points to the evolutionary nature of construing and to the idea that the total self-concept amounts to a subsystem in construct theory terms. The statement that the self-theory "is part of a broader theory which he holds with respect to his entire range of significant experience" is a neat rephrasing of the idea of a subsystem within a total personal construct system.

However, there is an interesting break in the line of argument when the notion of the purpose of self-theory as being "to optimize a pleasure/pain balance" is proposed along with the argument that the self-theory also facilitates "the maintenance of self esteem." These are notions in a language other than that used to describe the process of the building of a self-theory and, indeed, seem to derive from a different psychology. Thus we have the split between a process which is seen in one set of terms and a purpose which is seen in another, biologically derived, set of constructions, with no integration between the two other than to argue that one is *"for"* the other. Intriguingly enough, the third purpose for this self-theory building, "to organize the data of experience in a manner that can be coped with effectively," seems to be a purpose which is appropriate to theory building (and thereby self-theory building) and which maintains the integrity of the whole argument. In this respect this third purpose parallels Kelly's Fundamental Postulate in personal construct theory: "a person's processes are psychologically channellized by the ways in which he anticipates events." More specifically, it reads like Kelly's Choice Corollary: "a person chooses for himself that alternative in a dichotomized construct through which he anticipates the greatest possibility for the elaboration of his system." In short, theories are designed to elaborate themselves, or more specifically, when the "theory" is a person, persons are designed to elaborate themselves.

Clearly it would take more than seven maids with seven mops and the statutory half year to investigate the implications of this kind of argument. However, a first step can be taken if we accept as a central thesis the construct theory argument that the construing of self, like other kinds of construing, must be elaborated and unfolded over time as validational fortunes vary. We can, therefore, test the crude hypothesis that in younger children, we will find a less elaborated and thereby less effective construing of self. It is this implication, that the construing of self becomes more effective with age, that we attempted to subject to test.

TESTING THE CHILD'S CONSTRUING OF SELF

The population studied consisted of 36 working-class children in an English primary school. They were randomly selected from the school register in six age and sex groups so as to comprise six 5-year-old boys, six aged 7, six aged 9, and equivalent groups for girls.

Each group of six children met and chatted informally with the psychologist until they seemed happy with the situation, and then 10 questions were put to them. They were encouraged to answer each question one at a time and their answers were tape recorded. There had been some previous playing with the tape recorder to make it a familiar part of the situation. The questions, with a sample five-year-old's answer for each from the transcripts, are given below.

1. What do you do at school?
   "We have prayers and we do things about Jesus and God."
2. What games do you play?
   "At home sometimes I play hopscotch."
3. What do you want to do when you grow up?
   "A student. Learn to teach people sums. The little ones."
4. What do you like to do on holiday?
   "Swimming in the sea with no armbands on."
5. What is your best friend like?
   "It's a boy. He's got quite long hair. He's nine. Sometimes he's naughty and sometimes he's good."
6. What is the most frightening thing you know?
   "When my Daddy smacks me."
7. What is your teacher like?
   "She's got short hair and she teaches us to be quiet and do sums."
8. What do you like best on television?
   "Cartoons. They're funny. They're really things for children."
9. What do you think of grown-ups?
   "When you're hurt sometimes they cuddle you. They won't let you have sweeties when you want them."
10. What sort of boy (girl) are you?
    "Sometimes I'm naughty, sometimes I'm good. Sometimes I get sent to bed though. When I'm naughty I cry and when I'm good I help my Mum."

All the children's answers to these questions were tape-recorded and exactly transcribed. From the transcriptions all circumstantial clues as to the identity of the speaker (e.g., references to proper names, jobs of parents, addresses, and so forth) were eliminated. The answers were then re-recorded in a single adult voice and in a randomized order.

Four months after this first question and recording session each child was interviewed individually. He was reminded of what had happened in the first session and was told that he would be played a recording of the exact words that were spoken by him and the five other children, in answer to each question in turn. He was then played the six answers to Question 1, *twice through*. Afterward he was asked which of the six statements was the one that he had made.

He was further asked why he thought that his selected statement came from him, which of the other five statements he was quite sure was not his, and finally why he was sure that the indicated statement was not his. The same procedure was followed in relation to each of the 10 questions. Everything that the child said in this session was tape-recorded and transcribed.

Predictions and Modes of Analysis

Insofar as personal construct theory argues that *self* is a construction which is elaborated over time and in terms of varying validational fortunes, then we can hypothesize an elaborative process. The argument could take the form that with increasing age, the constructs the child has about himself will increase in number, in range of convenience, and in strength and variety of implications. Therefore, the child will be able more readily to recognize himself, as distinct from other people, with increasing age.

The appropriate operational prediction in terms of this experiment is that older children will more frequently recognize their own statements. The relevant data are shown in Table 1.

Table 1
Number of Their Own Statements Correctly Identified by Children

Age in Years	Boys	Girls	Total	Total Possible
5	11	29	40	120
7	25	25	50	120
9	27	33	60	120

Note: Accuracy of identification is shown for the three age and sex groups (out of a maximum of 10 correct per child, with 6 children in each age and sex group).

Chi square examination of these data shows that, although there is no significant difference between adjacent age groups, the 5-year-olds differ significantly from the 9-year-olds in accuracy of own statement identification ($p < .02$) and the trend with age is satisfyingly linear.

Although, at ages 7 and 9, boys and girls are not significantly different on this measure, there is a significant sex difference (chi square $p < .01$) at age 5, with the 5-year-old girls performing impressively and the 5-year-old boys still very much at sea with this kind of task.

It was rare for any child to identify as "not what I said" something he had actually said, and only 26 such errors were made in the entire series. These errors were fairly evenly distributed across age and sex groups.

The data broadly support the "elaboration" hypothesis.

On Being "Individual"

In construct theory terms man is not a passive predictor of his universe and thereby not a passive predictor and analyzer of himself. He invents himself. He is continually conducting behavioral experiments with his world, and it is in the interaction between his expectations and the actions in which they are embodied that validation or invalidation takes place and his system elaborates. Where *self* is concerned we can argue from this to the proposal that in order to recognize oneself, one must first do something that is recognizable; in order to differentiate oneself, one must do something which, in one's own terms, is different. Posing the problem in its extreme form, if you say what others say and do what others do, how will you recognize your own words and deeds? It is in this sense that construction is reflexive and cyclic.

Ideally we should test this prediction out in terms of the child's *own* construing of his statements as being more or less differentiated in terms of their content and quality (i.e., as being "unusual" in terms of his construct system). However, it is difficult to find ways of doing this without either giving clues or providing informative surveys of the material to the child. (On reflection, this is a nonsensical statement. The children could have been asked, after the identification task was completed, which of the statements *they* considered "unusual" and which "ordinary." This would largely have avoided contamination between the two tasks and provided more germane data than are here offered.)

The cruder form of the hypothesis was tested by having all the statements of the children rated by three adult judges for "individuality." The three judges were asked to consider each statement in turn and say whether or not they felt it was a somewhat unusual or individual response differing from the common run of responses of the children in some way. The three judges had an average interjudge agreement level of 80% in rating statements as being "individual" or "less individual," which indicates that there is commonality in judgments in this area and opens up the possibility that what was seen as individual by the adult judges may reflect something which would also be seen as individual in the terms of the child's construction system. Those statements which had been rated by two or more judges as being "individual" were deemed "individual" for the purpose of this analysis. The prediction was that the children in the groups would more often correctly identify their own "individual" statements than they would correctly identify their own "less individual" statements. Of the 59 statements judged "individual," 34 were correctly identified and 25 were not correctly identified, whereas of the 301 statements judged "not individual," 116 were correctly identified and 185 were not correctly identified. Chi-square analysis therefore supports the prediction ($p < .001$).

The converse prediction, that children would more accurately identify as "not mine" the "individual" statements, was not significantly true of the data, though the "not mine" task presented so little difficulty to the children that it seems no very effective measure.

How Do I Know It Is Me?

If we accept that construing of self elaborates as the whole construct system elaborates, then we would expect to find extending strategies for recognizing self as the child grows older. For example, perhaps the most direct strategy for recognizing one's own statement is to remember its concrete terms, whereas to infer that a statement is yours because it is the kind of statement that you are likely to make, you being the kind of person you see yourself as being, seems a more complex strategy.

Studies which relate to this assertion in that they argue that "psychological" constructs are relatively late in developing have been conducted by, for example, Brierley (1967) and Little (1968). A question worth raising here is, In what sense can we assert that younger children lack "psychological" constructs? It might be more appropriate to see them as not yet having sharply differentiated subsystems for dealing with construing in "physical" terms and construing in "psychological" terms. Thereby they may be using the same constructs in what to us is an omnibus fashion to serve "physical" and "psychological" purposes. To the child, events which for us constitute separate and dualistic worlds may be within the range of convenience of the *same* global constructs.

In terms of the data available in this study, it can be argued that 5 out of the 10 questions asked of the children invite more psychologically framed responses—Questions 5, 6, 7, 9, and 10. We might therefore predict, in terms of a later development of a separate "psychological" subsystem hypothesis, that answers to these questions would be recognized more easily as the child grows older.

The data from the study were examined and it was found that the 5- and 7-year-old children correctly identified 14.5% of their responses to "psychological" questions, and 23% of their responses to "nonpsychological" questions, where 9-year-old children identified 25.8% of the "psychological" and 24% of the nonpsychological" questions. Although the results are tilted in the direction of the prediction, this is not a significant difference.

Here we are analyzing the data in terms of questions which we think invite a psychological type of construction. This is a somewhat second-order way of getting at the issue of whether the children actually use such a subsystem for identifying their own statements. A more direct test is to examine the responses themselves. The children had been asked, both when selecting responses as their own and in stating that given responses were definitely not their own, to explain their reasons for their selection, and these reasons were taped and transcribed. They were studied and nearly all of the responses could be put into one of seven categories. These categories, with examples of the way in which the child justified his choice of "mine" or "not mine," are as follows:

1. The statement was identified by reference to an *activity* which the child says he does or does not undertake.
   E.g., "Cos I hardly ever watch matches. I only watch important matches."
   "Cos I always play at home and it's my hobby."
2. The child made a simple reference to *good or bad* features of the subject of the response.

"Well, because we've got a nice book corner and she says you can go and get a book."

"Cos sometimes she's nice to me and sometimes she shouts at me."

3. The response was *remembered* as belonging to the child or being someone else's statement.

"I just remember."

"That was Alison's answer."

4. The statement contained a reference to something which the child *liked or disliked*.

"Well, cos I like doing sums and I usually do them and ask for more sums."

"Cos I don't like murder films. I keep dreaming about them and I have bad dreams."

5. The statement was simply *repeated* in some form.

"Cos the police are poofs."

"Cos sometimes Mummy is nice and sometimes she's not."

6. The statement was said to be *"psychologically"* appropriate to the child or to someone else or to be "psychologically" inappropriate to the child or to someone else.

"I don't think I could ever kill a human being." (The child was denying that the statement "I want to be a soldier" was his.)

"Cos cartoons, for instance, are not my style. I can watch them for five minutes and get bored."

7. The statement was said to contain a feature which was *impossible* from the point of view of the child or which was *certain* from the point of view of the child.

"Cos my Mummy and Daddy aren't like that."

"Cos my best friend had ginger hair, sort of ginger black."

Table 2 shows by age group the frequency of use of these various strategies for identifying statements.

A *k* sample chi-square examination of the frequency of use of the various strategies shown in Table 2 indicates that they do vary significantly frequently over age ($p < .001$). Examination of the contents of the table suggests that children make progressively less use of simple memory, whether they see good or bad features in the elements of the statement, or whether they see the activities indicated in the statement as ones which they undertake or not. In complementary fashion, older children made more use of like-dislike aspects of elements in the statement, its general psychological ap-

Table 2

Frequency of Use of Different Strategies for Identifying
"Me" and "Not Me" Statements

Strategy used	5-year-olds	7-year-olds	9-year-olds
1. Activity undertaken or not	48	15	18
2. Good or bad feature of the element	15	13	5
3. Remembered	82	29	22
4. Like-dislike some aspect	33	67	64
5. Simple repetition of statement	11	13	13
6. "Psychologically" appropriate or inappropriate	8	49	54
7. Impossibility of certainty of an aspect	40	54	63
8. Unclassifiable	3	0	1

propriateness to them, and the impossibility or certainty of the assertion as far as they are concerned.

This experiment and the way in which we view the data raise the question of whether construct theory paints a "developmental stages" portrait of the child. Is Kelly advancing an argument essentially like that of Piaget? Obviously any description of continuous change can have "cutoffs" written into it so that "stages" are delineated. However, construct theory can usefully be viewed as standing in contrast to "stage" theories. For example, while we can denote the development of a subsystem of "psychological/personality" constructs by the child as a stage, it can perhaps better be viewed as simply a case of the child's total system differentiating yet one more subsystem with its own range of convenience and internal structure. Thus we are arguing that the personal construct system, from the beginning of life, essentially gets bigger, its scope extends; but its nature, in terms of manifesting superordinate and subordinate constructs, elaborating in terms of varying validational fortunes, being defended from chaos by hostility and so forth, does not change. From this point of view the failure of the child to provide an adult-approved answer to a problem is seen not as a case of the child simply failing but as working, perhaps successfully, at the answer to the question *as it is seen* in the child's terms. Consider the typical problem in which child is asked which of two trains made up of wooden blocks has more carriages, and he picks up the one made up of larger blocks, even though both have an equal number of blocks. Certainly, in terms of one kind of arithmetic construing, he has failed; but if he intepreted the question to be of the order, which train is the "bigger" or the more "impressive," then he has answered truly. If we envisage a construct system as being complete from its inception and from then on enlarging its scope, we become more concerned with the kinds of "truth" which can be achieved by the construct system/person at given times, in given circumstances, and less concerned with the fact that it is not providing the same "truths" as our own system or the adult "normative system."

Further Conversations

From each age and sex group of six children, the child who had proved most effective in identifying his own recorded statement and the child who had proved least effective were interviewed individually. With each child the discussion ranged around five questions, as follows:
1. In what way are you different from others?
2. How long have you been different?
3. Do you like being yourself or would you like to be someone else?
4. What sort of person would you like to be?
5. How do we become different?
The interviews were tape-recorded and transcribed. On a sample as small as this it is foolish to perform statistical analyses, but a careful working through of the transcripts convinced us that the differences between children in how effectively they can elaborate their construing in this area relate more to age than they relate to whether the children had done well or badly in identifying their own statements. As an illustration of this, we can consider in a little detail the responses to the question "How do we become different?" Children here were broadly asked how it comes about that people differ from each other in a variety of ways.
The responses of the 5-year-olds (accurate identifiers marked plus and less accurate, minus) were : (i +) "Well, I don't know about

that," (ii —) silence, (iii —) "Because you can't get all the same people," and (iv +) "I haven't a clue."

The 7-year-olds were much more articulate in response to the question. Overall, they produced arguments relating to the disastrous consequences that would ensue if we were all the same and variations on the theme that we are inevitably different. In one case there was a very tentative groping for the idea that we become more different as or because we do different things. Verbatim, the four replies of the 7-year-olds to the question "How do we become different?" were as follows:

(i +) "Because if we all thought the same it wouldn't be much good, would it? We would all be thinking the same, we would all try to do it, we wouldn't have enough builders, or if we decided to be builders there would be too many men and they would all be doing this and that and the other, other people's things."

(ii —) "Because some people grow fast and some people don't grow fast." (This child had mentioned differences in height in answer to "In what way are you different?")

(iii +) "We are all different altogether, we are not born the same, we don't look the same."

(iv —) "Because we all do different things, we all write differently, and we have all got our own ways of doing things, you know."

The 9-year-olds seemed to be trying to work with the idea that it is different experiences which make us different, and one of them, child iv (who was the only child to achieve a perfect record on identifying his own statements), seemed to be trying to hint at a cyclic notion of experience creating differences which in turn made for further different experiences.

The verbatim responses of the 9-year-olds were as follows:

(i —) "Because God wanted us to be different. Because if we were all the same we wouldn't know if we were each other, would we?"

(ii +) "I don't know, just the way we grow up. The things we do, it makes a difference. We change different."

(iii —) "We just are. Different schools."

(iv +) "Sometimes it's if when they were young they came across something that taught them right off or something, or running, they might not be very good at it. They wouldn't like it. Or say some can't dance. They don't like dancing."

The answers to the question "How are you different from others?" ranged from the citing of physical characteristics (height, voice, face, and so forth), activity and preference differences ("I'm not too keen on too many blankets on my bed"; "I'm good at drawing pictures"), to what might be called personality constructs, often of a trait type ("I'm not quiet and dreamy"; "I think different thoughts"), and one child made a tentative reference to the idea of alternate views of others as being somehow involved ("Some people think I'm good and bad and others don't").

In answer to the question "How long have you been different?" almost all the children saw their differentiation from others as dating from birth, and only one dated it to the beginning of school. They did not elaborate their reasons for this belief.

When asked "Do you like being yourself?" all but two children were pleased to be themselves—one would like to be Jill "because she's funny, she's nice" and the other would like to be Tracy "cos she's got a nice long garden."

When the children were pressed further on this question of "Do you like being yourself?" and asked if they were someone else what sort of person they would like to be, the younger children were more likely to name a specific person they would prefer to be. The reasons given for their choices were mainly that the alternative self had privileges not enjoyed by the subject. Older children tended to talk about a generalized ideal alternative self who was specified in terms of desirable physical or psychological characteristics.

The material provided in these interviews, like that coming from the earlier interviews, supports and illustrates the idea that the child's construing of self progressively elaborates. From a personal construct theory point of view, it is a reasonable possibility that this elaboration could be further assessed and defined in terms of the increasing use of constructs with wider ranges of convenience, possibly an earlier use of preemptive and constellatory constructs and a later use of more propositional constructs, and a steady increase in the multiplicity of implication of constructs. An important feature of this elaboration might be the achievement of meta-constructions about processes and change and finally the recognition of the reflexive nature of construing.

A further line of speculation about the evolution of self-construing might concern the degree to which varying patterns of family relationship and differing modes of formal education help or hinder the elaboration of constructs about self.

ADULT CONSTRUING OF CHILDHOOD SELF

In response to the following request, 33 adults wrote accounts of how they became aware of *self* in childhood: "Think about how you became aware of yourself as an individual when you were a child. Write an account of any experience or experiences (events, situations, ideas) which significantly contributed to your developing a feeling of being a separate individual, a "self," during your childhood."

The traditional question which psychologists tend to ask when confronted with material of this kind is, Are they lying? The question is not usually phrased so brutally, but this seems to be the import of the continual stress on the unreliability of subjective report, tendency to confabulation, defensiveness, distorting effects of time on memory, social desirability bias, and so forth. Our view of this, which is about as supportable as the alternative view, is that the people who wrote these passages for us made a genuine attempt to say something informative and significant about the ways in which they became aware of self when they were children and that they are the only really well informed experts on the topic. The kind of careful thought that they put into this is of value and is likely to be, in any sensible definition of the term, "true." Additionally, there is the interesting point that insofar as adults believe that they discovered self in relation to certain events or themes, then this will be a composite part of their continuing idea of themselves and will be, by that token, significant.

There are, of course, a multitude of ways of construing very rich data of this kind, but we will use it to enlarge the ideas set out in the introduction about the ways in which the concept of self is elaborated. Inevitably, our adults repeatedly demonstrated the inadequacy of our summary of elaborative themes, but they will serve as a starting point.

The brief essays made two general points manifest. It becomes very clear that it is easier to see them in terms of people elaborating a construct of self versus others rather than arriving at a concept of self. Virtually all the passages made reference to a contrasting of themselves with other people, or with the universe in general, as a central experience. Sometimes the experience is formalized for the child by a game such as that intriguing psychological invention, "blindman's buff": "I was playing blindman's buff . . . and the lost feeling when I had been blindfolded seemed to set up a very much I—*them* situation. The isolation of what I felt as a lost feeling made me aware of what it was like to be outside of, or in a sense 'not belonging' to, the group. Instead of just tagging along I suddenly thought this game depends on what I do—I cannot follow the leader here, I don't want to be called silly—if only I can find my way to someone I know at this party—someone I might recognise fairly easily. With this feeling of separateness came a feeling of 'power' and 'independence': I can play the game as it should be."

Secondly, it is intriguing that virtually all of the people who volunteered to write these short essays wrote in terms of particular events rather than making references to ongoing processes and themes. It may be that if we try and reach back as far as we can, and most of the contributors groped for very early memories, then we return to the land where meanings are carried by incidents rather than abstracted into ideas about process.

The discovery of self by way of the privacy of consciousness was sharply illustrated in a number of the accounts. This, in turn, took various forms. Some referred to the discovery that internal experience cannot be overheard: "The first time I had been away from home alone . . . I very easily remembered thinking, after a couple of days, that I had done all sorts of odd things which, even if my Mother was thinking of me, she wouldn't know until I had told her."

Many of the accounts spoke movingly of the privacy of consciousness in the form of loneliness. One told of being sent to a Swiss sanitorium at the age of 3 and of being confused by the strange language that the people around her spoke and of her parents leaving her behind and going away on the train: "But it was that memory of standing on the station, the feeling of helplessness, despair, and of being abandoned which is as vivid to me today as it happened then—and always has been. I remember it was a sunny day, I remember feeling quite small and thinking that the ground seemed very close. I remember the feelings I experienced then as mine and that it was I who was alone."

Sometimes circumstances added identity to solitude: "I remember getting lost in the Fun Fair and being panic stricken in the middle of a large crowd. I was found and brought somewhere, where my name was announced over the loudspeakers. Although I was still wailing I remember being very proud hearing my own name."

The integrity of our experience and the way we discriminate what is relevant to us from what is not is sharply illustrated and can be discerned in a passage such as the following: "At about the same age I became aware, not only of the world, of its several countries, but also beyond. I knew nothing tangible about there being other objects in that beyond, but I knew that they were there, the void they were in went on and on without any form of enclosure. The lack of enclosure more than frightened me and I wondered at myself in this vastness and what I now know to be called infinity." This can be seen as a portrait of a child confronting the contrast between the little that he knows and understands and can be part of and the vast universal *other* that lies beyond.

There was no direct reference, in any of the passages, to the acquisition of a sense of *continuity* over time. We can argue that the act of these adults in setting down these very early experiences as matters of great moment is itself an acknowledgment of their continuity over time. It may also be that the way in which the instructions were given pointed people towards a "starting point" and that they did not, thereby, feel called upon to examine the significance of biography as such.

Self experienced as a causal agent, as being responsible, was a theme of very many of the passages, though interestingly enough the experience of failure was cited as equally significant. Possession in this context seemed to be itself a significant act. A neat yet complex example: "Perhaps the first time I remember that I had a vague feeling of self was when playing with one of the children and we exchanged toys. On returning home the distinction between my toys and the toys belonging to others was pointed out and it became obvious that life was not so simple as it had appeared. There was a difference between what others had and what I had and there was therefore a distinction between them and me."

Intriguingly, a sense of causality and control, and thereby self, appears in situations where the person has, for practical purposes, collapsed. One person described an experience at age 5 where she was due to go on stage in a school play and suddenly burst into tears of total fright: "Panic sticken, I bawled my eyes out and my sister took me backstage to Miss W. People tried to comfort me after my initial fright and I remember Miss W. seeming upset and saying she wondered what had upset me. She came up to me and almost pleadingly asked would I do it [i.e., go on stage] and I remember the feeling that I could say yes or no, I could decide as me not just what I was told to do. This lady was asking me, not my sister, who was usually volunteered into pacifying me at school. I felt very surprised and also felt that I had been treated as a person and somehow felt a person."

Perhaps anger can be construed, at one level, as the experience of causality, an experiment in being the agent: "One early memory connected with identity which scared me was the day I got so angry in playing with my doll that I shook and shook and shook her. I was on my own and I can remember how I took fright at how much vehemence was in me. I hadn't been aware of that strength of feeling. I realised I could have torn her to bits if I'd gone on. . . . It's one of the vivid memories and it was me, no one else, no twin etc. involved." That last sentence is worth a second reading.

A complex example, involving the experience of deceit and elaborating the theme of control and assertion with an awareness of others' views of oneself, is evidenced in the following passage: "Another memory of a discovery of a separate 'me' was the day when I deliberately tripped my younger brother and then pretended to my parents that this silly child kept falling. My deceit was discovered and this seemed to be the first appreciation that I wasn't just the 'good little girl' which seemed to be an imposed character, she had a nasty side too. Though it wasn't pleasant to have this nasty bit made known there was a positive side and that was that this was definitely 'me' and not what others saw me as. It seems that it was important for me to differentiate myself from my brother in the eyes of my parents."

This last passage raises the issue of seeing others by analogy with oneself and seeing oneself as seen by others and as being not as others see one. This is frequently put forward as vital to one's recognition of self. Sometimes it takes a relatively simple form in the experience of being compared: "At seven years being described by relatives—mother, father, and even grandmother—as being 'different from others' (grandmother: 'Where did you get *her*?'). This was reinforced in boarding school by the same type of comment, 'Both your sisters are so good, model girls, etc.'"

Sometimes the experience of others' judgment was made more intense by the context in which it took place and the form in which it was expressed. One writer was evacuated from London during the war and then, like so many evacuee children, was up for selection by the residents of the safer area: "The next day we were paraded in a quiet residential road and the good citizens of Yeovil came out of their houses and looked us over. It was just like a cattle market, not the survival of the fittest but the picking of the less scruffy. I can remember a hot feeling spreading right through my body; a feeling of fear in case I wasn't chosen, of resentment I suppose, although I was too young to realise it, a feeling I was *me* and that from then on it was just me, looking after myself, on my own."

This contrasts with the equally salient effect of the experience of others' intense concern: "I really felt a self when I went through a terrifying experience of nearly drowning in water in a flooded boiler-house. I fell into this, face down, and possibly the oilskins I wore kept me afloat. My father rescued me and the next part I remember was being in a mustard bath with both parents extremely concerned. I suppose it was their concern which really made me feel a self."

There is an echo here of the way in which some schizophrenics formerly seemed to recover their sense of self after the now blessedly discarded treatment of deep insulin coma. The patient felt the daily *intensity* of concern of doctor and staff, generated by the fear that the coma might not be reversible. One wonders if perhaps this was the essence of the treatment for the so-called schizophrenic.

A point not made in the Bannister-Fransella summary of self experiences but noted by Allport is the knowledge of one's body as separate from the rest of the world—we live within a sealed envelope of skin. It may be that this is so early and basic an acquired construction that it was too obvious for our people to cite as a source of conviction of self. Just as the fish forgot to specify water when he was asked to describe his environment, our sense of bodily separation is equally taken for granted except in the rare instances where we lose it temporarily for any reason. Interestingly enough, there were some examples of the fact that the modalities in which a child may experience the distinction between his own body and that of others may be lost to us and consequently by adults. Consider the following: "I can remember when still sleeping in a cot in my parents' room my mother giving me a drink in the middle of the night and my objecting because I said 'it has your smell on it.' My mother was very angry and hurt by this, and I was surprised, because it seemed very obvious to me that each person had their own particular smell. (I lost the ability to make this distinction thereafter.)"

A further omission from the Bannister-Fransella list is that a key point in the construing of self is the achievement of reflexivity, the point at which the person is able to reflect on his notion of self and to construe his constructions about himself and others' constructions of him. The achievement of such a meta-level is apparent in some of the passages and most commonly seems to involve the initial experience of privacy and the derivation of further hypotheses about the insides of others, their limitations, commonalities, and so forth.

Consider the following: "When I was three years old my older brother was told to go to the next village and collect an empty barrel and bring it back. He took a wheelbarrow to fetch it in and took me along with him for the walk. On the way back I got into the barrel, which in turn was standing in the wheelbarrow, and was wheeled along in this way by my elder brother, crouching down in the barrel. At some point in the journey my brother met a man he knew and stopped to talk to him. I was crouched down in the barrel and suddenly realised with great clarity that I could hear this man speaking but he didn't know I was there, he didn't know I could hear him, and that I was able to know about him without him knowing about me. In some way this sticks in my mind as one of the times I realised that I was an individual, that I was a self. It was the knowledge that I could observe someone without them knowing that I was observing them. It was to do with being secret and in myself."

Here the notion of a secret seems to be the basis for a reflexive experience, both the notion of being secret and of overhearing secrets. Sometimes there is a cyclic me-them-me quality about such experiences: "At four years of age I remember being very anxious of being me when one day I came down to the drawing room and heard my grandmother tell the assembled family, exactly in the words I had used, the way I had a short time previously spoken to myself in the bathroom when washing my hands and all the time talking loudly to my reflection in the mirror. I remember being very aware of myself as a person, when looking in the mirror, and pleased about it; however, later, in the drawing room, feeling cheated and not quite sure, but on reflection, reconsidering my earlier experience in the bathroom and regaining my equilibrium."

Returning to the essential quality of contrast, of the construct being *self-other*, it is notable that a recurrent theme of the passages is comparison with and judgment by others. One writer pinpointed this by describing an occasion on which he was mocked by his father for his failure to correctly wire up a radio he was given for Christmas: "It was from incidents like this that I learned I was a stupid and ignorant person. (I recount this incident because I believe that events that teach one what sort of person one is make one aware of one's self as an individual.)"

This thought reaches toward the construct theory contention that we achieve a picture of ourselves by filtering others' constructions of us through our constructions of them. To be called timid by someone you consider rash to the point of madness is one thing. To be called timid by someone you have always thought a mouse is quite another.

Since Kelly argues that we may best seek definition in the contrast between the two poles of a construct, we might finally consider how and why a sense of self might be only poorly achieved. Time and again, in grid "mappings" (Bannister & Mair, 1968) of the construct systems of adult psychiatric patients, a variety of weakly delineated "selves" has been manifest. Some experience distances between "self as I am" and "ideal self" so great that the ideal must surely be a fantasy rather than a plan—or else the ideal is seen in terms quite unrelated to those used to interpret present self, and inference from one to the other seems impossible. In some grids, self has been a construct almost without implications or has been seen as the grave of the person's hopes: "like I am" and "like I used to be" are permanently identical. Sometimes only one pole of the construct is elaborated, as in Fransella's (1972) stutterers who had a truly rich vision of "self as stutterer" and only the most impoverished notions of "self as fluent speaker." In yet others, several compartmentalized "selves" are evident, with no constructs effectively bridging the sealed worlds within the one person.

Much is known, publicly and experientially, about how a child's picture of himself might become distorted, and we can readily translate both common sense and formal psychology into construct theory terms. Consider the plight of the child of wildly inconsistent parents—parents whose behavior veers and swings between them and within each, the sort who might later get themselves described as "mystifying" or "double binding" or "teaching distorted meanings." The child faces the fearsome task of elaborating a notion of what he is when any expectations he develops are likely to be invalidated or proved irrelevant. Thus he may be alternately treated in similar situations and for similar efforts on his part as *important* and then *unimportant*, or as *sensible* and then *idiotic*, or as *lovable*, and then *repulsive*. The child is not just struggling to avoid acquiring a picture of himself as "unworthy," he is in danger of failing to acquire a picture of himself at all. Imagine the equivalent position where constructs about the physical world are concerned. Suppose we were to build a world of trick objects for the infant—place him forever in a universe where collapsible furniture, mirrored images, conjurer's boxes, liquifying solids, and illusionist's lighting created a mad and unpredictable physics. We readily recognize that an infant so placed would have small chance of elaborating that construing of shape, distance, solidity, conservation, and so forth so lovingly catalogued by developmental psychologists. He would fail to "grasp" his world. The building of "trick" psychological environments is, sadly, no rare occurrence.

Even if the child's early family cosmos is relatively stable, it may yet encourage him to develop notions of self which are too specialized, too designed to fit the family, so that when he moves to school he may be faced with interpersonal events that are entirely outside the range of convenience of his constructs. His discrimination of say situations in which he should be *obedient* and situations in which he should be *independent* may not serve his purposes when he is faced with an expanded world. Again, he may have validated at home a construing of self which is bound to be invalidated at school. If the boy has been brought up to see himself in "girlish" terms (of dress and manner and speech and activities), then school may massively disprove his expectations. If the family has taught him to see himself as essentially and always "forgivable," then this theory may collapse under the counterweight evidence of the playground. At such times the child may suffer guilt, in Kelly's sense of the term—an awareness of dislodgment of the self from core role structure. He finds that he is not the self that he had pictured, for the expectations derived from that picture are not fulfilled.

The educational system itself varies in its provision of opportunity to experience, experiment with and elaborate self (Bannister & Salmon, 1975 and Salmon, 1970). Primary schools in England, probably more than any segment of the system up to and including universities, often provide rich opportunities for the child to locate his own nature. The life of the primary school child often abounds in free painting, extensive project work, story telling (with its free offer of figures to identify with and against), creative games, and an approach informed by the idea that the child is not so much to be stocked with knowledge as to be encouraged to discover—and the discovering of the world is the context in which self is discovered. Later schools place the emphasis more and more on "objective knowledge," on "facts" which the child must not handle personally. Indeed, he will be rebuked and fail his examinations if he strives to take a personal and self-relevant view of history or science or even language.

Finally, it may be that the form of construing is more vital than the content if an elaboratable understanding of self is to be achieved. Kelly distinguishes between preemptive and constellatory constructs on the one hand and propositional constructs on the other. A preemptive construct takes the form, "if this is an X, it is *nothing but* an X." Thus the child schooled in this form of construction might be locked into a content as in "if I am a Jew (naughty boy, bright lad at school, sissy), then I am *nothing but . . .* " Constellatory construing rigidly sets the implications of an interpretation so that the child may gain elaboration of a fixed kind. "If I am clever, then I am admired by adults, not good at games, dedicated to hard work, not very popular with other kids . . . " Propositional construing is essentially "as if" in nature. "I can see myself as if, *among other things,* I were a tough kid, a clown, a rebel (or whatever)." This is the freest form of construing and offers perhaps the greatest chance of gaining an identity which is not also a prison.

Geneticists and environmentalists, in their extreme moods, are agreed that the child has no fundamental surprises for us. He is either unpacking his genetic suitcase and clothing himself in its contents or tamely marching to the drumbeat of external stimuli. Kelly would have us see the child's behavior, as we should see our own, as a continuous experiment. Perhaps no part of this creative endeavor is more pressing or more impressive than the invention of self.

1. Dr. Bannister is currently a member of the Psychology Department of High Boyds Hospital, Ilkley, Yorkshire, England.

REFERENCES

Allport, G. W. *Becoming*. New Haven, Conn.: Yale University Press, 1955.

Bannister, D., & Mair, J. M. M. *The evaluation of personal constructs*. London: Academic Press, 1968.

Bannister, D., & Salmon P. A personal construct view of education. *New York University Education Quarterly*, 1975, **6** (4), 28.

Bannister, D., & Fransella, F. *Inquiring man*. Harmondsworth, Middlesex: Penguin, 1971.

Brierley, D. W. *The use of personality constructs by children of three different ages*. Unpublished doctoral dissertation, London University, 1967.

Epstein, S. The self-concept revisited. *American Psychologist*, 1973, **28** (5), 404–416.

Fransella, F. *Personal change and reconstruction*. London: Academic Press, 1972.

Kelly, G. A. *The psychology of personal constructs*. New York: Norton, 1955.

Little, B. R. Factors affecting the use of psychological v. non-psychological constructs in the Rep. Test. *Bulletin of the British Psychological Society*, 1968, **17**, 55.

Salmon, P. A psychology of personal growth. In D. Bannister (Ed.), *Perspectives in personal construct theory*. London & New York: Academic Press, 1970. Pp. 197–221.

Interpretive Man:
The Enlarged Self-image

Alvin W. Landfield
University of Nebraska–Lincoln

*T*his article evolved from a more delimited consideration of the person in relation to Professor George A. Kelly's Organization Corollary. That which began as a preoccupation with certain studies of construct organization within this corollary grew into a series of short essays which have been grouped together here: Science, Psychology, and Paradoxical Man; The Personal Construct as a Way of Knowing; Consistent Man; The Organizational Process; and The Construction of Meaningfulness.

The first essay contains a brief statement on science and psychology which illustrates man's paradoxical nature as he actively searches for unity and certainty as well as contrast and challenge. The contrasting theme of man's interpretive nature is elaborated in the section on the personal construct as a way of knowing. Alternative ways of viewing behavioral consistency are presented in the next section, showing that personal construct theory is more than a consistency formulation only (see Maddi, 1972). Processes of organization are also introduced in the consistency section and elaborated further within the context of research on the differentiation and hierarchical integration of personal construct systems. Here, we take a step beyond cognitive complexity or measures of construct differentiation by introducing a measure of hierarchical integration of construct systems which is called ordination. In the final section, studies are reviewed which support the use of rating-scale polarization as a measure of meaningfulness, a type of measure essential to the determination of construct ordination.

The theme that binds together these seemingly varied sections is the person and the assumption that man has the capacity to interpret as well as to react. It is this self-image of interpreter and creator that psychologists should take more seriously. The five essays are presented to encourage scientists to expend more effort in the pursuit of that interpretive quality of man which is excluded from many psychological studies.

SCIENCE, PSYCHOLOGY, AND PARADOXICAL MAN

The development of a science may be defined by the creation and re-creation of a professional language for that science. The history of a science begins with prescientific or lay conceptions which then are supplanted by the more unitary, precise, technical, heuristic, and divergent terminology of the scientist. Where prescience ends and science begins may be difficult to judge, since the science of one age may be construed as the prescience of the next. Moreover, there may be disagreement about the existence of a centralizing paradigm for that science. Although there is such disagreement in psychology, most psychologists presumably would refer to themselves as scientists.

Even though the particularized language of a science is comprehensible primarily to those trained in the speciality, scientific words and conceptions filter back eventually into common language and become part of the broader culture and its folklore. This process of cultural assimilation of scientific and quasi-scientific language is seen most strikingly in relation to American psychology, where undergraduate courses have proliferated, community book stores carry numerous titles in the field, and popular magazines exhibit a plethora of psychological speculations suited to everyman.

That the educated layman would be deeply interested in learning more about his own behavior and insistent that some of his questions should be answered in the context of science is understandable and has many implications. His interest may counterbalance the perseveration of scientists who tend to elaborate theories and methods too far removed from everyday experience. His interest may challenge the psychologist to widen the scope of his investigations, to encompass man's feelings, beliefs, and values. His multifaceted and changing interests may encourage the psychologists to continue his more molar as well as his molecular approaches to behavior.

Although laymen with some knowledge of psychology may exert beneficial and corrective influences on the field, it might be argued, conversely, that the rapid assimilation of psychological conceptions into the common language of a culture can restrict the theorizing and experimentation of psychologists in that culture. The psychologist is encouraged to investigate only that which is understood or valued by his culture. This restriction to that which is accepted by one's culture might not be fully appreciated by the psychologist who has internalized these restrictions within his personal value system.

Just as there may be scientific words and conceptions filtering back into the common language of a culture, a similar process may occur as scientists in one field become aware of the conceptions of scientists in another field. For example, certain ideas of the physicist have become popularized in psychology. Psychologists may refer to physics as they discuss the nature of science and the methods that should be employed in psychology. However, psychologists do not agree about the essence of physics. They may remark about the imagination of the theoretical physicist, the preciseness and clarity of his molecular studies, or the ways in which he combines theoretical skills with observational technique.

The interactions between layman and psychologist have broadened the contextual base of psychology. In like manner, the dialectic between the physical scientist and the psychologist has encouraged the psychologist to take a closer look at the nature of science and the nature of a science most suitable for psychology and for psychologies. As psychologists consider more carefully the nature of science and how it relates to psychology, one can only speculate about how they would "psychologize" and "scientize" about the following quotation:

> The suddenness of the discovery, coupled with the totally unexpected properties of the particle are what make it so exciting. It is not like the particles we know and must have some new kind of structure. . . . The discovery is abstract. We don't know what it means. . . . [Theorists] are working frantically to fit the particle into the framework of our present knowledge of the elementary particle. [Richter & Ting, 1974]

A psychologist might show an indifference to the physicist's feeling of excitement, his conception of newness, or his wish to relate new meanings to the old. Then again, the psychologist could wonder about the nature of the relationship between excitement and the experience of the unexpected, the correlates of a fascination for the abstract in contrast with the concrete, and the ambivalence about forming new meanings which is suggested by frantic efforts to place that which is excitingly new within better-known structures of knowledge. The psychologist could also theorize that the apparent ambivalence about the old and the new highlights a central theme in man's paradoxical psychology—his oppositional nature in contrast to his persistent search for unity.

These two aspects of man have not been ignored by psychologists. Gibson (1970) and Singer (1966) conceptualize man's search for certainty and consistency. Rychlak (1968), focusing on the dialectic, states the case for man's oppositional and interpretive nature.

The search for unity in science is given a strange twist by Lancelot Whyte (1957), a British philosopher, who defines science as "a non-rational search for unity in facts which are not facts" (p. 49). Blumer (1972), taking a dialectical position on the nature of reality, criticizes the scientist for his absolute and unitary approach to the independent variable:

> The indifference of variable analysis to the process of interpretation is based apparently on the tacit assumption that the independent variable predetermines its interpretation. This assumption has no foundation. The interpretation is not predetermined by the variable as if the variable emanated its own meaning. If there is anything we know, it is that an object, event, or situation in human experience does not carry its own meaning: the meaning is conferred on it. . . . Now the question arises, how can variable analysis include the process of interpretation. [P. 251]

The paradoxical nature of man, as he actively searches for both certainty and challenge, is highlighted in Heisenberg's (1972) statement that greater truths may be found in the "deeps of obscurity," and the omission of all that is unclear would probably lead to "completely uninteresting and trivial tautologies" (p. 213). Although Heisenberg found challenge in obscurity, other scientists seem less open to the unknown, more quickly placing difficult problems and phenomena beyond science. In this respect, they are not really so different from laymen who withdraw from conflicts which they can not resolve. Kuhn (1962) suggests that scientists, as a rule, prefer to work out of a single paradigm and to focus their attention on those problems which the paradigm can best resolve. Only when they cannot extend their paradigm, under pressure of having to resolve important new problems, will they turn to a different paradigm. Scientists and ordinary human beings sometimes prefer the comfort of unity and certainty found in traditional dogma, religion, scientific theory, and method, and they tend to avoid the antithetical feelings, rules, and behaviors implicit in their traditional choices. In this preference for the comfort of unity and certainty, scientists and laymen may ignore their own interpretive natures. That man should not ignore his interpretive nature is suggested by Bridgman (1954), Oppenheimer (1956), and Dubois (1974).

One may hypothesize that it is man's nature to seek unity and certainty. However, even as unity and certainty allay man's feelings of anxiety, his dissatisfactions and boredom, coupled with his curiosity, lead to questioning those unities and certainties which contribute to his security. Unity provides the comfortable context within which meaning is stabilized. Contrast performs a dual function of providing a context for change in that unity as well as a dimensional framework within which one may comprehend his particular position.

If man functions in both unifying and contrasting ways and plays the role of both interpreter and reactor in relation to his experience, how can the psychologist, as a scientist, approach this complex and paradoxical organism?

It seems apparent that Professor George A. Kelly (1955) attempted to answer this question with his *Psychology of Personal Constructs*. He first made the *analogy* between scientist the man and man the scientist, assuming *observational, interpretive,* and *predictive* characteristics for both of them. He then ingeniously elevated *contrast* to a central place in his system, assuming it as a fundamental process of all men, and defined his *personal construct* in a manner which simultaneously encompassed the generalizing and differentiating natures of man. The context of the construct was broadly defined and the methods of eliciting it were illustrative rather than confining. Emotions and feelings, interpreted most personally at the level of the individual's own construction, also could be understood most abstractly by the psychologist as he applied the Kellian innovative interpretations of anxiety, guilt, fear, threat, and hostility. The psychologist's appreciation of behavior was tied to his inferences about man's conceptions, and these conceptions, although deceptively easy to obtain from personal description, could be inferred from any behavior. Although acts of choice were seen as occurring within the person's own system of contrasting anticipations, these anticipations were *not* assumed to be identical with the precise, molecular, objectified, and controlled predictions of the laboratory scientist. The validation of interpretations was seen against the background of the person's own system, a system that could be more idiosyncratic than public, more emotional than logical, and, above all, dimensional as well as unitary.

This emphasis on constructive man was created deliberately as a contrast to the popular psychology of the time—reactive man. Kelly challenged us to make inferences about valuing and thinking man and provided us with a theory, sufficiently abstract, within which to encompass a variety of life orientations, values, and selves. He defined the personal construct psychologist as one who accepts the constructions of his subjects as a base from which to theorize and to anticipate their behavior. Using his subject's constructions as a base for his inferences, the psychologist may theorize about his subjects and create subordinate formulations within the broad outlines of the theory.

Self-image and the Scientist

Kelly's construction of his theory revealed a preoccupation with his own self-image as a scientist when he suggested that the psychologist should not separate himself from his subject matter. Kelly reasoned that scientists and their subjects have much in common and extended an invitation to all of us to imagine ourselves as active, interpretive beings, creating dichotomus or dimensional structures of personal meaning, and ceaselessly, although not obviously, experiencing the continuities, discontinuities, and themes of our own lives.

Drawing the analogy between scientist and common man allows the psychologist to pose questions which he would not ordinarily ask. Since the psychologist is man, one may ask about the origins of his theories and how his theories account for his own behavior. If one is interested in self-image, it may be fruitful to inquire how a formal theory of personality or general behavior is related to the theorist's own self-image or to his anti-image. A study by Lazarus (1971) suggests that professionals do function within contrasting models of man. In this study, Lazarus surveyed 20 behavior therapists who were receiving personal therapy. Curiously, none of these behavior therapists sought help from behavior therapists. One client commented, "I have decided to give the opposition a fair try." Another commented, "My therapist is a beautiful human being and that means more to me than his theoretical orientation" (pp. 349–350). Explaining this contrast of "action in support of self" and "action in support of others" seems clearly within the province of science and personal construct theory. In any case, it is fun to speculate about how the personal values and anti-values of a Freud, Skinner, Rogers, or Kelly may have influenced their particular careers.

Although the psychologist understandably may not wish to probe too deeply into the personal value origins of his own formal theorizing, it is legitimate to inquire whether the propositions of one's general theory can be used to explain one's own theoretical behavior. The application of a general theorist's frame of reference to his own scientific behavior makes sense within a philosophical position taken by Oliver and Landfield (1962), who state, "In a science, reflexivity occurs in those conclusions which assert something about the processes whereby they have been derived. . . . To derive conclusions from evidence a man must think. Thus to assert that thought is of this or that nature, is to say something about the nature of the process whereby this conclusion has been derived" (p. 114).

In stating that the general theorist should be willing to apply his own theory to himself, as a scientist, Oliver and Landfield did not assume that the process would be easy. They also did not suggest that the theorist should bare his soul to his colleagues. The reflexive argument points to the idea that the theorist should have *some concern* about his role of scientist within the context of his own theory of human beings. That Kelly experienced this concern is eloquently stated in a letter to S. I. Hayakawa,[1] in which he describes his efforts to understand himself in terms of his own expressed theoretical orientation:

> A number of years ago . . . I was struck by the fact that every psychology textbook I read contained at least two theories of personality. The first theory was expounded, usually in the first chapter of the textbook, as an explanation of the way "science" sets about its task. But this description of scientific activities may properly be regarded as a description of the behavior of

1. G. A. Kelly to S. I. Hayakawa, September 30, 1963.

scientists—or at least an effort to describe the behavior of scientists. Hence, it is, itself, a theory of personality, limited, of course, supposedly to scientists.

Having got this out of his system, the author then usually went ahead to describe the psychology of the rest of us poor mortals in terms quite unlike those he had used to describe the personality of the elite. Partly in rebellion to this, I suppose, I set about the task of developing a theory of personality in which I suppose I echoed one of the mottos of the Protestant Reformation. Instead of saying "every man his own priest," I proposed that we regard "every man his own scientist." The pathways into which this effort led me have proved, in the main, to be amusing and, I hope, more or less profitable.

At least I am sure now that one can take the model of the scientist and use it as a general personality theory and that such a theory has a special relevance to psychotheraphy and to certain innovations in the way psychotherapists go about their business.

THE PERSONAL CONSTRUCT AS A WAY OF KNOWING

When Kelly (1955) defined the personal construct as an awareness of how two things are alike in a way that differentiates them from a third, he encompassed several aspects of knowing. First of all, one knows along a dimension extending from precise verbal symbolization to levels of understanding which may be preverbal, difficult to express in words, identified with raw feelings, and sometimes expressible in movement, gesture, and sound. Although most research on the personal construct has focused on verbal formulations, Kelly succinctly stated that "construing is not to be confounded with verbal formulation" (p. 51). Nevertheless, he constructed the Repertory (Rep) Test for the highly verbal investigator and his equally verbal subjects. However, Kelly did not intend that the constructs elicited by this instrument would be treated as the equivalent of all constructs within the system.

Two other aspects of knowing are encompassed by Kelly's appreciation of two complementary operations defined by contrast and generalization within and across contexts of time. In regard to man's capacity to generalize and contrast, Kelly stated,

> A construct which implied similarity without contrast would represent just as much of a chaotic undifferentiated homogeneity as a construct which implied contrast without similarity would represent a chaotic particularized heterogeneity. The former would leave the person engulfed in a sea with no landmarks to relieve the monotony. The latter would confront him with an interminable series of kaleidoscopic changes in which nothing would ever appear familiar. [P. 51]

Kelly's appreciation of this relationship between generalization and contrast placed him apart from students of concept formation who traditionally have defined the concept as the grouping of similarities. They have paid scant attention to contrast. One of Kelly's theoretical contributions to the concept formation literature was to enlarge upon this understanding of conception by pointing out that one must know what is excluded from a group in order to know what should be included in that group. Contrast as a way of knowing was given special emphasis when he argued that man would have no appreciation of darkness without a contrasting awareness of lightness. Moreover, he would have little appreciation of friendship unless, at the same time, he could have some awareness of what is excluded from that friendship.

Michael Wallach (1959) may have supported this "Kellian" position on contrast when he stated as a conclusion to his research, "Attention to a contrast class would seem to be one important mechanism for making such selections, since choosing one or another contrast class tends to influence the number and kinds of properties in whose terms we define the class of interest" (p. 19).

Ogden (1932), focusing on the meaning of opposition and its historical significance, theorized that opposition is a fundamental human and linguistic experience, and that symbolization of polarities is related to body symmetry—to the early differentiation of vertical sidedness and horizontal directions of left and right. Kephart (1960), a psychological researcher, supported Ogden's theory about body symmetry by demonstrating that confusion in laterality is related to difficulties in learning to read and write. He states, "Our first information about the coordinates of space comes from the kinesthetic awareness of differences in our own body, and chief among these directional differences is the right-left differentiation" (p. 23). That understanding of opposition is acquired early in childhood is supported by Bloom (1970). She presented evidence that children between the ages of 19 and 25 months may comprehend the dualities of existence and nonexistence, acceptance and rejection, and affirmation and denial.

Taking a broader cultural perspective on contrast, we may become aware of the great dialectics in history, observing that man's progress through time is definable by controversies in politics, religion, art, and science. Great ideas seem sharpened by controversy, argument, and contrast.

Personality theorists have all shown an interest in man's contrasts. Jung (Jacobi, 1951) perceived opposites as a source of psychic energy, as an explanation of sudden shifts in behavioral balance, and as a projection of unrecognized characteristics. Adler (1931, 1964) noted that opposites in behavior can have the same meaning. Menninger (1963) talked about common cultural oppositionalities such as life-death, good-evil, forces of light and darkness, yang and yin, assimilation and accommodation, anabolism-catabolism, synthesis-disintegration, and constructiveness-destructiveness. Freud (1952), devoting his attention to man's inner conflicts, wrote,

> It is important to begin early to reckon with the fact that the mind is an arena, a sort of tumbling ground, for the struggles of antagonistic impulses; or to express it in non-dynamic terms, that the mind is made up of contradictions and pairs of opposites. Evidence of one particular tendency does not in the least preclude its opposite; there is room for both of them. The material questions are: How do these opposites stand to one another and what effects proceed from one of them and what from the other. [P. 80]

Even as Freud talked about man's contrasts and conflicts, he did not elevate the idea of contrast to a central position, but tended to subordinate it to the particular contents of his theory.

Theorists have noted that man tends to avoid the contrasting aspects of himself. Freud, of course, talked about defenses against hidden impulses—impulses and aspects of one's nature of which one might be ashamed. Kelly stated that we make decisions within pairs of contrasts, choosing one pole over the other one and focusing more consciously on the pole of choice than its opposite. It may be hypothesized that man becomes most aware of the contrasts to his choice at the point of disenchantment with it, in the contexts of survival, boredom, and play.

The Dichotomy

The idea of contrast captured the attention of scientists; however, the conception of thinking as a dichotomous process was unpalatable for some of them. Such men as Korzybski (1933) and Johnson (1946) opposed the idea that duality could have a constructive purpose. They tended to equate the dichotomy with primitive, unscientific thinking which implied absolutism, simplicity, rigidity, and absence of change. The amusing aspect of this controversy over Aristotelian dichotomies and Galilean gradations was the rigidly dichotomizing behavior of the general semanticist as he outlined the evils of the dichotomy. In this context, Korzybski's publishing company carries the interesting title, the International Non-Aristotelian Library Publishing Company.

The modern general semanticist, such as Weinberg (1959) or Hayakawa (1949), has assumed a more moderate position on the dichotomy. Hayakawa understands the motivating nature of the duality, perceiving that strong positions and commitments are necessary to initiate important undertakings, and that final decisions often involve dichotomies. Weinberg rewrites Aristotle's three laws. The law of identity, "A is A," becomes "A may be assumed to remain constant for the sake of discussion." The law of the excluded middle, "Anything is either A or not-A," becomes "Anything may be classified as either A or not-A." Finally, the law of non-identity, "Something cannot be both A and not-A," becomes "Something should not be classified both as A and not-A at the same time in the same context" (pp. 82–83). Restructuring Aristotle's laws in this manner emphasizes the process of abstracting and recognizes that it is the person who does the labeling, and that anything may be understood in other ways—depending on one's purpose. Contrast and change are both caught within these new definitions, and the similarity of Weinberg's position to that of Kelly becomes apparent.

Kelly (1955), even as he focused on the dualities of man, did not believe that dichotomous thinking is necessarily absolute, although a person can use his dichotomies in this way. He also did not assume that dichotomies are simple, although one might think, feel, and behave in simple, dichotomous ways. Within personal construct theory, one can think like a Galilean or an Aristotlian, yet share a feature common to all men, that feeling, thinking, and behaving are intrinsically matters of contrast.

Perhaps it was the extreme dialectical position of Korzybski that set the stage for the later emergence of such reconciling positions as those of Weinberg and Kelly. Such a hypothesis, if tenable, suggests that meaningful reconciliations of opposites occur when the dialectic is sharp and oppositions become most clear.

Defining Contrast

Although we may comprehend contrast in our lives, how does one define it? Obviously, it must be personal rather than something found in a dictionary of antonyms. Moreover, even as difference is an important aspect of contrast, important contrasts tend to form dualities. Perhaps one could define contrast in meaning as a personal awareness of a striking or important difference, a type of difference which implies the possibility of polar opposition or conflict; that one pole of a difference may either cancel out or balance the other one; and that the contrasting poles can be linked together or be combined in some way. Defining contrast in this way then suggests the criteria of meaningfulness, oppositionality, and duality of togetherness.

Awareness of a contrast in meaning is not just another way of saying that something is different from something else. Contrast implies the meaningful experiencing of an oppositional difference. It also implies that oppositional poles may be linked together or combined in some manner. Many differences do not meet these criteria of meaningfulness, oppositionality, and duality. For example, the statement that elephants are different from violins is not very striking or important, nor does it suggest a duality. However, if we were to observe an elephant and a violin within the same zoo enclosure most of us would sense the absurdity of it, find it humorous, and be very curious about why anyone would place a violin in the elephant's cage. The experience would be perplexing but, nonetheless, strikingly meaningful at the moment. Directly experiencing the realistic and absurd togetherness of most unlikely companions does meet the criteria of meaningfulness, oppositionality, and duality, although the physical togetherness of elephant and violin represents only a momentary duality and therefore cannot be equated with those more enduring dualities such as pleasure and pain, life and death.

CONSISTENT MAN

If the idea of knowing through personal constructs were applied to all men, what difference would this conception make in the interpretation of man's behavior? In this essay, the reader will be asked to reevaluate the issue of behavioral consistency within the framework of personal construct theory.

Old debates never die, they just reappear in different forms. Recently, several investigators of personality have revisited the issue of the generality versus the specificity of behavior in the context of their observations that people behave inconsistently, lacking cohesiveness and stability in their personalities and behavior. Block (1973), in his effort to explain inconsistency, questions the ways in which psychologists conceptualize it. He points out that "the behaviors being contrasted and correlated may not all be significant or salient for the individual" (p. 73). Block's argument is extended by Bem and Allen (1974) when they state that consistency must be sought in the study of the person, taking into consideration his viewpoints. In this regard, their position is similar to that of Kelly (1955). Perhaps Mischel (1973a) has been most instrumental in reviving the debate on generality as he emphasizes the power of the situational context, notes the failure of trait psychology, and observes that the human mind functions as a reducing valve "that creates and maintains perceptions of continuity even in the face of perpetual changes in actual behavior" (p. 76). Reading further in this chapter, one gets the impression that for Mischel, situation-specific behavior is the rule rather than the exception and man's struggle to organize and to integrate his life experiences may be more of an afterthought and rationalization than a guide to future behavior. However, in another manuscript, presumably a later one, Mischel (1973b) seems to present a broader and more tempered position on personality consistency when he accepts the value of three different perspectives on psychology: first, the psychologist's constructions of conditions and procedures such as conditioning, reinforcement, and stimulus control; second, the psychologist's constructions of mediating conditions such as the person's constructs, values, and rules; and third, the psychologist's constructions of the subject's phenomenology.

It also is apparent that Mischel (1973b) has some appreciation of the personal construct view when he states, "Obviously the impact of any stimulus depends on the organism that experiences it" (p. 262), and again when he states, "Clearly, different persons may group and encode the same events and behaviors in different ways. At a molar level, such individual differences are especially evident in the personal constructs individuals employ and in the kinds of information to which they selectively attend" (pp. 267–268).

Even though Mischel has an appreciation of the personal construct, he did not indicate that the personal construct might encompass the three perspectives of psychology, namely, the conditions needed to modify behavior, mediating variables of the person, and phenomenological impact. If the psychology of personal constructs had been his theory of choice, he might have noted that the Kellian alternative to reinforcement, the validation and invalidation of constructions, neatly captures the idea that the investigator may never be in complete control of the stimulus since it properly belongs to the subject who construes it. He also might have observed that the personal construct is more than something caught in the web of a conventional personal construct grid. Emotions, feelings, and phenomenological influences can be understood in relation to the personal construct, since it is defined as a dimension of awareness. Finally, he might have emphasized man's interpretive nature as being the focus of a psychology of personality. Situations are constructions of man and the significance of them must be understood in relation to the interpretations placed upon them.

Consistency and Personal Construct Theory

Understanding consistency within personal construct theory is not a simple matter. First of all, Kelly stated that it is not consistency for consistency's sake nor even self-consistency that man seeks: "Rather it is his seeking to anticipate the whole world of events and thus relate himself to them that best explains his psychological processes.

If he acts to preserve the system, it is because the system is an essential chart for his personal adventures, not because it is a self-contained island of meaning" (p. 59). On the same theme, Kelly again writes, "It is not mere certainty that man seeks; if that were so, he might take delight in the repetitive ticking of the clock. More and more he seeks to anticipate all impending events of whatsoever nature" (p. 58). At one point, Kelly relates the process of an expanding universe to play, delight, surprise, and laughter. He then states, "However, more serious play can be risky, eluding verbal description and encouraging the spectator to feel unsympathetic with what he perceives as a 'shapeless mass'" (p. 999). Kelly's position suggests that even as creative behavior can have direction and purpose, the objective observer and the consistency psychologist may fail to perceive it in others as they look for reliability in specific responses or only within their own personal construct systems. Abstracting the moving theme challenges the observer to take inductive leaps and to wonder what it means to be the other person.

As Kelly enlarged upon his ideas of a moving universe, he suggested that one should look for an optimal rather than a maximal stability of the personal construct system. Continual, although not necessarily extensive, change in the system would be anticipated. Also, by assuming that man chooses in the direction of an increased elaboration and definition of his system, Kelly introduced the idea of consistency in the direction of change. In this instance one would have to judge consistency at a more abstract level. Taking this more abstract approach to change helps us understand, for example, the frustration of the world traveler who is forced by circumstances beyond his control to settle permanently in a small, isolated community.

Embracing the idea of ordinal relationships among constructs, Kelly's Organization Corollary underlines the importance of measuring consistency with respect to different levels of abstraction and molarity. One might expect that the dimensions of a person's awareness would be more stable than particular behaviors and self-descriptions encompassed by those dimensions. In other words, one expects the more encompassing, superordinate structures of the personal construct system to be more stable than subordinate elements within those structures. In the context of this idea of superordination-subordination in construction, Kelly differentiated slot change from organizational change. Slot change or side change refers to the movement in construction or behavior from one pole of a construct to its contrast. Kelly hypothesized that slot change would be more stable if it occurred within the context of modifications in construct relationship and hierarchy, that is, organizational change.

The significance of organizational change was studied by Levy (1956), who hypothesized that constellations of interrelated constructs would be more resistant to change than constructs which are unrelated to other constructs within the system. In this ingenious study of constellatory and propositional constructs, Levy found an inverse relation between "the range of interdependency of a construct and its susceptibility to change following predictive failure" (p. 58).

Placing constructs along a dimension of greater and lesser meaningfulness provides another context within which the psychologist can measure consistency. Kelly hypothesized that core constructs which have greater significance for the person's psychological life and death will be more resistant to change than peripheral constructs. Varble and Landfield (1969) provided suggestive evidence that, in the context of psychotherapy, clients show more self-ideal discrepancy change on less important or peripheral than on more important or core constructs.

Kelly also hypothesized that a construction of change would expedite change. Starting from this idea, Hass (1974) postcoded the change content of personal constructs contributed by two religious subgroups, one committed to the status quo and the other one committed to slow or moderate change. Specifically, Hass studied a nationally publicized dialectic between two groups belonging to a branch of the Lutheran church. Leaders of the church sharply polarized around the issue of change, one group being absolutely opposed to any change in church doctrine and theology. The other group was open to slow or moderate change. Results of the postcoding procedure revealed a significantly greater use of change construction in the sample of pastors belonging to the change group. These subjects more often described acquaintances along dimensions connoting openness and closedness to experience ($p < .001$).

Kelly's Fragmentation Corollary emphasizes the idea that incompatibilities at one level of the personal construct system may be compatible at a higher order of personal theory. Employing this type of conception may help to explain how a marital argument can lead to the dissolution of a marriage in one instance and to an affirmation of the relationship in another case. In the first instance, a marital partner might construe ambivalent feelings as validating a poor relationship. In the second case, ambivalent feelings might be interpreted as supporting the importance of the other person and the need for better communication.

It seems apparent that the issue of consistency-inconsistency within the framework of personal construct theory becomes a question of understanding the varying contexts of behavioral stability, integrity, and change. We have mentioned several contexts which relate to the organization and content of the personal construct system. There is another context which refers to the situation, the situation as construed by both the subject and his investigator. The situation for the subject is an interpretation made within his personal construct system. The investigator hopes that his subject's interpretation of the situation will coincide with his own intentions, or conversely, that the investigator's interpretation of the understandings of his subject will validly reflect how the subject is construing the situation.

An illustration of how an experimenter may try to ensure that his subject's interpretation of the situation will coincide with the investigator's intentions is provided by Willis (1961). Willis operationally defined the dimension of maturity-immaturity, located subjects who agreed with the definitions, and also importantly used the construct in describing self and others. Subjects then were exposed to actors playing mature and immature roles and expectancies, roles, and expectancies which conformed to the operational definitions agreed upon by subjects and investigator. Now this focusing on the interpretations of both subject and experimenter is time-consuming and may not lead to a proliferation of manuscripts. Nevertheless, such experimental efforts may represent a more profound psychology in which subject consistency and change will be studied within shared frameworks of communication and value.

THE ORGANIZATIONAL PROCESS

The study of individual *frameworks* of communication and value is a particular focus of personal construct theory. In this regard, Kelly (1955) stated that a primary characteristic of man or scientist is his capacity to create organizing themes for his life. "Each person characteristically evolves, for his convenience in anticipating events, a construction system embracing ordinal relationships between [bipolar] constructs" (p. 56). This corollary, which focuses on hierarchical relationships among dimensions of contrast, implies that taking perspective and making decisions requires higher order construction within the personal construct system. In describing the relationships among constructs, Kelly used such terms as superordinate, subordinate, contrast linkage, core, peripheral, constellatory, and propositional. It is these last two ways of describing construct relationships—constellatory versus propositional—that encouraged the early research on cognitive complexity. And it is these two conceptions which will be given special attention as we extend our own research beyond cognitive complexity as it is currently defined by the process of differentiation.

Kelly defined the constellatory construct as one which fixes the other realm memberships of its elements and illustrated it by referring to typological and prejudicial ways of thinking. In contrast to constellatory construction, he defined the propositional construct as one which carries no implications regarding the other realm memberships.

Propositional and constellatory thinking may be comprehended by considering a Rep Test grid in which a subject records contrasting ideas about his acquaintances—for example, friendly versus unfriendly, honest versus dishonest—and then rates each acquaintance within these dimensions of personal meaning. Imagine this subject equating his personal construction of friendship with honesty. His friendly acquaintances are always honest. His unfriendly acquaintances are always dishonest. This relationship also may be reversed, so that honesty implies friendliness and dishonesty implies unfriendliness. It is this very tight relationship between the two constructs that points to constellatory thinking. One does not have to experience the other person's honesty to know that he is honest. All one needs to experience is that the person is friendly. One does not have to experience the other person's friendliness to know that he is friendly. If you know that he is honest, he then must be a friendly person. In contrast to this example of constellatory construction, a subject may employ person descriptions of friendship and honesty without equating them or perceiving any necesssary relation between them. In this instance, one may speak about these constructs as propositional with respect to each other. If friendship and honesty also are unrelated to other dimensions of the person's experience as well as unrelated to each other, one may refer to these constructs as propositional with respect to the system—that part of the system which we have measured.

Regarding the usefulness of propositional construction, Kelly writes, "throughout our discussion of the Psychology of Personal Constructs, we have attempted to rely heavily upon propositional constructs, as contrasted with . . . the dogmatic thinking implied by the use of constellatory constructs" (1955, p. 15). This quotation is separated by only several sentences from the following statement: "if a person attempted to use propositional thinking exclusively, he might have considerable difficulty in coming to any decision as to what the relevant and crucial issues were in any situation" (pp. 155, 166). Implied in these two sentences is the hypothesis that the excessive use of either constellatory or propositional thinking is related to problems in decision making and of maladjustment. Those problems which are associated with the excessive use of either constellatory or propositional construction can be interpreted as an inability to discriminate complexly along a dimension of significance. The rigid, impulsive behavior of the highly constellatory person may be traced to the simplicity of his system within which significance is but two-leveled, that is, all or none. The confused behavior of the highly propositional person may be linked to the cluttered nature of his system. In his case, a hierarchy of significance has little meaning.

Kelly's discussion of the problems inherent in an excessive dependency on either constellatory or propositional construction and his emphasis on ordination or hierarchical relations within a construct system point to the limitations of research programs devoted only to understanding cognitive complexity. Cognitive complexity which emphasizes only differentiation does not capture the essence of Kelly's Organization and Fragmentation corollaries, in which the hierarchical organization of constructs is of critical importance. Kelly's more elaborate approach to construct organization became evident when the present author encountered difficulties with his own measure of complexity, a differentiation score which sometimes failed to discriminate between complex, well-adjusted subjects and others who seemed most confused. This inability to discriminate between two classes of highly differentiating subjects encouraged a more thoughtful consideration of Kelly's Organization Corollary and a painstaking review of the literature on cognitive complexity. The results of this return to theory and a review of the literature are reported in a manuscript by Leitner, Landfield, and Barr (1975). In this manuscript, the more complex position of Kelly is elaborated, along with a discussion of methods and findings of complexity studies. These authors comment on the limitations of typical measures of cognitive complexity, including Landfield's (1971) functionally independent construction (FICcp) score. They also introduce a measure of hierarchical integration called ordination (Ocp), a measure which can be used in conjunction with the FICcp measure of construct differentiation. In the next section, I will elaborate on the general nature of both the FICcp and ordination scores. After pointing to certain correlates of the FICcp score, I will show what happens when FICcp is combined with ordination. Readers interested in a fuller description of the derivation of FICcp and Ocp scores and research with these scores are directed to the volume by Landfield (1971), the review by Leitner, Landfield, and Barr (1975), and a manuscript by Landfield and Barr (1976). Third-generation computer programs for obtaining the FICcp and Ocp scores are also available on request.

Functionally Independent Construction (FICcp)

The FICcp score is based on a modified Rep Test (Landfield, 1971) where the subject rates his acquaintances within dimensions that are anchored by the subject's own social descriptive language, that is, his personal constructs. The resulting grid may be of different sizes, depending on how many acquaintances are rated and how many bipolar constructs are used. Typically, a 15-by-15 grid is employed, with 15 acquaintances being rated on 15 constructs. However, in our research with the interpersonal transaction group which will be discussed later, a 10-by-15 grid was employed, since self and nine other group members were described within fifteen constructs.

Rating of acquaintances within bipolar constructs may be done in two ways. In one procedure, the subject rates his acquaintances as 1, 2, N, or ?, depending on whether he describes an acquaintance at the first pole (1) of his construct or the contrast pole (2), is uncertain about how to apply the construct to his acquaintance (?), or cannot apply the construct to a particular acquaintance (N). The investigator treats the N and ? ratings as instances of nonapplication, which are assigned the score of zero. Using this scoring system, each acquaintance is defined as 1, 2, or 0 within each construct.

In the second procedure, constructs from a Rep Test are used to anchor 13-point scales (......*......), which the subject uses to rate his acquaintances. Although the subject may use any of the scale points, the investigator collapses each construct scale to three points: first pole (1), contrast pole (2), and midpoint (0). One may interpret the N and ? ratings used in the first procedure as being somewhat similar to the midpoint ratings in the second procedure, although subjects may attach any meanings they wish to the midpoint rating. In a recent study of ten subjects, Hasenyager (1975) found the sum of N plus ? ratings significantly related to the midpoint ratings ($p < .05$) on the 13-point scales.

In both of these scaling procedures, the final triadic scoring is consistent with Kelly's Range Corollary, which states that constructs may have different ranges of application. Even as Kelly stressed the Range Corollary, he conveniently ignored it when he introduced the grid form of the Rep Test. This compromise allowed him to develop a nonparametric factoring technique with a range of application that did not include triadic scoring. That Kelly was uncomfortable with his decision is shown by the following quotation:

> The assumption which is specific to the grid form of the test is that all the figures fall within the range of convenience of all the constructs. . . . This may not be a good assumption in all cases; it may be that the client has left a void at a certain intersect simply because the construct does not seem to apply one way or the other. [Kelly, 1955, p. 271]

Experience with our modified forms of the Rep Test procedure in which subjects use nonapplication ratings or ratings signifying less meaningfulness suggests that the Range Corollary should be taken more seriously.

Continuing our discussion of scoring procedures, we use grid row rating patterns as operational definitions of descriptive construct dimensions (c) and column rating patterns as operational definitions of people (p). Each row pattern is related to the other row patterns and each column pattern is related to the other column patterns. After all rows and columns have been interrelated, these two matrices of relationship are used in determining the functionally independent construction score, or FICcp. This process of deriving the FICcp score from construct relationships can be illustrated. A subject's grid shows that his descriptive construct dimensions 1, 2, 3, 4, and 5 are unrelated to each other, directly or inversely, and also are not related to other descriptive construct dimensions on the grid. *Each* of these five constructs is assigned a score of 1. Constructs 6, 7, 13, 14, and 15 are interrelated, each construct with the other four constructs, but not to other constructs on the grid. This cluster is assigned a score of 1. Constructs 8 and 9 are related to each other but not to other constructs. This cluster is assigned a score of 1. Finally, construct 10 is related to construct 11, and construct 12 is related to construct 11 but not to 10. This cluster, in which all constructs are not interrelated, also is assigned a score of 1. Now the scores for the five independent constructs are added to the scores for the three independent clusters. The final score for descriptive constructs, or the FICc, is 8. This score then is combined with the FICp (for people) score and the final FICcp score has a possible scoring range of 2 to 30, or a scoring range of 2 to 25 if a 10-by-15 grid is employed. Procedures used for assessing grid relationships and determining the FICcp score are described in detail by Landfield (1971), and an improved computer program prints out the final FICcp scores and shows all construct relationships, direct or inverse, for all columns and rows.

Research on the FICcp score indicates that it is relatively stable for periods of one month (Landfield, 1971). It is particularly stable for a sample of experienced psychotherapists. Very high scores, that is, more units of construction, in the range of 21 to 30, may be associated with serious suicidal behavior, as shown by Landfield (in press) in a student population and by Elliot (1972) in a psychiatric population. Evidence for generality of the FICcp score was found in a study by Slane and Craig (1975), who obtained a significant relationship between scores based on two very different grids ($r = .66$, $p < .01$). Acquaintances were described on one grid and environmental contexts of space and form, for example, "your room," on the second grid.

A clinical study by Landfield of five alcoholics being treated in a detoxification center revealed a tendency for these persons to obtain either very low scores (below 5) or very high scores (21 plus), suggesting either tightly organized systems or systems in which constructs are unrelated. One loosely organized person was a binge drinker, suggesting a linkage to our findings on serious suicidal intent. A content analysis of their constructs revealed an overwhelming emphasis on ideas of morality and hard work, a finding that prompted a colleague to comment, "If I had those constructs, I'd drink more, too." Clinical observations of some depressive patients who were given Rep Tests suggest that people with depressions can be either highly undifferentiated or highly fragmented persons. Perhaps it is the fragmented depressive that is more likely to be a suicidal risk. These clinical observations, although limited, suggest that a gross behavioral label can have several underlying interpretations, with different implications for treatment. It seems reasonable that the clinician might be more concerned about conceptual disorganization in one type of alcoholic or depressive person and, alternatively, more concerned about excessively tight organization in another type of alcoholic or depressive person.

A study by Sadowski (1971) points to an interesting relationship between the FICcp and the way in which a person responds to a confusion questionnaire. In this questionnaire, subjects were asked to respond with *yes, no,* or *uncertain* to such items as: I am an indecisive person; I usually know where I stand on things; I consider myself a disorganized person; I am not easily confused; Many people confuse me; You never really know if people are going to act as you expect them to; and, My world is all in bits and pieces. In using this questionnaire, Sadowski differentiated between admitted confusion and manifest confusion, in which the person was uncertain about whether or not he was confused. Her findings point to a relationship between higher differentiation scores and manifest confusion, that is, the greater use of uncertainty ratings in both male and female groups ($p < .05$). A relationship also was found between higher FICcp scores and admitted confusion in the female group ($p < .01$). The zero order correlation in the male group suggests that males either were less aware of their confusion or were less willing to admit to it. In showing a relation between confusion and the FICcp score, Sadowski gives some support to the studies on suicidal intent in which the investigators hypothesized a disorganization of the personal construct system.

Although the FICcp score of construct organization may have certain implications for personal confusion when the score is very high and for behavioral rigidity when the score is very low, the

FICcp score does have limitations. First of all, it does not give sufficient information about construct ordination or the ways in which constructs are related in hierarchy. Moreover, the conventional Rep Test, used in conjunction with the FICcp score, sometimes does not tap the person's most significant and organizing constructions. That significant constructions may not be tapped by the Rep Test was suggested by Kelly when he stated that constructs should not be confounded with words. Certain constructions may be preverbal. They also may be better expressed by sounds and gestures than by words. Moreover, other techniques, such as the Pyramid Procedure (Landfield, 1971), Mood Tags (Landfield & Rivers, 1975), and an Emotional Construct Rep Test,[2] in which subjects respond with "feelings I am filled with," may be more useful for eliciting constructs which are emotionally toned and more spontaneous.

It seems apparent that a complex, well-organized subject who is unable to verbalize his more significant constructions might obtain a very high FICcp score which could be mistakenly interpreted as confusion. This problem of interpreting the high FICcp score is compounded when one considers that the FICcp measure, like most complexity measures, gives more information about conceptual differentiation than hierarchical integration or ordination.

Kelly succinctly pointed to the importance of ordination in his Organization and Fragmentation corollaries. In discussing ordination as a central feature of organization, Kelly introduced the construct of superordinate-subordinate structures. This implies that one structure may subsume another. Relationships between constructs then may be viewed in both horizontal and vertical ways, between constructs at similar and at different levels of abstraction. Relationships between constructs at different levels of abstraction point to what Kelly referred to as construct ordination.

Now the measurement of ordination can be approached in a variety of ways. One way might be to create techniques for eliciting the more elusive constructs, expecting that in some instances these constructs would relate to certain independent constructions from conventional Rep Tests. Constructs which seemed most propositional on the conventional Rep Test might well cluster about certain superordinate structures if such structures could be elicited.

2. Research in progress by Paula Golden at the University of Nebraska–Lincoln, 1976.

Our choice was an approach which does not demand that the psychologist elicit additional constructs. Instead, the investigator makes inferences about whether the person can use his own descriptive constructs and his acquaintances from the Rep Test at different levels of significance or meaningfulness. We reasoned that a person who conceptualizes feelings, ideas, and people at different levels of significance can make such discriminations *only* if there are integrating conceptions within which he may order these differences in significance. To the extent that the person is more ordinated, that is, able to employ more levels of meaningfulness, one may assume that the person is utilizing certain integrative, higher order conceptions, even though these conceptions do not appear on the conventional Rep Test. The idea of making inferences about conceptual structures which cannot be directly assessed may be discomfitting, but nonetheless scientific.

Assuming, Hypothesizing, and Fragmenting Man

Psychology as it really happens is not so neat, and our first attempts to develop an ordination measure began with different ways of measuring functionally independent construction which were related to our earlier discussion of propositional and constellatory thinking. It was reasoned that an excessive use of propositional construction on the conventional Rep Test might mean that the person does not have ways of organizing his constructions that will allow him to make decisions in regard to that which has greater and lesser meaningfulness. Even if the psychologist could tap the more elusive constructions, these too might be more propositional in nature. Likewise, the person who employs only constellatory construction, where constructs are all tightly related, might be seen as lacking higher order construction. If the psychologist could tap more of his constructions, they too might be tightly interwoven with his more accessible constructions.

Working from this logic, we used two different criteria of relationship between construct dimensions—a very stringent one, defined by 14 overlapping cells, with 15 as a perfect score, and a very minimal criterion, defined by 11 overlapping cells. A very low FICcp score obtained when using a very stringent criterion of relationship suggests that the person may be highly constellatory in his thinking, having only a few units of construction with limited possibilities for an organizational hierarchy. A very high FICcp score obtained when using only a very minimal criterion of construct relationship suggests that the person may have little capacity for relating his feelings, ideas, and people.

In addition to the very stringent and minimal criteria for assessing construct relationships, we also used a moderate criterion of 12 overlapping cells. Using this moderate criteron in conjunction with the stringent one permitted a differentiation between two kinds of highly organizing people, those who may be aware of exceptions to their construct relationships and those who tend to be unaware of exceptions. The former group may be characterized as hypothesizers, since the awareness of exceptions tends to encourage the checking out of relationships. The latter "constellatory" group may be characterized as functioning more at the level of assumption, since tight interrelationships among constructs do not encourage further testing of those relationships.

Proceeding now to the level of measurement, it was reasoned that *assuming man* would show little differentiation among his descriptions and people when a stringent criterion of construct relationship is employed. In other words, there would be few exceptions to his construct relationships. Illustrating this point, imagine that friendliness is associated with honesty to such a degree that to know a person's friendliness leads one to assume his honesty. The relationship does not have to be tested. In contrast, it was reasoned the *hypothesizing man* would show low differentiation at the moderate criterion level and high differentiation at the stringent level of construct relationship. To illustrate this point, imagine that friendship is related to honesty, but not too tightly, allowing for some instances in which a friendly person may be dishonest. Thus, the hypothesizing person, functioning at an optimal rather than a maximal level of relationship, remains open to exceptions and to a continual testing of his feelings, associations, and ideas.

In sharp contrast to the assuming and hypothesizing styles of construct organization, a third style is best characterized by the term, fragmentation. *Fragmenting man*, perseverating with an exclusively propositional focus, unable to relate his dimensions of meaning within the same or across different levels of abstraction, may be defined by high differentiation of his constructs when the criterion of relationship is minimal.

Even as these three styles of organization and their measurements showed promise, we still wanted a measure of ordination which was independent of the FICcp measure of construct differentiation. The search for an ordination measure was expedited when we encountered a few subjects with elevated FICcp scores, that is, high differentiation, who also were judged capable of making thoughtful and efficient value choices. The ordination score, based on information about how well a person can differentiate along a scale of meaningfulness, will now be described briefly. A discussion of ordination also is found in the manuscript (Leitner et al., 1975) cited at the beginning of this section.

Ordination (Ocp)

Our measure of ordination, the Ocp score, is obtained by asking a subject to rate himself and his acquaintances on 13-point scales which are anchored by personal constructs. However, in the analysis of ordination, in contrast to the derivation of the FICcp score, the subject's ratings are not reduced to sidedness and midpoint ratings. Instead, the full range of scoring is used by assigning a score of zero to the midpoint and by scoring the other scale points as different levels of extremeness or meaningfulness, from 1, on either side of the midpoint, to 6, at the extremes. The extremity rating as a measure of meaningfulness is supported by a series of studies conducted by Bonarius (1970) and by the investigations of Cromwell and Caldwell (1962), Isaacson and Landfield (1965), Landfield (1971), and O'Donovan (1965). These studies as well as other studies of rating scale polarization will be reviewed in the section on the construction of meaningfulness.

Continuing our explanation of ordination scoring, if we want to know the ordination level of a particular *descriptive construct*—for example, humorous versus dull guy—we note how the subject has rated himself and others on this construct. If the person has used four different levels of extremeness—for example, scale points 0, 2, 3, and 5—a score of 4 is multiplied by the difference between his highest and lowest ratings (5), and the ordination score is 20. If we want to obtain the ordination level of a particular *acquaintance* described by the subject, we observe how he has rated that person across his 15 descriptive constructs. Again, the number of rating levels used is multiplied by the high-low rating difference. In summary, the ordination score for a descriptive construct or for a rated acquaintance encompasses levels of meaningfulness and range of meaningfulness. A correction factor for excessive use of a particular rating is explained in the review manuscript by Leitner, Landfield, and Barr (1975). The final ordination score, Ocp, is found by first averaging the different descriptive construct ordination scores (Oc) and the different acquaintance ordination scores (Op), and combining these two averages into Ocp. The highest possible average ordination score for descriptive constructs (c) or people (p) is 42. Therefore, the upper limit for the Ocp score is 84.

Combining the Ocp with the FICcp

Returning now to the earlier discussion of construct differentiation and integration, we combined the FICcp and Ocp scores by establishing four combinations of these measures: (1) low integration (o) with low differentiation (FIC); (2) high integration with low differentiation; (3) low integration with high differentiation; and (4) high integration with high differentiation. High and low were determined by scoring above and below the group mean (see Table 1).

Table 1
Four Combinations of FICcp and Ocp Scores

Quadrants

1. Low Integration (0), Low Differentiation (FIC)	2. High Integration (0), Low Differentiation (FIC)
3. Low Integration (0), High Differentiation (FIC)	4. High Integration (0), High Differentiation (FIC)

1. Low within and between construct differentiation.
2. High within and low between construct differentiation.
3. Low within and high between construct differentiation.
4. High within and between construct differentiation.

The terms *integration* (O) and *differentiation* (FIC) which designate our quadrants in Table 1 can be confusing, since the FIC measure of differentiation, which is more orthogonal in construction, and the O measure, which has implications for the capacity to integrate hierarchically, both involve a process of differentiation. A within-construct differentiation in *meaningfulness* occurs in the integration measure. A between-construct differentiation in *type of meaning* occurs in the differentiation measure. Until we find better ways of designating the four quadrants, the terms *integration* and *differentiation* will be used, referring to two kinds of differentiation which have different organizational implications, one for differences among constructs, the other for integrative capacities. The differentiation (FIC) measure of between-construct difference refers to what some psychologists understand as cognitive complexity.

We hypothesized that persons scoring high in differentiation but low in integration will show interpersonal confusion. Moreover, other subjects will be confused by such persons. Persons scoring high in both differentiation and integration will not show interpersonal confusion. However, other subjects may find them difficult to understand at the beginning of a relationship with them. Even as they may be better organized, they are complex and it will take longer to know them.

Persons scoring very low in both differentiation and integration, that is, more simply organized, will tend to be more rigid in their social adjustments. Social maladjustment will be more apparent among those who either are very low in both differentiation and integration or are high in differentiation but low in integration. Persons scoring low in differentiation but high in integration will not show interpersonal confusion and they will, in turn, be well understood by others at the beginning of a relationship as well as later.

The Interpersonal Transaction Group

These hypotheses were considered within the framework of the interpersonal transaction, or IT, group. This group as initially developed by Landfield was used with normal college students. One primary purpose of the IT group was to provide a context within which to study the development of interpersonal understanding among unacquainted persons. Another primary purpose was to integrate more natural interactive processes with more formal research assessments derived from personal construct theory. A secondary purpose was to provide constructive experiences in which group participants might learn more about themselves, others, and their interrelationships.

In its original form, ten participants attended eight 2-hour sessions. Except for Sessions 3 and 8, which were research sessions, group members primarily interacted with one another in dyads. After simple instructions were given for what was to be "shared" in the dyadic interactions, members rotated from one dyad to another until each person had engaged in conversation with all members of the group. The order of dyadic interactions was predetermined, and each interaction was of very short duration, from 6 to 8 minutes. The general nature of the conversations was the same for all dyads and the emphasis throughout these sessions was placed on trying to share and to understand one another without being critical. The instructions—for example, to share an important value—were general enough so that members could feel they were in control of what was talked about even as they were asked to engage in certain conversations. When subjects are asked to state what they do *not* value as well as what they do value, the contrasting nature of the personal construct is most evident. Finally, the emphasis on sharing and understanding, in contrast to confrontation, is congenial with Kelly's (1955) Sociality Corollary: "To the extent that one person construes the construction processes of another, he may play a role in a social process involving the other person" (p. 95).

In addition to the technique of rotating dyads, an important feature of each session was the Mood Tag experience. At the beginning and end of every session, each person was asked to write on a slip of paper *how he felt at the moment* and also *how he did not feel at the moment*. He then taped this paper, which included his first name, to his clothing and circulated among other group members. The Mood Tag may be viewed as a way of eliciting personal constructs of an emotional nature.

The formal research format for the IT group involved eliciting a set of personal constructs prior to the first meeting. These constructs were then placed at the poles of 13-point rating scales and were used in rating self, others, and predictions of self and others' expectations. Now, several measures may be derived from these ratings. First of all, meaningfulness of scale and person rated is reflected in the polarization or extremeness of ratings on these personal construct scales. A measure of empathy also may be derived by asking each member to predict how others will rate themselves, predictions being made on the other person's scales. In this latter measurement, the 13-point scale is reduced to 3 points: left side (1), middle (0), and right side (2). The reason for reducing the scale to one of sidedness and midposition can be illustrated. Take the example of Person *A*, who rates himself on his own personal construct scale at position *plus* 2, but is predicted by Person *B* at *plus* 5 and by Person *C* at *minus* 1. Using a scale of *minus* 6, to 0 to *plus* 6, Persons *B* and *C* predict Person *A* equally well. However, Persons *A* and *B* are more in agreement because they understand *A* on the plus side. Moreover, assigning greater weight to sidedness and duality makes good sense within the Dichotomy Corollary of personal construct theory. Therefore, our 13-point scales are reduced to 3 points when we wish to measure a person's ability to predict on his own constructs or on the constructs of others. As stated previously, the 3-point system is also used if we wish to obtain an FICcp organization score from these data. However, the assessment of meaningfulness as inferred from rating scale polarization involves the use of the entire scale, scored from 1 to 6 on either side of the midpoint (scored 0).

Data from four IT groups were used in a study of the FICcp (differentiation) and the Ocp (integration) scores. Two groups were comprised of college students. One of these groups seemed to have attracted several rather maladjusted individuals. Two additional groups were comprised mainly of persons who were apprehended by the police for drunken driving.[3] Members of these latter groups varied considerably in age and socioeconomic background as well as in severity of their problems. The format for these four groups was somewhat similar for the first eight sessions. However, the alcoholic problem groups were extended to 20 sessions and the treatment aspects of these groups were of concern to the investigators, Landfield and Rivers (1975). Since the number of paticipants in these groups was small and we needed to maximize the range of organizational scoring, subjects from these four groups were combined for the analysis of construct organization.

3. This research was partly supported by a grant from the University of Nebraska Graduate Research Council.

One of the interesting features of the organizational scoring used in the study is that both the FICcp and Ocp were based on descriptions of immediately present group members rather than on past and absent acquaintances. Furthermore, within each group, persons described were the same except for the self. It should also be noted that the two organization scores were derived from the same construct scales. However, there was no reason to expect a relation between the two scores, since the FICcp score is derived primarily from construct sidedness and the Ocp score is based primarily on degree of response. The relation between these two scores was not significant ($r_s' = .26$).

Relating the FICcp and Ocp organizational scoring to other IT group measures was accomplished by taking a quandrant approach to our data. As previously stated, the quadrants were defined by high-low differentiation on the one axis and by high-low integration on the other, high-low being determined by the mean of the distribution. We placed other scores, such as positiveness of self and others, meaningfulness of self and others, and predictive accuracy, within these quadrants and observed the differences. The method is quite exploratory, and end-of-group comparisons may suffer from the fact that testing in two groups was done at the eighth session, whereas testing in the other two groups was completed at sessions 17 and 18.

The question of greatest concern was how to distinguish between two hypothesized classes of high differentiating people: the confused, maladjusted persons on the one hand and the coping, better adjusted persons on the other. It was our hope that hierarchical integration or ordination might be the key to separating these two groups. In the next subsection, we begin with a clinical discussion of persons in Quadrants 3 and 4, our two classes of high differentiating subjects.

FICcp and Ocp Analysis

First, taking a clinical perspective on persons in Quadrant 4, those high in differentiation and integration, and persons in quadrant 3, those high in differentiation but low in integration, we observed the following: Persons who remain in Quadrant 4 were described primarily as healthy, mature people. For example, one person was described by the investigators as "strong, level-headed and well-liked." A second group member was described as "well-organized, likable, and clear-cut about where she is going." A third was considered "a good healthy farm boy with integrity of person." A fourth member was described as "highly creative, well-balanced, and mature." Only one person who remained in Quadrant 4 was labeled as highly maladjusted at the beginning of the group. This fifth person, a member of an alcohol problem group, significantly improved. His confusion, as described by Landfield and Rivers, may well have been their own confusion about him. His improvement was not anticipated.

The most suicidal person is found in Quadrant 3. He described his life as "looking through the wrong end of a telescope, and the telescope was becoming longer." Two students, located in this quadrant at both the beginning and end of the group experience, could be described as excessively concrete. One of them seemed withdrawn and "schizy." A fourth person in this quadrant seemed quite superficial and unstable. Bar hopping was one aspect of her "flightiness." Another member of this quadrant seemed acutely confused at the beginning of the group. However, this person modified her life style in a rather dramatic and constructive way, a change that was accompanied by an increase in ordination and a shift to the third quadrant. Generally, persons beginning in Quadrant 3, those who presumably could not integrate their high complexity, seemed most maladjusted. These data support the hypothesis that complexity which is uncorrelated with integrative processes will be found in the context of difficulties in social decision making.

Positiveness of self and others. Proceeding to formal research measures, we begin with positiveness of self, or "good" ratings, defined by the number of personal construct dimensions on which a person rated himself on the preferred side. In this analysis, we did not find a significant difference at the beginning of the group experience between the two quadrants defined by high differentiation. However, at the end of the experience, on second testing, high differentiating and integrating persons obtained significantly higher positive scores than high differentiating but low integrating persons ($F_p = .05$).

Switching from self to conception of others, low differentiating persons in Quadrants 1 and 2 assigned positive ratings to others more often at both the beginning and end of the group experience ($\chi^2 = 4.9, p = .05; \chi^2 = 7.5, p = .01$). This difference between the combined Quadrants 1 and 2 versus 3 and 4 was accounted for primarily by Quadrant 3 members who assigned fewest positive ratings to others. In this regard, we found that high integrators of Quadrant 4 assigned positive ratings significantly more often to other group members than low integrating persons of Quadrant 3 at the beginning of the group experience ($\chi^2 = 4.5, p = .05$). This trend also apparent at the end of the group experience, failed to reach statistical significance. Summarizing these findings, it can be inferred that persons who either are more simply organized or more complex with higher ordination tend to view others in more positive ways than persons who are complex, but handicapped by an inability to integrate their complexities.

Meaningfulness of self and others. The next variable, called meaningfulness, must be interpreted carefully, since rating scale polarization is used in the assessment of both self-other meaningfulness and ordination. That the problem of contamination may not be serious is supported by the lack of significant correlations between meaningfulness of self or others and ordination.[4] Moreover, it is the number of different levels of rating scale polarization that contribute to the ordination score, whereas meaningfulness attributed to self or others is found by adding the polarization scores of the different rating points. This may be illustrated by a person who uses all 7 of the rating scale points as he describes himself on 15 construct scales. Although this person obtains the highest ordination score on self that is possible, 9 of his 15 ratings could cluster at any one of the 7 rating levels of meaningfulness. Therefore, meaningfulness of self could vary as ordination remains high. Using another illustration, a person using only 2 of the 7 rating scale points in describing himself will have a very low ordination score on self. If he uses rating scale points 5 or 6 on all 15 constructs, his self-meaningfulness will be very high, whereas his self-meaningfulness will be very low if he uses only rating scale points 1 and 0.

Even as there may not be a significant relationship between

4. *Self meaningfulness and ordination:* Group 4: $r_s = .22, p = .52; r_s = -.16, p = .64$; Group 5: $r_s = -.51, p = .12; r_s = -.34, p = .32$. *Meaningfulness of others and ordination:* Group 4: $r_s = .53, p = .11; r_s = .24, p = .49$; Group 5: $r_s = -.35, p = .31; r_s = -.14, p = .70$.

meaningfulness attributed to self or others and ordination, excessively high scores or excessively low scores on meaningfulness point directly to low ordination. A person who scores all sixes or all zeros on meaningfulness cannot obtain a high ordination score, since he functions at only one level of meaningfulness. This lack of independence of the ordination and meaningfulness scores, when meaningfulness is excessively high or excessively low, has interesting ramifications for O'Donovan's (1965) hypothesis that neurotics are polarizers; schizophrenics are depolarizers; and normals are both, discriminating between that which is more and less meaningful. In other words, normals are more ordinating than neurotics or schizophrenics, and perhaps all emotionally maladjusted persons share a common deficiency—an inability to integrate their personal constructs in hierarchy.

Focusing now on self-meaningfulness, that is, rating scale polarization as the person rates himself, we found that high differentiating but low integrating persons in Quadrant 3 obtain lower self-meaningfulness scores than persons in the other three quadrants. These differences between Quadrant 3 and each of the other three quadrants are most significant at the end of the group experience (all $F_p = .02$). When meaningfulness of others is considered, persons in Quadrant 3 again receive lower scores than persons in the other quadrants at the beginning (all $F_p = .05$) and at the end of the group experience (all $F_p = .01$). One may hypothesize that confused people do not perceive themselves or others in highly meaningful ways.

Predictive accuracy. A third type of analysis focused on the person's ability to predict accurately how each group member would rate him, all predictions being made on the other person's constructs. The task of entering the other person's construct system and construing how the other person thinks was suggested by the Sociality Corollary, "to the extent that one person construes the construction processes of another, he may play a role in a social process involving the other person" (Kelly, 1955, p. 95). Results of this analysis show that at the beginning of the group experience, high differentiating and integrating persons in Quadrant 4 are better predictors than high differentiating but low integrating persons in Quadrant 3 ($\chi^2 = 4.6, p < .05$). Using only the ordination or hierarchical integration score, it was found that persons high on integration at the beginning of the group experience are more accurate predictors of how others view them within the construct frameworks of other group members ($\chi^2 = 4.2$, $p < .05$). When this analysis is reversed, that is, to show how well the group can predict the person, the person's lower differentiation score is related to greater ability of the group to predict how the person will rate members of the group ($\chi^2 = 5.5$, $p < .02$).

Apparently, at the beginning of group experience, high integrating persons did a better job of predicting the views of others than did low integrating persons. However, the predictive ability of the group as a whole was related to the differentiation level of the person being predicted, persons with lower levels of differentiation being more predictable. This latter finding is consistent with other studies of cognitive compexity (Leitner, Landfield, & Barr, 1975).

Applying these findings to the low integrating and high differentiating members of Quadrant 3, one may infer that they are handicapped in two ways. First of all, their lack of integrative skills is associated with more difficulty in understanding how others view them. Second, their greater complexity is associated with being less understood by others.

Finally, we analyzed the relation between construct organization and empathy, defining empathy as the person's accurate predictions of the self ratings of other members of the group on *their* constructs. Results of this analysis show that high differentiating persons are significantly less empathic at the end of the group experience ($\chi^2 = 6$, $p < .02$). Although not significant, there is a trend for persons in Quadrant 4 to predict better than persons in Quadrant 3. Putting these findings into the terminology of cognitive "complexity," or differentiation, less complex persons are more empathic than more complex persons. Furthermore, complex persons who are more hierarchically integrated tend to be more empathic than complex persons who are less integrated.

Although firm conclusions will not be drawn from these limited data, the evidence, consistent with theory, is sufficiently clear-cut to suggest that the linkage of high differentiation of the personal construct system with low ordination may point to the inability to encompass the complexities of life. Lower feelings of self-regard and regard for others, decreased self-meaningfulness, and less ability to predict the views of others tend to be associated with persons in Quadrant 3, who are high in differentiation but low in hierarchical integration of their constructs.

The hypothesis that subjects who score very low in both differentiation and integration will show symptoms of maladjustment received partial support when the two most extreme subjects in Quadrant 1 were considered. Both persons, judged most maladjusted and least changed in their groups by the investigators, were most anxious throughout the experience and highly critical of the group process. Moreover, both persons obtained elevated self-meaningfulness scores at the beginning of the group. Self-polarization scores of 82 and 88 out of a possible 90 points were much above other scores, pointing directly to a lack of self-ordination in the context of high egocentricity. The high extremity ratings on self and the low self-ordination score, that is, few levels of meaningfulness, contributed support to O'Donovan's (1965) position that neurotics are polarizers who are unable to distinguish between levels of greater and lesser importance for themselves.

A most interesting implication for further research on ordination was suggested by Leitner (personal communication). He observed that Landfield has related the excessive use of propositional thinking to serious suicidal intent and Bannister (1962) had related it to schizophrenic thought disorder. Leitner then hypothesized that the ordination level of suicidals would be higher than the ordination level of schizophrenics, arguing that Kelly's view of suicide as an act of dignity points to some limited ability to organize at least part of one's personal construct system, even as the system is deteriorating.

Combining measures of integration and differentiation also may resolve a number of controversies among those who investigate cognitive complexity. For example, in the area of impression formation (see Leitner, Landfield, & Barr, 1975), the nature of the relation between cognitive complexity-simplicity and change in impression formation is unclear. Some authors report that simple subjects change less when exposed to discrepant information. Others report the opposite. These contradictory findings might be explained if more information were available on the integrative capacities of these subjects.

In conclusion, our research on ordination shows that lumping subjects together on the basis of cognitive differentiation can be very misleading and points to the critical need for new methodologies which encompass the dual processes of hierarchical integration and differentiation, a duality which is central to the psychology of personal constructs.

THE CONSTRUCTION OF MEANINGFULNESS

Our method of inferring ordination within the personal construct system requires the assumption that meaningfulness of descriptive constructs and persons described within these constructs can be measured. In particular, ordination is inferred from different levels of meaningfulness as measured by rating scale polarization on personal construct dimensions. This relation between meaningfulness and scale polarization, which is so essential to our measurement of ordination, will now be reviewed. However, prior to this special review, meaningfulness will be considered in the context of several other methodologies.

The personal construct psychologist may assess meaningfulness in numerous ways. He can ask the person to rank people, feelings, ideas, and situations. Although it may be somewhat tedious for the subject, a paired-comparison method may be used. Another approach is called "death of a construct." In this procedure, the subject is asked to imagine the disappearance, one at a time, of descriptions and persons in his life. Then again, one may observe on the Rep Grid that a certain acquaintance or descriptive dimension is most interrelated with other acquaintances or descriptions. In this case, the psychologist assumes greater importance for that which is most central to personal construct organization. The Rep Grid may also be used in conjunction with elaborate statistical devices which uncover clusters and factors. An implications grid procedure by Hinkle (1965) gives information about superordinancy of construction when a subject feels that an imagined change on one construct will necessitate change on another construct. If change on construct A implies change on construct B, but change on B does not imply change on A, one may infer that construct A is superordinate to B. Moreover, one may assume that construct A is more meaningful or significant because of the superior position and influence of this construct in the hierarchy. Questions about how you know a person in a certain way or why a person behaves a certain way may also point to constructs of greater and lesser meaningfulness. Perseveration in the use of certain constructs on the Rep Test may indicate greater significance. Of course, one may directly ask the subject to discuss what is of greatest and least importance about people. Then again, one may make inferences about constructs and their relative importance for the person from his speech patterns, gestures and emotional reactions. Finally, one may infer meaningfulness from rating scale polarization as the person rates himself and others on 13-point scales which are anchored by his own constructs. It is this latter method of assessing meaningfulness which requires discussion, since it is the base from which we infer ordination of constructs.

O'Donovan (1965), in his review of the rating extremity response, stated that rating scale polarization has been explained in two primary ways. First, it is a sign of pathology. Second, it signifies meaningfulness. Rather than perceiving these two interpretations as mutually exclusive, O'Donovan reconciled them by hypothesizing that polarizers tend to be neurotic, depolarizers tend to be schizophrenic, and the tendency to both polarize and depolarize is the mark of normality. Stating that normals both polarize and depolarize is congruent with our position that the capacity to assign greater and lesser meaningfulness to people, descriptions, emotions, ideas, situations or behaviors is essential to the decision-making process. Neither extreme polarizers nor extreme depolarizers make distinctions among levels of meaningfulness. As a consequence, one finds the rigidity of overreaction in the polarizer and the rigidity of underreaction in the depolarizer. Restating this in terms of personal construct theory, the polarizer and depolarizer are handicapped by a lack of hierarchical integration or ordination in their construct systems; that is, they lack multiple levels of meaningfulness.

Hamilton (1968), in a later review of extreme response styles (ERS), noted that researchers try to control for response styles and recommended that ERS be studied by methods which use a high degree of stimulus ambiguity. The aim is to free the extreme response from content bias. Implicit in this aim is the feeling that the extreme response constitutes a hazard for researchers. In contrast to Hamilton's position, the personal construct researcher, working from the Dichotomy Corollary (Landfield, 1971), deliberately tries to elicit the extreme response in a context of greatest meaningfulness—the person's own language system. Thus, what one scientist may seek to control and eliminate, another scientist may wish to nurture.

Although O'Donovan reviewed the rating extremity response in some depth, Hamilton considered his viewpoint only briefly. After presenting O'Donovan's position that meaningful stimuli are linked to greater rating scale polarization, he made the statement, "However, the present review (Hamilton's) has shown that when meaningless stimuli are presented, individual differences in extreme responding occur which are quite stable over time" (p. 200). The "however" at the beginning of this statement suggests that "meaningful" responding to meaningless stimuli is a refutation of the O'Donovan position. Apparently, Hamilton reasons that if subjects can respond to that which is obviously meaningless by responding more extremely, these subjects are not really perceiving meaningfulness. Rather, they are simply responding with a particular kind of response style which has no implications for meaningfulness. The underlying assumption made here, that the stimuli *really* are meaningless, is reminiscent of the logic that was used by investigators of frustration. One impedes the ongoing response, defines this blockage as frustration, then observes how different people react to frustration. The assumption is made that the meaning of this blockage is the same for each person. The idea that persons may not feel frustrated or even be aware of the intended blockage does not concern the objectively minded psychologist, particularly if, for him, science is a matter of aggregates in which exceptional instances may be ignored, discounted as noise, or eliminated by proper choice, training, and control of one's subjects.

The logic of the "objective" psychologist makes little sense to those who assume that the stimulus is an interpreted one and that meaningfulness of the stimulus or frustration from it are in the eye of the beholder rather than in the absolute possession of an all-knowing psychologist. In this context of stimulus interpretation, the work of Rychlak (1966) is intriguing. Taking a more idiographic stance in which he used subjects as their own controls, Rychlak found greater rated meaningfulness (reinforcement value) of certain nonsense syllables to be related to improved paired-associate learning. Apparently, even nonsense syllables can vary in meaningfulness, and subjects may vary from one another as to which syllables are more and less meaningful to them. Perhaps that which is meaningless to the "objective" psychologist sometimes can be meaningful to his subjects.

Turning now to studies of rating scale polarization, Bonarius (1970) provided a most definitive series of investigations in which he employed a sophisticated interaction model of person, scale, and object described. In these studies, he showed how polarization increases when the person rates significant people on his own construct scales. Mitsos (1961) reported that subjects rate more extremely on Semantic Differential scales which they designate as most meaningful to themselves in thinking about people. Cromwell and Caldwell (1962) found more extreme ratings of acquaintances on own constructs in contrast to others' constructs. O'Donovan reported a tendency for more extreme ratings to be associated with verbal reports of greater meaningfulness.[5] Landfield (1965) found that subjects rated more extremely on preferred scales. Isaacson and Landfield (1965) reported that personal construct scales were placed closer, that is, more polarized, to both self and not-self than were Butler-Haigh Q-Sort statements. Moreover, even negative personal construct poles were placed at the like-self end of the self versus not-self scale. Not only does this study support rating scale polarization as a measure of meaningfulness, but it also suggests that if psychotherapists wish to make negative interpretations to their clients, they might experience less resistance from them when criticisms are placed in the context of the clients' own negative language.

Another study by Isaacson (1966) showed a relation between construct rankings, extremity ratings, and ratings of certainty of position. Bamber (1972) reported that her subjects rated present friends more extremely than past acquaintances. Ourth and Landfield (1965) and Landfield (1971) described a study in which they asked psychotherapists and their clients to rate each other on their own and the other's constructs at the beginning of therapy. Premature termination was shown to be related to less extreme ratings of the other person when one's own constructs are used. In a study of two kinds of scaling procedures, Hasenyager (1975) asked ten subjects to fill out a modified Rep Grid in which they rated each acquaintance as 1 (left side of construct), 2 (right side), N if he could not apply a particular construct dimension to an acquaintance, and ? if he could not decide which construct pole best applied. These same subjects also were asked to rate their acquaintances a second time, using 13-point scales with a starred midpoint. Hasenyager then correlated the use of the N and ? ratings on the grid with the use of the midpoint and 1 ratings on the 13-point scales. He found that N (not apply) ratings on the grid were significantly related to the midpoint or zero ratings on the 13-point scales ($p = .01$). The ? ratings were more correlated with the 1 ratings on either side of the mid-point than with the mid-point ratings. Hasenyager's study

---

5. D. O'Donovan, Polarization and meaningfulness in 6,300 value judgments (unpublished manuscript, University of Missouri, 1964).

supports the interpretation of less meaningfulness at the midposition of the construct rating scale.

Meaningfulness and the IT Group

Information regarding the correlates of rating scale polarization is also available from research with the interpersonal transaction (IT) group, a research format introduced in a previous section and developed in greater detail in another article by Landfield and Rivers (1975). Members of the IT groups were asked to rate themselves and others on personal construct scales and to predict how other group members would rate themselves toward the beginning and at the end of the group experience. As stated previously, meaningfulness was measured by rating scale polarization on the 13-point construct scales. However, predictive accuracy was determined in relation to sidedness and midpoint ratings on the same scales.

Meaningfulness and interpersonal transaction will focus on the relationships between different kinds of rating scale polarization and the following variables: favorable ratings of others, feelings of comfort and acquaintanceship, empathy of the person for the group and the group for the person, change in self-conception as measured by slot and range change, and the person's favorable view of himself. Unless stated otherwise, reported findings are based on analyses of the two longer-term Groups 4 and 5 which met for 20 sessions. In regard to statistical probabilities, a two-tailed test was used in all analyses.

Favorable ratings of others. An important feature of the interpersonal process is the degree to which persons understand one another in favorable ways. In the IT groups, favorableness was measured by the total number of personal constructs on which the person assigned favorable ratings to other group members, favorableness being determined by the person himself. In the case of groups 4 and 5, members rated each construct pole as positive, negative, or neutral. That favorableness of construct pole as determined by the subject may be different from favorableness as understood by external judges is supported by the disagreement between the opinions of eight judges and IT group members on 15% of the constructs used by group members. For example, judges *incorrectly* assigned *favorableness* to the following descriptions: a scientist, a wee bit self-centered, dependent on others, outward, experienced, unemotional, hard-nosed, and predictable. Judges *incorrectly* assigned *unfavorableness* to: concerned with self, average intelligence, headstrong, emotional, idealistic, innocent, and unpredictable.

In this first analysis, the relation between favorableness toward others and meaningfulness attributed to them at the beginning of the group experience was close to significance in Group 4 and highly significant in Group 5 ($r_s = .48$, $p = .14$ and $r_s = .78$, $p = .006$). This relationship disappeared at the end of the groups ($r_s = .24$ and $r_s = .00$). That one may attend more meaningfully to those perceived initially in very favorable ways makes sense; however, the decrease of this relationship should be understood in the context of the special nature of the IT group. Since this group process features dyadic interactions, members can not avoid one another. As a consequence, there will be a "deepening" of understanding even between those who do not view one another so favorably.

Comfortableness. Another important aspect of the interpersonal process is the degree of comfortableness one feels in relation to another person. Comfortableness in the short-term IT Groups 1 and 2 was measured by asking each member to designate two group members, one with whom he feels most comfortable, the other one with whom he feels most uncomfortable. It was hypothesized that the subject would rate the person with whom he felt most comfortable more extremely than the person with whom he felt most uncomfortable. Placing this hypothesis within the Choice Corollary, the person elaborates that end of a contrast on which he can best extend and define his system or himself. The comfortable acquaintance seemingly would allow the person greater freedom for such extension and definition.

In this second analysis, a significant number of members of each group attributed greater meaningfulness to the comfortable person at the *end* of the 8-week experience. Nine members of each 10-member group showed greater polarization on the comfortable person ($x^2 = 6.4$, $p < .02$). However, this relationship was significant in only one of the groups at the beginning of the group experience.

Acquaintanceship. Even in the IT groups, members will feel that they are better acquainted with certain members than with others.

Acquaintanceship, assessed only in Group 2, was measured by asking each member to designate two persons in the group, one whom he knows best and one whom he knows least. In this context of acquaintanceship, it is logical to expect that persons would assign greater meaningfulness to group members with whom they feel best acquainted. This expectancy was upheld. At the beginning of the group, 9 members were more polarizing on their best-known choices $(x^2 = 6.4, p < .02)$. Eight of the 10 members were more polarizing at the end of the group $(x^2 = 3.6, p < .10)$.

Empathy. A central issue in psychotherapy is how well a therapist can understand his client from the client's own viewpoint. In a typical investigation of empathy, the client fills out a questionnaire, usually of a *yes* or *no* response variety. Then the therapist fills out the same questionnaire as he thinks his client has done it. In this illustration, empathy is restricted to the language framework of the investigator. In contrast to this approach, we asked group members to enter the personal construct systems of other group members and predict how the other person might rate himself in relation to his own values, that is, personal constructs. Two kinds of analyses will be reported on the prediction of the other person's self-ratings. First, one can look at the total predictive accuracy score for each person in relation to the nine other group members. Second, one may reverse the procedure and observe how well the nine other members, as a group, predict the self-ratings of each person. In the first instance, one may speak of the person's empathy for the group. In the second instance, one focuses on the group's empathy for the person.

Analyzing the *person's empathy for the group,* we found that members of Groups 4 and 5 who attributed greater meaningfulness to other members were also more accurate in predicting how others would rate themselves on their own personal construct scales at the end of the group experience $(r_s = .63, p = .05$ and $r_s = .77, p = .01)$. When the focus is the *group's empathy for the person,* greater attribution of meaningfulness to the person by the group was accompanied by higher group accuracy in predicting how the person would rate himself at the end of the group experience $(r_s = .53, p = .11$ and $r_s = .66, p = .03)$. These results make sense if we assume that knowing may have some linkage to prediction. Just as meaningfulness in science has *some* relation to prediction, interpersonal meaningfulness may be related to prediction of people, particularly when this prediction is defined as the ability to enter the language worlds or construct systems of other persons and to understand correctly how they will construe themselves.

Two additional correlates of group empathy for the person were found. First, the group predicts more accurately the self-images of persons who have rated themselves more extremely on their own construct scales at the end of the group experience ($r_s = .63, p = .05$ and $r_s = .75, p = .05$). Secondly, the group predicts more accurately in relation to persons whose self-meaningfulness tends to be greater than the average meaningfulness which they assign to others in the group. In other words, persons who assign greater meaningfulness to themselves than to others at the end of the group experience tend to be more predictable as they rate themselves on their own construct scales ($r_s = .82, p = .004$ and $r_s = .61, p = .06$). These findings suggest that persons who are more certain of their own roles, presumably behaving in more definitive and open ways, allow the group to understand them better than persons less certain of their identities.

Change in self-conception. Slot or side change is defined as a rating reversal from one side of a construct scale to the opposite side. Range change is defined as a switch in rating from the midpoint to a side or from a side to the midpoint of a scale. Using slot and range changes, change in self-conception was determined by adding the number of constructs on which one or the other change occurred. Speculating about the correlates of change in self-image, one might expect that greater initial meaningfulness of self would be related to greater resistance to change in self-image. In the language of personal construct theory and the Choice Corollary, the person who is extending his understanding of himself in some highly meaningful direction will tend to continue in its direction. At this point, the reader is reminded of the finding by Isaacson (1966) that extremity of position is related to certainty of position.

In regard to the hypothesis that self-change will be negatively related to initial self-meaningfulness, we found that initially higher self-meaningfulness was related to less slot and range change from the beginning to the end of the group process ($r_s = -.54, p = .10$ and $r_s = .74, p = .01$). It was also observed that initially greater self-positiveness was related to less slot and range change ($r_s = -.92, p = .002$ and $r_s = -.76, p = .01$). This finding introduces the final topic, the correlates of favorable ratings of the self.

Favorable ratings of the self. Counting the number of construct dimensions on which the person rated himself on the favorable side, we found that more favorable self-ratings were related to the group's attribution of greater meaningfulness to the person at the beginning and end of the group experience (Beginning: $r_s = .73, p = .02$ and $r_s = .59, p = .07$; End: $r_s = .70, p = .02$ and $r_s = .81, p = .004$). Related to this finding is the observation that the group's rating of meaningfulness of the person is correlated with the group's rating of favorableness toward that person (Beginning: $r_s = .75, p = .01$ and $r_s = .94, p = .002$; End: $r_s = .91, p = .002$ and $r_s = .86, p = .002$). Restating these findings, greater self-favorableness is related to greater attribution of meaningfulness to the person by the group. Furthermore, the group's ratings of favorableness toward the person are related to the group's ratings of meaningfulness of that person. However, the relationship between self-ratings of favorableness and meaningfulness is not significant (Beginning: $r_s = .49, p = .14$ and $r_s = .46, p = .17$; End: $r_s = .60, p = .06$ and $r_s = .31, p = .33$). This information on the correlates of favorable self-ratings suggests that the relationship between self-regard and meaningfulness is more interpersonal than intrapersonal. That meaningfulness of self and self-regard might not be highly related in groups of maladjusted persons makes sense. A person can dislike himself, yet be quite certain of his identity.

Reflections on the IT Groups

These analyses of the extremity rating response in the interpersonal transaction groups not only point to the usefulness and construct validity of rating scale polarization as a measure of meaningfulness, but also give the reader a glimpse of the kind of information that may be generated by the fusion of personal construct methodology with a new approach to the study of interpersonal process. Perhaps one might think of the IT group as a laboratory for the personal construct theorist and researcher.

A negative finding. The arguments in this section on the construction of meaningfulness all point to rating scale polarization as a measure of meaningfulness. However, Warr and Coffman (1970) provide an interesting contrast in their study of personal and supplied constructs. They asked subjects to rate the same acquaintances on sets of 12 elicited and 12 supplied construct dimensions. In sharp contrast to other studies, their finding that personal dimensions are not rated more extremely than supplied dimensions suggests that the investigator may sensitively provide meaningful symbols for his subjects. This possibility is suggested by Kelly's Sociality Corollary. Warr and Coffman may well have been enacting sensitive social roles in relation to their subjects and their construct systems. Alternatively, it is possible that these authors may have elicited more peripheral and less significant constructs from their subjects. In this event, provided constructs might be as useful or even more useful than the subjects' own constructs.

That these investigators may have provided significantly useful constructions for their subjects is also a possibility if we assume that the personal construct is not merely a verbal label. Most of us have had the feeling, "I wish I could have said it that way." Such feelings suggest that sometimes the verbalizations of others may better symbolize our own dimensions of awareness, our personal constructs. However, the possible usefulness of other people's symbols should not blind us to individuality in construct label and meaning. The current weight of evidence tends to encourage the investigator to demonstrate that his rating tasks are most pertinent to the phenomena that he is studying, pertinence being defined, in part, by the investigator's appreciation of the communication processes of his subjects as individuals as well as in aggregate. Such an individualized approach may demand more effort from the investigator, but does point more directly toward understanding people than does the mere accumulation of .05 p levels.

In summary, the evidence is strong that rating scale polarization on personal construct scales relates to meaningfulness. Furthermore, this relationship supports our use of the polarization measure in the assessment of the hierarchical integration of construct systems, a method of assessment called ordination.

A FINAL STATEMENT ON INTERPRETIVE MAN

The psychologist's image of man typically is that of the reactor, a sometimes useful but limited picture of the human being. The enlarged image of man, the subject of this chapter, places man's reactions within an interpretive model, a self-image implicitly held by most investigators of behavior but one which they may not apply to the subjects of their studies.

The present manuscript reflects the work of an investigator who became intrigued with Kelly's ideas of interpretive man after heavy exposure to Watsonian conditioning theory as an undergraduate. Admittedly, the student initially found conditioning theory quite challenging. It provided a new perspective on man and neatly explained behavior. However, Professor Kelly provided a new challenge when he asked this graduate student what psychology was all about. The student proceeded to tell him about conditioning theory. Kelly listened carefully, then remarked, "That is interesting and is one way in which psychologists understand human beings. However, there may be other ways of understanding the person as well."

This was the investigator's introduction to constructive alternativism, a philosophical position which is equally applicable to person and scientist, and within which processes of interpretation are given special value. These are the processes that the investigator has tried to share with his readers, reflecting something of the nature of the investigator and his constructions of personal construct theory, in the hope that they also provide a valid conception of other people.

REFERENCES

Adler, A. *What life should mean to you.* New York: Blue Ribbon Books, 1931.

Adler, A. *The individual psychology of Alfred Adler.* Edited by H. L. & R. Ansbacher. New York: Harper & Row Torchbook, 1964.

Bamber, M. Threat and meaningfulness in the development of friendship. Unpublished master's thesis, University of Missouri, 1972.

Bannister, D. The nature and measurement of schizophrenic thought disorder. *Journal of Mental Science*, 1962, **108**, 825–842.

Bem, D., & Allen, A. On predicting some of the people some of the time: The search for cross-situational consistencies in behavior. *Psychological Review*, 1974, **81**, 506–520.

Block, J. Some reasons for the apparent inconsistency of personality. In H. Mischel & W. Mischel (Eds.), *Readings on personality.* New York: Holt, Rinehart & Winston, 1973. Pp. 72–75. (a)

Bloom, L. *Language development: Form and function in emerging grammars.* Cambridge, Mass.: MIT Press, 1970.

Blumer, H. Sociological analysis and the variable. In Irwin Deutscher (Ed.), *What we say/What we do.* Glenview, Ill.: Scott, Foresman, 1973. Pp. 246–259.

Bonarius, J. C. J. Personal construct psychology and extreme response style: An interaction model of meaningfulness, maladjustment, and communication. The Netherlands: University of Groningen, 1970.

Bridgman, P. W. Remarks on the present state of operationalism. *Scientific Monthly*, 1954, **79**, 224–226.

Cromwell, R. L., & Caldwell, D. R. A comparison of ratings based on personal constructs of self and others. *Journal of Clinical Psychology*, 1962, **18**, 43–46.

Dubois, R. The humanizing of humans. *Saturday Review World*, December 14, 1974, p. 80. Reprinted from R. Dubois, *Beast or angel.* New York: Scribner, 1974.

Elliot, T. Conceptual styles of suicidal psychiatric patients. Unpublished doctoral dissertation, University of Missouri, 1972.

Freud, S. *A general introduction to psychoanalysis.* New York: Washington Square Press, 1952.

Gibson, E. J. The ontongeny of reading. *American Psychology*, 1970, **25**, 136–143.

Hamilton, D. L. Personality attributes associated with extreme response style. *Psychological Bulletin*, 1968, **69**, 192–203.

Hasenyager, P. The relationship between neutral responses on the role construct repertory test versus the extremity rating scale. Unpublished manuscript, University of Nebraska, 1975.

Hass, L. Personal construct systems and theological conservatism: A study of conservative Lutheran pastors. Unpublished doctoral dissertation, University of Nebraska, 1974.

Hayakawa, S. I. *Language in thought and action.* New York: Harcourt, Brace, 1949.

Heisenberg, W. *Physics and beyond.* New York: Harper & Row, 1972.

Hinkle, D. N. The change of personal constructs from the viewpoint of a theory of implications. Unpublished doctoral dissertation, Ohio State University, 1965.

Isaacson, G. I. A comparative study of the meaningfulness of personal and common constructs. Unpublished doctoral dissertation, University of Missouri, 1966.

Isaacson, G. I., & Landfield, A. W. The meaningfulness of personal and common constructs, *Journal of Individual Psychology*, 1965, **21**, 160–166.

Jacobi, J. *The psychology of C. G. Jung.* (Rev. ed.) New Haven, Conn.: Yale University Press, 1951.

Johnson, W. *People in quandaries: The semantics of personal adjustment.* New York: Harper, 1946.

Kelly, G. A. *The psychology of personal constructs.* Vols. 1 & 2. New York: Norton, 1955.

Kephart, N. C. The slow learner in the classroom. Columbus, Ohio: Charles E. Merrill, 1960.

Korzyski, A. *Science and sanity.* Lakevill, Conn.: International Non-Aristotelian Library Publishing Company, 1933.

Kuhn, T. S. *The structure of scientific revolutions.* Chicago: University of Chicago Press, 1962.

Landfield, A. W. Meaningfulness of ideal, self and other on client and therapist constructs. *Psychological Reports* 1965, **16**, 605–608.

Landfield, A. W. *Personal construct systems in psychotherapy.* Chicago: Rand McNally, 1971.

Landfield, A. W. A personal construct approach to suicidal behavior. In P. Slater (Ed.), *Explorations of Intrapersonal Space.* London: Wiley, 1976.

Landfield, A. W., & Barr, M. A. Ordination: A new measure of concept organization. Unpublished manuscript, University of Nebraska, 1976.

Landfield, A. W., & Rivers, P. C. An introduction to interpersonal transaction and rotating dyads. *Psychotherapy: Theory, research, and practice,* 1975, **12**, (3), 366–374.

Lazarus, A. A. Where do behavior therapists take their troubles? *Psychological Reports,* 1971, **28**, 349–350.

Leitner, L. M., Landfield, A. W., & Barr, M. A. Cognitive complexity: A review and elaboration within personal construct theory. Unpublished manuscript, University of Nebraska, 1975.

Levy, L. Personal constructs and predictive behavior. *Journal of Abnormal and Social Psychology,* 1956, **53**, 54–58.

Maddi, S. R. *Personality theories: A comparative analysis.* Homewood, Ill.: Dorsey Press, 1972.

Menninger, K. *The vital balance.* New York: Viking Press, 1963.

Mischel, W. Continuity and change in personality. In H. Mischel & W. Mischel (Eds.), *Readings on personality.* New York: Holt, Rinehart & Winston, 1973. Pp. 75–84. (a)

Mischel, W. Toward a cognitive social learning reconceptualization of personality. *Psychological Review,* 1973, **80**, 252–283. (b)

Mitsos, S. B. Personal constructs and the semantic differential. *Journal of Abnormal and Social Psychology,* 1961, **62**, 433–434.

O'Donovan, D. Rating extremity: Pathology or meaningfulness. *Psychological Review,* 1965, **72**, 358–372.

Ogden, C. K. *Opposition: A linguistical and psychological analysis.* Bloomington: Indiana University Press, 1932.

Oliver, W. D., & Landfield, A. W. Reflexivity: An unfaced issue in psychology. *Journal of Individual Psychology,* 1962, **18**, 114–124. Reprinted in ETC.: *A Review of General Semantics,* 1963, **20**, 187–210.

Ourth, L., & Landfield, A. W. Interpersonal meaningfulness and nature of termination in psychotherapy. *Journal of Counseling Psychology,* 1965, **12**, 366–371.

Oppenheimer, R. Analogy in science. *American Psychologist,* 1956, **11**, 127–135.

Richter, B., & Ting, C. C. New elementary particle find excites physicists. AP release, *Lincoln* (Nebr.) *Sunday Journal and Star,* November 17, 1974.

Rychlak, J. F. Reinforcement value: A suggested idiographic intensity dimension of meaningfulness for the personality theorist. *Journal of Personality,* 1966, **34**, 311–335.

Rychlak, J. F. *A philosophy of science for personality theory.* Boston: Houghton-Mifflin, 1968.

Sadowski, A. Personal construct organization: Correlates in behavior and experience. Unpublished master's thesis, University of Missouri, 1971.

Singer, J. E. Motivation for consistency. In Shel Feldman (Ed.), *Cognitive consistency: Motivational antecedents and behavioral consequents.* New York & London: Academic Press, 1966. Pp. 47–73.

Slane, S., & Craig, G. Constructions of the interpersonal and physical environment. Paper submitted to the Environmental Design Research Association 6 Conference at Lawrence, Kansas, April 1975.

Varble, D., & Landfield, A. W. Validity of the self-ideal discrepancy as a criterion measure for success in psychotherapy: A replication. *Journal of Counseling Psychology,* 1969, **16**, 150–156.

Wallach, M. A. The influence of classification requirements on gradients of response. *Psychological Monographs,* 1959, **73** (No. 8).

Warr, P. B., & Coffman, T. L. Personality involvement and extremity of judgment. *British Journal of Social and Clinical Psychology,* 1970, **9**, 108–121.

Weinberg, H. L. *Levels of knowing and existence: Studies in general semantics.* New York: Harper, 1959.

Willis, F. The movement interpretation of threat and level of self-acceptance. Unpublished doctoral dissertation, University of Missouri, 1961. Also, *Dissertation Abstracts,* 1961, **22**, 17–19.

Whyte, L. L. Can we grow geniuses in science? *Harper's,* June 1957, pp. 45–50.

New Approaches to the Analysis of Personal Constructs in Person Perception[1]

Seymour Rosenberg
Rutgers University

I am pleased to participate in this year's symposium, which is devoted to current developments in personal construct theory. My own research interests in lay conceptions of personality have developed from quite another tradition, that of person perception within the domain of social psychology. Yet, the substantive questions with which I am concerned and the methodological problems that I encounter in the empirical study of lay conceptions of personality—or "implicit personality theory," as it has been dubbed in social psychology—are strikingly similar in detail to those of personal construct theory. I hope to demonstrate these similarities in this paper as I describe the approaches we have developed to study implicit personality theory.

I hope also that this symposium, while advancing the development of personal construct theory, will facilitate contact between social psychologists interested in implicit personality theory and personal construct theorists. I believe that increased communication between the two groups can do much to advance our understanding of how a person views himself and others as psychological beings, and of the role that these perceptions play in everyday social relationships.

1. This research was supported in part by NSF Grants GS-40265 and BNS 76-10675, and in part by a research grant from the Rutgers University Computer Center. A number of the ideas and methods on which the research is based were developed during a research leave, supported in part by an SSRC fellowship. I would also like to acknowledge the help and dedication of two students, Sam Kingsley and Moonja Kim. Their involvement in this research has been indispensable to me both in the development and clarification of many of the guiding ideas and in the laborious collection and analysis of the data.

INTRODUCTION

Implicit personality theory refers to a person's everyday beliefs about personality. This belief system includes the traits that he perceives as characteristic of himself and others—traits having to do with intelligence, integrity, sociability, attractiveness, maturity, and so on—and his beliefs about the interrelations among these traits.

The "theory" is characterized as "implicit" because it is inferred from the person's descriptions and expectations about people rather than being stated by him as a formal theory. Furthermore, it is unlikely that most individuals could organize their categories and beliefs about their relations into an explicit system.

The psychological phenomena referred to by implicit personality theory are also of central interest to personal construct theorists. Although the range of personal construct theory is not limited to interpersonal perception, much of the explication of the theory as well as the actual empirical work is in terms of how a person views himself and others as psychological beings. This shared substantive interest has not, by itself, led to much contact between personal construct theorists and social psychologists—at least if we are to judge by the limited number of mutual citations in the literature to date.

There is, however, a growing interest and awareness by each group of the work of the other. I believe that this is due in part to a gradual *convergence in method* and in part to a shared interest in the development and elaboration of a *theory* of interpersonal perception.

What follows in this section is an introduction to each of these two topics. The subsequent sections describe in detail our current methods for studying an individual's implicit personality theory and the implications for theory of our findings to date.

Convergence in Method

Until recently, social psychologists have relied almost exclusively on fixed-format instruments such as check lists and rating scales to study lay conceptions of personality. The trait categories that are used in these instruments are usually selected by the investigator on a fortuitous basis and, as a consequence, may fail to include important categories used by the person in his everyday life. Free-response methods in which the respondent describes persons with terms of his own choosing have also been used in social psychology from time to time but primarily to ascertain the kinds of general categories that show up in such descriptions; that is, the extent to which people refer to appearance, emotional adjustment, interests, etc. (Beach & Wertheimer, 1961; Dornbusch, Hastorf, Richardson, Muzzy, & Vreeland, 1965; Yarrow & Campbell, 1963). Only recently have the individual trait terms and their occurrences in free-response descriptions been extracted and analyzed as a belief system (Jones & Rosenberg, 1974; Jones, Sensenig, & Haley, 1974; Pervin, 1976; Rosenberg & Sedlak, 1972a, 1972b).

In contrast, Kelly and other personal construct theorists have long been advocating free-response instruments from which to extract and interpret a person's interpersonal constructs. The rationale for those instruments and the way they are analyzed is to be found in the basic tenets of the theory. The research instruments of personal construct theorists are exemplified by the repertory grid methods originally devised by Kelly (1955), and the variations subsequently introduced by other investigators.

Still, there are features in most versions of the grid method that may constrain an individual's response unnecessarily and hence lead to a more fragmentary representation of his view of people. I am thinking, in particular, of grids in which the psychologist chooses the role figures to be described (and they are small in number), in which the individual is required to verbalize the contrast for a construct, and in which the selection by the psychologist of role triads to elicit constructs may have certain biasing effects on the final set of constructs obtained.

Kelly (1955, pp. 270–273) was aware of the fact that these constraints involved certain assumptions about the representativeness of the role figures and of the sorts (triads), and about the "stability of conception"—that is, that the subject "does not shift ground between writing his emergent poles and listing his implicit poles." The possible limitations of the original instruments, which were intended only as illustrative of an open-ended approach, have in fact motivated the subsequent development by personal construct theorists of a number of modifications. A summary of the more recent grid methods is available in Bannister and Mair (1968).

The instruments that are described in this paper for the study of implicit personality theory do not have the limitations referred to above. Still, any method, no matter how "free" it appears to be, prob-ably introduces certain biases in the data base. The question is, What are the values and limitations of any particular method? Clear-ly, a continuing critique of data-gathering methods in these terms is a very worthwhile activity.

My own study of implicit personality theory started with trait sorting, a fixed-format method in which the subject is asked to describe several persons he knows by sorting personality trait names into different groups, each group representing a different person (Rosenberg, Nelson, & Vivekananthan, 1968; Rosenberg & Olshan, 1970). We supplied the trait terms that the subject sorted. Nevertheless, we thought that we had freed up the situation con-siderably over most other fixed-format methods because the subject could select the people to describe and because our method of scaling analysis did not require that we prejudge the dimensions of personality perception.

It soon became apparent, however, to me and to some of my col-leagues that we didn't know enough about lay concepts of personali-ty to select a representative set of trait terms for use in discovering the dimensions of personality perception. Nor did we have a defensi-ble empirical procedure for developing such a set of terms. In the face of this ignorance, multidimensional (or factor-analytic) studies in pursuit of the basic dimensions of implicit personality theory yield an incomplete product at best—you cannot get out of a multidimentsional analysis what you did not put in.[2]

As a consequence, we began to shift to free-response methods by asking each of a sample of individuals to describe in his own terms a number of people he knows, some personally and some by reputation (Rosenberg & Sedlak, 1972b; Jones & Rosenberg, 1974). The most frequently occurring trait categories in these ad-lib descriptions were selected for clustering and multidimensional scaling. The co-oc-currence of these traits in the free-response protocols were ag-gregated across the different subjects. The resulting structures revealed the modal categories and dimensions of our college student

2. We have recently reopened the question of how to compose a represen-tative set of terms from the categories and dimensions found in the extensive free-response descriptions of our subjects. One of our current studies is con-cerned with a comparison of the structure obtained from such a composite vocabulary with that obtained from the subject's own free-response vocabulary.

sample, that is, their concern with competence and achievement (e.g., *intelligent, hard-worker* vs. *unintelligent, lazy*), social skills (e.g., *outgoing* vs. *introverted*), friendship and acceptance (e.g., *friendly, helpful, loving* vs. *cold, selfish*), and interpersonal integrity (e.g., *honest, sincere* vs. *liar, phony*).

The trait structures obtained from aggregated free-response data were inadequate, however, in two ways. First, they are not as clear as those obtained when subjects are asked to describe the same number (≈10) of people using only the traits that occur frequently in the aggregated free-response descriptions (Sedlak, 1971). Apparently, free-response data yield a less stable measure of trait-relatedness than does a fixed-format method (using the same traits) when each of the subjects describes only a handful of people he knows. Second, the structures based on aggregated data represent only the commonly used categories and dimensions in the subject sample. Nor can the differences among subjects be reliably ascertained when only a handful of descriptions is obtained from each subject.

Our attention then shifted to a serious consideration of how to obtain an adequate data base to study the trait structure of single individuals. In an initial study, an individual's view of people was extracted from completely naturalistic descriptions (Rosenberg & Jones, 1972). By naturalistic descriptions, I mean descriptions that are not in response to any contrived arrangement between subject and investigator. Ordinary conversation can provide naturalistic personality descriptions but is generally not a feasible data source. Therapy protocols are perhaps more feasible because they are easier to record and usually have a high density of interpersonal perception and affect. Literary materials are perhaps the most easily obtained source of naturalistic descriptions and can be particularly valuable when the writer's life is well documented. Thus, the Rosenberg and Jones (1972) study is of an author, Theodore Dreiser, whose writing is heavily laced with character descriptions and about whom much is known.

We demonstrated, with the analysis of a sample of Dreiser's short stories, the feasibility of extracting a person's view of people from completely naturalistic materials and representing it in at least a quasi-formal manner. The Dreiser study also demonstrated the value of analyzing single individuals. The trait structures obtained from his writings revealed dimensions that were central in his life and personality. Moreover, except for the evaluative dimension, these could not be readily recast into dimensions such as the semantic differential that typically emerge from aggregated group data. Even in the case of evaluation, the traits valued by one person are not necessarily those valued by another: for Dreiser, unconventional traits were highly valued and conventional traits abhorred (Swanberg, 1965)—hardly a universal attitude.[3]

It is important, however, that this research go beyond the study of literary and other public figures, psychotherapy patients, or persons who happen to provide a convenient naturalistic data source in their letters or diaries (for example, Allport's *Letters from Jenny*, 1965). The use of naturalistic materials of people who provide these convenient records is not only scientifically hazardous when used exclusively, but is also economically prohibitive. The task of extracting trait descriptions from fiction, speeches, verbatim transcripts, and letters is extremely laborious and time-consuming. It is clear, therefore, that the analysis of naturalistic materials needs to be supplemented with a feasible method for studying fairly large numbers and varieties of people, each in detail.

As a consequence, a free-response instrument was gradually developed that is both simple and economical to administer and that yields stable measures of trait co-occurrence. This development was guided by the caveat that the solicited descriptions approximate as closely as possible the descriptions that might be found in everyday life. I shall describe, in the section on methodology, the various alternatives that were considered and their relation to naturalistic materials and Rep Grid descriptions. The particular format now being used most extensively will be described in detail.

The use of data from individuals who are cooperative and available, as opposed to writers and public figures, can have some other advantages as well. One is that we can readily obtain other psychological information from them. Another advantage is that we are able to extract interpersonal affect data in addition to trait perceptions. That is, in addition to describing the traits he sees in himself and others, each person can describe the feelings that the

3. The type of analysis used in the Dreiser study would seem to be of value to psychohistorians. Such an analysis requires, however, that the person's writings contain an adequate amount of psychological description. Unfortunately, politicians—a favorite among psychohistorians—are often opaque in their views of people, at least in public. Candid expressions, such as those found in the "Watergate tapes," are often not readily available to the researcher.

different people elicit in him, also in terms of his own choosing. The motivation for collecting this affective information is to explore the relations, which I expect to be close ones, between trait perception and interpersonal feelings. The argument Epstein (1973) makes, for example, for studying the relationship of emotion to self-conception certainly seems as cogent for interpersonal conceptions as well. That is, the function of these conceptions "is to make life livable, meaning emotionally satisfying. Thus, the self-theory . . . does not exist apart from the emotions, and to a large extent the opposite is also true" (p. 415).

Our interest in the detailed study of an individual has thus brought us very close indeed to the long-standing concerns of personal construct theorists, and the methods we have evolved both to gather and to analyze data contribute much to the converging interests to which I referred earlier.

Theory: Structure and Content

The focus on individuals does not mean that I have abandoned the search for "universals" in implicit personality theory—that is, the ways in which individuals are similar in their psychological conception of people. This search takes two forms.

One is in the nature of the structures themselves, and is exemplified by the search for a general representation of implicit personality theory. The second is in the content that different individuals share in their conception of people. The concern with both types of commonality can be found in personal construct theory as well.

With regard to structure, personal construct theory is itself a structural theory that is intended to be universal in conception. As Kelly (1955) stated, "We have used the subject's own system of axes, yet we have abstracted them in ways which permit us to subsume them within our own system. Thus we have not bogged down in the particularistic approach" (p. 318).

Social psychologists have not developed formal structural models of implicit personality theory. There are, of course, the general psychometric models inherent in the social psychologist's use of a particular computing algorithm to represent the interrelations within a set of trait descriptions. In general terms, the use of multidimensional scaling to represent the structure of implicit personality theory assumes that a person thinks of personality differences among individuals in terms of gradations in each of a set of basic trait properties. Alternatively, the use of clustering assumes that the person thinks of differences among individuals in terms of more or less distinct personality types. These two general types of models have been used to represent implicit personality theory (Rosenberg & Sedlak, 1972a) and may, of course, be mixed in various ways (e.g., Torgerson, 1965). In any case, these models are not psychological conceptualizations of the processes underlying the beliefs and feelings associated with interpersonal perception.

Kellian theory is the only serious attempt that I know to formalize the "structural" aspects of person perception in psychological terms. It has guided my own analyses of implicit personality theory with concepts such as construct-contrast (as distinct from dimension), superordinate relations among constructs, and so on. The results that have been obtained and that will be reported in this paper suggest that the concepts of construct theory are indeed very useful in representing the structure of implicit personality theory. These results, involving as they do the use of clustering and scaling, also demonstrate the intimate connection between the psychometric models of the social psychologist and the structural concepts of the personal construct theorist.

The concern with content in personal construct theory is expressed, not only in the theory by the Commonality Corollary, but also in Kelly's programmatic research suggestions for extracting "group factors" from a set of individual grids. One of his suggestions is that the grids "be stacked one above the other and a common factor extracted." In the context of contemporary psychometric developments, both the commonalities and the differences could be represented within a single scaling analysis (Carroll, 1972; Carroll & Chang, 1970; Horan, 1969; McGee, 1968; Tucker & Messick, 1963). The application of these analyses requires that the roles described be the same from individual to individual, a condition satisfied by most grid methods. In contrast, the data-gathering methods described in the next section do not require the use of a common set of roles. Thus, it has been necessary to develop other approaches to the analysis of content.

Alternative approaches to the analysis of *free-response* content are still in the early stages of development. The first step has been to summarize recurrent areas of content in the form of a category system that subsumes the trait terms found in free-response descriptions (e.g., Beach & Wertheimer, 1961; Dornbusch et al., 1965; Landfield, 1971; Yarrow & Campbell, 1963). Such a summary, based on descriptions elicited by the free-response method described in this paper, is presented in the latter part of the paper. The category system (quite tentative, as yet) proposed in this paper turns out to be quite similar to that developed by Landfield (1971) within the framework of personal construct theory. The latter part of the paper also outlines some speculative ideas on the universals of content, that is, on the type of content categories that subsumes the interpersonal perceptions of any particular individual.

METHODOLOGY

Data Gathering

The open-ended format my colleagues and I used in our initial applications of the free-response approach (Jones & Rosenberg, 1974; Rosenberg & Sedlak, 1972b) is the forerunner of the current methods described below. The problem with the initial work is that we had adopted the traditional practice, admittedly easier, of designing our studies so that they required only an hour or so of laboratory time from each of the subjects. The consequences, which I have already noted, are that the data base obtained from a person is inadequate for extracting his belief system and that aggregating individual protocols to achieve added stability reveals only the modal categories and dimensions of the group. The solution to the first problem is obvious: enlarge the data base obtained from each individual. The second problem vanishes because pooling, while of possible value for some purposes, is no longer motivated solely by the need to achieve stability in the data base.

The current free-response methods require that each individual participate from 10 to 25 hours, depending on the particular method and individual. All of the methods require that an individual describe in his own terms a sizable sample of people that he knows, one at a time, and that he list as exhaustively as possible the characteristics he perceives in each of these people and the way each makes him feel. The person is asked to formulate his trait perceptions and feelings in the form of discrete units, but not necessarily single words.

Two variants of this general format were explored: (a) the person cumulates a trait and feeling list as he describes people—that is, when he uses a trait or elicited feeling to describe one person he is asked to judge the presence of this trait or elicited feeling for all his other people; or (b) the person starts anew in describing each of his people.

We finally settled on the first variant for much the same reasons that the Rep Grid is preferred to the Rep Test as a research instrument (Bannister & Mair, 1968; Kelly, 1955). On a priori grounds, the second alternative would seem to be closer to a natural situation—still, it probably results in the more fragmentary type of record that is obtained from naturalistic literary material (e.g., Rosenberg & Jones, 1972). It appears to be difficult for a person to give a description that is both spontaneous and comprehensive. Still, the second format is the method of choice when the investigator is interested in the order in which constructs emerge in a natural description of a person and in what this order may reveal about the processes underlying person perception (Jones et al., 1974).

At first, the subjects consisted of a handful of individuals who were willing to volunteer their time, partly out of curiosity about the work and partly in return for learning about their view of people, as represented by a clustering and scaling analysis of the descriptions. A number of individuals were eager to participate, but motivation usually flagged because of the length of the task. It became apparent that an alternative method for recruiting subjects was necessary for this type of commitment.

One feasible alternative I have found is to incorporate the research into my advanced undergraduate seminar in personality research. Each student participates as a subject during the first third of the semester. There are no assigned readings or formal lectures during this period. In the remaining part of the course, the student analyzes and interprets his own data using various psychometric and statistical techniques, including multidimensional scaling, clustering, and regression analysis. Each student and I also discuss his material in a series of individual sessions—for my part, to help clarify certain aspects of the results and to provide ideas for improving the collection and analysis of the data. The content of students' protocols is not discussed in class in order to preserve the confidentiality of their material. The nature of the course and its requirements are made explicit to the students before they enroll.[4]

I would like now to describe in more detail the method that was used with a sample of 16 students, 6 males and 10 females. Unless otherwise noted, the findings and observations reported later in this paper are based on these data. In order to distinguish the students from the people they describe (and out of habit), I will refer to the students as "subjects."

Each subject first listed at least 100 people from his life. To facilitate this task and to provide a balanced sample, the subjects were provided with a 7-page booklet, each page with one of the following headings:

1. *All persons in household during childhood and adolescence.*
2. *All persons who were close or intimate* in the *past* but not present.
3. *All* persons you *knew well* but were not close or intimate—in the *past* but not present.
4. Persons who are *close* or *intimate*—in the present.
5. Persons you *know well* but are not close or intimate—in the *present.*
6. *Current acquaintances known at least one year* (limit 25).
7. *Persons known by reputation only* (limit 10).

Subjects were reminded on several pages of the booklet to "Be sure to include persons you may not like, may not find interesting, attractive, congenial, etc." because our previous work revealed a bias against listing and describing such people.

In spite of protestation from several subjects that they did not know 100 people, almost everyone's final listing exceeded 100, often by 25 to 50 additional names. In order to limit each subject's final protocol to a relatively uniform number of people, the initial listing

4. The inclusion of this task in the seminar provides not only a data base from highly motivated individuals, but is an excellent pedagogical experience for the students as well. Because their own personal material is involved, students learn the technical aspects of data analysis as well as the substantive issues with an ease and depth that I am unable to produce when I rely only on reading, lecture, and discussion—as I do in my graduate seminar. Many students also find the task of describing people they know informative from a personal standpoint and the protocol itself appears to be a rich source of information for students to learn about their interpersonal life. As we improve the techniques for analyzing these data, the yield for the individual appears to improve also.

was reduced to this figure when necessary by asking the subject to delete the persons he knows least well.

The description of each person on a subject's list consisted of two distinct parts: (a) the physical and psychological traits that he thought to be characteristic of the person; and (b) the feelings elicited in the subject by the person described. These two parts were kept separate, since the meaning and intent of a term is quite different, depending on whether it refers to a trait or feeling; for example, a person described as *happy* (trait) may or may not make the subject feel *happy*, and vice versa.

Subjects were instructed to make the trait and feeling judgments on a 3-point scale. For traits:

  0 means the trait is not descriptive of the person, but does not necessarily mean that the person possesses the opposite trait [in order to indicate that the person possesses the opposite trait, the subject was instructed to add the opposite as a separate trait term];
  1 means the person possesses the trait to a noticeable degree but need not describe the way the person is all the time;
  2 means the person possesses the trait to an extreme degree but need not describe the way the person is all the time.

A similar scale, appropriately worded, was used for the feelings:

  0 means the person does not make (or has not made) you feel this way;
  1 means the person makes (or has made) you feel this way to a noticeable degree;
  2 means the person makes (or has made) you feel this way to an extreme degree, but need not make you feel this way all the time.

The instructions also suggested that the same person can have a variety of traits—even those considered "opposite" in meaning. Similarly, the same person can elicit "opposite" feelings at different times.

The rationale for a 3-valued scale comes from experience with pilot subjects, where it was found that additional values added little information while adding considerably to the subject's chore. Most pilot subjects reported that they could make the distinctions they wished with 3 values, whereas a 2-valued scale, 0 and 1, was too limiting.[5]

The following precautions were taken to reduce biases introduced by the order in which people were described and the content of these descriptions:

1. The order in which the 100 people were to be described was randomized with the restriction that each of the first three sets of seven people be a uniform sample from the seven categories listed above. The 22nd, 23rd, and 24th "persons" to be described were three different selves: "me-now," "me-past," and "me-ideal." The order in which the remaining people were described was completely random. A subject was free to add at any time during the data collection names of significant people he had forgotten in his initial listing. These people, usually no more than two or three, were put at the end of the randomized list.

2. Before systematically describing any of the people on his list, each subject prepared two "starter lists," one of traits and one of feelings. The starter lists served not only to reduce biases in content that might be associated with the first few people on the list but also to help get the subject started. A subject prepared his starter list for traits by considering the *last* 20 people on his randomized list and recording the first five traits that came to mind for each of these people, including physical features he thought particularly noticeable or important. Similarly, he prepared a starter list for feelings by recording five feelings and emotions that each of the last 20 people tend to elicit in him. Each starter list was a random composite of the recorded terms, with duplicates removed. (Alternative methods for generating starter lists were first explored with pilot subjects but abandoned because they introduced biases of their own. They included asking the subject to list terms he thought he used frequently

5. The use of an additional alternative, *not relevant*, was explored with 3 of the 16 subjects. These 3 subjects were asked to use this alternative when they judged that a trait or elicited feeling on their cumulative lists was not relevant (as opposed to not descriptive, which is 0) to the person described; for example, *beard* to describe a female. The rationale for exploring subjects' use of this alternative is quite similar to Kelly's (1955, pp. 271–272) notion that certain constructs may have a limited range of convenience. Different individuals appeared to interpret *not relevant* quite differently, however. One female subject used it only for the few heterosexual traits and feelings in her descriptions of other females. Another subject used *not relevant* almost to the exclusion of 0. The value of providing this alternative is questionable in either case.

or making a large list of terms available to the subject from which he could select a starter list.)

3. A subject systematically alternated between trait and feeling descriptions. The following schedule was devised for each subject: he started with trait descriptions for the first five people on his list, followed by feeling descriptions of the first ten people on the list. He switched back to trait descriptions and alternated them with feeling descriptions such that after persons n through $n+9$ were described by traits, persons $n+5$ through $n+14$ were described by feelings.

The descriptions were collected on a computer terminal tied into the Rutgers University time-sharing system. The computer was programmed (Livingston & Kingsley, 1976) to do the following: (a) present the subject with his randomized list of persons, one at a time; (b) present for each person the trait (or feeling) terms previously entered by the subject, including the starter list; (c) record the subject's judgment (0, 1, or 2) of the person on each term; (d) record any new trait (or feeling) term that the subject wishes to add to his vocabulary of terms; (e) re-present for judgment the persons already described, when a new trait (or feeling) term is added.

Thus, the computer eventually contains a Person $\times$ Trait and Person $\times$ Feeling matrix for each individual, as shown in Figure 1.

	TRAITS								**FEELINGS**						
	1	2	.	.	j	.	.	t	1	2	.	.	k	.	.	f
1				.								.			
2				.								.			
.				.								.			
i	.	.	.	.	X_{ij}				.	.	.	.	Y_{ik}		
.															
n															

FIG. 1. Form of the data matrix obtained from each subject.

The total number of trait terms in the sample of 16 individuals ranges from 56 to 123, and the total number of feelings ranges from 34 to 91.

Short Version

Is it possible to obtain a stable trait and feeling structure from a subject with less than 100 descriptions? If so, how many people are required to give us about the same structure as that obtained from the descriptions of $\approx$ 100 people?

To answer these questions, a plot was made of the number of traits and feelings that a subject added as he completed the descriptions of his list of people. Eight of the nine subjects in a test sample each added a *total* of only one or two terms to their trait and feeling list after they had described the first 35 people. For practical purposes, therefore, a subject's vocabulary is elicited by the first 35 people listed, using the stratified random procedure described above. The "distance" between traits and feelings (the input measure for scaling described in the next subsection) based on these 35 people was then correlated with the "distance" based on $\approx$ 100 people. The correlations ranged from .79 to .93 with a median of .90. Thus, a sample of 35 people can often provide a good approximation of the trait and feeling structure obtained from the 100 people.

It should be noted, however, that this "short version" does not give as comprehensive a picture of the people that a subject knows. It is also less likely to yield as stable a picture of the basic categories (clusters) of people in the subject's view of people.

Structural Analysis[6]

Relatedness Measures

Most methods for representing the structure of a set of related entities require, as input data, a number for each pair of entities reflecting how closely they are related. A large variety of measures

---

6. Additional notes on the analytic methods described in this section are given in the Appendix.

have been developed to describe the "proximity" between the entities of a rectangular matrix of the sort shown in Figure 1. The matrix contains two distinct types of entities for which a relatedness measure may be calculated: the rows (people) and the columns (traits and/or feelings). The same method of calculation is usually appropriate for either rows or columns. In either case, the measure between any two entities reflects the similarity or dissimilarity in their two profiles of scores.

The choice of a particular measure depends on several considerations. For example, covariance or correlation is the appropriate choice for factor analysis, whereas a distance-type measure is the usual choice for clustering and multidimensional scaling. Another consideration in the choice of a relatedness measure is whether the rectangular data matrix contains qualitative or quantitative variables (or some mixture of the two). However, the choice of an appropriate measure is also ad hoc, to some extent. As Sneath and Sokal (1973) have commented, after an extensive discussion of resemblance measures, "But when all is said and done, the validation of a similarity measure by the scientist working in a given field has so far been primarily empirical, a type of intuitive assessment of similarity" (p. 146).

The measure currently being used to analyze the data from the open-ended format described in the previous section is the δ-measure first devised for the study of Dreiser (Rosenberg & Jones, 1972). This measure was specifically designed to ignore "negative matches," that is, the co-occurrence of any two zero values in the two profiles. The rationale for ignoring negative matches is that a large number of joint absences of traits, for example, can distort the estimation of similarity between two people. The distortion can be especially serious in completely naturalistic descriptions such as the Dreiser data, where most of the traits are thinly scattered over a large number of people. Numerical taxonomists in biology, who also encounter this problem in measuring the similarity among distantly related organisms, have devised similar measures of distance (Sneath & Sokal, 1973, p. 131).

There is another approach to this problem when the data are not naturalistic. When using the repertory grid or the open-ended format described above, the investigator can simply require that the subject use fewer zeroes. Bannister (1959) has suggested, for example, that the subject be instructed to place half the people in his

Rep Grid at each pole of the construct. Alternatively, instead of making 0 or 1 judgments, the subjects can be instructed to rank order the people on each construct (Bannister, 1963). I have preferred not to impose such restrictions on subjects (for one thing, such restrictions would require a radical alteration of the format) but instead to correct the problem, to the extent that it exists, in the choice of a distance measure.

The δ-measure has another property which should be noted. The measure gives weight not only to direct similarity between the profiles of two entities, but also to their indirect similarity. With traits, for example, the measure weights not only direct co-occurrence between traits i and j but also the fact that i and j may co-occur independently with a third trait k. That is, a subject may have described one person with traits i and k but not with j and other persons with traits j and k but not with i. Thus, the measure incorporates both direct and indirect co-occurrences that exist between any given pair of traits.

The reasons for adding indirect co-occurrences to the distance measure are several. In naturalistic data, it compensates for the likely possibility that a writer will not use synonymous terms to describe a character, at least to the degree that reflects their psychological proximity. Whether the data are completely naturalistic or not, indirect co-occurrence seems to add stability to a distance measure because it contains additional information about the relations between entities.

An interesting possibility worthy of careful study is that indirect co-occurrences, being a highly unobtrusive measure, puts entities into closer proximity than the subject is willing or capable of acknowledging directly. For example, a subject may "censor" certain negative traits and feelings in describing certain people, perhaps out of guilt, yet the terms he does use to describe these people do co-occur with sufficient regularity in the descriptions of other negatively evaluated people (about whom there is little or no guilt) to put the two groups into the same large cluster.

The discussion here of relatedness measures is necessarily brief and incomplete and is intended primarily to explicate our particular choice of a distance measure and some of the basic considerations involved. A number of excellent summaries of relatedness measures are available for readers who are interested in the technical aspects of this topic (e.g., Green & Carmone, 1972; Sneath & Sokal, 1973).

The equation for calculating the δ-measure is available in the original paper (Rosenberg & Jones, 1972).

Two-Way Clustering

The output of a *hierarchical clustering* is a sequence of partitionings (clusterings) of the entities (Johnson, 1967; Sneath & Sokal, 1973). Each partitioning of the entities, say traits, consists of nonoverlapping clusters or groupings of the traits. The hierarchical relation among partitionings means that the nth partitioning in the sequence contains a union of two clusters from the $(n-1)$th partitioning. Each successive clustering is produced when an increasingly larger δ-measure is taken for putting traits into the same cluster. Thus, the procedure starts with each trait in its own cluster and ends with all traits in one cluster.

Let us consider first the application of hierarchical clustering to the traits and feelings *together*. A cluster may thus consist of a mixture of traits and feelings—and many clusters are indeed such mixtures. The grouping of certain traits and feelings into one cluster means that the presence or absence of one of these traits or feelings in the description of a person is likely to indicate the presence or absence of the other traits and feelings in the same description, within certain limits, of course. As we shall see, the observation of what trait and feeling categories are associated with one another is one of the interesting consequences of combining them into one analysis.

The same clustering algorithm, with the δ-measure for each pair of people as input data, also groups the ≈ 100 people into a smaller and more manageable number of people clusters. The presence of people in the same cluster means that the subject characterizes them similarly and feels similarly about them.

The clustering of traits and feelings and of people, when combined into one representation, displays many of the regularities in a subject's protocol. Such a display is obtained simply by regrouping the rows (people) and columns (both traits and feelings) in Figure 1 according to the results of the two separate clusterings. Such a permutation of both rows and columns, based on clustering, is called a "two-way clustering." (Alternative algorithms for two-way clustering are described by Hartigan, 1975).

An example of such a permutation is shown in Figure 2. The data for this matrix were obtained from one of the 16 subjects, identified as MA, who is a male, age 19, and single at the time he participated in the study.

Because of space limitations, the matrix was split vertically, using the first branching in the hierarchy as the basis for splitting. The terms in each branch were then reproduced on a separate page. Also, because of space limitations, the additional branching of the hierarchy is not shown. Instead, horizontal and vertical lines are used to separate the more distinctive clusters among the people and among the terms, respectively.

Note that the permutation of rows and columns according to the clustering analyses tends to produce rectangles within the data matrix consisting of 0's, of 1's, or of 2's, thus displaying the pattern of traits and feelings characteristic of each cluster of people.

The rows and columns in Figure 2 have also been rearranged from negative to positive according to MA's evaluative ratings. These evaluative ratings were obtained by asking MA to rate each of his people and each of his trait terms on a 7-point likableness scale. He also rated each of his feelings on a 7-point pleasantness scale.

Kendall's τ between MA's liking of his people and row location is .82; the τ between MA's evaluative ratings of the terms (likableness for traits and pleasantness for feelings) is .76. Apparently then, one of the main features of the clustering structure in Figure 2 is evaluation. Note, for example, that the first branching of terms more or less cleanly separates the negative (part 1 of Figure 2) from the positive (part 2 of Figure 2) terms. As we shall see in a later section, a similar separation occurs in a multidimensional configuration of the terms, and this result obtains for other subjects as well.

The structure is not completely explicable, however, in terms of a single dimension such as evaluation; that is, the columns in Figure 2 are not a simple ordering from most negative to most positive terms. (The same is true for people.) There are other interesting and important structural properties inherent in these data. The analyses described below—dominant-residual analysis, contrast analysis, and multidimensional scaling—are intended to extract and represent these structural features.

Dominant-Residual Analysis

This analysis was motivated by the frequent presence of several rather odd juxtapositionings of traits and feelings in the clustering solution. For example, there is a cluster in Figure 2 (part 1)

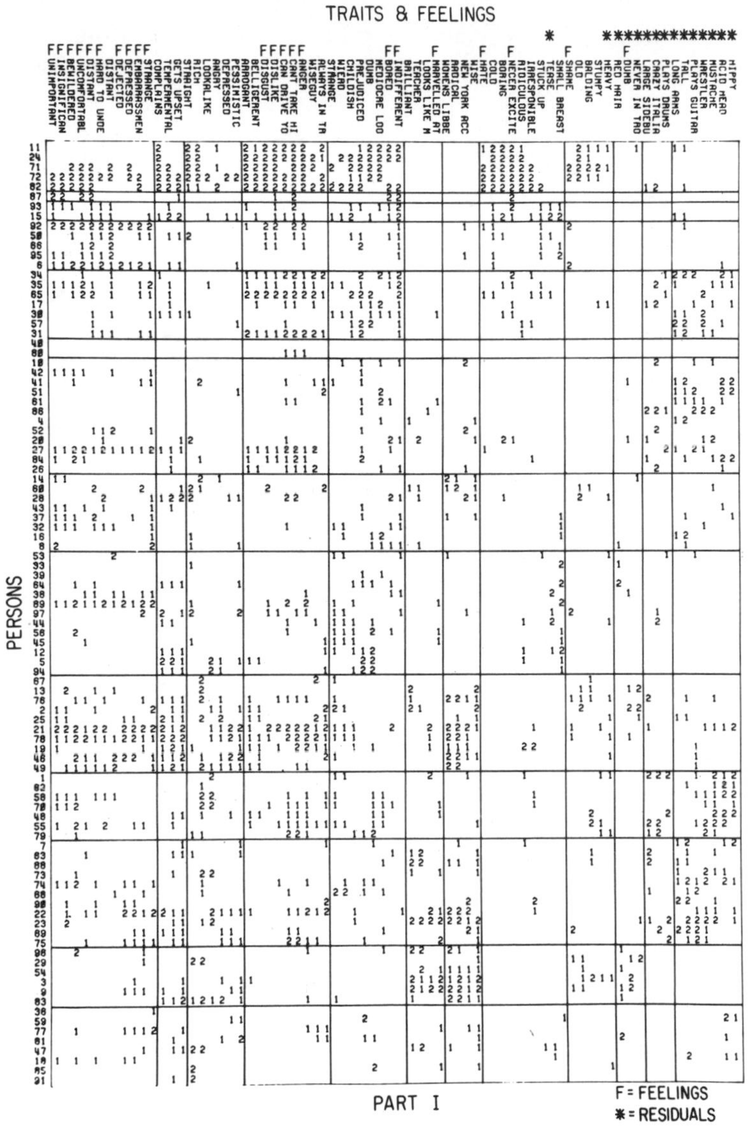

FIG. 2. Two-way clustering of subject MA's data matrix.

TRAITS & FEELINGS

PART II

F = FEELINGS
* = RESIDUALS

PERSONS

consisting of *red hair, dumb* (feeling), *never in trouble*. While the grouping of the last two terms may be understandable (their actual co-occurrence suggests otherwise, a point to be discussed later), their grouping with *red hair* seems odd. The actual frequency of co-occurrence (relative to their non-co-occurrence) of *red hair* with either *dumb* or *never in trouble* does not reveal much of a relationship with either of them. Yet, certain traits and feelings, instead of remaining as isolates, merge with one another and/or within an otherwise meaningful grouping and can confuse the conceptual homogeneity of a cluster.

The problems highlighted by MA's data are present to some degree in all of the protocols we have collected and analyzed. Physical traits (not all!) such as *red hair* are but one source of the problem. There are often other relatively isolated traits in a person's descriptions of people (e.g., MA's *tennis player*) in that, while he notices and reports them, he gives few if any traits that go with them. That is, there seems to be no elaborate belief system associated with these types of traits. These isolated trait categories appear to be similar to Kelly's (1955) *superficial constructs* or *excessively impermeable constructs*. Sometimes, there also exists in a protocol small highly meaningful clusters of traits and feelings that are relatively unrelated to the majority of terms, but because they are in the minority, these small clusters fail to be adequately grouped and represented in a clustering (and low-dimensional scaling) of the total set of terms.[7]

If the conjectures just discussed about the underlying structure are valid, one strategy for dealing with the problem of relatively isolated traits and feelings is to form two (or more) subsets of traits and feelings, one representing the major constructs in the belief system and the other consisting of the "isolates." Separate analyses of each subset may then provide a clearer picture of the psychological

7. Does a multidimensional configuration of the traits and feelings do a better job of separating relatively unrelated terms? The answer is probably yes, because in a space of sufficiently high dimensionality there is room for terms that do not belong together to separate from each other. While a solution of high dimensionality may be adequate to the task, there remains the problem of identifying the homogeneous clusters within the space. Clusters can, of course, be identified by mapping the results of a hierarchical clustering onto the space. However, as we have already noted from the clustering shown in Figure 2, such a mapping would not effectively isolate a trait such as *red hair* even if the trait were relatively isolated spatially.

dimensions in both the dominant (majority) structure and whatever structure is present in the remaining minority of traits and feelings. The question is how to effect this partitioning without involving the psychologist in the task of judging which traits and feelings belong in which subset. The dominant-residual analysis is a method, based on statistical criteria, that we are using to obtain such a partitioning.

The method currently being used was suggested by James Rohlf, a biologist who has encountered similar problems in the numerical taxonomy of animals based on a large and *heterogeneous* set of the animals' characteristics (here, traits and feelings). This method is simpler than the statistical procedure I have described elsewhere (Rosenberg, 1975). The results of the two different methods are quite similar. Nevertheless, it should be noted that while either method of partitioning traits and feelings is useful in clarifying the content of an individual's protocol, they are ad hoc procedures and additional work is necessary to understand more fully the nature of the partitions they produce.

The dominant-residual analysis consists of the following: A measure of dominance is calculated for each trait and feeling reflecting its relation to all the other traits and feelings in the subject's protocol. This measure is obtained by first calculating a contingency χ^2 for the given trait or feeling versus each of the other traits and feelings. The dominance measure for a given term is based on the sum of all these contingency χ^2's. When the dominance values for all the terms are ordered from most to least dominant, there is usually a distinct discontinuity at the lower end. The terms are partitioned into dominant and residual subsets using this discontinuity as the cutting point.

Figure 3 schematizes the decomposition of the total set of traits and feelings into dominant and residual subsets. The figure also schematizes the additional structural analyses described in this section and their relation to the partitioning.

Finally, it should be noted that the clustering of people based on the dominant traits and feelings would yield a clustering similar to that derived from all the terms. That is, the more dominant traits and feelings strongly determine the way the people have been clustered. They are termed dominant because they do, in fact, dominate the measured distance between people, as well as composing the most salient dimensions in the trait and feeling space. On the other hand, the clustering of people based on the residual terms is likely to yield a new grouping of the people.

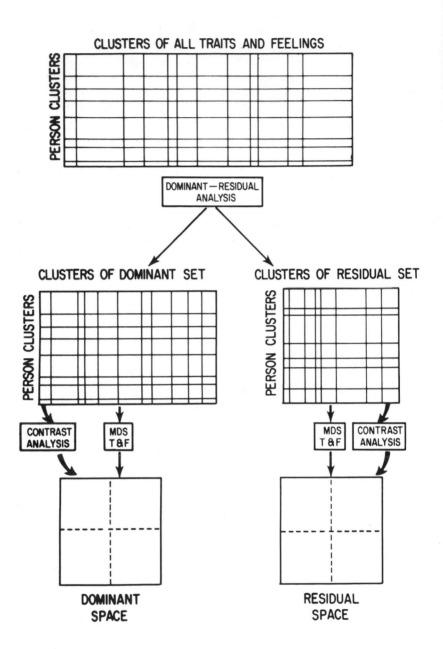

FIG. 3. Scheme of the structural analysis of a subject's protocol.

Contrast Analysis

The search for contrasts among the trait and feeling clusters was inspired by Kelly's proposition that psychological constructs exist in dichotomous form. The reader should, however, take note of at least two important differences between the way these contrasts (dichotomies) are identified in our data and the way they are obtained in the Rep Grid.

First, the poles of the contrasts we identify are clusters of traits and feelings, unlike the Rep Grid, where the dichotomies consist of pairs of single terms or phrases. It turns out that many of the clusters are composed of traits and feelings that could conceivably form more than one construct-contrast pair in the Rep Grid. For example, one of MA's positive clusters consists of *faithful, understanding, sympathetic, warm, kind, intelligent, bright, responsible, admiration* (feeling) which might appear as two (or more) constructs in the Rep Grid, one referring to a concern for others and the other to intellectual competence. Of course, the factorial analysis of the Rep Grid might result in the fusing of these two constructs into one factor that corresponds, more or less, to the grouping obtained from cluster analysis. Nevertheless, differences in methods of data analysis probably result in some differences in the general construct-contrast "factors" that emerge.

Second, unlike the Rep Grid, our format does not ask subjects to form the construct-contrast pairs. Instead, the opposite of a cluster(s) of traits and feelings is empirically identified from the co-occurrence data. That is, a high positive correlation between two (or more) clusters results in their being grouped on one side of a dichotomy; a high negative correlation between two (or more) clusters is the basis for linking them into an opposing pair. Nor does this linking method assure that an opposite will be found for every cluster or group of clusters. That is, clusters are found which do not have a high negative correlation with any other clusters in the protocol. This finding does not, however, refute Kelly's proposition about the dichotomous form of constructs. The opposing pole may simply not be present in the protocol—a fact which, as Kelly pointed out, may have psychological interest.

Finally, regardless of the data-gathering method, the use of clusters rather than single terms to represent the poles of a dichotomy has distinct advantages in interpreting personal constructs. The fact that a single term (or pair of contrasting terms) has several meanings is well known. How does the psychologist, limited by his own construct system, understand a subject's language? As Kelly (1955) noted, the general answer is to note the contexts in which a term occurs—other terms, accompanying nonverbal acts, and so on. A cluster of terms provides such a context for reducing their ambiguity. To cite but one example, for one of our subjects (FB, whom we shall discuss in detail later) *stubborn* appears in the same cluster with *independent, successful, determined, industrious, efficient, practical*, making it unlikely that she is referring to a negativistic (and negative!) trait.

Multidimensional Scaling

This part contains a brief overview of multidimensional scaling. Readers interested in a more complete but nontechnical description of scaling and its application to person perception may consult Rosenberg and Sedlak (1972a). A somewhat more technical discussion of scaling is available in Green and Carmone (1970), and recent technical advances in this area are described in Shepard, Romney, and Nerlove (1972). The particular computer algorithm that we use for scaling is KYST (Kruskal, Young, & Seery, 1973).

The input measure for multidimensional scaling is the same as that for clustering—the δ-measure described earlier. However, multidimensional scaling, in contrast to clustering, generates a spatial configuration of the traits and feelings (or people). A configuration is sought by the computer algorithm so that the interitem distance in the configuration corresponds to the input measure of relatedness. Since the correspondence is rarely perfect but does improve as more dimensions are used, an important question is determining the appropriate number of dimensions for representing the input data. Do the entities fall on a line (one dimension), a plane (two dimensions), etc.? Two criteria are commonly considered in answering this question.

One criterion is that the multidimensional solution consists of as few dimensions as possible. The usual procedure for determining minimal dimensionality is first to obtain a one-dimensional solution, a two-dimensional solution, and so on up to some number of dimensions considered more than sufficient for the input data. A badness-of-fit measure, termed *stress*, is also calculated for each solution. The stress measure is essentially a normalized sum of squared residuals in which 0% stress means that a perfect monotone relation exists between input and output distances. Stress necessarily decreases or remains unchanged with increasing dimensionality, since the fit must improve (or remain unchanged) when more dimensions are used to represent the input data. The *rate* at which stress decreases with increasing dimensionality is useful, however, in determining optimal dimensionality. For example, even though the program will arrange the traits on a line, a plane may be required to capture adequately the distance relations in the input data. The stress measure would usually reflect this fact by decreasing sharply in value between the one- and two-dimensional solutions. If additional dimensions are superfluous—for example, a three-dimensional solution when a two-dimensional solution is adequate—little drop occurs in the stress measure. For the sake of parsimony, the dimensionality after which there is little improvement in fit is chosen as the optimal dimensionality.

The second criterion for estimating the appropriate dimensionality is the psychological interpretability of a configuration. The general rule is that if an n-dimensional configuration can be satisfactorily interpreted but the $(n + 1)$-dimensional configuration reveals no additional meaningful structure, it may be appropriate to stop at the n-dimensional configuration. A variety of empirical aids are available for interpreting a configuration (Rosenberg & Sedlak, 1972a; Shepard, 1972), some of which will be illustrated in the next section.

The relation which is schematized in Figure 3, between the contrasts we extract and the multidimensional scaling of traits and feelings, is also clarified in the next section.

INDIVIDUAL PROTOCOLS—A SAMPLING

The first part of this section describes in detail the results of a structural analysis of each of four subjects protocols, using the methods described in the previous section. Because of the voluminous amount of material involved, the analysis of all 16 subjects cannot be presented in this detail in the present paper. Nevertheless, as we shall see, all four subjects exhibit a number of important similarities, and this gives me confidence that these similarities are indeed quite general. The analysis of all 16 subjects will be made available in published form at a later date.

The structural analysis focuses primarily on the dominant traits and feelings of the four subjects. The reason for this is that the dominant-residual analysis identified only a handful of heterogeneous residual terms in three of the four protocols—hardly worth further analysis. The multidimensional configuration of the residual terms is examined for the one subject whose residual set is sufficiently large to warrant such an analysis. The nature of his residual set and the ways in which it differs from his dominant set illustrate the role of the dominant-residual analysis in clarifying a subject's protocol.

The next section, Toward a Theory of Content, is concerned with the content of the protocols. A category system for the traits and traitlike feelings, based on the data from all 16 subjects, is proposed, along with some speculations for the development of a general theory of content.

Dominant Structure

The traits and feelings in the dominant structure of each of the four subjects are listed in Tables 1, 2, 3, and 4. Two of the subjects are males and two are females. The subject's sex can be identified from the identification initials in the heading of a table; that is, M— is a male subject and F— is a female subject.

The terms in each table are grouped into clusters, according to the clustering analysis. The clusters are grouped, in turn, according to the contrast analysis.

The contrasts are labeled alphabetically. Contrasts in which there is an explicit opposite are listed first. The contrasts are listed in the order of their dominance level. Contrasts without an explicit opposite follow. Again, these latter contrasts are listed in the order of their dominance level. When there are two or more clusters on one side of a contrast, they are listed from most positive to most negative.

Most of the poles in Tables 1–4, whether they have an explicit opposite or not, are labeled as either "positive" or "negative." The basis for these labels is that in each subject's overall hierarchical

Table 1

Results of the Contrast Analysis of MA's Dominant Traits and Feelings

CONTRAST A ($d = 15$)
Positive Pole
    wonderful
    fantastic
    *wonderful
    *fantastic
    *great
(1) *love to be with
    *close
    *easy to under-
        stand
    *worthwhile
    *important

    sincere
    likable
    *friendly
    *like to be with
    *good
(2) *happy
    *respect
    *like
    *interest

    faithful
    understanding
    sympathetic
    warm
(3) kind
    intelligent
    bright
    responsible
    *admiration

Negative Pole
    mediocre
(3) *indifferent
    *bored

    strange
    weird
(2) childish
    dumb
    prejudiced

    irresponsible
    ridiculous
(1) cold
    boring
    *never excited me
    *hate

CONTRAST B ($d = 12$)
Positive Female Pole
    sweet
    pretty
(1F) sexy
    nice-smelling

    large eyes
    shapely
    cute
(2F) big breasts
    beautiful
    good kisser
    *passionate

Negative Female Pole
(1F) stuck up
    small breasts

Positive Male Pole
    individualistic
    clever
    optimistic
(1M) talkative
    easy going
    humorous
    *made me laugh

    nice guy
(2M) handsome
    powerful
    tough

CONTRAST C ($d = 13$)
Positive Female Pole
    exciting

    great smile
(1F) *sad
    *jealousy

    *love
    *exhilarated
(2F) *exciting
    *excited

CONTRAST D ($d = 13$)
Negative Pole
    argumentative
    obstinate
(4) grouchy
    unpredictable
    *wonder

    arrogant
    belligerent
    always in trouble
    wise guy
(3) *disgust
    *dislike
    *can drive up wall
    *can't take some-
        times
    *anger

    straight
    rich
    lookalike
(2) angry
    depressed
    pessimistic

    complains
(1) gets upset
    temperamental

CONTRAST E ($d = 12$)
Negative Pole
    *dejected

Table 1 *(Continued)*

(3) *depressed	CONTRAST F (d = 12)	(2) teacher
*embarrassed	*Negative Pole*	looks like me
*strange	stumpy	*marvelled at
	(1) old	
distant	balding	
*hard to under-		CONTRAST H (d = 10)
stand		*Pole*
*unimportant	CONTRAST G (d = 11)	great laugh
(2) *insignificant	*Positive Pole*	ham
*bewildered	wise	knucklehead
*distant	(1) New York accent	(1) nuts
*uncomfortable	women's libber	drug user
	radical	pot head
(1) *shame		boozer
	brilliant	

Note: d is average dominance level of the terms in a contrast. Value is —log p (see Appendix).

* indicates feeling terms.

Table 2
Results of the Contrast Analysis of MB's Dominant Traits and Feelings

CONTRAST A (d = 14)	(3) high need power	submissive
Positive Pole	manipulative	(1) interested in
honest	egocentric	other's feelings
sensitive to others		quiet
*good	overconfident	
(1) *happiness	fooling self	*Positive Pole (Opposite)*
*sympathetic	oral character	impulsive
*compassion	(2) loud mouth	(1') *cynical
*friendship	immature	*altruism
	boring	
interested	talks behind you	CONTRAST C (d = 14)
kind		*Negative Pole*
(2) helpful	obnoxious	*sorrow
easy to get along	(1) dishonest	*pity
friendly	*disgust	*ashamed
amiable		(3) *threatened
	CONTRAST B (d = 12)	*immature
Negative Pole	*Positive Pole*	*insecure
authoritarian	innocent	*rejection

Table 2 *(Continued)*

		scholarly	CONTRAST G ($d = 11$)
(2)	*antipathy	*esteem	*Positive Pole.*
	*sick	*admiration	fun-loving
			*self-confidence
(1)	*anger	leadership	*intelligent
	*little	(3) *awe	(1) *scholarly
		*eager to learn	*maturity
			*powerful
CONTRAST D ($d = 13$)			*secure
Positive Pole			
	realistic	CONTRAST E ($d = 12$)	CONTRAST H ($d = 10$)
	aware	*Negative Pole*	*Negative Pole*
	mature	obsessive	manic depressive
	self-confident	(1) compulsive	(1) quickly
	skillful	stern	changeable
(1)	intelligence	obsessive/	materialistic
	smart	compulsive	insensitive
	high need ach		
	diligent worker		CONTRAST I ($d = 9$)
	*respect	CONTRAST F ($d = 11$)	*Negative Pole*
	*philosophical	*Positive Pole.*	(1) scatterbrained
		novel	
	sophisticated	(1) love	CONTRAST J ($d = 8$)
	meticulous	*pride in	*Negative Pole*
(2)	reserved	association	(1) mammoth size

Note: d is average dominance level of the terms in a contrast. Value is $-\log p$ (see Appendix).

* indicates feeling terms.

Table 3

Results of the Contrast Analysis of FB's Dominant Traits and Feelings

CONTRAST A ($d = 16$)	*understanding	natural
Positive Pole.	*helpful	fun-loving
*closeness		(3) friendly
*proud	*friendship	*humor
*secure	*happy	*interested
*confident	(2) *accepted	
(1) *concern	*at ease	giving
*involved	*intelligent	(4) loving
*attractive		loyal

Table 3 *(Continued)*

---

*love
(5) *accomplished
*influential

Negative Pole
aloof
(1) condescending
*distant
*uneasy

CONTRAST B ($d = 15$)
Positive Pole.
secure
(1) intuitive
mature
*admiration

Negative Pole
lonely
insecure
(4) immature
defensive
*annoyance

pushy
(3) aggressive
confused
*pity

*anger
(2) *frustration
*upset

arrogant
pedantic
*dislike
(1) *hurt

*unaccepted
*discouraged
*depressed

CONTRAST C ($d = 14$)
Positive Pole
dependable
responsible
honest
proud
active
confident
(1) patient
understanding
thoughtful
considerate
happy
rational
*respect

independent
successful
determined
(2) industrious
efficient
practical
stubborn

Negative Pole
irresponsible
(1) lazy
irrational

CONTRAST D ($d = 11$)
Positive Pole
serious
(1) inhibited

sensitive
attractive

(2) shy
sophisticated

Positive Pole (Opposite)
extroverted
spontaneous
(1') uninhibited
dominating
selfish
extravagant

CONTRAST E ($d = 14$)
Negative Pole
(1) *defensive
*introspective

CONTRAST F ($d = 12$)
Positive Pole
(1) thrifty

CONTRAST G ($d = 10$)
Positive Pole
imaginative
(1) talented
creative

CONTRAST H ($d = 10$)
Negative Pole
(1) emotional
dependent

CONTRAST I ($d = 9$)
Negative Pole
(1) secretive
*indifference

Note: d is average dominance level of the terms in a contrast. Value is $-\log p$ (see Appendix).

* indicates feeling terms.

Table 4

Results of the Contrast Analysis of FC's Dominant Traits and Feelings

CONTRAST A (d = 16)
Positive Pole.
    sweet
    *relaxed
    *loving
    *closeness
(1) *uninhibited
    *comfortable
    *warmth
    *spontaneity
    *happy

    cute
    happy
    *lightness
(2) *playful
    *entertaining
    *hip
    *respected

    easy-going
    gentle
    good-natured
(3) kind
    friendly
    *friendly
    *confident

    loving
    romantic
    intuitive
    a dreamer
    perceptive
(4) understanding
    *fraternity
    *openness
    *fondness
    *honesty
    *frankness
    *caring

    emotional
    caring
    sensitive

(5) *gentle
    *sensitivity
    *understanding
    *kind

Negative Pole
    spoiled
    childish
    controlling
    egotistical
    self-centered
    bourgeois
    macho
    domineering
(2) *superficial
    *cautious
    *unsettled
    *uneasiness
    *interrogated
    *competitive
    *inhibited
    *uncomfortable
    *defensive

    fake
    *mistrust
(1) *coolness
    *guarded
    *dislike
    *disgusted

CONTRAST B (d = 15)
Positive Pole
    strong
    mature
    independent
    introspective
(1) hard-working
    clever
    intelligent
    serious
    intense
    *serious
    *intense

    talented
    globally
    passionate
(2) abstract
    philosophical
    introspective

Negative Pole
    narrow-minded
    superficial
    dull
    immature
(1) dependent
    fearful
    stagnate
    *boredom
    *numb
    *pity

CONTRAST C (d = 14)
Positive Pole
    carefree
    earthy
    mellow
    political
(1) successful
    *mellow
    *admiration
    *extroverted
    *important

Negative Pole
    demanding
    hot-tempered
    uptight
    insecure
(1) neurotic
    narcissistic
    possessive
    *inspective
    *aloof

Table 4 *(Continued)*

CONTRAST D (*d* = 12)
Positive Pole.
    talkative
    aggressive
(1) attractive
    outgoing
    humorous
    *amused

    gregarious
(2) extroverted
    *childish

Opposite Pole
    depressive
    nervous
(1) a loner
    introverted
    *consoling

CONTRAST E (*d* = 14)
Positive Male Pole
    exciting
    *giddy
(1M) *security
    *excited
    *romantic
    *sexually aroused

    sexy
(2M) sensuous
    *sexy
    *dramatic

CONTRAST F (*d* = 14)
Positive Pole
    impulsive
(1) restless
    reckless

    eccentric
(2) crazy
    fragile
    *cosmically
      connected

CONTRAST G (*d* = 13)
Pole
    hyper
    stubborn
(1) strong-willed
    moody
    *hyper

CONTRAST H (*d* = 13)
Negative Pole
    crafty
    *nervous
    *clumsy
(1) *frustration
    *drained
    *puzzled
    *depressed

CONTRAST I (*d* = 11)
Negative Pole
    *possessive
    *jealous

    *hurt
(1) *bitter
    *inferior
    *stupid
    *insecurity
    *upset

CONTRAST J (*d* = 11)
Positive Pole
    *mature
(1) *aggressive
    *quick-witted
    *witty

CONTRAST K (*d* = 9)
Negative Pole
    straight
    naive
    inhibited
(1) shy
    passive
    mothering
    *protective

    scatter-brained
(2) subordinating
    *superior

CONTRAST L (*d* = 8)
Negative Pole
    *shy
(1) *passive
    *political

Note: *d* is average dominance level of the terms in a contrast. Value is $-\log p$ (see Appendix).

  * indicates feeling terms.

clustering, the positive clusters merge to form one major grouping and negative clusters merge to form a second major grouping—just as we observed in Figure 2 for subject MA. Evaluatively neutral or ambiguous clusters sometimes form a third major grouping. Neutral or ambiguous poles are not labeled as either positive or negative in the tables.

The positive, negative, and neutral groups can be conveniently displayed without reproducing the entire hierarchical clustering. These three groups of clusters can be displayed within the multidimensional configuration, as we shall see in a moment.

The justification for contrast analysis from a psychological point of view requires more than a listing of single contrasts. In the dominant set, for example, these contrasts seem to be the psychological building blocks of an evaluative gestalt. It is this type of structural significance of contrasts that Kelly (1955) seemed to have in mind when he proposed the concept of dichotomous constructs and postulated a superordinate relation among these constructs in his Organization Corollary. However, Kelly's notion of "superordinate relation" is not sufficiently explicated to provide a detailed model of the organization among several interrelated contrasts, considered simultaneously.

A multidimensional configuration of contrasts and the clusters that comprise them is *one* way of representing the relations among contrasts.

The two-dimensional configurations of the clusters that comprise each of the contrasts are shown for each of the four subjects in Figures 4, 5, 6, and 7. The four figures correspond to Tables 1, 2, 3, and 4, respectively. Each cluster of traits and feelings is represented by a point—the average location of the traits and feelings that comprise that cluster. For example, in Table 1, MA's most positive cluster in Contrast A—*wonderful, fantastic, . . . worthwhile, important*—is represented in Figure 4 by the point labeled (A, + 1).

The grouping of clusters into positive, negative, and neutral, to which I referred earlier, is also shown in each of the figures. Positive traits and feelings are in one part of the space and negative traits and feelings are in another part. This observation is readily verified empirically by fitting the subject's likability ratings for traits and his/her pleasantness ratings for feelings to the configuration. (This is not to suggest, however, that "likability" and "pleasantness" are necessarily the best ways of labeling the evaluative dimension, a point that will be discussed later.) The best fitting axis for each property is shown in the figures. (See Rosenberg & Sedlak, 1972a, for a description of the fitting procedure.) The angle between the

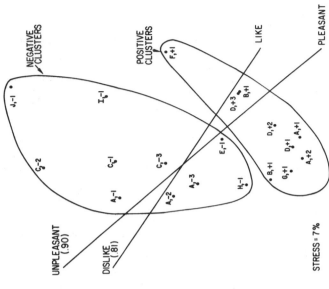

FIG. 5. Subject MB's two-dimensional configuration of the clusters of his dominant traits and feelings. (The content of each cluster is given in Table 2.)

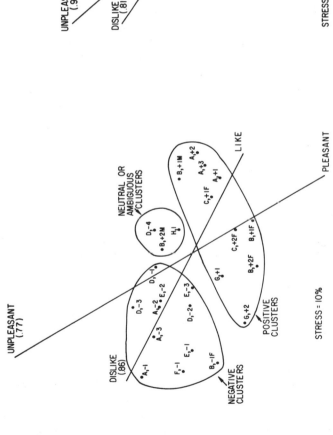

FIG. 4. Subject MA's two-dimensional configuration of the clusters of his dominant traits and feelings. (The content of each cluster is given in Table 1.)

axis for likableness (traits) and the axis for pleasantness (feelings) varies from 5 to 32 degrees in the four two-dimensional configuratins. These small angles simply indicate that, in general, positive traits and feelings tend to go together and that negative traits and feelings tend to go together.

The value associated with each axis in the figures is a multiple R which indicates the degree to which the property actually corresponds to the location of the traits (or feelings) in the configuration. The multiple R is quite high in most cases. Nor do the R values shown in the figures necessarily represent a maximum—only a maximum when the multidimensional solution is constrained to two dimensions. For example, MA's multiple R for pleasantness increases from .77 to .84 in three dimensions. Similarly, FB's multiple R for likableness increases from .71 to .83 in three dimensions. There is little question that evaluation is a very strong general (superordinate) dimension in all the configurations, apparently the most permeable of constructs.

Are there other general dimensions more or less orthogonal to evaluation? If there are, they do not reveal themselves as readily by inspection as the evaluative dimension does. According to the stress (badness-of-fit) values, an adequate representation of the input distance data requires a space of at least two dimensions. In fact, a more adequate representation of the input data usually requires a space of three dimensions. The configurations presented here (Figures 4–7) are in two dimensions because of the problem of representing, on a flat piece of paper, all the information shown in these figures for configurations of higher dimensionality. Apparently, the multidimensionality is required to accommodate the interrelated contrasts within the positive and negative traits and feelings. A subset of the clusters within the positive (or negative) set does sometimes form a construct-contrast pair—for example, the sex contrast within MA's Contrast B. However, it is not clear whether the different evaluative contrasts are themselves implicitly ordered along some general psychological dimension or dimensions.

In summary, the multidimensional model can be viewed as a model in which there is a superordinate contrast—evaluation—composed of subordinate contrasts whose relations are represented by their proximity in the space. I am using evaluation here to explicate the model, but the structure being discussed is quite general—any psychological dimension with interrelated contrasts can be accommodated by this model.

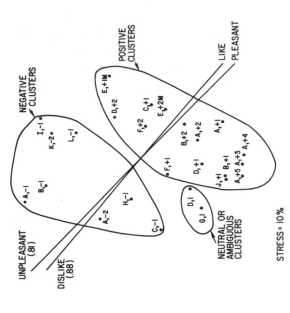

FIG. 7. Subject FB's two-dimensional configuration of the clusters of her dominant traits and feelings. (The content of each cluster is given in Table 4.)

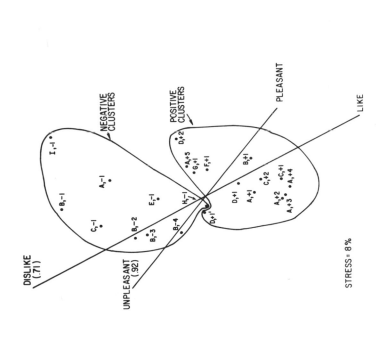

FIG. 6. Subject FB's two-dimensional configuration of the clusters of her dominant traits and feelings. (The content of each cluster is given in Table 3.)

A multidimensional configuration of contrasts provides only a first approximation to representing their interrelations. That is, relative proximity in a multidimensional space may be the result of a variety of relations among scaled terms. Multidimensional scaling places the terms in a space on the basis of their overall profile similarity. Except for revealing a general superordinate contrast such as evaluation, multidimensional scaling does not seem to help in discovering additional superordinate relations among the contrasts that comprise the evaluative gestalt.

What is an alternative approach for discovering the relations among contrasts? I have just begun to take up this question. I plan to examine contrasts two at a time, using two-way clustering, in an effort to discover the relations between them. Nor do I think that it will be necessary to pick pairs of contrasts haphazardly. I think that the most dominant contrast (Contrast A in Tables 1–4) is a superordinate contrast, from which the others may be "hanging off" as subordinates.

"Anatomy" of a Contrast

I would now like to show, with a couple of illustrations, the structure *within* a contrast. This can be done with a two-way clustering that is limited to the content of a single contrast. Two contrasts were selected where both poles are present in the subject's protocol.

Figures 8 and 9 show the two-way clustering for the first two of MA's contrasts. The rows and columns of Contrast A (Figure 8) are permuted according to likableness. The rows of Contrast B (Figure 9) are permuted according to sex and the columns according to evaluation within sex.

Figure 8 shows a number of properties of Contrast A that are of interest structurally. First, we see that the dichotomy is graded, with the extremely positive people receiving both the positive and very-positive traits and feelings. Similarly, (but not as extensive in content) the extremely negative people are not given any positive attributions. Second, there are clusters of people about whom MA is ambivalent: they are given both positive and negative traits and feelings but not the extreme ones. Third, the subject's rating of "likableness" does an adequate, but not optimal, job in ordering the rows and columns to form the type of diagonal to which I am referring. That is, the

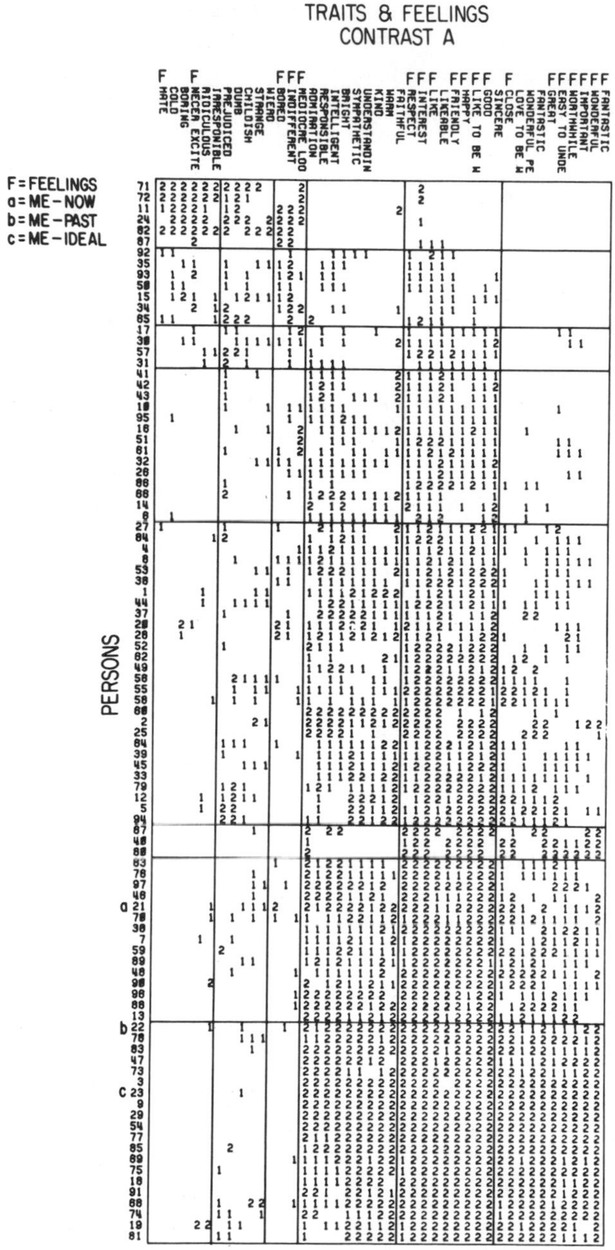

TRAITS & FEELINGS
CONTRAST A

F = FEELINGS
a = ME – NOW
b = ME – PAST
c = ME – IDEAL

PERSONS

FIG. 8. Two-way clustering of subject MA's most dominant contrast (Contrast A, Table 1).

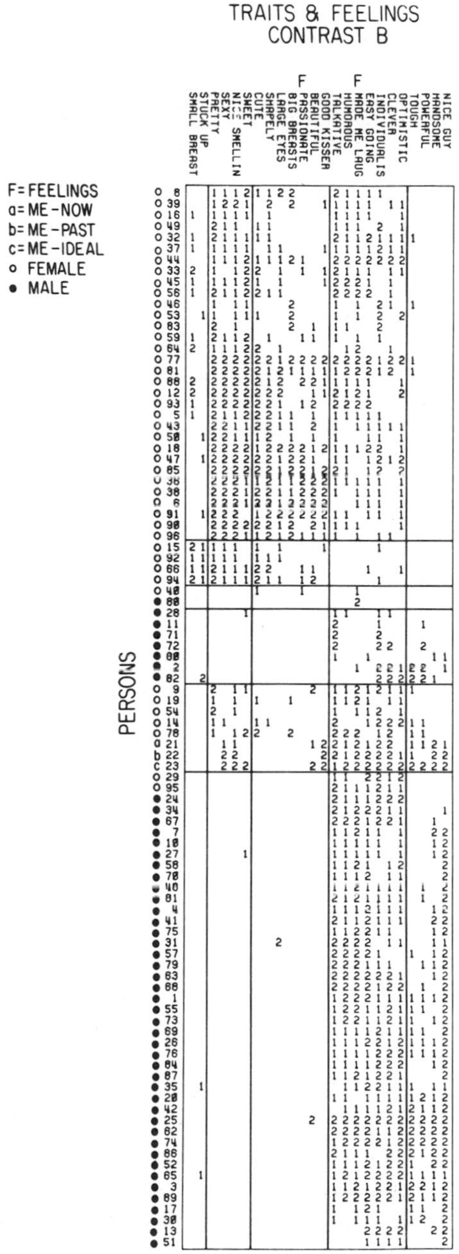

TRAITS & FEELINGS
CONTRAST B

F = FEELINGS
a = ME - NOW
b = ME - PAST
c = ME - IDEAL
o FEMALE
● MALE

PERSONS

FIG. 9. Two-way clustering of subject MA's sex contrast (Contrast B, Table 1).

subject's underlying evaluative construct is only being approximated with the concept of "likableness." Finally, the location of the selves are shown. They are all positive, but "me-now" is not as positive as either the past or ideal self. The location of other significant figures is not shown, although this would be of considerable interest in a systematic analysis of the composition of people clusters.

The structure of the sex contrast in Figure 9 is particularly clear and requires little comment. It is interesting to note that the three selves are not in the all-male cluster of people but are instead in a cluster with five females. I have been offered a number of dynamic interpretations of this result. The structural information does not, per se, provide a basis for resolving which interpretations are the more valid ones.

The two contrasts displayed in Figures 8 and 9 suggest two general types of relations between the clusters that comprise a bipolar contrast: *subset/superset* and *disjunctive*. The subset/super-set relation is most clearly exemplified in Figure 8 by the last two column clusters; that is, the last column cluster *(close, love to, . . . wonderful, fantastic)* implies the presence of the next to last column cluster *(respect, interest, . . . good, sincere)*, but not vice versa. The disjunctive relation is clearly exemplified in Figure 8 by the first and last column clusters; that is, the presence of one cluster implies the absence of the other, and vice versa. There is also the *equivalence* relation between terms *within* a cluster. These three general types of relations—subset/superset, disjunctive, equivalence —were also identified by R. D'Andrade (unpublished manuscript) as the basic relations in a belief structure concerned with folk disease terms (D'Andrade, Quinn, Nerlove, & Romney, 1972).

What is the nature of the beliefs that give rise to these various co-occurrence patterns? Consider the equivalence relation. Why do two (or more) traits that seemingly refer to different content areas end up in the same cluster? Is it that the people described by the subject happen to have such combinations but the subject doesn't believe that these traits necessarily go together: for example, the people we happen to know both speak and write English but we can imagine people who do one but not the other? Or does the subject "believe" that one trait implies the other and vice versa? Or are trait clusters the result of linguistic habit? These questions are also applicable to the disjunctive relation, except that in this case we would ask whether the subject believes that a trait in one cluster implies the absence of a trait in another cluster, and vice versa. In the case of a subset/superset relation, does the subject believe that the presence of one cluster of traits is a necessary but not sufficient condition for the presence of another cluster of traits? Or, again, is it the result of the particular people the subject knows?

A variety of empirical strategies is available for answering these questions. One of the more promising possibilities is the application of Asch's (1946) classic paradigm for studying personality impressions. Basically, the application of this paradigm would be as follows. The investigator describes a hypothetical person with a subset of traits (and feelings) from the subject's own vocabulary. The investigator then tests for the impressions formed with another subset of his traits (and feelings). The particular terms chosen for the stimulus set and for the test set are determined by the type of relation under study.

Suppose, for example, we took the stimulus and test terms from the same cluster. If the subject believes that they actually imply each other, he should attribute the test terms to the person described. Also, interchanging which are test terms and which are stimulus terms should make no difference. This finding would not rule out linguistic habit as an explanation, but a definitive test of this possibility has long eluded investigators in this area (D'Andrade, 1965; Loehlin, 1961, 1967; Mulaik, 1964). If we took stimulus and test terms from two clusters that stand in a subset/superset relation, we could test whether the subject actually makes asymmetric inferences that correspond to this relation.

I think that the questions posed above about the nature of the beliefs that give rise to the various co-occurrence patterns are of fundamental importance to a comprehensive analysis of implicit personality theory. I don't believe, however, that these questions could have been sensibly approached empirically until the structural analysis had been developed to identify the contrasts and to display the various relations that exist within a contrast.

Residuals

The structure of the residual set is instructive when it contains an adequate number of terms for a structural analysis. A useful consequence of such an analysis from a methodological standpoint is

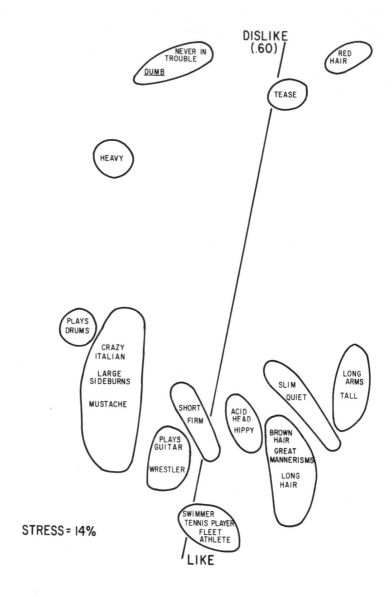

FIG. 10. Subject MA's two-dimensional configuration of his residual traits and feelings. The results of a clustering analysis are also shown in the configuration. The underlined term is a feeling; the remaining terms are traits.

to compare the content and structure of the residual set with that of the dominant set; that is, to verify that the partitioning is not merely a statistical artifact but does, in fact, represent different aspects of person perception.

MA's residual set of 26 terms is sufficiently large to warrant such a structural analysis. His two-dimensional configuration of residual terms is shown in Figure 10. The results of a clustering analysis of these terms are also shown in Figure 10 by listing the terms in a cluster within an enclosed area. The exact location of individual terms within each cluster area is not shown in the configuration. While this information could have been shown, there is very little lost by not doing so. It is well known that the small distances in a multidimensional configuration are not very reliable.

First, we may note that the content of his residual set contains a large number of physical traits (e.g., *red hair, slim, heavy*, etc.) and traits that refer to athletics and certain specific skills (e.g., *tennis player, plays guitar*, etc.). Evaluation, although present from a statistical standpoint, is considerably weaker in the residual set than it is in the dominant set; that is, the R of .60 for likableness is statistically significant but considerably smaller than the R of .86 for the same property fitted to the dominant terms (see Figure 4). Moreover, the R for the residual terms does not increase substantially in higher dimensions; even in five dimensions, the R is only .67.

Second, the importance of the residual traits is apparently less than that of the dominant terms. This was verified by asking MA to rate (on a 7-point scale) the importance of all the traits on his final list. A t test comparing the importance ratings of the dominant terms with those of the residual terms yields a value of 6.65 ($p < .001$). The average importance rating for the dominant traits is 4.6 and for the residual traits 2.0, where 1 is least important and 7 is most important.

Third, feeling terms are almost completely absent from the residual terms.

Finally, I would like to return to the question of whether the dominant-residual analysis identifies and removes the traits and feelings that confuse the conceptual homogeneity of certain clusters. Let us look at the data from Subject MA. The residuals are identified in Figure 2 with an asterisk. On an intuitive basis, at least, removing residual terms from certain clusters increases the conceptual homogeneity of certain clusters. Also, when the residual terms alone are reanalyzed with hierarchical clustering, new groupings emerge that make a number of the residual clusters in Figure 2 a less confusing conglomerate. To cite but one example, note in Figure 10 that *red hair* becomes an isolate while *dumb* (feeling) forms a two-element cluster with *never in trouble*.

The value of removing the residual terms from the total set obviously depends on the composition of a particular subject's protocol. For MA, it proved highly useful. For other subjects, where the number of residual terms is small, the partitioning is not as crucial.

TOWARD A THEORY OF CONTENT

As we have already seen, a general evaluative dimension appears in the structure of all four of the subjects that were selected for detailed analysis. The fact is that, without exception, evaluation is the strongest general dimension in the structure of each of the 16 subjects in the total sample.

The evaluative dimension found in these protocols is, of course, the same as Osgood's evaluative factor. This raises the question of whether Osgood's three semantic factors—evaluation, potency, and activity—can provide the basis for a content theory of person perception. The evidence from a number of studies summarized by Rosenberg and Sedlak (1972a) indicates that, while the semantic differential provides a satisfactory interpretive scheme for structures obtained from fixed-format methods it does not hold up as well in naturalistic or free-response data. Except for evaluation, which shows up as a strong dimension regardless of the data-gathering technique, semantic differential factors are weakly represented and/or are not orthogonal to evaluation in free-response data. This conclusion also seems to be supported by the findings described in the present paper. As I noted earlier, the multidimensionality in the subjects' structures seems to be required in order to accommodate the interrelated but distinct content within the positive and negative traits and feelings, rather than to represent additional general dimensions orthogonal to evaluation. The fact that the three semantic differential factors emerge from fixed-format studies may be due to the way investigators sample trait terms and/or to the aggregation of data over subjects. In any case, these three factors do not seem to provide a universal basis for interpreting the content of person perception.

What is a reasonable alternative to a set of general psychological dimensions to characterize the content of person perception? One possibility is in the analysis of the content that comprises the evaluative dimension. That is, although the content of the evaluative dimension varies from subject to subject, there are recurrent areas of content—areas that refer to competence, maturity, integrity, sociability, and so on. The ubiquity of the evaluative dimension and the presence of recurrent evaluative content provide the beginnings of an alternative approach to a theory of content.

I would like to turn, therefore, to a tentative categorization of the traits and the traitlike feelings (e.g., *intelligent, mature, attractive, warm*) that the 16 subjects frequently report in their affective descriptions of themselves. This categorization is not intended to include all the affects such as *anger, fear, excitement*, etc. that may be associated with a subject's perception of certain traits in others. The category system for traits and traitlike feelings is summarized in Table 5, with positive and negative examples of each.

Our work on a category system for the trait terms found in these protocols is very similar in intent to Landfield's (1971) investigations into the content of personal constructs in the Rep Grid. There is, in fact, considerable overlap between his category system and ours, although the exact wording of certain categories may be different. The overlap is particularly notable because the two systems were derived independently and from different data bases. Landfield's empirical efforts to substantiate his system are much more extensive than our own, although much remains to be done to assure a system that adequately captures the meanings of the subject's language.

Nevertheless, I cannot resist at least some preliminary theoretical speculations about the underlying sources of the trait categories that are observed in the subjects' descriptions. I discern at least two important areas of self-concern that are reflected in an individual's perceptions of self and others. These two areas of concern are, for want of better terms: (a) *being accepted, intimate;* (b) *being competent and successful in certain domains.*

Some evidence for this dichotomy in person perception can be found in an early study by Rosenberg et al. (1968). The results of a reanalysis of the data in that study using cluster analysis are

Table 5

*Major Categories for Traits and Traitlike Feelings in a
College Student Sample*

Categories	Positive Examples	Negative Examples
Intellectual Competence and Achievement	intelligent talented knows a lot	unintelligent ignorant
Maturity	mature	immature childish
Attractiveness (male & female)	handsome beautiful attractive shapely good physique	ugly fat unattractive
Integrity	honest sincere truthful	dishonest insincere liar phony
Sociability	friendly warm witty social sensitivity	unfriendly cold dull social insensitivity
Concern for Others	kind generous sympathetic	unkind unsympathetic
Psychological Stability	"together"	neurotic

summarized in Figure 11. The major clusters of traits that emerged
are shown in the figure. The first branching partitions the traits into
two groups, one positive and one negative. The next partitioning
within each group appears to correspond to the distinction proposed
above, and the clusters are labeled as "Social Clusters" and "Competence Clusters," respectively. The third partitioning shown in
Figure 11 reveals certain additional distinctions within each of the
four major groupings. Additional subgroups would be revealed if
the entire hierarchical clustering were displayed in the figure.
However, the content of the terms used by Rosenberg et al. (1968) is

not as extensive as that found with the current free-response method. A number of general trait categories listed in Table 5 are either weakly represented or not present at all among the terms listed in Figure 11. The reason is simply that the trait vocabulary was selected by the investigators for a fixed-format method and not by the subjects themselves. While this limitation underscores the value of the free-response approach, the major groupings that emerged from the Rosenberg et al. (1968) study support the general thesis outlined above.

In the free-response protocols described in this paper, the concern within acceptance and intimacy is also reflected in traits such as *friendly, warm, kind, sympathetic, loving* (and their opposites) and in feelings that express similar traits in the self with respect to certain others, that is, feeling *friendly, warm,* and so on. The students' concern with competence and achievement is reflected in the perception of intellectual accomplishment, maturity, and perhaps attractiveness and interpersonal integrity as well. Outer-directed feelings such as *awe, admiration,* and *respect* (*envy,* also) on the positive side, and *contempt* and *disgust,* on the negative side, identify particular areas of competence and achievement that are important to a subject. The free-response feeling protocols also allow us to observe directly a subject's concern with his own competence (self-worth), sometimes with and sometimes without explicit mention of the traits in the self or others that are associated with these feelings: *worthwhile, proud, important* versus *inferior, shame, guilt, unimportant.*

I should note that the two basic concerns outlined above—and indeed the various content categories listed in Table 5—are generally interwoven psychologically. This is not to say that individuals cannot distinguish between competence and acceptance, or among the constructs within each of these two general domains. However, many of the clusters that are observed in the data are mixtures of two or more content areas. Of course, individuals differ in the extent to which they separate content in their everyday perceptions. A few highlights and examples from Tables 1 to 4 will suffice to illustrate these points.

In all four cases, the positive pole of the most dominant contrast (Contrast A) refers primarily to traits of sociability and concern for others. Feelings of friendship and concern are also found in this contrast. Additional content in Contrast A varies somewhat from subject

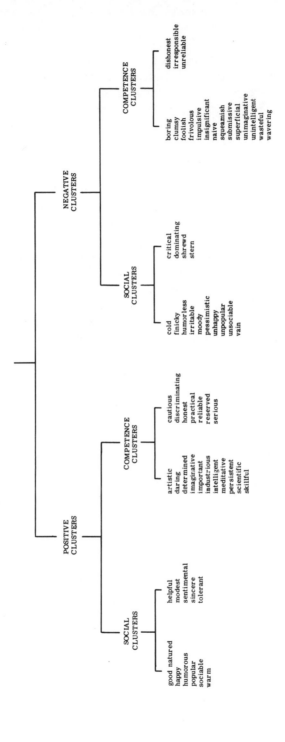

FIG. 11. Major clusters of the traits used in the Rosenberg et al. (1968) study.

to subject. For some, intellectual competence and integrity are included in Contrast A; for others, these categories, particularly intellectual competence, are part of other contrasts. In MB's protocol (Table 2), intellectual competence is in Contrast D; in FB's protocol (Table 3), intellectual competence is in Contrast G; for FC (Table 4), it is in Contrast B (and, as in MB's protocol, it is mixed with maturity). Sexually related contrasts, when they occur, tend to be most pure in content. This type of contrast appears in the protocols of two of the four subjects: MA (Contrasts B and C) and FC (Contrast E). Finally, the perception of psychological stability appears in some cases but rarely forms a separate contrast.

A category system for the content of perception and speculations about the link between interpersonal perception and self-concerns are but the first steps in constructing a theory of content. While no one set of studies can provide a definitive answer to the nature of content universals, I do believe that the cumulative effect of a number of studies, each involving a sample of individuals from a different population, will be instrumental in developing and elaborating a general theory of content. The concern with maturity, for example, which is frequently observed in college students, may undergo interesting age related changes. The self-concerns of an individual may always include conceptions of what one is like (and should be like) during any given chronological period, but maturity in older adults (and young children) is not necessarily expressed in terms of *dependable, responsible, serious, childish, egocentric,* and *demanding.*

FUTURE DIRECTIONS

The work described in this paper gives rise to a variety of methodological and theoretical questions, a number of which have already been mentioned. These questions will be summarized in the first part of this section. The methodological developments that have been described also provide new tools for studying the relations between implicit personality theory and everyday social interaction. The nature of these relations, with special attention to the possible connections between implicit personality theory and the acquaintance process, will be taken up in the second part of the section.

Methodological and Theoretical Questions

On the methodological side, there is the need for (a) a continuing analysis and critique of data-gathering methods (including the use of completely naturalistic methods as one way of "checking on" laboratory-based formats and their analyses); (b) a better understanding of the ad hoc methods of dominant-residual analysis and contrast analysis. I shall not dwell any further on these problems here, since they have already been discussed earlier in the paper.

On the theoretical side, there are many interesting and diverse questions. These questions can be classified into three general areas: (a) structural theory, (b) a theory of content, and (c) the relations between implicit personality theory and the information-processing models of the social psychologist.

With regard to structural theory, one of the key tasks is to develop detailed models to represent the structural relations among and within contrasts—in effect, to elaborate Kelly's concepts of dichotomous constructs and the superordinate relations among them. One approach to the investigation of structural relations among contrasts, which was outlined in the paper, is an empirical and conceptual analysis of pairs of contrasts, guided by the idea that the most dominant contrast may be playing a key role in these structural relations. Relational concepts such as superordinate/subordinate, disjunctive, and equivalence for the analysis of a single contrast—the "anatomy" of a contrast, as it was termed—were also outlined. In this connection, a number of questions were also raised about the beliefs that underly the structural patterns found in a contrast, and a research paradigm was proposed, based on Asch's (1946) classic work, for answering such questions.

With regard to a theory of content, little is known about the universals of content in interpersonal perception. The cumulative effect of studying populations different from college students would be of considerable help in discovering the basic content categories of person perception. I have also speculated in the paper that the content of an individual's perception of self and others is the result of the individual's self-concerns, and that a knowledge of these self-concerns would explicate the content of person perception.

Relations between self-concerns and implicit personality theory can be studied directly and is, in fact, the subject of a doctoral thesis being conducted in our laboratories by Sam Kingsley. The first step in this research has been to identify the elements and relations of an individual's self-conception—his *implicit self-theory*, as we have dubbed it. We assume that a self-conception actually consists of a set of multiple selves, and that each self can be identified by the way an individual perceives himself vis-à-vis another person that he knows. One could also include self-conceptions of the individual when he is alone in various situations, but the social selves are likely to reflect the most important aspects of self-conception. Thus, the methods for studying implicit self-theory parallel those developed for studying implicit personality theory. That is, the individual describes his perception of himself with each of a number of people that he knows. Actually, the feeling protocols described earlier in this paper can be viewed as elements in the structure of implicit self-theory, particularly when they include traitlike terms (e.g., feeling *intelligent, attractive, bossy*), which they usually do (see Tables 1–4). These feeling protocols are often fragmentary, however, in the number and range of traitlike terms, and more explicit self-characterizations are necessary for a complete analysis. The structure and content of these self-characterizations may then be compared directly with those obtained from the individual's descriptions of others.

With regard to the third set of theoretical questions—the relations between implicit personality theory and information processing models—I do not have much to say except to register the need to connect these two domains. The integration of the information-processing models of the social psychologist with structural and content theory promises to be a difficult, albeit worthwhile, task, as we discovered in a recent workshop devoted to this problem (Anderson & Rosenberg, 1975). By "information processing," I am referring to the work of N. H. Anderson and others (see Anderson, 1973, for a recent review) who have developed highly sophisticated models of how an individual combines information about a stimulus person to form an overall impression. A related concern but quite different in its mode of conception is that of Schmidt (in press). He is attempting to develop a theoretical account of how an individual infers the motives and plans of another from the other's acts. In short, what are the relations between a person's observations of another (the "stimulus" side), the way he processes this information, and the beliefs he holds about people?

Implicit Personality Theory and Social Interaction

The connections between implicit personality theory and other important social psychological phenomena is an essential task for future research. A number of ideas for studying these connections, with particular reference to the acquaintance process, are outlined in the remainder of this section.

The acquaintance process is a continuous psychological process of an individual vis-à-vis another. A key feature of this process is the social decisions that the individual makes. Social decisions involve, in most general terms, the choice between approach (interacting with the other) and avoidance (not interacting with the other). Ambivalence is a combination of these two choices and is distinguishable from indifference, which is the absence of approach-avoidance conflict. Approach and avoidance are assumed to coordinate with the superordinate dimension of evaluation (positive and negative, respectively) found in the structural analyses. Ambivalence is also found in the structures as combinations of certain positive and negative trait and feeling clusters. (See, for example, the positive and negative traits and feelings associated with certain people clusters in MA's dominant contrast, Figure 8.) These coordinations provide the first link between structure and social decisions.

Concepts of approach and avoidance imply that interpersonal behavior is concerned with the attainment of certain positive experiences and the avoidance of certain negative ones. It is assumed that these experiences can be particularized (classified) in terms of the attainment or avoidance of specific interpersonal feelings— friendship, happiness, excitement, fear, sadness, love, respect, self-respect, worthlessness, anger, and so on. Thus, the "goals" of interaction for an individual are assumed to coordinate with the affective categories found in an individual's structure.

Social decisions are made as a consequence of interaction, and/or on the basis of indirect information about the other when interaction does not or cannot occur, as, for example, from descriptions by a third person, or from mass media. The perceived characteristics of the other elicit the feelings referred to above, and hence determine the social decisions that the perceiver makes.

The trait terms in an individual's protocol are assumed to refer to these perceived characteristics (behavior configurations, really). Since everyday trait language is not very precise and since the subject is probably not exhaustive in his coding of relevant characteristics, we have only a hazy idea of what referent behavior is actually being encoded by the perceiver. The particular characteristics in another that elicit certain feelings (or constellations of feelings) also vary from individual to individual. A "bossy person," for example, may make one individual angry and another individual depressed. Thus, the inclusion of feelings into the structure of implicit personality theory may yield clearer relationships between social interaction and implicit personality theory than the trait structure alone.

If this general framework relating structure and interaction is correct, it should be possible to trace the acquaintance process in terms of the traits and feelings that an individual attributes to other people. As an individual becomes acquainted with another, the other would be expected to move from one existing cluster of people (the row groupings in a two-way clustering) into another, eventually reaching some stable location.

There are a number of interesting questions about the nature of these movements. How soon does a new acquaintance reliably match the characteristics of an existing people cluster? What are these initial clusters? How predictable is a shift from one people cluster to another, given the present location of the acquaintance?

While it is possible to answer these questions by studying the acquaintance process in everyday life, it usually takes a long time for impressions to firm up and stabilize. A more feasible possibility is the use of an encounter-group format, because the acquaintance process is compressed into a relatively short period and involves significant aspects of the other. Also, all the individuals involved are available for study, not just the perceiver.

If we obtain each individual's structure before the group is formed, using the methods described in this paper, and then obtain his descriptions of the group members at periodic intervals, it is possible to locate each person in the encounter group in terms of the perceiver's existing clusters. Methods for locating new persons in a structure have been developed by statisticians and extensively applied by the numerical taxonomists (Sneath & Sokal, 1973, ch. 8). Their applications stem from an interest (analogous to ours) in identifying with formal methods the location of an organism within an existing taxonomic system. These methods also include estimates of the probability of a correct identification, which, in our application, indicates the reliability of the assignment of an acquaintance to a people cluster. Thus, the location of an acquaintance and the temporal course of the acquaintance process can be expressed with a good deal of precision.

In terms of the trait and feeling structure, I would conjecture that the location of an acquaintance is reliably determined first in the subject's most dominant contrast (i.e., Contrast A, Tables 1–4), and then in certain other contrasts. Moreover, I think that the evaluative location of the acquaintance within the most dominant contrast is predictive of his evaluative location in other contrasts. Other contrasts, depending on their content, may or may not be relevant to a particular acquaintance. A heterosexual contrast, for example, which is evaluative is not relevant to same-sex acquaintances. The temporal course of the acquaintance process can be tracked in terms of the contrasts in the subject's structure.

REFERENCES

Allport, G. W. *Letters from Jenny.* New York: Harcourt, Brace & World, 1965.

Anderson, N. H. Cognitive algebra: Integration theory applied to social attribution. In L. Berkowitz (Ed.), *Advances in experimental social psychology* (Vol. 7). New York: Academic Press, 1973. Pp. 1–101.

Anderson, N. H., & Rosenberg, S. Workshop on Mathematical Approaches in Person Perception. Final report to the National Science Foundation, 1975.

Asch, S. E. Forming impressions of personality. *Journal of Abnormal and Social Psychology,* 1946, **41,** 258–290.

Bannister, D. An application of personal construct theory (Kelly) to schizoid thinking. Unpublished doctoral dissertation, University of London, 1959.

Bannister, D. The genesis of schizophrenic thought disorder: Re-test of the serial invalidation hypothesis. *British Journal of Psychiatry,* 1963, **109,** 680.

Bannister, D., & Mair, J. M. M. *The evaluation of personal constructs.* London: Academic Press, 1968.

Beach, L., & Wertheimer, M. A. A free-response approach to the study of person cognition. *Journal of Abnormal and Social Psychology,* 1961, **62,** 367–374.

Carroll, J. D. Individual differences and multidimensional scaling. In R. N. Shepard, A. K. Romney, & S. B. Nerlove (Eds.), *Multidimensional scaling: Theory and applications in the behavioral sciences.* Vol. I. *Theory.* New York: Seminar Press, 1972. Pp. 105–155.

Carroll, J. D., & Chang, J. -J. Analysis of individual differences in multidimensional scaling via an n-way generalization of "Eckart-Young" decomposition. *Psychometrika,* 1970, **35**, 283–319.

D'Andrade, R. G. Trait psychology and componential analysis. *American Anthropologist,* 1965, **67**, 215–228.

D'Andrade, R. G., Quinn, N. R., Nerlove, S. B., & Romney, A. K. Categories of disease in American-English and Mexican-Spanish. In A. K. Romney, R. N. Shepard, & S. B. Nerlove (Eds.), *Multidimensional scaling: Theory and applications in the behavioral sciences.* Vol. II. *Applications.* New York: Seminar Press, 1972. Pp. 9–54.

Degerman, R. L. Transformation of a dendrogram to fit a specific left-to-right ordering. *Classification Society Bulletin,* 1973, **3**, 33.

Dornbusch, S. M., Hastorf, A. H., Richardson, S. A., Muzzy, R. E., & Vreeland, R. S. The perceiver and the perceived: Their relative influence on the categories of interpersonal cognition. *Journal of Personality and Social Psychology,* 1965, **1**, 434–440.

Epstein, S. The self-concept revisited: On a theory of a theory. *American Psychologist,* 1973, **28**, 404–416.

Green, P. E., & Carmone, F. J. *Multidimensional scaling and related techniques in marketing analysis.* Boston: Allyn & Bacon, 1970.

Hartigan, J. A. *Clustering algorithms.* New York: Wiley, 1975.

Horan, C. B. Multidimensional scaling: Combining observations when individuals have different perceptual structures. *Psychometrika,* 1969, **34**, 139–165.

Johnson, S. C. Hierarchical clustering schemes. *Psychometrika,* 1967, **32**, 241–254.

Jones, R. A., & Rosenberg, S. Structural representations of naturalistic descriptions of personality. *Multivariate Behavioral Research,* 1974, **9**, 217–230.

Jones, R. A., Sensenig, J., & Haley, J. V. Self-descriptions: Configurations of content and order effects. *Journal of Personality and Social Psychology,* 1974, **30**, 36–45.

Kelly, G. A. *A theory of personality: The psychology of personal constructs.* New York: Norton, 1955.

Kruskal, J. B., Young, F. W., & Seery, J. How to use KYST. Unpublished manuscript, Bell Telephone Laboratories, 1973.

Landfield, A. W. *Personal construct systems in psychotherapy.* Chicago: Rand McNally, 1971.

Livingston, J., & Kingsley, S. QUERY: An interactive computer program for the collection of checklist data. Behavior research methods & instrumentation, 1976, **8** (4), 391–392.

Loehlin, J. C. Word meanings and self-descriptions. *Journal of Abnormal and Social Psychology,* 1961, **62**, 28–34.

Loehlin, J. C. Word meanings and self-descriptions: A replication and extension. *Journal of Personality and Social Psychology*, 1967, **5**, 107–110.

McGee, V. E. Multidimensional scaling of N sets of similarity measures: A nonmetric individual differences approach. *Multivariate Behavioral Research*, 1968, **3**, 233–248.

Mulaik, S. A. Are personality factors raters' conceptual factors? *Journal of Consulting Psychology*, 1964, **28**, 506–511.

Pervin, L. A. A free-response description approach to the analysis of person-situation interaction. *Journal of Personality and Social Psychology*, 1976, **34**, 465–474.

Rosenberg, S. Applications of clustering and scaling in the investigation of a person's "implicit theory of personality" from naturalistic data: Progress, problems, and possibilities. Talk presented at joint meeting of the Psychometric Society and the Classification Society, University of Iowa, April 1975.

Rosenberg, S., & Jones, R. A. A method for investigating and representing a person's implicit theory of personality: Theodore Dreiser's view of people. *Journal of Personality and Social Psychology*, 1972, **22**, 372–386.

Rosenberg, S., Nelson, C., & Vivekananthan, P. S. A multidimensional approach to the structure of personality impressions. *Journal of Personality and Social Psychology*, 1968, **9**, 283–294.

Rosenberg, S., & Olshan, K. Evaluative and descriptive aspects in personality perception. *Journal of Personality and Social Psychology*, 1970, **16**, 619–626.

Rosenberg, S., & Sedlak, A. Structural representations of implicit personality theory. In L. Berkowitz (Ed.), *Advances in experimental social psychology* (Vol. 6). New York: Academic Press, 1972. Pp. 235–297. (a)

Rosenberg, S., & Sedlak, A. Structural representations of perceived personality trait relationships. In A. K. Romney, R. N. Shepard, & S. B. Nerlove (Eds.), *Multidimensional scaling: Theory and applications in the behavioral sciences*. Vol. II. *Applications*. New York: Seminar Press, 1972. Pp. 133–162. (b)

Schmidt, C. F. Understanding human action: Recognizing the motives and plans of other persons. In J. Carroll & J. Peyne (Eds.), *Cognition and social behavior*. Potomac, Md: Erlbaum Press, in press.

Sedlak, A. A multidimensional study of the structure of personality descriptions. Unpublished master's thesis, Rutgers University, 1971.

Shepard, R. N. A taxonomy of some principal types of data and of multidimensional methods for their analysis. In R. N. Shepard, A. K. Romney, & S. B. Nerlove (Eds.), *Multidimensional scaling: Theory and applications in the behavioral sciences*. Vol. I. *Theory*. New York: Seminar Press, 1972. Pp. 21–47.

Shepard, R. N., Romney, K. A., & Nerlove, S. B. (Eds.), *Multidimensional scaling: Theory and applications in the behavioral sciences.* Vol. I. *Theory.* New York: Seminar Press, 1972.

Sneath, P. H. A., & Sokal, R. R. *Numerical taxomony.* San Francisco: Freeman, 1973.

Swanberg, W. A. *Dreiser.* New York: Scribners, 1965.

Torgerson, W. S. Multidimensional scaling of similarity. *Psychometrika,* 1965, **30**, 379–393.

Tucker, L. R., & Messick, S. An individual differences model for multidimensional scaling. *Psychometrika,* 1963, **28**, 333–367.

Yarrow, M. R., & Campbell, J. D. Person perception in children. *Merrill-Palmer Quarterly,* 1963, **9**, 57–72.

APPENDIX: NOTES ON METHOD

Reordering a Hierarchical Clustering

The order in which clusters are placed is not uniquely determined by hierarchical clustering. This means that certain regularities in the data can be displayed by permuting the clusters according to some relevant property of the entities that have been clustered.

A sample of data from one of the subects (MA) is used to illustrate such a permutation. The sample data were obtained by selecting the first 24 people on MA's randomized list and the first 30 items on his trait list. Figure A1 shows an unordered version of a two-way clustering of this matrix with the hierarchical clustering of rows and columns, each represented as a tree.

The tree that is drawn next to the rows, for example, may be viewed as a "mobile" in which the two clusters hanging off any mode can interchange position. Thus, for example, the first 3 people can change places with the 2 people after them; the first 5 people with the 13 people after them; and so on. Many such interchanges are possible. The same type of interchanges can be made for columns; for example, the first 7 traits can change places with the 3 traits after them; the first 10 traits with all the traits after them; and so on.

Figure A2 shows the results of permuting both the rows and columns of Figure A1 according to MA's evaluative ratings. In the case of the rows, MA was asked to rate each person according to how much he liked the person. For the columns, MA was asked to rate

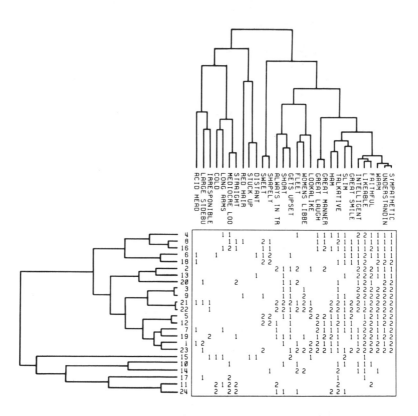

FIG. A1. Two-way clustering of 24 people (rows) and 30 traits (columns) from Subject MA's protocol.

each trait according to whether a person possessing the trait would be liked or disliked. Both sets of ratings were obtained on a 7-point scale. The permutation of the rows, as shown in Figure A2, maximizes the correlation (Kendall's τ) between the subject's likableness ratings of the people and row location (top to bottom). The same is true for the columns; that is, the τ between the likableness ratings of the traits and column location (left to right) is at a maximum. The permutations are constrained only by the nodes of the hierarchical trees, as noted above. In this example, the τ for rows is .77, and for columns .88. The algorithm for permuting a hierarchical tree so as to maximize τ is from Degerman (1973).

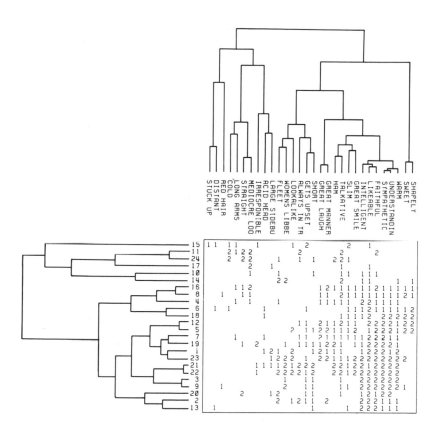

FIG. A2. A permutation of the two-way clustering shown in Figure A1 according to Subject MA's evaluative ratings of people (rows) and of traits (columns).

Dominant-Residual Analysis

A measure of dominance is calculated for each trait and feeling reflecting its relation to all the other traits and feelings in the protocol. This measure is obtained by first calculating the contingency χ^2 for the given trait or feeling versus each of the other traits and feelings. That is, for any trait t_i, there are the following contingency tables and each yields a χ^2.

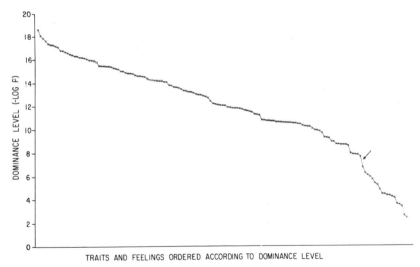

All of the contingency χ^2's for trait t_i are then summed. The dominance measure is $-\log p$, where p is the probability level of the sum of the contingency χ^2's. Traits and feelings with the largest $-\log p$ values are the most dominant. When the traits and feelings are ordered from most to least dominant, there is usually a distinct break or discontinuity at the lower end. This can be seen in Figure A3, where MA's traits and feelings are ordered from most to least dominant along the abscissa with the $-\log p$ measure shown as the ordinate. The cutting point selected to partition the terms into a dominant and a residual set is shown in the figure with an arrow. The procedure is repeated for the dominant set to see whether additional traits and feelings "fall out." For MA, four more terms became residuals. A third run yielded no additional residuals.

FIG. A3. Level of dominance (ordinate) of Subject MA's traits and feelings, with terms ordered from most to least dominant along the abscissa.

We are currently working on the development of an objective procedure for determining a cutting point. We are considering a curve-fiting procedure (possibly a linear fit) for plots such as Figure A3 which weights each $-\log p$ value in proportion to its size; terms with the lowest $-\log p$ values are eliminated if they fall below the fitted curve. The dominance values of each of the remaining terms are then recalculated for this subset of terms alone; the curve-fitting is repeated and terms are eliminated as before. This procedure is repeated until no further deletions can be made.

Contrast Analysis

The following steps are used to identify contrasts in a subject's protocol. The subject's traits and feelings are first grouped into clusters, according to the results of a clustering analysis. Scores are then calculated for each person described for each cluster; a person's score for a cluster is the sum of his ratings (0, 1, or 2) on each of the traits and feelings in that cluster. The correlation of these cluster scores across persons is calculated for each pair of clusters. Positive and negative correlations are then separately standardized so that each set has the same mean and standard deviation. A clustering (unweighted average method, Sneath & Sokal, 1973) of the clusters is obtained using the *absolute* values of the standardized correlation coefficients as input data. The reason for the standardization is that the positive correlations before standardization are higher on the average than the negative correlations; as a consequence, clustering based on unstandardized absolute values yield no contrasting clusters—the positive correlations dominate the clustering analysis. Finally, each of the major groupings of clusters is examined to determine which clusters in the group are positively correlated and which are negatively correlated. Clusters within a group that are positively correlated are located on the same side of the dichotomy; clusters that are negatively correlated are located on opposite poles of the dichotomy.

It might be noted, parenthetically, that we first attempted to identify contrasts by the same type of statistical criterion we used to identify the residuals, that is, by the level of dominance of the terms in a cluster. We did not obtain clear contrasts in a number of cases, although we found a strong relation between the average level of dominance of a cluster and its opposite. In a sense, then, the contrast analysis described above is a continuation of the dominant-residual analysis (that is, a kind of partitioning based on dominance), although the statistical methods we actually use to identify contrasts are not based on the dominance level of the cluster members.

Metaphors for Living[1]

Miller Mair

Crichton Royal Hospital,
Dumfries, Scotland

O ver the last twenty years personal construct theory has become well known but has remained little understood. People often become excited by aspects of the theory, but then it seems to slip away somehow and they can remember only general impressions or particular catch phrases. Many seem to find it difficult to make much use of construct theory ideas in practice. Even when practice does follow on interest, it seems more often than not to boil down to some exercise in repertory grid use which may differ from older test procedures in some respects but in general perpetuates concern with measurement which the scientific tradition in psychology has long applauded. In this way much of the spirit of excitement, surprise, scope, and daring in Kelly's writings (Kelly, 1955, 1969) seems to be lost.

There are many reasons why we might find Kelly's theory a difficult one to grasp. It is, for example, very unusual in the *form of its presentation.* No other psychological theory has been expressed as a "fundamental postulate" with a supporting cast of "corollaries." It is difficult to know what to do with twelve such assertions, other than learn them by heart and repeat them whenever the occasion arises. In addition to this the theory is couched in remarkably *abstract terms.* We find none of the familiarity or warmth of words like "reward" or "punishment," "pleasure," "pain," or "sex." You find yourself instead dealing with cool, unusual things called "constructs" which have to do with "anticipation," "validation," and "abstraction." What is presented as a "personal" approach seems to be conveyed in terms which are impersonal, formal, and far removed from the sorts of experiences most of us have in everyday life.

It is also disconcerting since it seems to be *both a theory of action and a theory for action.* On the one hand it provides a frame of

1. I wish to express my gratitude to the Netherlands Institute for Advanced Study in the Humanities and Social Sciences (NIAS), Wassenaar, Netherlands. Much of the thought and reading which formed the basis for this essay was undertaken during a fellowship year at the institute in 1971–72.

reference within which we can represent various forms of human action, but on the other Kelly seems to be inviting, even luring, the reader into action in pursuit of concerns of personal importance. In getting us involved in such action on our own account Kelly seems to be suggesting that this theory may serve both as a springboard or launching pad and a framework within which we may chart and make sense of the ventures we undertake. This dual function of his theory is likely to be difficult to understand and disturbing for the psychological scientist taught to distance himself from his inquiries and to build up a respectable pile of evidence before risking new steps in pursuit of his concerns.

One further consideration which contributes to difficulties in coping with personal construct theory is that *it is not just a "theory" but a "psychology"* which Kelly is proposing. Many seem to forget this startling claim and write chapters or books comparing personal construct *theory* with other theories, but very little attention seems to have been paid to the more fundamental task of conceptualizing and comparing *psychologies.* Such a task would involve the specification of whole sets of usually unacknowledged and unnoticed values, assumptions, aims, beliefs about the nature of the world and our possible knowledge of it, criteria for evaluating experiences and events, and the like. An undertaking of this kind lies outside the scope of my present concerns, not to mention my competence, but I suspect that personal construct theory will remain something of an enigma until we can formulate more adequately our understanding of the kind of psychology which is needed to support it.

My aim here is to look at a few aspects of personal construct psychology with the hope that, by approaching from a different direction, we may be able to see some of the features which make this an unusual psychology and at the same time provide it with a tradition which it would seem to be extending. My intention is first to lay aside personal construct psychology and to look instead at the older notion of *metaphor*; since this topic is still fairly unfamiliar in psychology, I will discuss it at greater length than is strictly necessary for my present argument. Then, through the use of metaphors, we will look again at some of Kelly's ideas which seem to be contributions towards a *psychology of living* rather than merely a psychology of behavior.

AN INTRODUCTION TO METAPHOR

Our common speech is littered with metaphor. We speak of feeling "dull" or "high," "bright," "rough," "depressed," "light in the head" or "heavy in the heart," "sharp," "keen," "hard," and "soft." All these are metaphors, though they have often "faded" and need attention drawn to them if they are to be momentarily revived. Our everyday speech sometimes "bubbles," "sparkles," and "glows" with metaphors which "trip" off the tongue to give our expression "clarity" and "warmth," "vibrancy" and "punch."

In poetry, of course, metaphor is vital and omnipresent. T. S. Eliot (1936) speaks, for example, of the "the yellow fog that rubs its back upon the window panes," as if the fog were some kind of animal. Norman McCaig (1972) speaks of male pigeons on the roof as "wobbling gyroscopes of lust." Kathleen Raine (1970) likens "time" to a storm at sea when she writes, "Time blows a tempest—how the days run high, deep graves are open between hour and hour."

In philosophy we find that a limited number of "great metaphors" underlie much of the thinking throughout the centuries about, for instance, the nature of mind. One of these is the idea of consciousness as an impression. Thus the phenomenon of knowledge was viewed as if it were a trace of some kind imprinted on a wax tablet. This metaphor, deriving from Greece and surviving through the Middle Ages, is still apparent in ordinary speech when we talk of someone as "making a deep impression" on us or of "hammering a point home." Another of the great philosophic metaphors coming into vogue after the Renaissance was that of the mind as a container and our experience in consciousness as the contents of this container.

Religious thinking through the ages is also rich with metaphor concerning man's relationship with God. One view suggested that the relationship might best be viewed as that between a king and his kingdom, another as that between a clockmaker and a clock. A third approach was to make sense of the relationship as if it were like that existing between one person and another. Yet another was to think of the relationship as like that between an agent and his actions or a self and his body. Barbour (1974) notes a further metaphor suggested by A. N. Whitehead in which God's relation to the world is viewed as if it were like that between an individual and a community.

In all the sciences metaphor is readily apparent. Physicists talk of light sometimes as if it were "waves" and sometimes as "particles."

Biologists are concerned with the "genetic code," and its "grammar" and "punctuation." Engineers talk of metal as if it suffered "fatigue."

In considering society and politics, the state has been thought of in different metaphoric terms at different times. At one time it was viewed as if it were a "body" with the king as the head and the other groupings in society as other organs and limbs of the "body politic." Hobbes describes the state as if it were a many-jointed monster, a leviathan. Rousseau suggested a different metaphor for the state and the relations between the persons comprising it when he wrote about "the social contract."

And of course the use of metaphor does not stop outside the boundaries of psychology. Everywhere you look in psychology you find metaphors peering back at you, very often pretending not to be there at all. So we find man viewed variously as if he were an animal, a machine of various kinds (formerly more mechanical and now often electronic), a battleground of warring forces, a pawn of biological and social circumstances, a plant which requires the right conditions to foster healthy growth, or even as if he were rather like a scientist. From the most "hard-nosed" and "hard-headed" approaches to psychology to the more humanistic and "soft" we find metaphoric thinking everywhere apparent.

THE IMPORTANCE OF METAPHOR

Widely differing views on the importance or otherwise of metaphor have been expressed throughout the centuries. In general the classical view was that metaphor was characteristic of the language used in poetry, and poetry was a special kind of activity quite distinct from logic and rhetoric. Poetry made a lot of use of metaphor, but even there, metaphor was thought of essentially as a kind of decoration or embellishment placed on top of ordinary language. Metaphor was considered an extra garnish which, if used too freely, could make ordinary language too much like poetry, and obviously that would not be a good thing at all! Hawkes (1972) points out that behind this view were two basic assumptions about language and its relation to the "real" world. First, it supposes that language and reality, or words and the objective world to which they refer, are quite separate things. Second, it holds to the belief that the *manner* in which something is said does not significantly affect or alter *what* is said. The belief here is that there are "bare facts" and there are a variety of ways of talking about these which are completely separable from them.

In developing this line of thought Aristotle showed his concern for good style and correct, clear use of language by warning against the unsatisfactory ambiguity involved in poetic language generally and the use of metaphor in particular. But in spite of sometimes seeming to consider metaphor almost as a vice, Aristotle did also have some appreciation of the power of metaphor. In the *Poetics* he went so far as to say that "the greatest thing by far is to have a command of metaphor." He went on in the same passage to say, "This alone cannot be imparted to another: it is the mark of genius, for to make good metaphors implies an eye for resemblances." I. A. Richards (1936), one of the greatest modern writers on metaphor, started his discussion of the subject in his *Philosophy of Rhetoric* by applauding and elaborating Aristotle's insight that "a command of metaphor" may be of tremendous importance in life as well as literature and disagreeing completely about the impossibility of imparting it to others.

For centuries after Aristotle, metaphor was castigated in various ways and even became a matter of religious debate. The Puritans concerned with Plain Style in the early seventeenth century sought to banish sinful extravagance in language. Hawkes (1972) points out that "Plain delivery" of the word was the aim, and "painted eloquence" was seen as an enemy of the truth. The content of speech or writing was considered more important than form and was seen as quite separable from it. So far did this attitude progress that at the end of the seventeenth century Samuel Parker advocated an act of Parliament to forbid the use of what he called "fulsome and luscious" metaphors. Even Dr. Johnson at times seemed to consider metaphor as an abuse of language.

It was among some of the poets of the romantic movement that a radically different approach to understanding metaphor gained ground. They inclined to the view that metaphor had an organic relationship to language as a whole and emphasized its tremendous importance for giving expression to imagination. Metaphor was no longer considered as a mere ornament added to language but as a fundamental way of *experiencing* the facts. Shelley talked of metaphor as "a way of thinking and of living; an imaginative projection of the truth." Because of this he considered it to be "at the heart of the 'made'." Wordsworth stressed that for him there was no essential difference between the language of prose and that of poetry, and both he and Shelley noted the linking or integrating function of the mind through the medium of metaphor. But it is perhaps Coleridge who is best known and most trenchant in his examination of "the perception of similitude in dissimilitude" and more generally for the entire "manner in which we associate ideas." Coleridge struck a revolutionary note in his concern with metaphor as Imagination in action. I. A. Richards (1962) points out that Coleridge's view of the mind was revolutionary in that he rejected the idea of it being passive in its recording of given "reality" but instead described it as "an active, self forming, self realising system" which creatively adapted and gave shape to the world, almost "making it up" as it went along. "Language," says Coleridge, "is framed to convey not the object alone, but likewise the character, mood and intentions of the person who is representing it." For Coleridge, as Hawkes (1972) points out, "Imagination stretches the mind, then because it 'stretches' reality by the linguistic means of metaphor. Given this, metaphor cannot be thought of as simply a cloak for a pre-existing thought. A metaphor *is* a thought in its own right."

Coming to the present time, I. A. Richards is at once both one of the great modern champions of Coleridge and a person who, more than almost any other, has revived concern with and understanding of the possible importance of metaphor. Richards discarded the classical view as inadequate and allied himself with much in the romantic view of the significance of metaphor. He also warns that the serious study of metaphor may plunge us into very deep psychological waters and suggests that perhaps some awareness of this has contributed to the general neglect of the subject. After a discussion of words and meanings in the *Philosophy of Rhetoric* (1936), he claims that metaphor is the "omnipresent principle in language" and notes that "we cannot get through three sentences of ordinary fluid discourse without it."

Richards suggests that the traditional view only noticed a few of the modes of metaphor and even then limited the term *metaphor* to only a few of these. "And thereby," he says, "it made metaphor seem to be a verbal matter, a shifting and displacement of words, whereas fundamentally it is a borrowing between and intercourse of *thoughts,* a transaction between contexts." Thus he presses forward the notion of metaphor as not just a verbal affair but something fundamentally involved in the way we think, this in turn being fundamental to the way we live. In pursuing this line we find ourselves dealing not with literary matters alone but with issues central to psychology and human functioning. "In asking how language works," Richards says, "we ask about how thought and feeling and all the other modes of the mind's activity proceed, about how we learn to live and how that 'greatest thing of all,' a command of metaphor—which is great only because it is a command of life—may best, in spite of Aristotle, 'be imparted to another'."

Like a number of other writers in recent years, Richards used the term *metaphor* in a sense which went well beyond a mere playing with words. For him the term was appropriately applied to all kinds of cases where we may use words compounded together and speak of one thing as though it were another. But he went further than this "to include, as metaphoric, those processes in which we perceive or think or feel about one thing in terms of another." He proceeds even further to a powerful, but tantalizingly brief, sweep around broader horizons still. In this often quoted passage he presses the relevance of metaphor right to the center of personal and interpersonal living.

A "command of metaphor"—a command of the interpretation of metaphors—can go deeper still into the control of the world that we make for ourselves to live in. The psychoanalysts have shown us with their discussions of "transference"—another name for metaphor—how constantly modes of regarding, of loving, of acting, that have developed with one set of things or people, are shifted to another. They have shown us chiefly the pathology of these transferences, cases where the vehicle—the borrowed attitude, the parental fixation, say—tyrannizes over the new situation, the tenor, and behavior is inappropriate. The victim is unable to see the new person except in terms of the old passion and its accidents. He reads the situation only in terms of the figure, the archetypal image, the vehicle. But in healthy growth, tenor and vehicle—the new human relationship and the family constellation—co-operate freely; and the resultant behavior derives in due measure from both. Thus in happy living the same patterns are exemplified and the same risks of error are avoided as in tactful and discerning reading. The general form of the interpretative process is the same with a small scale instance—the right understanding of a figure of speech—or with a large scale instance—the conduct of a friendship. [Pp. 135–136]

Many others have written on the importance of metaphor, but this should be enough to illustrate the kinds of views expressed and the general changes which have come about in the appraisal of metaphor. One point which I wish to stress here is that Richards and many others view metaphor as having both broad relevance and deep significance for many aspects of human functioning. The time seems to have passed when metaphor was considered as merely some decorative or distasteful embellishment of style.

SOME USES OF METAPHOR

So it seems that metaphor is considered of some significance in human affairs, but what does it do for us? What functions does it serve? Many uses have been discussed by writers on the topic, and I will try to convey some of those which seem most often mentioned.

One general function of metaphor is to clothe the unknown with something more familiar, to reach out for what is unknown but dimly sensed through the medium of some familiar aspect of the known. Thus Marias (1967) talks of "metaphor as a mental tool, that is, a means of knowing the reality which can be known in no other way." Owen Thomas (1969) points out that "man constantly seeks to circumscribe the unknown" and goes on to say that "the attempts to define the unknown must begin with the known"; it is on this premise that he leads into his discussion of metaphor. Donald Schon (1963) gives detailed consideration to metaphor as a means of entering the unknown for invention and discovery. The use of metaphor, or as he terms it, the "displacement of concepts," is for him central to the development of all new concepts and theories. He goes on to say that "the process is nothing less than our way of bringing the familiar to bear on the unfamiliar in such a way as to yield new concepts while at the same time retaining as much as possible of the past."

The metaphors we choose intentionally or implicitly adopt as ways of reaching new understandings or for approaching the future, or some novel event or person, can have important implications for us. Turbayne (1962) indicates this when he suggests that an effective metaphor acts as a "screen" through which we look at the world. It acts as a filter on the facts, suppressing some and emphasizing others. It "brings forward aspects that might not be seen at all through another medium." Thomas (1969) notes something similar when he considers metaphor as a base for action, and the kinds of things we do, the sensitivities and priorities we elaborate, will depend on our choice of a metaphorical base.

It is suggested, then, that while metaphor may be a way of making sensible, available, and even controllable some new aspects of reality through more familiar forms, it does not offer up new meanings ready-made, clean-cut, and complete. There is usually some *ambiguity* and an *invitation* to pursue possible meanings, possible paths to further meanings still only implicit but unrealized in the new comparisons. Schon (1963), in discussing both models and metaphors, for example, considers them both not solutions to problems but "programmes for exploring new situations." "Neither models nor metaphors," he says, "subsume analogous situations under general concepts already formulated; instead they both intimate a similarity not yet full conceptualized. One is asked, as it were, to find features of the old in the new; one is offered new ways of looking at a phenomenon." Barbour (1974) indicates that while it has sometimes been suggested that a metaphor may be translated exactly into other more literal language, he and many other writers cannot accept this view. He suggests that a metaphor cannot be replaced by a set of equivalent literal statements because it is "open ended." With the use of metaphor, no limits can be set as to how far the comparisons involved may be extended, and therefore it cannot be paraphrased because it has an unspecifiable number of potentialities for articulation. He suggested further that a metaphor is not merely an illustration of an idea already explicitly spelled out, but a suggestive "invitation" to the discovery of further resemblances and differences. This incomplete, invitational, response-seeking feature of metaphor was also recognized by Coleridge, who felt that vital metaphors require a response from the receiver as an act of "completion," just as a play needs some kind of response from an audience.

This leads us to consider a further vital function of metaphor, namely, its importance in all aspects of *communication*. Many writers comment on the intensification of experience and language involved in the use of metaphor. Hawkes (1972) notes that the deliberate use of metaphor "intensifies language's characteristic activity, and involves, quite literally, the creation of 'new' reality." The imaginative use of metaphor can create vibrancy, immediacy, and vigor in both the making and expression of meanings. So metaphor gives "life" to our discourse.

It has also been suggested by many that metaphor can be used for the expression of feelings since it seems to have the quality of conveying at the same time both ideas and feelings. It not only shows new ideas or aspects but brings out new ways of feeling when it is used effectively. Metaphors also evoke images and can be conveyed in imagery, and Barbour (1974) suggests that metaphors often have emotional and valuational overtones. They call forth feelings and attitudes in a dynamic way so that the very language in use becomes an event in itself and not merely an account. Thus he suggests that metaphors influence our attitudes as well as our perceptions and interpretations of events.

Concerning the receiving end in communication, Thomas (1969) notes that comprehension or understanding of what we are involved in, saying, or claiming "fades" in direct proportion to the loss of effective metaphors or the effective use of metaphor. Reider (1972) and others talk also of the importance of metaphor as a way of interpreting what others mean. He talks of metaphor as "the most economic condensation of understanding of many levels of experience." The power of metaphor in therapeutic communication is also stressed by Haley, Jackson, and others of their orientation. Haley (1971) points out that "one of the most interesting aspects of the attempts to change people is the fact that the use of metaphors or analogies seems especially central to the process of therapy." Haley regards the patient's problems as an acted-out metaphor and argues that "the goal of therapy is to change the communicative behavior of the person; to change his metaphor."

Metaphor is important in communication well beyond the limits of verbal exchange. However, the function of metaphor within language is of such importance that it has been emphasized many times. Hawkes (1972) points out that. I. A. Richards, Owen Barfield, and Philip Wheelwright all consider metaphor to be central in language. Similarly, Christine Brooks-Rose suggests that the process of metaphor is located at the "heart of language" and both defines and refines it, and she suggests that through this process it refines and defines man himself. But it is not just within the formal structure of language that metaphor is considered important. Hawkes (1972) indicates that the very underpinnings of our languages are metaphorical in their presuppositions. He points out that in some languages it is just not possible to make the sorts of statements, or think the sorts of thoughts, that can be achieved in other languages. He points out that English contains metaphorical devices in its grammar which impose a system of spatial and temporal relationship on objects and events, while certain other languages and cultures do not. Our tense system makes us break up experience in terms of past, present, and future, while languages which have nothing like this system do not impose this aspect of "reality" on all their users. "Presuppositions such as these," he says, "affect our lives as part of a 'reality' which exists, concretely, 'brutally' and 'out there' beyond us."

So we come to an aspect of metaphor repeated often in writing on the subject, namely, that metaphor is a vital means whereby we both discover and create the realities of our lives and our world. "I believe that the universe is covered with a patina of interpretations," says Marias (1967), "and most of these interpretations are metaphors. Only we tend to forget this." He goes on to suggest that if our metaphors, our interpretations, were different in any instance we would assess situations differently and act differently in relation to what we took to be the "real" state of affairs. He goes so far as to claim that "metaphors are the foundation of everyday reality." Wallace Stevens sums up this view of the relation between reality and the use of metaphor when he proposes that "reality is a cliché from which we escape by metaphor." Finally, Hawkes (1972) concludes his excellent overview of metaphor by recognizing that all explanations of metaphoric functioning are oversimplified, and he finishes by saying that "in the long run the 'truth' does not matter because the only access to it is by means of metaphor. The metaphors matter: they are the truth."

BEING USED BY METAPHOR

But everything is not rosy in the metaphoric garden. Problems accompany the use of metaphor. Thomas (1969), while indicating that we use metaphor to circumscribe the unknown, went on to note that by so doing, by setting boundaries around our perceptions, our awarenesses, we can and do thereby also limit what we see even as we highlight certain features. Kenneth Burke (1954), in drawing attention to some of the dangers in the use of metaphor, invokes Veblen's concept of "trained incapacity." This is "that state of affairs whereby one's very abilities can function as blindnesses." So also in the use of metaphor, our very skill in the use of particular ways of sorting and interpreting reality may be a major impediment to our being able to reach for new meanings or being able to cope with changing circumstances. We may thus be caught and fossilized by the very power available to us in particular metaphors, and this may be particularly likely if we fall into the "great danger of analogy," which is that we take a similarity as evidence of an identity, if we come to believe that our particular metaphoric view of reality is in very truth reality itself.

Turbayne (1962) is one of the writers who most clearly recognizes both the powers and the pitfalls of metaphor. He insists that there is a great difference between using a metaphor and taking it literally, between using a model and mistaking it for the thing modelled. "The one is to use a disguise or mask for illustrative or exemplary purposes; the other is to mistake the mask for the face." So it is that after the disguise or mask of metaphor has been worn for a considerable time, it tends to blend with the face and it becomes extremely difficult to "see through" it. If metaphor is used "without awareness," says Turbayne, then we become victimized by it rather than empowered. In a sense, therefore, metaphor only exists where it is actively recognized, otherwise it is "hidden" and likely to be taken for reality itself.

Turbayne goes on to argue that the tremendous pervasiveness of mechanical explanations in the western world is one glaring example of being victimized by metaphor. He accuses Newton and Descartes, among others, of being "unconscious victims of the metaphor of the great machine." He suggests further that through their confusions in this manner of taking metaphor for reality, they have impregnated the whole consciousness of the western world with this same confusion. He proceeds to "undress" the metaphor of mechanism and to show that it can be dispensed with. To do this he elaborates an alternative metaphor in place of "mechanism"—the metaphor of nature as if it were a language—and to show how this can account for aspects of perception which were previously difficult to explain. His primary intention in this excercise is not to advocate his new metaphor but rather to make us more aware of the metaphors we use in explorations of "reality" so that we may be less likely to join the legions of those who have fallen victims in mistaking their own pretences for final truths.

The warnings given by Turbayne can be taken a little further. As noted earlier, Haley (1971) considers the problems presented by patients in therapy as if they were metaphors. More recently, Wright (1976), approaching the topic from a psychoanalytic perspective, suggests rather that metaphor and symptom should be distinguished. He views both metaphors and symptoms as symbolic structures which present one thing in the semblance of another, but he argues that while the symptom "conceals" and leads to a "restriction" of view, the metaphor "reveals" and leads out towards new possibilities. For Wright, a metaphor "is a product of an ego that is going towards a problem and attempting to grasp it," while a symptom "is a product of an ego that is turning away from a problem and refusing to see it." Thus he suggests that "whether symptom or metaphor arises depends on the *attitude of the ego* that is confronted with the problem." Thus, while in Turbayne's terms symptoms could be regarded as instances of being used by metaphor, Wright is bringing to our attention the possibility that very often "being used" may not be the passive thing it seems. Often when we are "victimized" by metaphor we may in fact be "willing" victims of our own metaphors or of those offered to us in the traditions of our culture. Often we may be *active perpetrators* of the victimization which ensues from the misuse of metaphor. It may be that we already have not only a considerable facility in the use of metaphor for elaborative ventures but similar skill in turning away from problems to be used by the metaphors we might otherwise command. Thus from consideration of both the uses and abuses of metaphor it may no longer seem so strange to suppose that "a command of metaphor" may turn out to be "the greatest thing by far."

BUT WHAT IS METAPHOR?

So far I have largely skirted round the question of *what* metaphor is or *how* metaphors function. We have seen already that there have been considerable changes in the importance attributed to metaphor through the centuries, and ideas of what consititutes metaphor have changed accordingly. For Aristotle and many after him, metaphor involved giving a thing a *name* that really belonged to something else. It was a verbal exchange or crossover. The Oxford Dictionary reflects this traditional view in defining metaphor as "the figure of speech in which a name or descriptive term is transferred to some object to which it is not properly applicable." The word *metaphor* itself derives from the Greek and means literally "a carrying across." It is in this limited verbal sense, as a figure of speech, a kind of intentional verbal mistake, that most of us are likely to have encountered metaphor in language or literature classes in school. We are likely to have met it especially in relation to poetry as a way of playing with words to achieve certain dramatic or other effects.

Two major changes then took place over the centuries, and especially during the romantic period, which have influenced many modern views on metaphor. First of all, the forms of language used in poetry, which Aristotle separated off from other forms of discourse, have increasingly been accepted as essentially similar to the kinds of language we use every day. Second, and accompanying this change, there has been a fundamental reappraisal of the importance of metaphor for human understanding. This has extended our appreciation of its scope and mode of functioning well beyond the purely "verbal" transpositions noted by Aristotle. Many writers have tried to grasp some satisfactory conception of metaphor and how it works. In this connection it is attempts to understand "metaphoric functioning" rather than any specific "metaphor" which will concern us here.

One good example of an extended or more generalized concern with the mode of functioning of metaphor is provided by Donald Schon (1963). His suggestion is that "in at least one of its senses the process of metaphor is nothing more or less than displacement of concepts." As we have noted already, he goes on to say that for him the "displacement of concepts" is central to the development of all new concepts and that the metaphoric process is "nothing less than one way of bringing the familiar to bear on the unfamiliar, in such a way as to yield new concepts while at the same time retaining as much as possible of the past." Schon in fact chooses to restrict the term *metaphor* to the results of the process of displacement, so for him displacement is the mode of operating while metaphors are the things thrown up thereby.

Thus metaphor, the process of metaphor, involves displacement, transposition, a carrying across of concepts from one kind of event to apply to another. But it cannot be viewed simply as a "conceptual" affair. Richards (1936), as we have seen, was concerned to extend the scope of metaphor, and he suggested that metaphor was a "borrowing between and intercourse of thoughts, a transaction between contexts." So he emphasizes "thinking" rather than "concept formation," and for him "thinking" is often used as a shorthand way of referring to the "mind's activity" in general. Through this means he extends understanding of the functioning of metaphor, the process of metaphor, into realms of feeling and activity as well as thought and language. It is also worth noting that Richards emphasizes the active nature of the metaphoric process, and rather than talk of some bland or passive transference, he uses words like "transaction," "borrowing," and "intercourse."

Turbayne (1962) is also concerned with widening the classical meaning of metaphor. Like Richards, he seeks to go well beyond the transfer of "names" suggested by Aristotle. He suggests we could better view the process of metaphor as the "presentation of the facts of one category in the idioms appropriate to another." He insists further that metaphor need not be expressed in words and that activities of many kinds, if they involve the presentation of the facts of one category in idioms appropriate to another, can legitimately be considered metaphorical. Thus he holds that the artist, for example, who "speaks" in paint or clay can be considered to be speaking in metaphor, just as for Haley, the patient who "speaks" in terms of "complaints" and "problems" is considered to be functioning metaphorically also.

Turbayne also stresses another important feature of metaphor which is often obscured. In metaphoric functioning, he points out, there is a "pretence that something is the case when it is not." He stresses that in metaphoric functioning we are in a sense making a mistake by acting *as if* one thing were really something which it is not. Thus, for Turbayne, in metaphoric activity we are somehow representing the facts *as if* they belonged to one logical type of category, or range of types of categories, when they actually belong to another. In this way he suggests that an effective metaphor acts as a "screen" through which we look at the world; it filters the facts, suppressing some and emphasizing others, bringing into prominence some aspects that might not be seen at all through another medium.

As we have noted already, Turbayne warns that what may be called a "screen" or "filter" can readily become more like a "disguise" or "mask" which hides, obscures, and confuses rather than clarifying, highlighting, and revealing.

Turbayne, Hawkes, Thomas, Richards, and others also stress the breadth of their conceptions of metaphor by considering as variations of metaphor all the forms of speech which have traditionally been distinguished. Thus *simile* (where the "like" or "as if" aspect of metaphor is stated more evidently), *synecdoche* (where a part of something is "carried over" to stand in place of the whole thing, as in speaking of "hands" on a ship rather than "men"), *metonymy* (where the name of one thing is transferred to take the place of something else with which it is associated, as when speaking of "the Crown" rather than "the monarch"), *catachresis* (where a thing which has no name is given a name belonging to something else, as in using ordinary words in a technical sense), and *oxymoron* (where two words or ideas which are not only incompatible but nearly contradictory in essence are linked, as in saying "the cold fire of his eyes") are all forms of metaphoric functioning. So also *allegory* can be seen as an extended metaphor or combination of many interrelated metaphors in the form of a story or drama, and *fable, parable*, and *myth* can also be included. *Personification* is also regarded as a form of metaphoric functioning where inanimate objects or abstract concepts can be treated as if they possessed human features. In a similar way *paradigms* and *models* can be viewed as specially elaborated forms of metaphoric functioning.

A further important point about metaphor is made by Owen Thomas (1969). He suggests that, strictly speaking, only man can "make statements" which are not true, and we often state ideas in terms which are logically contradictory. So in metaphor we are really making a "mistake" or a "series of mistakes" to some end. But Thomas reminds us that we need to have some systematic and accepted structuring of events, otherwise it would be impossible to make such "mistakes." Language is such a complex, systematic structure whose rules, grammar and syntax give coherent form to our world, though no language encapsulates the ultimate forms of reality. Through metaphor or the kind of "mistake making" which metaphor involves, we break the "rules" in various ways and so stretch the boundaries of our understanding. Such "stretching" is done by *both* keeping the rules *and* breaking them. A "command of metaphor" would seem then to involve some skill in breaking the rules, but this can only be done by having and respecting conventions which can be broken. As in some modern poetry, jumbles of metaphors with little or no structure against which to highlight the invention of new meanings may result in strain and confusion (thus possibly, after all, forming an effective metaphor of much of our modern experience of living) and we may be in danger of losing both the "baby" of new meanings with the "bath water" of accepted forms. So it is well not to forget what Schon (1963) pointed out clearly, namely, that metaphor has both a *radical* function in forging new possibilities and a *conservative* function of preserving what is good and sustaining in the forms of the past.

SOME METAPHORS OF METAPHOR

Wallace Stevens pointed out that there was "no such thing as a metaphor of a metaphor." However, before turning to look at some aspects of personal construct psychology from the perspective of metaphor, a brief look at some partial metaphors about aspects of metaphoric functioning may be useful.

Consider first the parts which compose the metaphor. I. A. Richards seems to have been one of the first modern writers to recognize the need for some clear terminology for talking about the component parts of any metaphor. He insists that the word "metaphor" be used for the whole double unit rather than any part of it. He suggests, further, that the "underlying idea or principal subject" be called "the tenor." The basic analogy which is used to embody or carry the tenor, the "general drift" of the discourse, he refers to as "the vehicle." These elements transact with each other, and their "transaction" is the meaning of the metaphor. Terms such as these facilitate more precise discussion of aspects of metaphoric functioning, but they must still be used lightly, with some delicacy, if we are to avoid destroying every metaphor by routinely ripping it into two necessary and identifiable parts. William Empson (1953) indeed claims that any clear-cut distinction between tenor and vehicle can often hardly be maintained when the number of "possible" meanings offered by any metaphor increases, without any one necessarily becoming clearly dominant over the others and thus identifiable as "the tenor."

Rather than focusing on the constituent parts of metaphor, Philip Wheelwright (1962) suggests another way of talking about metaphoric functioning. He suggests that there are two main modes of operation of metaphor. On the one hand there is the outreaching and extending of meaning by means of comparison, which he refers to as *epiphor*. On the other hand there is the creation of new meanings by means of juxtaposition and synthesis, which he refers to as *diaphor*. Another approach is that of Sperber, quoted by Rowe (1975), who was interested in the dominant metaphors which spring from deep-seated features or tendencies in any person's mind. These could act as "centres of expansion," continuously suggesting further similes and metaphors for the description of other experiences, or as "centres of attraction," whereby the person continuously calls on and enlists analogies from other contexts to help describe and elaborate centrally important metaphors with maximum precision, freshness, and variety. Thus he considers a twofold movement of metaphors—from and towards a person's emotional center.

A different kind of overview of metaphor, or metaphor concerning some aspects of metaphor, is that provided by Kenneth Burke in *A Grammar of Motives* (1945). He talks of metaphor as providing and using a "perspective." "Metaphor," he says, "is a device for seeing something in terms of something else. . . . a metaphor tells us something about one character considered from the point of view of another character. And to consider A from the point of view of B, is of course to use B as a perspective upon A." Thus, when one person tries to see things from the point of view of another, to feel what the other feels, he is in Burke's sense involved in the process of metaphor whereby he tries to shift his base in order to gain a new perspective on the realities of the world.

Finally, here it should be noted that *association*, long stressed within psychology, is what one writer termed a sine qua non for semantic change generally and for the making and understanding of metaphor in particular. But mere association is not enough, nor is any view of association of a mechanical kind whereby billiard balls collide or mutely fall together into the same pockets of the mind. The association involved in metaphor seems to require active or interactive participation for both its creation and interpretation. C. K. Ogden's comments, quoted by Burke (1954), seem relevant here. He suggests that "the governing principle in association is the direction of interest, and contiguity only works inside this principle. Clearness and consecutiveness of thinking, in other words, depends primarily upon clearness in our interests. Perhaps most of the blunders of thought are due to confused and mixed interests." This seems therefore to suggest that the life concerns of the individual, his "interests," have to be considered and identified if we are to understand association in general and metaphor in particular.

METAPHORS AND CONSTRUCTS

Perhaps enough has now been said about metaphor, its possible importance, uses, and modes of operating to make it clear that there are numerous similarities here with the concerns expressed in personal construct psychology. My intention in presenting so many of the ideas of other people on metaphor has been to make it apparent that the seemingly separate worlds of literature, poetry, art, invention, and the use of language on the one hand and the psychological account of human action developed by George Kelly on the other have, in fact, a great deal in common. While personal construct psychology may still be an unusual creature within "scientific" psychology, it has a very familiar air if approached, in part at least, from the perspective of all the work on metaphor which is found within a more "literate" tradition. Because of this family resemblance we may hope for some more fruitful cross-fertilization and development of personal construct psychology than seems so far to have been achieved within the psychological and "scientific" world where we have mostly tried to contain it.

Many writers emphasize that metaphor is an important way by which we create new meanings, making sense and alternative sense where there was little or none before. Metaphor, in short, is a means of entering the unknown through the gateway of the known. Kelly was also concerned with just this matter, and indeed, his paper on "The Psychology of the Unknown" (1963) was an essay on "how man, from his position of relative ignorance, can hope to reach out for knowledge that no one has yet attained." Kelly went so far as to say he regarded this confrontation with the unknown as "a primary problem for the psychologist," though he doubted if many of his colleagues saw it that way.

In this "reaching out" Kelly was uncertain whether we might

better consider reality to be "out there" or "deep within us," but he took the view that we never know reality completely. All our knowledge is approximate and is subject to revision as more fruitful approximations are invented. Similar views are expressed by writers on metaphor. They also see man as not only "uncovering" but "making" our realities by means of the "interpretations" we place on events. Both Kelly and writers on metaphor suggest that all our approaches to reality are through the "screens," "goggles," or "masks" which we construct.

We noted earlier the comment by Wallace Stevens to the effect that reality is a "cliché" from which we can escape by the use of metaphor. Kelly echoes a similar concern when he notes that to "transcend the obvious" is the basic problem for man. For Kelly, we do this by "construing" and "reconstruing" reality, but he makes it clear that we cannot hope to "reconstrue" events if we are convinced of the inescapability of our present interpretations and actions. Kelly here lays great stress on the need to adopt a kind of "invitational" mood in our language so that we can take our statements as invitations to exploration rather than mere assertions of hard necessities. We noted a similar invitational aspect of metaphor. In metaphor, also, we noted the importance of *as if*, or the willing use of make-believe. Kelly likewise placed *as if*, or "hypothetical thinking," at the center of his approach as a vital means whereby invitations to new explorations, new actions, or new meanings could be explored without overwhelming guilt or threat.

Metaphor has been described as a tool or instrument for both extending and clarifying language and other aspects of our living, as a way of reaching for what is new while preserving aspects of the old, as providing bases for action and experience. All these echo concerns found in Kelly's writings on construing. In our discussion of metaphor we noted that it could be a means whereby "perceptions" and "conceptions" could be identified and altered but also "attitudes" expressed and "emotions" formed and conveyed, all at the same time. All this is also reflected in Kelly's writing on the nature of constructs. He was particularly concerned to break down the old boundary lines in our thinking which had become traps ensnaring us in the belief that our own fictions of "feeling," "thought," and "will" were necessary divisions in reality itself.

But just as we can be used by metaphor or metaphor may be used to close down rather than open up new possibilities, so also, Kelly makes clear, constructs are avenues of freedom or ruts which prevent new movement. Our construct systems, according to Kelly, offer us a network of pathways for movement, but we cannot strike out across country unless we can build new paths, new constructions, to carry such movement. I. A. Richards also points out that we may be directed as much by the metaphors we are avoiding as by those we are using intentionally. This again reminds us of Kelly's injunctions to listen for what the person is *not* saying as well as what he is drawing attention to by affirming. Furthermore, according to Kelly, much of our living is likely to be an acting out of nonverbal or preverbal constructs operating below the grasp of our awareness. Again we found in the discussion of metaphor the danger of being tyrannized by metaphors when we become unaware of what they are and how we are using them. Our comprehension of ourselves or others fades as our awareness of the metaphors we are using diminishes, just as such comprehension increases as we appreciate the constructions which inform our actions or the actions of others.

This list of similarities between metaphor and construing could readily be extended, but these similarities in no way imply identity of interest. Metaphors are not constructs and "construct" is not just a new name for "metaphor." As we have noted, metaphor involves "sort-crossing," that is, making a kind of "mistake" whereby you think about, view, feel, or act in relation to one thing as if it were really some other kind of thing. Although no sharp distinctions can be drawn, constructs, on the other hand, are talked of more as "sortings" rather than "sort-crossings." The practical task through which constructs are elicited is a "sorting" task whereby the person seeks ways in which "two things are alike and different from a third." Sorting of this kind is a way by which a person attempts to be "appropriate" or to structure the "conventions" of his life. Sort-crossing, on the other hand, is a sorting activity which breaks the "conventions" and through which the person apparently becomes "inappropriate" in order that he may perhaps become "appropriate" in a different way.

A construct also seems to be a more abstracted notion than metaphor; at least I think Kelly considered it so. It is also more clearly delineated than metaphor in being defined from the beginning as a particular dimension of similarity/difference, while metaphor is more multifaceted, less directional, and more ambiguous.

In addition to all this, metaphor and construct are generally discussed in different kinds of contexts and derive from different areas of discourse. They carry therefore different kinds of connotations which are likely to affect our use of them and thinking about them. Thus, for me at least, constructs often seem linear, directional, geometrical axes of reference which seem hard, straight, angular, intellectual, and "digital." Metaphor, on the other hand, often carries an aura of associations which are flowing, colorful, sinuous, sensuous, surprising, ambiguous, inviting, warm, rich, protean. However, since the similarities in concerns are so striking, differences in emphasis and association such as these may be suggestive of further developments in our consideration of personal construct theory. Metaphor and its study has a very long history within the realms of poetry, literature, art, religion, and invention, while constructs were born into a modern world of psychology which had devoted itself to a hard-line scientific tradition valuing measurement, precision, mathematics, prediction, specification, and objectivity. Perhaps by viewing personal construct psychology only within this kind of scientific tradition we may blind ourselves to possibilities inherent in this new psychology and fail to consider what science itself may yet become if it begins to be able to incorporate more of the diverse forms of human life and concerns.

It could almost be argued that personal construct psychology is a psychology of man as a maker and user of metaphor. However, my present aims are much more modest, since I want only to highlight some aspects of personal construct psychology through the use of metaphor in the hope that some features of the kind of psychology we may here be dealing with can thereby become more apparent.

ASPECTS OF PERSONAL CONSTRUCT PSYCHOLOGY

George Kelly made a point of trying to specify some of the major assumptions he was making about the nature of our relations to and involvement with "reality," but he was a little less clear in specifying a number of other aspects of his approach, which may account for some of the difficulty many people seem to have in coming to terms with his psychological perspective. I want here to draw attention to four suggestions which he seems to me to be making concerning man and the nature of inquiry. I want to do this through the use of a number of metaphors which make it clearer why Kelly's position may be problematic for many of us and clearer also what kind of "party" we are letting ourselves in for if we accept his "invitation" to pursue our personal concerns through the framework he offers. The metaphors I've chosen involve considering "man" *as if* he were a "mystery," and "inquiry" *as if* it involved "making" and "making up," "venture," and "indwelling." None of this includes much consideration of the main content of the *theory* as enshrined in the fundamental postulate and corollaries, but rather the broader context within which the theory is presented.

After this, and again through the use of metaphor and some of the considerations raised in the changing understanding of metaphor, we will look briefly at a few further issues in the kind of psychology Kelly has outlined.

Man as a Mystery

It may not be immediately apparent on first reading Kelly's writings that he ascribed no essential nature to man, but rather talks of the ways in which he proceeds, the ways in which he reaches out for events by construing their replications. But since "ways of proceeding," "events," and "replications" are all constructed by man himself, we are left wondering about what his nature may be. Kelly tells us, in discussing the fundamental postulate, that "the person" is to be central and not any bits or pieces of the person. The fundamental postulate states therefore that "a *person's processes* are psychologically channelized by the ways in which he anticipates events." A distinction is made between "person" and "processes" and his "ways" of anticipating events, and thereafter the whole focus of the theory is on further understanding of "the ways" by which the mystery of the "person" and his "processes" is made manifest. As in the fundamental postulate, so in nearly all the corollaries, the "person" is mentioned and placed at the center. Thus, "A person anticipates . . . " (Construction Corollary), "Persons differ . . . " (Individuality Corollary), "A person chooses . . . " (Choice Corollary), "A person may successively employ . . . " (Fragmentation Corollary). But still the kind of nature which this "person" has who chooses, employs, anticipates, and differs is left unspecified.

Similarly, in defining his constructs concerning transition, Kelly talks repeatedly of "awareness"—awareness of dislodgment, awareness of incidental or comprehensive change, awareness of events lying outside the range of one's constructs. Who is "aware" of all these things? It is the "person" of course, but again, what sort of creature is that?

As mentioned earlier, Kelly thought that one of the vital tasks for man was to "transcend the obvious," to break out of the "cliché" which we tend to make of our reality. So at the center of his psychology is a huge question mark concerning the nature of man: a mystery, rather than any suggestion of a pat answer or a comfortable conclusion. In contrast to this, many of the approaches to man in much of psychology have been so simplified and apparently "conclusive" that they have stunted the imagination and obscured the freedoms of generations of psychologists. Rather than sensing and respecting man as an astonishing mystery, we seem often to have turned him instead into a "cheap thriller" or an "open and shut case."

In recognizing and suggesting that we approach man as a mystery, Kelly is not proposing either a defeatist or an obscurantist position. He is saying rather than man is an endless mystery which we have repeatedly been making different things of throughout the centuries. We have seen something of his struggles and sufferings and something of the things he has created and destroyed. We have seen the terrible heresies of one age becoming the commonplace assumptions of the next. Man has made many different things of himself in different times and in different places.

Because of considerations such as these, Kelly suggests that if we are to make something more of the mystery of man—or any man—we should not limit ourselves by considering him only within the fleeting moments of a psychological experiment, or in the first five years of life, or even within a ten-year follow-up. Kelly suggests that we may be able to gain a fuller perspective on the possible nature of man if we consider him within the span of his own life and, beyond that, within the sweep of the centuries. At any moment each man is suspended somewhere between his own birth and his own death, but also between the birth and death of the human race, the birth and death of the world, and more. If we only view him within very narrow limits of time and place we may dismiss many human struggles as trivial or neurotic which may appear in a different light if we consider a wider context and a longer journey.

The whole direction and thrust of Kelly's concern is with what man may yet make of himself, with what he may yet turn out to be. The position Kelly took was that we do not yet know what man may become. He is limited by the limits of his own daring and ingenuity. A major task for psychology, therefore, is to extend that ingenuity and provide means whereby we may dare to attempt what previously would have seemed impossible. Personal construct psychology itself has to be considered in relation to aims such as these.

Inquiry as Venture

The metaphors of "adventure," "exploration," and "quest" seem to reflect something of the spirit which permeates much of Kelly's writing. Kelly indeed claimed that this approach in psychology was an invitation to "immediate adventure," since he was suggesting that we can make ourselves and can make ourselves differently if we so choose. He took the position that we are not bound by our conditioning or our family dynamics, or delineated completely by our heredity, *unless we choose so to be.* He is thus inviting us to consider seriously that we can *be* different if we go out and *do* differently, we can *become* different by *acting* differently. We are probably limited in many ways, but we do not know for sure what these limits may turn out to be when we challenge them with imagination and determination. Our imagination or ingenuity is something we can work to develop, whereas we may scarcely think this worth pursuing if we suppose our limitations are *preordained* and *in nature.*

This invitation to venture is a difficult one to cope with, since it puts up to question all our accepted reasons for not being as different as we so often claim we want to be. It raises the uncomfortable possibility that we might ourselves be determining that our fate be thought of as already determined, we might ourselves be digging the very graves which with increasingly desperate cries we claim are getting deeper and are threatening to swallow us completely. This may be an uncomfortable possibility to face, but there is worse to come if we try to translate Kelly's invitation into practice. If we dare to step out of our usual ruts or beyond the safe and familiar routines of our lives, we are liable, very quickly, to find ourselves experiencing considerable distress in many forms, which Kelly terms "anxiety," "guilt," "threat," and "fear."

The kind of venture which seems to me to assume a central place in personal construct psychology is not of the "big game hunting" or the "conquering Everest" variety. It is something both more homely and more audacious. What Kelly seems to be advocating is something like "life on the frontier"—living on the frontiers of your experience rather than within cosily settled conventions or as a more-or-less willing victim of the demands of tradition. You can almost hear the "wagon trains moving westward," seeking new pastures and more space for living, as you read Kelly's writings. Venture of this kind, even if it may seem to be on a very small scale, if it is to persist in the face of dangers and deprivations, requires the kind of courage described by Paul Tillich (1952) in *The Courage to Be* or the "anchorite and eagle courage" rather than "courage before witnesses" referred to by Nietzsche (1911).

One of the unusual features of Kelly's psychology is that the constructs he outlines to subsume experiences of change and transition are not so much accounts of what we are like, but are rather forewarnings, anticipations, preparations for what we are likely to experience *if* we venture even a little beyond the security of our settled ways. His "constructs of transition" are like warnings and strategies for recognizing and perhaps coping with trials and terrors awaiting each venturer as he lays himself at risk by crossing the boundaries of the known within his own life.

So what kinds of experiences are we likely to have to cope with if we accept Kelly's invitation to venture, if we begin to "move out west"? Even before the journey properly begins we may experience a sense of panic sweeping through us. We may sense that once we leave the safety of "home," things may never be the same again, that *we* may never be the same again. This terror may scream to us to be sensible, to stay at home, to hold to what we have and know, to leave well alone. This is *threat*. It is described by Kelly as "the awareness of an imminent comprehensive change in one's core structures." Many ventures big and small stop just here, often before they have really begun. Therefore if we are to be able to accept Kelly's invitation to venture, we will have to learn both how to recognize and to cope with such threat. This may itself be no easy matter and may be sufficient to discourage all further attempts at movement.

If we overcome this first hurdle and manage to move out a little into what is for us "unknown territory," all may go well for a time. Then, as the strange emptiness and noises of the unknown get through to us as we clutch our favorite protective blankets, we may be gripped by an undermining sense of "being at sea" or "being lost." We may experience all sorts of alarms and panics which unsettle the very foundations of our normally accepted understandings of ourselves and the world. All this is *anxiety*, which Kelly described as "the awareness that the events with which one is confronted lie mostly outside the range of convenience of his construct system." Anxiety is meaninglessness, the loss of any adequate way to structure our experience of ourselves in relation to the world. It is to some degree an inevitable accompaniment of venture, and not only courage but some skill in *making* sense where there is nonsense and confusion is needed. The acquisition of some such skill seems a necessary prerequisite if venture of the kind Kelly is suggesting is to be pursued beyond the first few steps.

Many more specific dangers are likely to loom up which are fairly clear and identifiable. These dangers, which do not leave us victims of the unsettlement of anxiety or the disruption of threat, may be experienced as *fear*. This, for Kelly, is "the awareness of an imminent incidental change in one's core structure." Though no major challenge to the way we constitute or make sense of ourselves or the world is at stake here, ways of coping with fear need also to be learned if such dangers are to be overcome and the venture continued.

But even if we manage to deal with experiences such as these, we may still find ourselves with a deep sense of disorientation, wondering what has become of the person we used to be and used to know. We may find ourselves no longer able to recognize or even own the kind of person we are beginning to become. This is the experience of *guilt*, which Kelly describes as "the awareness of dislodgment of the self from one's core role structure." This sense of loss of self may be so traumatic as to leave no apparent ways back to some secure sense of what we used to take ourselves as being. The extreme danger here is not from other people or external dangers but from suicide as a desperate attempt to provide a solution, even though it proves to be a final solution. Because of this, the development of ways of coping with "guilt," which is the sense of "sin" involved in new ventures, is vital if the invitation to personal venture is accepted and is to be carried to some constructive conclusion.

Because he thought it so important that any venturer learn to explore and come up with new kinds of solutions, Kelly included in his "training manual" the outlines of two strategies for tackling problems with honesty and openness. The first of these he called the *creativity cycle*. The "loosening" phase of this involves the skills of backing off from an immediate problem, looking around, loosening up, taking a fresh perspective, free associating, getting more possibilities available for consideration. Thereafter the various tactics or skills involved in the "tightening" phase have to be brought into operation, whereby some particular possibility is clarified and sharpened so that it can be acted on and the resulting outcome evaluated and the procedures thereafter modified as necessary.

Intersecting with this particular strategy is another which Kelly refers to as the *c-p-c cycle*. This involves "circumspection" (looking around for new possibilities), "pre-emption" (selection of particular possibility), and "control" (the decision or choice which precipitates the person into action). Only the most general outlines of these two strategies are provided by Kelly, and a great deal of detailed work would have to be done with them if they are to become personally effective approaches to action. Thus again, preparation for ventures seems to involve considerable work in becoming proficient in the use of strategies such as these.

In considering adventure, I suggested that Kelly's concerns were "homely" as well as "audacious." What may seem to an onlooker as a modest, homely venture, if venture at all, may however be for the person involved something of terrifying uncertainty within his particular world. You will not appreciate the terrors and dangers facing me in any venture unless you understand what I am risking, or what in Heinrich Ott's (1967) words, is "ultimately at stake" for me. In any venture you put yourself at risk to some degree, and while an invitation to venturesomeness is offered by Kelly, it would seem not unreasonable to treat it with caution. Much may be at stake.

Understanding as Making and Making Up

The metaphor of "making," and indeed "making up," is fairly explicit in Kelly's writing. Thus, in the very word "construction" Kelly is perhaps suggesting that we view our inquiries, our ventures *as if* they involved making, building, designing, planning, erecting (and perhaps some of his own early interest in engineering is reflected here). At first sight it would seem that this emphasis on making, on the man-made, would fit in well with our manufacturing types of society. But it has not yet turned out to be so, and perhaps a little further elaboration of the metaphors may give some clues as to why this may be.

Before doing this, though, it is well to remember that Kelly talks of "making" always within the wider context of the ultimate mystery of man and his world. So, unlike those who emphasize the use of more mechanistic metaphors of man in psychology, Kelly is concerned with the ways in which we *make* means by which to *realize* something of the mystery of our as yet unrealized and even unimagined possibilities. Anything but the most superficial acknowledgment of the central mystery of man seems to be shunned by most psychologists and especially by those who consider themselves most "realistic" and "scientific." Thus, the tenor of the times is often to approach our subject matter with little respect and with the general assumption that there are only a few more hitches to be sorted out before we have his "real nature" trapped and tamed. All this tends to mean that we create methods of inquiry which aim to pin man down as quickly and effectively as possible so that we may claim to predict and control him, rather than giving our energies to developing, to *making*, means whereby he may be helped to *make* more of himself.

"Making" for Kelly was clearly a kind of "do-it-yourself" activity, and making things by and for yourself in this way is a lot harder, more time-consuming, frustrating, and demanding than buying or borrowing the "ready-made" hand-me-downs of your culture. But learning to make, not merely things, but your very self seems to be what Kelly was suggesting. He proposed in fact that his philosophical position could be described as one of "ontological responsibility." For him the underlying task of man was to undertake increasing responsibility for his own actions, even those he may presently consider irrational or beyond his control. Learning to assume such responsibility is clearly a serious undertaking, since it involves taking into our own hands all the duties and problems of *making* our own way in the world and the demanding, endless challenges of *making* the means whereby we may be able to *make* something more of ourselves than we have so far achieved.

"Making" also involves many phases of activity which we can

readily forget when we become accustomed to living by "inherited" or "ready-made and polythene wrapped" methods. It involves getting and preparing the materials, planning the sequences of how things should be done, recognizing that things cannot be rushed and time is involved, appreciating that it involves skill in the use (even the making) of the tools by means of which we can work on the materials in producing the results we are seeking. All this requires a real valuing of the thing being made and a respect for the tools, materials, and means whereby it is being made. Thus it is perhaps not so surprising that Kelly's invitation to "make" ourselves and our meanings in the world has been received with less than avid enthusiasm.

There is another point which should also be made here which emphasizes still more the enormousness of the task waiting for us if we consider entering the "homemade-person" business. As soon as we begin we are likely to find ourselves slap up against the question: *What* should we make of ourselves? Each person has to ask what he should try to be, or simply, as Kelly puts it in "A Psychology of the Optimal Man" (1969), "what ought he to be?" Since there is no one around other than the person himself to give an answer to this question, the responsibility and the uncertainty remain his own. This kind of choice may again be a sufficient reason to justify abandoning the whole venture of making one's own way.

But all this is only to touch the very edge of the disturbance to our settled ways which Kelly is suggesting. It seems to me to be one of Kelly's vital contributions to psychology that he stresses that "making" very often involves "making up." If we get involved in "making ourselves" or "making our own sense of the world," we will find ourselves concerned with "invention" and not just the shoring up of already prepared structures. Kelly (1969) suggested, in "The Language of Hypothesis," a new mood for the use of language—the invitational mood—which would be useful here. Using language in this way we would not refer to fixed realities, as with the indicative mood, but would invite exploration of alternatives, as when we ask, "Suppose we regard the floor as if it were hard," or "Let us view your father as if he were shy." Statements such as these, says Kelly, leave "both the speaker and the listener, not with a conclusion on their hands, but in a posture of expectancy—suppose we regard the floor as hard, what then?" Such an approach to language and reality orients one to the future and not merely to the present or the past.

"It invites the listener to cope with his circumstances . . . in new ways." Kelly goes on further to say that make-believe is indeed an essential feature of science and that science tends to make progress by scientists entertaining propositions which appear initially to be quite preposterous.

This same kind of concern with "as if" is involved in metaphor, and the same kind of invitation to pursue the "fictions of mankind" was outlined in some detail by Vaihinger (1924) in *The Philosophy of "As If"*. But are we in any position to *accept* such an invitational mood, to approach the world *as if* it were our oyster, a cuddly teddy bear, or a hair shirt of fiendish efficiency? Once again I think this turns out to be a more demanding kind of invitation than may at first appear.

Many people, when invited to think or act *as if*, find this an almost unintelligible suggestion. Their attitude may be summed up as, "What is the case is the case and there is no point in denying it." With this view it may well seem ridiculous to suppose that "hard realities" could ever be approached or constructed differently. But what Kelly is suggesting is not naive optimism but rather that we may be limited primarily by the degree of our own and our society's ingenuity in inventing and daring to explore alternative possibilities of how we might take things to be.

If the invitation is taken up it seems often to get stuck after the first improbable step. "So what if I do consider my father to be shy rather than uncaring, what then? That still doesn't alter the fact that he has made me so miserable." What seems to be needed here is skillful alternation between "as if" thinking and *if . . . then* thinking. The *if . . . then* mode of thinking is the more commonly discussed one whereby we make use of the accepted rules of language and logic, work out implications, and consider relevant evidence in support of our propositions. The *if . . . then* form is just as important as the other but rests on it and follows after it. While a considerable amount of attention has been paid to this type of approach—*if* such and such *then* such and such follows—in psychology, the *as if* mode has been largely ignored or left implicit and therefore confusingly vague. We seem generally to be less sure of what to do and where to go from our first steps in *as if* thinking, or make-believe, than with the more bounded and familiar routines of *if . . . then*.

Often, also, if our first excursions in *as if*—pretence or make-believe—seems to open up some new idea or prospect for us, we are liable to consider this as now constituting "the answer" or "the truth," subject of course to its surviving various *if . . . then* kinds of tests. In Turbayne's (1962) sense it is here that we are again in danger of being used by the metaphors we have just invented. The danger is in confusing our metaphors, or inventions, with reality itself. If we do this we are likely to tie ourselves down to our new interpretations, our new pretences, just as we were tied down to the old ones.

But if we get this far in the use of *as if* thinking and acting, then an alarming alternative to accepting the "new view" as the "new reality" may open up. The alternative that may be borne in on us is that all our interpretations are subject to change, that we know nothing for sure and certain. An awareness of this gaping possibility whereby we and the world seem *nothing but* a patina of make-believe, pretence, and fictions can be tremendously threatening. It may undermine one's whole sense of the solidity of existence and the world. Thus, if you pursue the *as if* approach past the first few stages, you may suddenly be aware that you are headed for nowhere and nothingness, groundless subjectivity where everything might be this or might be that, but nothing is known for sure. No wonder most of us don't get beyond this point very often, and no wonder Kelly's innocent-looking invitation to think *as if* has not been taken up with very obvious alacrity.

I suspect Kelly is inviting us to just this kind of experience of groundlessness, but not merely to this. The awareness and acceptance that all our present understandings are likely, in the course of time, to prove inadequate and subject to change does not mean that they are of no use to us. What it probably does mean is a change in our attitude towards what we presently take to be reality. It may mean that if we are to avoid both the dangers of being willing victims of our metaphors and finding ourselves awash in a frightening sea of shifting uncertainties, then we have to learn how to take the further steps involved in *committing ourselves* to our "best" interpretations or pretences. This means learning to entrust ourselves to and with those of our constructions which seem to offer us, in so far as we are able to judge, most scope and understanding, grasp and meaning in our continuing living. Kelly's concern with "commitment" should perhaps thus be seen as a necessary accompaniment of his invitiation to think "as if." But again it makes life difficult in some respects since, in psychology at least, we have done little to elaborate *how* people learn to commit themselves to work out the possibilities of particular positions. Such work may prove necessary if Kelly's invitation to make-believe is to be accepted.

So it seems we may be letting ourselves in for a lot of problems if we take up this invitation. We may have to learn how to pretend, how to pretend to take our pretences seriously as we act through and in relation to them, how to entrust ourselves (the continuing mystery of whatever we may turn out to be) to the frail vehicle of some of our seeming "best" pretences. This life of passionate pretence and revision of pretences seems to be something like what Kelly is inviting us to consider. Such a view of life is at odds with our commonly accepted understanding of honesty and openness, direct dealing, and belief in the obvious. What it seems to imply is that in some sense our most "honest" searching for understanding of ourselves, others, or the world we live in may be possible only through willing "deception," by making intentional "mistakes" and then by learning for a time to deceive ourselves about our deceptions by acting as if they were truth itself. Such a view would make Sartre's (1956) discussions of "bad faith" and Fingarette's (1969) lucid, penetrating account of self-deception of considerable importance in a psychological understanding of honesty and make-believe. They would similarly be directly relevant to a fuller appreciation of the nature of Kelly's invitation to think "as if."

Knowing as Indwelling

It is important to remember in all this that Kelly was concerned to outline a strategically fruitful *psychological* approach to the understanding of man. His advocacy of venture was in relation to making something of the continuing mystery of *man*. But just as the explorer in the outside world will achieve some understanding of peoples he meets on his journeying if he *lives among* them for a time, so the personal venturer will only gain intimate knowledge of himself or others by getting close to them in some way, by getting under their skins. Kelly refers to this matter in his essay "Psychotherapy and the Nature of Man" (Kelly, 1969). "With all respect to the psychologists who erect systems between themselves and their fellow men," says Kelly, who considers himself as guilty as any in this matter, "the next step in this discussion is to point out that the closer one gets to persons the closer he gets to the nature of man. Granted, of course, that getting close to a person does not guarantee that you will understand him!" He goes on to point out that "if you never get close to him it is doubtful that you can ever develop a very perceptive scheme for understanding him." Similarly, in "The Psychology of the Unknown" (Kelly, 1963), when he talks of the vital importance of *involvement* for psychological understanding, he reminds us that

> if a man, say a psychologist, remains aloof from the human enterprise he sees only what is visible from the outside. But if he engages himself he will be caught up in the realities of human existence in ways that would never have occurred to him. He will breast the onrush of events. He will see, he will feel, he will be frightened, he will be exhilarated, and he will find himself feared, hated, and loved. Every resource at his disposal, not merely his cognitive and professional talents, will be challenged. So involved will he be that, in order to survive, he will have to cope with his circumstances inarticulately as well as verbally, primitively as well as intelligently, and he will have to pull himself together physically, socially, biologically and spiritually.

Not only Kelly, but also the philosopher of science and former professor of physical chemistry, Michael Polanyi (1958), shows appreciation of the significance of involvement for knowing and understanding. He discusses it, though in the context of science, mathematics, the arts, and religion, and speaks of both "dwelling in" and "breaking out" from immersion in the subject matter of concern or contemplation. Both phases of the activity are vital if, in our earlier terms, we are to avoid being used by our metaphors, or if we are to avoid losing ourselves within only one phase of the creativity cycle. Kelly similarly recognizes the importance of "breaking out" in his insistence on the necessity of "reconstruction" in addition to involvement and commitment. However, I want to focus here on "indwelling" or "involvement," since this aspect of experiencing is so often ignored in psychology. "A true understanding of science and mathematics," suggests Polanyi, "includes the capacity for a contemplative experience of them." He goes on to talk also of music and dramatic art and of how a teacher should enable a pupil "to surrender himself to the works of art." "This is neither to observe nor to handle them, but to live in them." Later he also claims that "the impersonality of intense contemplation consists in a complete participation of the person in that which he contemplates and not in his detachment from it, as would be the case in an ideally objective observation."

So here we find ourselves again confronted with suggestions which run counter to much that psychologists as scientists have been taught about the necessity of "detachment" and "separateness" between knower and known, inquirer and subject. Indeed, one of the tasks facing us in trying to understand Kelly's psychology of personal constructs is that of learning to "indwell" or "live in" our experience of ourselves and others. One form of metaphor, namely, *personification*, may be specially useful here. Personification involves treating events, experiences, things, and feelings *as if* they were persons with whom we are engaged in some kind of relationship. In using this metaphoric mode it is possible sometimes to "enter" and sense, *as if* from the "inside," some of our experiences which may otherwise remain external to us, separated, little known, or threateningly unformulated. Thus, with appropriate preparations being given, it is possible, for example, to consider a concept like the "future" *as if* it were a "person" we are going forward to meet, and to find out thereby what kind of "person" this seems to be and what kind of "relationship" we have with each other. This is a sort-crossing task which can result in surprising insights for the person involved concerning his approach to life and the kinds of problems he is experiencing, even if inarticulately, in his everyday affairs. Or again, a heavy smoker may be invited to think of "cigarettes" *as if* they are a "person" he is meeting many times each day of his life, and this improbable task can sometimes lend to insights and personal knowledge which might not be forthcoming with more direct questioning.

Consider a little more fully one example of a stammerer who is losing his stammer but still sticks on some words sometimes, and he is asking if he may just have to accept that he will always have a slight speech impediment. After some practice with *as if* thinking, he was able to consider his residual stammer *as if* it were a "person" he was having some dealings with. Through this strange cross-sorting he sensed that it was *as if* his irregular speech was a small boy who had been shut away in some kind of room or prison for a very long time. This small boy, it seemed, was determined to make sure that something of him was heard, even though he was not given any direct voice in the man's affairs. To the stammerer it seemed that this small boy felt things very deeply, though the man himself had always tried to keep his feelings in check throughout his life. So the small boy made his presence felt through disruption of the man's speech in all kinds of situations where the man was attempting to gloss over or hide his feelings or deny their existence. Both the stammerer himself and I, listening to him, felt we were here beginning to deal with something of importance in his life, even though it arose in this curious form of make-believe.

Examples of this kind of use of personification can readily be multiplied, but in the few examples I've mentioned the people involved did seem able to "get into" some aspects of their "problems" in ways which might not have been possible had they remained at the level of "obvious reality." One way of understanding how this might be is to suppose that each of us *as persons* is able to respond to all sorts of circumstances *to the extent of our capacities as persons.* We are not necessarily limited in *our* ways of dealing with events by the more restricted characteristics or capacities which we ascribe to the things or events themselves. I can respond to all kinds of circumstances to the limits of *my* capacities, whatever they may be, and am not restricted in my ways of responding by the limits of *the thing* I am dealing with. Thus unless we can provide ourselves with the opportunity and means of understanding our relationship with events in some ways which are as broad and complex as we are ourselves, we may sometimes not be able to make any adequate sense of our apparently "irrational" concerns.

The ploy of "getting into" our experiencing of some events by the use of personification can be elaborated further. Consider the stammerer a little more. He is able to "describe" the "little boy" who has been kept a "prisoner" for many years, but he can then be invited for a time to *be* this boy rather than his more elaborate usual self. This step is likely not to be possible without preparation, since an unusual mode of experiencing is being suggested. The person is being invited to shift the center of his awareness so that he is thinking and feeling *as if* from within the "boy" rather than from his customary perspective. In this particular instance our patient begins a bit falteringly, softly, to talk of feeling neglected and ignored, of feeling tremendous rage at times at never being allowed a voice or say in affairs. He says how he feels very deeply about things, both passionate hatred as well as love. He feels that his feelings of love and affection especially are ignored and neglected by the person of the stammerer, who seems frightened of them and shuts him away. He goes on haltingly to say that he has always loved this person of whom he is a part and can never leave him until these feelings of his can be both recognized and expressed by the person as an integral part of himself. In the course of all this the stammerer is near to tears, he is clearly very moved by what he finds himself saying and feeling. He feels he has been involved in exploring something which he had scarcely been aware of and had no way of recognizing or approaching.

Whether he is then able to *make* further use of this kind of experience is another matter. I am merely offering it here as an instance of *indwelling*, as living in and from an aspect of his experience which in a way didn't even exist before the metaphor of personification was introduced as a vehicle for elaborating his present awareness. Personification is only one way of extending our skills in "living in" aspects of our experience, but it seems to be especially relevant in considering personal construct psychology. This seems so because at the center of Kelly's thinking is the *person*, and personal *experience* is a fulcrum around which the powers of the individual are exercised. Even though the person may be a continuing and living mystery, *greater understanding of the mystery may be gained by entering and using the mystery itself*, the form of the personal, rather than escaping into *premature* objectivity. In personification we are attempting to penetrate a mystery by using the form of the mystery itself. Even though we are not yet able to articulate many of the powers and possibilities of the personal, we need to develop means whereby we can *use* these powers to make available to us knowledge and understandings which do not present themselves in logical, prepacked forms. Unless we can make better ways of dwelling in and breaking out from aspects of our awareness, we may fail to make what we might of many of our personal possibilities.

It might seem to some that the use of personification is a very retrograde step in psychology. It may seem like bringing back homunculi of many kinds, as well as witches, hobgoblins, and gremlins, when so much effort has been exerted in replacing such as these by "objectivity" and reason. However, this would be to miss the point. I wonder if we had to rush into preemptive objectivity because we knew no other way of combating the tyranny of metaphors which we mistook for direct claims about reality. Provided that we persist in remembering that we are engaged in forming and discovering something of our reality through interpretation and reinterpretation, then we may be able to tread safely on dangerous ground where previously we were liable to be sucked down into believing that our own fictions were direct accounts of naked reality. Realities of a psychological kind are involved, but these can be constructed only as we live in *and* break out from our metaphoric self-deceptions.

The use of personification can extend far beyond the account I have given here. It is often readily possible for people to formulate aspects of their awareness *as if* different subselves were involved. In this way a person may be enabled to enter and elaborate his experience of himself and his relations both within himself and between himself and other aspects of the world in a manner which is quite different from the "external" view the person may generally have of himself. Such "selves" may be explored as varying and changing "communities," each person being himself a "community of selves" rather than a single unit closed like a clam. In identifying and living in different "selves" or groupings of selves within his own personal "community," a person may gain a living sense of the kind of "population" he includes, the manner of organization or controls exercised by aspects of himself, the sorts of fragmentations and separations which are operating, the kinds of rules of entry or exclusion which he may be enforcing in different aspects of his "community" without his general awareness. By means such as this a new perspective on many aspects of personal construct theory may also be obtained through the provision of some means of living in and from aspects of awareness, rather than taking only an external view of something abstractly considered as a personal construct *system*. From within, it may come to seem more like a *living community*, where aspects of structure and organization may be explored as living "realities" rather than treated as rather distant abstractions.

All this is, however, only a way of saying that "indwelling" seems to be a metaphor which we may need to explore if we are to "get into" aspects of personal construct psychology and if we are to gain more intimate knowledge of *the person* who is at the center of Kelly's concerns. Again the unusualness of this line of thought and action within general psychology may be another factor contributing to the difficulty we seem to have in making much that is new of the kind of psychology which Kelly seems to be inviting us towards.

A PSYCHOLOGY OF LIVING

So far, through the use of a number of metaphors, I've tried to indicate that there are aspects of Kelly's thinking which are unusual in the context of the mainstream of present-day psychology. Kelly seems to be inviting us to involve ourselves in inquiries of personal concern and thus to put ourselves at risk. Inquiry, in the sense in which Kelly uses the term, may involve the person fully and challenge all his talents and resources. Indeed, for Kelly it seems that "inquiry" is a metaphor for "living" itself rather than some separated activity whereby we detach ourselves from life and observe from a distance. Thus the metaphors for aspects of inquiry which I have already been considering—"making" and "making up," "venture," and "indwelling"—can similarly be treated as metaphors for aspects of living. Kelly suggests that by participating fully in and committing himself to such activities, a person may make something of his life and take responsibility for what he is making.

It is perhaps this reflexive perspective of *inquiry as living* and *living as inquiry* which makes personal construct psychology particularly awkward to handle alongside many other theories and approaches in psychology where "living" and "behavior" and "psychological inquiry" seem to be treated as separate kinds of events.

Kelly's psychology of *ways of living* has a number of emphases which distinguish it from, for example, a psychology of *behavior*. It concerns itself with the span of a person's life and the sense he is making within that span, rather than only or mainly with the outcomes of specific experiments. It involves us in dealing with things which matter to the persons concerned and not just or mainly with those issues which matter to professional inquirers. It focuses on the ways in which any person struggles to make something of himself and his circumstances through his actions rather than on his observed movements, traits, or traumas. It involves understanding of the person from his point of view and is intimately concerned with personal meanings, values, and commitments rather than detached observations and neutralized matters of "general" concern.

However, in pursuing the metaphor of *living as inquiry*, Kelly condenses many of his beliefs about both into the enigmatic wording of the fundamental postulate. Here I want to draw attention to two issues concerning living which are important for our understanding of Kelly's views on the nature of psychological inquiry. I want to suggest that Kelly was trying to develop *a psychology of questions* and a *psychology of means and manners* in personal action.

Consider first his interest in *questions*. Apart from talking of human life both for the individual and for mankind through the centuries as a *quest*, Kelly often talks *as if* "behavior" is our way of posing questions in the world. Questions are means and frameworks by and through which we anticipate events in forms bounded by our present understandings. With questions we reach out for and attempt to clothe with some familiarity the unknowns which lie ahead of us or outside our range of present comprehension. In personal construct psychology our attention is repeatedly directed to the questions a person may be asking through his whole living and not just in his words. It is assumed that little understanding has been attained of any person unless the fundamental questions which permeate and sustain his living have been recognized. Indeed, so central is a concern with questions in personal construct psychology that their importance for living and therefore also for inquiry is affirmed within the fundamental postulate of the theory. To highlight this particular meaning, Kelly's wording can be paraphrased to read, "A person's processes are psychologically channelized by his questions."

Questions and ways of asking questions set the limits on the kinds of answers which can be achieved. Something of the importance of questions can be noted by stepping outside personal construct theory for a moment. In her *Philosophy in a New Key*, which also stresses the importance of metaphor in human affairs, Susanne Langer (1951) clarified this point well in her beautifully illuminating overview of changes in philosophic thought through the centuries. She suggests that every age has its own philosophical preoccupations, and each age is distinguished by its "mode of handling problems, rather than what they are about." This mode of handling any problem "begins with its first expression as a question. The way a question is asked limits and disposes the ways in which any answer to it—right or wrong—may be given." In philosophy (as perhaps in individual lives), major movement comes not from piling up detailed answers to old questions, but eventually from rejecting the question in the old form and formulating different questions. Any particular way of formulating a question carries within its structure the hidden assumptions, which are more or less consciously taken as being truths. Professor Langer points out that though these assumptions are not usually stated by a person, "they find expression in the *form of his questions*." She goes on to say that "a question is really an ambiguous proposition; the answer is its determination. There can be only a certain number of alternatives that will complete its sense. In this way the intellectual treatment of any datum, any experience, any subject, is determined by the nature of our questions, and only carried out in the answers." She further suggests,

> In philosophy this disposition of problems is the most important thing that a school, a movement, or an age con-tributes. This is the "genius" of a great philosophy; in its light, systems arise and rule and die. Therefore a philosophy is characterized more by the *formulation* of its problems than by its solution of them. Its answers establish an edifice of facts; but its questions make the frame in which its picture of facts is plotted. They make more than the frame; they give the angle of perspective, the palette, the style in which the picture is drawn—everything except the subject. In our questions lie our *principles of analysis,* and our answers may express whatever those principles are able to yield. [P. 16]

Everything said here by Susanne Langer could refer also to the individual person and could be taken as a brilliant account of the importance of questions, which Kelly clearly recognized within the fundamental statement of his theory. For Kelly, an intimate concern with questions both precedes and provides the context of all answers, and answers for Kelly are "good" answers only insofar as they raise even better questions. Kelly's interest seems always to be aroused more by a man's questions than by his answers, and as we have already noted, he even suggested that we adopt an "invitational mood" in our language so that we might more readily approach our most familiar as well as other more unusual "answers" with a posture of expectancy, as questions rather than firm conclusions.

Kelly perhaps chose "the scientist" as an explicit metaphor for man because in our time the scientist is par excellence the person who has elaborated the art of asking penetrating questions in ways which have provided answers and further questions of astonishing beauty and power. Kelly's interest was not to turn everyone into formal scientists, but rather to draw attention to the essential human function of questioning and to encourage the elaboration of ways of clarifying and pursuing our questions which are most often acted rather than stated, implicit in our assumptions and deeds rather than consciously recognized and pursued in full awareness.

Kelly was of course also very much concerned with "getting answers" and with how people get answers for themselves. It was because of this that he stressed the direct relevance of the principles in the experimental methods of science for the posing and answering of questions in everyday life. However, for Kelly, questions are primary, since their form contains already the kinds of answers that can thereafter be attained. A psychology which emphasizes questions rather than answers inevitably raises problems for which no ready-made solutions are available. As yet no systematic means have been developed whereby we can readily identify, clarify, formulate, and reformulate the questions which may sustain, guide, or perplex our lives. Few books on psychological methodology give more than cursory attention to elaborating means whereby we may formulate and explore central questions clothed in our everyday concerns.

Kelly also seems to be proposing a *psychology of means and manners* in inquiry and living. He clearly recognized that the means we employ rank in importance with the ends for which we strive. In his "Psychology of the Optimal Man" (1967), Kelly states this concern plainly in discussing an example of a man who spends his time making as much money as he can. "What does it mean?" Kelly asks:

> Perhaps he is trying to insure his family against every conceivable hazard, or himself from the haunting fear of disclosing his own insufficiency. Whatever it is, his money making makes sense only in the light of his anticipations. But it also works the other way around. He may end up his life as a wealthy grasping man, himself his family's worst hazard and, as

a person, revealed as insufficient in more ways than when he started. The goal he so faithfully pursued turns out to be defined, not only by his ambition, but also by what he did to fulfill it. So for us all! *The events we attempt to anticipate may turn out to be contaminated by what we did to anticipate them.* [P. 248, italics added]

In other words the means we adopt and the manner in which we pursue our ends and give effect to our means modify the ends we aim for and themselves constitute a part of the ends we do achieve. The stress Kelly wanted to place on *means* is again expressed directly in the fundamental postulate of his theory where he states that "A person's processes are psychologically channelized *by the ways* in which he anticipates events."

In psychology generally there has been only a limited recognition that *the ways* in which we do things may significantly alter what we are doing. In accepting the conventional procedures of "scientific" inquiry within psychology we have adopted a set of stylistic rules whereby the investigator keeps himself anonymous, impassive, detached, and uncommunicative as regards his own beliefs, expectations, hopes, and intentions. Through this style of interaction with his subjects the experimenter hopes that his inquiry will thereby remain "pure" and avoid the "contamination" which would result if any other manner or style were adopted. Only relatively recently have severe doubts been cast on the general validity of this "correct" manner of approach in interpersonal inquiries. In psychology, just as in everyday life, it is unlikely that we can be most open, informative, and cooperative with someone who insists on being distant, impassive, uninvolved, impersonal, or uncommunicative. In psychological inquiry, as in ordinary life, the ways in which we pursue our concerns, the means we adopt, and the manners these involve modify the meanings we aim to create.

Something of this same kind of concern is highlighted by Watzlawick, Beavin, and Jackson (1968) when they outline five tentative axioms of human communication. In their second axiom they suggest that "every communication has a content and a relationship aspect such that the latter classifies the former and is therefore a meta-communication." That is, when we say or do anything we do so in some particular style or manner, and this manner modifies or qualifies what we are saying or doing. The resulting communication is then a mixture of the apparent message and the form or way in which it is constructed and conveyed. What Kelly also seems to be saying is that in all human inquiry, in all our actions in living, this intermingling of "content" and "manner" is always present. Just as the "tenor" and "vehicle" of a metaphor interact to create new meaning, so also in all our actions, what we do is transformed by how we do it. While our means, manners, and ends may not always be easily distinguished, they have to be recognized and explored in Kelly's psychology of living and in any psychological inquiry into living.

We noted earlier that the classical view of language and metaphor assumed that language (and perhaps also our other ways of making sense of events) and the "objective" world were quite separate things and also that the *manner* in which something is said (or otherwise acted out) does not significantly alter *what* is said (or done). In psychology we seem to have been working on something like these assumptions in inquiries into personal and interpersonal functioning. However, rather than talking of "Plain Style" which allows the "Truth" to appear unadorned by the seductions and fripperies of metaphoric extravagance, we have held instead to an equally puritanical "scientific method." By this standard means we have tried to cut through the "conceits" and "embellishments" of personal manners and styles in order to gain access to the "plain," "basic" laws of our human nature.

Kelly, it seems to me, is challenging this whole network of assumptions and is suggesting that in psychology we have to come to terms with the kind of alternative view which in earlier times, through the romantic movement, transformed our understanding of the role of metaphor in language and language in relation to our understanding of reality. He seems to be suggesting that our "ways of anticipating events" include both the means which we use and the ends towards which we strive and that both of these are in their turn intertwined with and transformed by the manner in which we both ask our questions and construct our answers. Both in living and in inquiry within psychology, we need then to develop ways in which we may be more sensitive to and respectful towards the diverse ways in which we and others fashion the styles of the realities within which we live. This again would seem to be no easy task, since only the very broadest terms within which such a psychology could be pursued have yet been conceived.

But it is not enough to recognize that the style or manner through which we deal with *present* events is an integral part of what they mean to us and what we intend in relation to them. Matters of manner and style seem also to be important in relation to *the ends* we seek as well as the *means* through which we seek them. When we probe into the unknown across the frontier of what we presently take to be the case, we are likely to find ourselves searching for "forms" in the haze of anxiety; we have to struggle to give "shape" to our inarticulate searchings; we must *formulate* some coherent understanding where there is at present only the uncertainty of shapeless possibility. How do we know in which direction to move, which possible patterns to trust and which to avoid? Might it not be that we are to some degree guided by our own sense of "good form," of "rightness of line," of "acceptable style"? Do we not structure our searchings through the "filters" of our own personal sense of "good style" or "good manners" or "good form"? While one person in relation to *his* questions may accept as adequate some explanation, solution, theory, or fact, another may well dismiss these as hopelessly inadequate in relation to the values which inform the pattern or style through which *he* reaches forward to give satisfying personal form to the "shape of things to come." The meanings we make and search for are shaped by the ways in which we anticipate events, and these ways include our questions and the manner in which we pursue them.

In advocating a psychology of *means and manners* Kelly seems thus to be directing our attention to the need to develop far greater psychological understanding of the questions we are asking in our everyday actions, and the manner, style, and form through which we create our relations with the world. He seems to be inviting us to consider the possibility that we need not necessarily be constrained or limited by a harsh, frequently ugly, and "puritanical" pursuit of the "plain, unvarnished facts." But once again, it seems to me, his invitation is no easy one to accept, since it suggests the need for fundamental reformulations in our approach to personal and interpersonal inquiry in psychology, and through the reflexivity which Kelly suggests between inquiry and living, in our manners of living too. We do not at present have in psychology many *ways* in which to identify and explore our questions, or represent and reform the manner in which we realize our intentions, or determine what we mean through the forms of our living.

AND SO . . .

I have tried to take another look at some aspects of personal construct psychology in the hope of removing some of the patina of familiarity which is already tending to hide the freshness of perspective George Kelly was struggling to create. My interpretations are inevitably a mixture of Kelly and me, but I hope something of the spirit of Kelly's questions and constructive answers has been illustrated even though I have bypassed most of the formal structure of his theory. Hopefully, also some of the abstract unfamiliarity of his thought can be made a little more accessible through the use of metaphor and the tradition of inquiry involved therewith.

Kelly seems to me to be offering us the outlines of a psychology of living which could considerably extend our understanding of psychological inquiry. Through making and make-believe, venture and involvement, he suggests that the mystery of man may be given new meanings. The alternative kind of psychology he indicates seems primarily concerned with our ways, manner, or style of reaching out towards ends through which we anticipate the realization of our intentions, which are themselves formed and reformed in the questions we pose in all our actions. It was Saint Augustine who said, "Let us know in order to search," and this same spirit informs Kelly's view of living as inquiry, as quest.

These insidious questions and gently insistent invitations to risk committing yourself to inquiries of personal significance are unlikely to find very ready acceptance in psychology, since they raise too many disquieting possibilities and too much threat to settled ways. Martin Foss (1949), in writing on *Symbol and Metaphor in Human Experience*, expressed something of what I feel about many of the "solutions" in terms of means and ends which we seem to have accepted in the mainstream of our modern psychology when he noted:

> The favorite answer of an age, however, is often one in which only a minimum of problems is preserved and which has been promoted to its place as favorite because it seems to render superfluous all further questioning. It closes all doors, blocks all ways, and just because of this permits the agreeable feeling that the goal has been reached and that rest is granted. [P. 1]

I hope it is apparent from what has been said here that Kelly has presented us with very many problems and numerous questions which we can scarcely yet ask, far less answer. Perhaps for some he has opened too many doors, which let in the cold draught of untamed reality and offered too many paths which lead into the unknown. If we are to avoid reducing his questions to technical clichés, we may find it useful to enrich our perspective on these concerns through a greater "command of metaphor." In so doing we may also build a bridge between the "arts" and the "sciences" and create a psychology which respects and offers some enrichment to the manner of our living and the form of our inquiry.

REFERENCES

Barbour, I. G. *Myths, models, and paradigms.* London: S. C. M. Press, 1974.

Burke, K. *A grammar of motives.* Berkeley: University of California Press, 1945.

Burke, K. *Permanence and change.* Los Altos, Calif.: Hermes Publications, 1954.

Eliot, T. S. The love song of J. Alfred Prufrock. In *Collected poems, 1909–1935.* London: Faber, 1936.

Empson, W. *Seven types of ambiguity.* (Rev. ed.) London: Chatto & Windus, 1953.

Fingarette, H. *Self-deception.* London: Routledge & Kegan Paul, 1969.

Foss, M. *Symbol and metaphor in human experience.* Lincoln: University of Nebraska Press, 1949.

Haley, J. Communication and therapy: Blocking metaphors. *American Journal of Psychotherapy,* 1971, **25**, 214.

Hawkes, T. *Metaphor.* London: Methuen, 1972.

Kelly, G. A. *The psychology of personal constructs.* Vols. 1 and 2. New York: Norton, 1955.

Kelly, G. A. The psychology of the unknown. Unpublished paper, Ohio State University, 1963.

Kelly, G. A. A psychology of the optimal man. In A. Mahrer (Ed.), *Goals of psychotherapy.* New York: Appleton-Century-Crofts, 1967.

Kelly, G. A. *Personality and clinical psychology: Selected papers of G. A. Kelly* (B. Maher, Ed.). New York: Wiley, 1969.

Langer, S. K. *Philosophy in a new key.* New York: Mentor, 1951.

Marias, J. Philosophic truth and the metaphoric system. In S. R. Hopper & D. L. Miller (Eds.), *Interpretation: The poetry of meaning.* New York: Harbinger Books, 1967. Pp. 41–53.

McCaig, N. Wild oats. In *Penguin modern poets*, Vol. 21. London: Penguin, 1972. P. 125.

Nietzsche, F. *The complete works of Friedrich Nietzsche* (O. Levy, Ed.). Vol. 4. P. 73, sec. 4. London: T. N. Foulis, 1911.

Ott, H. Hermeneutics and personhood. In S. R. Hopper & D. L. Miller (Eds.), *Interpretation: The poetry of meaning*. New York: Harbinger Books, 1967. Pp. 14–33.

Polanyi, M. *Personal knowledge*. London: Routledge & Kegan Paul, 1958.

Raine, K. The wind of time. In *Penguin modern poets*, Vol. 17. London: Penguin, 1970. P. 135.

Reider, N. Metaphor as interpretation. *International Journal of Psychoanalysis*, 1972, **53**, 463.

Richards, I. A. *The philosophy of rhetoric*. London: Oxford University Press, 1936.

Richards, I. A. *Coleridge on imagination*. (3rd ed.) London: Routledge & Kegan Paul, 1962.

Rowe, N. *Children's understanding and use of metaphor*. Unpublished M.Sc. thesis, University of Southampton, England, 1975.

Sartre, J. P. *Being and nothingness*. New York: Philosophical Library, 1956.

Schon, D. *Displacement of concepts*. London: Tavistock, 1963.

Thomas, O. *Metaphor and related subjects*. New York: Random House, 1969.

Tillich, P. *The courage to be*. London: Fontana, 1952.

Turbayne, C. M. *The myth of metaphor*. New Haven, Conn.: Yale University Press, 1962.

Vaihinger, H. *The philosophy of "as if."* London: Routledge & Kegan Paul, 1924.

Watzlawick, P., Beavin, J. H., & Jackson, D. D. *Pragmatics of human communication*. London: Faber & Faber, 1968.

Wheelwright, P. *Metaphor and reality*. Bloomington: Indiana University Press, 1962.

Wright, K. J. T. Metaphor and symptom: A study of integration and its failure. *International Review of Psychoanalysis*, 1976, **3** (1), 97–109.

The Interaction Model of Communication: Through Experimental Research Towards Existential Relevance[1]

Han Bonarius

University of Utrecht,
The Netherlands

> We presume that the universe is
> really existing and that man is
> gradually coming to understand it.
> By taking this position we attempt
> to make clear from the outset
> that it is a real world we shall be
> talking about, not a world composed
> solely of the flitting shadows of
> people's thoughts. But we should like,
> furthermore, to make clear our
> conviction that people's thoughts
> also really exist, though the
> correspondence between what
> people really think exists and what
> really does exist is a continually
> changing one. [Kelly, 1955]

*T*he quotation heading this article is from George Alexander Kelly, who made this statement twenty years ago as point of departure for his work, *The Psychology of Personal Constructs* (1955, pp. 6–7). In modern times, twenty years form a long period of history. Realize that in 1955, when Kelly presented his psychology, Ngo Dinh Diem had still to

1. It is a pleasure to express my gratitude to the following persons who, in one form or another, helped me clarify my thoughts: Freek Eland, Franz Epting, Ab Hesselink, Jan Hoekstra, Stans Hoppenbrouwers, Hans Koppenol, Steven Makkink, Marion Puts, Mariet Quanjel, T. Schipper, Lauri Waldman, Irene Wekker, Hannie Windemuller, and Renée Verhoeff.

become president of South Vietnam. Eisenhower was the president of the United States. Egypt was in the process of nationalizing the Suez Canal, which was followed by the English-French military intervention and the second war with Israel. In Hungary there was unrest leading to the bloodily suppressed uprising. Amazingly enough, the world has endured twenty more years in a similar way: wars, uprisings, revolutions, and suppressions have continued to occur. Mankind has also reached out for the moon and become aware of the limitations on this world's resources. A new consciousness has been growing, that of the interdependence of everything that happens in this world. What occurred in Vietnam has affected the whole world; what happens in the Middle East influences the life of people all over the world. The universe, as a whole, appears integral.

Kelly, in 1955, used the phrase "the universe is integral" as another abstract, theoretical statement—another starting point for his psychology of personal constructs. At present that statement is more than an assumption. It offers a comprehensive description of how we experience the world. Many people have become aware of the interdependence of the world's parts. Personally, I feel the need to reserve a large part of this paper to indicate the position of professional psychology in this world. This need is based upon the conviction that *men's thoughts not only passively reflect what exists in the universe, but also actively affect what is to happen.* As a matter of fact, I would like to add this conviction as another starting point to those first formulated by Kelly.

The assumption of the effectiveness of men's thoughts has ethical implications. Since the individual's thoughts or *constructions* have effect upon the real world, these thoughts and constructions affect other individuals. Thus, it is morally imperative to be explicit about one's thoughts, the more so since the space and the resources of this universe have to be shared with other people, with all of mankind. Only by making one's thoughts explicit and public are they open for discussion and can they be adjusted to the benefit of a larger world. Thus, this point implies the need for *clarification* and *communication* of what a person thinks. To the extent that individuals are under a moral obligation to test their thoughts through personal clarification and interpersonal communication, they can be held responsible for what they think and do.

Clarification and communication constitute the main theme of this contribution. It can even be argued that it is the central theme of psychology itself. Numbers of professional psychologists train their clients in the skill of interpersonal communication. Admittedly, some of us are working at a more mechanistic level with very disturbed patients or with mentally retarded persons. Usually, in the classical area of selection or in the more modern area of ergonomics there is little need to clarify the thoughts of the examined persons and of the experimental subjects. However, even in these last examples the professional psychologist himself is still under the scientific obligation to clarify himself and to communicate to the professional forum (De Groot, 1971) and to the larger public the scientific theories and the human values that guide his actions. Indeed, clarification and communication are the essential values of psychology both as a profession and as a science. In order to test the correspondence of the scientific theory and the professional activity with reality, clarification and communication take priority over even such established scientific rules as data collection, data description, quantification, and experimental manipulation.

The influence of psychology on the world is rather limited, if only because as a science it still focuses mainly on the white race and, as a profession, it still mostly services middle-class persons. However, within these unjustifiable limitations there is, since 1955, a definite movement away from the earlier preoccupations with isolated actions, reactions, and relations, towards the study and treatment of man-as-a whole, man-as-part-of-this-world, man-as-thinker. This change does not primarily originate in the progress of psychological theories and scientific research. Few, if any, of the older psychological theories have been abandoned simply because the related expectations were refuted by critical experiments. On the contrary, the "official science of psychology" does as yet hardly reflect the increasing involvement of the professional psychologist with personal growth, with interpersonal processes in education and therapy, and with the awareness of how certain conceptions of man keep him in captivity.

In 1964, Kaplan, writing on the philosophical part of human and professional thinking, introduced the distinction between "logic-in-use" and "logic-in-reconstruction." Similarly one could speak of a gap between "psychologic-in-use" and "psychologic-in-reconstruction." In 1955 Kelly narrowed this gap at an early stage by his introduction of the psychology of personal constructs. His theory concerns the formal aspects of the individual's system of person constructs, of the individual's personal thoughts. Kelly not only formulated a general theory, he also designed a series of techniques to study the content and the formal qualities of a given individual's personal construct system. Thus, as a theoretical psychologist Kelly was involved in psychological practice; as a professional psychologist, he reached out to improve the existing theories.

The purpose of the present paper is to contribute modestly to a further narrowing of the gap between "psychologic-in-use" and "psychologic-in-reconstruction." This will be done by presenting three topics. The first pertains to a critical analysis of professional psychological practice, especially with respect to personality assessment and clinical intervention. The question is posed again: to what extent is this psychological assistance based upon psychological theories and scientific techniques? The issue is clarified by locating psychological practice at the cross section between the scientific community and the society at large. The second topic pertains to the study of response style, in particular, extreme responding. On the basis of traditional, experimental research a partial theory of extreme rating is developed allowing for a very simple definition of the relevant aspects. The third topic concerns interpersonal communication, especially in regard to the communication of personal construct systems.

I am aware of the apparent different characters of these three topics. To me, the three issues are closely related. I like to see them as the parts of a triptych. The first panel, on professional practice is colored by philosophic analysis; the second, on extreme rating, by experimental method; the third, on interpersonal communication, by an explorative approach. This third panel forms the centerpiece of the triptych. In this part I try to demonstrate how experimental research of psychological phenomena so peripheral to human values as the tendency to use extremes of rating scales may provide the professional psychologist with a model indicating more relevant use of the traditional professional assessment and intervention techniques.

1. PSYCHOLOGICAL STATEMENTS: FROM PREDICTION TO COMMUNICATION

Here, then, is the real challenge: How can we foster a social climate in which some such new public conception of man based on psychology can take root and flourish? [G. A. Miller, 1969]

It is not a great exaggeration to say that until some years after 1955 the layman identified psychology with personality assessment and clinical diagnosis. The social role of a psychologist consisted of the administration of tests and writing of character descriptions. Factual changes in psychological practice preceded a change in the image of psychology as a helping profession. In the fifties, psychologists turned from projective techniques towards personality inventories. In the sixties, clinical psychologists moved away from general psychological assessment towards the functional analysis of more specific behavior, followed, usually, by tailor-made intervention concerned with changing that behavior.

These changes, although of different nature, both took place well within the limits of the classical conception of psychology as a positive science. The tremendous growth of psychology as a profession after World War I, and especially after World War II, may in fact be ascribed to its scientific methods. Like a member of the medical profession, the psychologist appeared to offer help and advice of high social and human value. His service is based upon actual knowledge of the human being. This knowledge is presumably collected by scientific research and its application is reserved to scientifically trained members of the professional community of psychologists. It is the exclusiveness of this community of scientific psychologists which makes that society, and individual persons have to pay a good price for their psychological services.

In Figure 1, the relationships between psychologists and (members of) society are presented schematically.[2] The professional psychologist (P) makes a psychological statement, or a set of statements, about the individual (I) The statement may have the form of a description (e.g., concerning intelligence or other personality variables) or a prescription (e.g., vocational advice, therapeutic advice). It is a *long-term statement* in the sense that it refers to relatively permanent aspects of the individual. The statement is reported to the individual himself or, as often in the case with children and patients, to persons in his direct surrounding who feel responsible for him. In Figure 1, this is reflected by the direction of the arrows from the "Statement Box." In all cases *the statement is essentially a prediction.* The validity of the statement depends on the

---

2. The following analysis has generality beyond the field of psychology in the area of other social professions, such as psychiatry and social work. However, the arguments are primarily illustrated by events from the area of psychology.

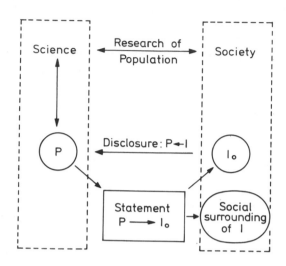

FIG. 1. The Predicting Model.

fulfillment of three conditions: the disclosure condition, the science condition, and the research condition.

The disclosure condition. A professional statement about an individual is only possible if the individual takes tests and/or answers interview questions. The disclosure condition is located in the factual relationship between a specific psychologist and individual, at the time of the psychological examination. The disclosed information flows from the individual to the psychologist. In Figure 1, this is reflected in the direction of the arrow between I and P.

The science condition. A professional statement about an individual is only valid if the information disclosed by the individual can be compared with standard knowledge of the population of which the individual is a member. In psychological practice this condition may be fulfilled by differential psychological knowledge with respect to personality variables (e.g., intelligence, need of achievement, etc.) or by general psychological knowledge with respect to personality processes (e.g., the effect of reinforcement upon behavior, the effect of feedback upon cognition, etc.). In both cases, this condition is concerned with the replicative aspects of human behavior, the objective aspects. The professional statement is one about the individual-as-an-object (Io). The science condition is located in the relationship between the specific psychologist and the scientific community of psychology. The science condition is stretched over a longer time period. It is limited by the professional experience of the practicing psychologist. This condition assumes periodic communication with the relevant issues between the scientific community and practicing psychologist. In Figure 1 this is reflected by the double-headed arrow between P and Science.

The research condition. A professional statement about an individual depends ultimately upon the continuation of theoretical and instrumental research. It is evident that the validity of the existing psychological knowledge deserves periodic scientific control, whereas new problems require fresh research. The research topics seem at first sight to be determined by science itself. Viewed from a longer time perspective it is evident that society concerns itself with certain problems and directs scientific research by selectively providing material and financial support. The historical development of psychological assessment more than illustrates this view. Naturally, science actively can and does influence society by reporting on theoretical and practical results. Thus, the research condition is located between society at large and the science of psychology. There is a two-way traffic of information, in Figure 1 reflected by the double-headed arrow between Science and Society. The research condition, quite evidently, is a permanent one.

The development of psychological assessment over the last hundred years clearly seems to support the presented analysis. The popularity of, for instance, intelligence testing can be ascribed to the predictive validity of the psychological statements. These statements are possible through our scientific knowledge of what is meant by the concept of intelligence, how it is measured, and how it is distributed in the population. This knowledge has been checked and improved by continuous research, and the essential parts of it have become common knowledge for society as a whole. Even the present rejection of projective techniques, which took place after scientific research had unmasked its lack of validity, supports the analysis more than it would seem to undermine the general belief in psychology. Society believes in the objective truth of psychological statements.

To professionals, however, the representation of Figure 1 may seem far too optimistic, even with respect to the issue of intelligence.

As professionals, we are well aware, regarding the disclosure condition, of errors in test administration; regarding the science condition, of the probabilistic character of IQ-scores; and regarding the research condition, of the rapid change of the criteria to be predicted. The validity and utility of intelligence testing may have been convincingly demonstrated over large numbers of persons. In the individual case, however, it is very well possible that the professional statement has little or no utility. Similar objections are even more true with respect to statements about personality variables and the dynamic aspects of human behavior. Indeed, one may question, as has often been done, whether objective psychological statements about individuals are possible at all. There are three fundamental arguments against the possibility of objective psychological statements as based upon scientific and empirical research. Since this is not the occasion to elaborate on method-ological issues, the arguments are here only given in brief.

The *first argument* concerns the nature of the subject of the psychological statement. Human beings are so complex that an entirely true and complete description of a person is impossible. Thus the psychologist must reduce the object of his study, the human being, to those aspects which psychology can adequately describe. It is said that the aspects which the individual himself feels are important are more often than not lost in this reduction.

The *second argument* concerns the influence on human behavior by the psychological examination itself. This argument is shaped after the well-known problem in physics that some of the smallest material particles cannot be observed directly because they would change in location and size under the influence of the X rays emitted by the electron microscope. By now it is a well-established fact in psychology that the specific situational context of the psychological examination exerts substantial influence on test performance.

The *third argument* is related to the epistemological discussion about the nature of "objective" statements. In science it is now generally accepted that "objectivity," in the last instance, is equal to social "convention." Bypassing the philosophical ramifications of this discussion, it seems that the social and public aspects of "objectivity" make questionable the possibility of scientific psy-chology. In psychology, the human beings which serve as objects of scientific study also take part in the judgment and evaluation of the objectivity of resulting psychological statements. Hofstee (1974) has recently elaborated on this argument. As he summarized it, human objects, unlike physical objects, have the disturbing quality that they talk back. In fact, they also undertake action to change the matter to which the statement refers. A dramatic example is given in Freud's statements on the repression of sexuality, which preceded a total change in sexual beliefs and sexual behavior.

In some form or another these arguments have played a role in the historical dispute concerning the scientific status and the human value of psychology. I have not the intention to reiterate at this time the historical discussions. It is sufficient to mention the early proponents of the human sides of psychology, Dilthey (1883) and Spranger (1950). The long European tradition of phenomenology, from Husserl's *Logische Untersuchungen* (1900) on to the Utrecht school of Buytendijk (1957) and his pupils (e.g., Van den Berg, 1955; Linschoten & Van den Berg, 1953; Kouwer, 1973) must also be completely skipped. However, a few lines must be spent on American phenomenology, a more recent development.

During World War II, Rogers, then at Ohio State University in Columbus and later at the University of Chicago, developed his nondirective approach (1942) and client-centered therapy (1951). In the American literature (e.g., Mischel, 1971; Hall & Lindzey, 1957) Rogers is classified as a phenomenological psychologist, as is the case with other American authors who have stressed the self-concept. Often (e.g., Mischel, 1971) the psychology of personal constructs (which Kelly developed at Ohio State University, after Rogers had left) is also labeled as phenomenological psychology. Incidentally, it is interesting to note the difference between American and European phenomenology. The first is focused upon the self and the experience of the inner feelings; the second upon the experience of the outer world. It may be argued that Kelly, with his theory of personal construction of this outer world, was more of a European than an American phenomenologist. At any rate, Kelly and Rogers share the therapeutic application of the phenomenological attitude. In fact, American phenomenology evolved naturally from therapeutic practice rather than from theoretical, arm-chair epistemology. Both Kelly and Rogers had realized that professional help should start from and be directed towards the unique, personal experiences of the individual. Perhaps this therapeutic application is the main reason for their increasing influence on psychology as compared to the diminished impact of European phenomenology.

For the psychologist who is attending the unique aspects of the individual, it is not possible to compare the data from a certain person with the norms of the population. That is to say, there is no standard mechanism available for attaching meaning to the disclosed personal material. The meaning can only be defined in interaction between therapist and client. The role of the therapist in the classical Rogerian approach is to hold up a mirror, for instance, by repeating and rewording the client's expression of his experience. The client himself actively determines the content of the interaction. In the Kellian approach the therapist invites the client to entertain alternative perspectives of his present surroundings. Together they discuss the specific times and locations that these alternative constructions are tried out.

Recently Hermans (1974), in the Netherlands, developed a technique, the "confrontation method." The format of the technique resembles that of paper-and-pencil tests. The individual is invited to make, in the presence of a professional, a list of important occasions, situations, and persons in his life. He then indicates the degree to which each of these value topics makes him experience feelings such as joy, inferiority, powerlessness, energy, and the like. In his interaction with the helper, the individual is confronted with his experience of the separate values and their interwoven aspects. With his confrontation test, Hermans departs from the predicting model (and his own empirical work of earlier date pertaining to psychometric measurement of the need of achievement). He explicitly defines the purpose of the confrontation technique as the facilitation of individual change by confronting the person with his individual system of values. Typically, his new approach is demonstrated and justified by the presentation of a few cases. This form of presentation is indeed typical for the phenomenological approach (and other approaches which stress the unique aspects of persons). In this respect Hermans is in the good company of Kelly, Rogers, and Freud, all of whom presented their viewpoints by means of case descriptions.

The treatment of the client as a unique person implies an important change in the relationship between psychologist and individual. The "Reflecting Model" (Figure 2) tries to show this

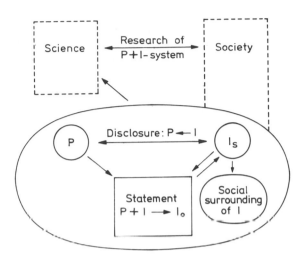

FIG. 2. The Reflecting Model.

change graphically. One may say that under the Reflecting Model, any statement, or set of statements, is the result of the interaction between the specific psychologist (P) and the individual (I). This interaction is reflected by the double-headed arrow between P and I. The statement itself concerns the individual who is disclosing himself. Usually it is the combined product of his expressions about himself and the reflections by the psychologist (see the "Statement" box). In producing the statement, the individual strives for clarification, and this clarification is tried out in the process of communication. The statement does not refer to the individual as a member of the population. Therefore, it does not carry predictive or even descriptive value. In contrast with the long-term statement under the predicting model, this is *a short-term statement*. Essentially, its immediate value is exploration of the self and the continuation of the interaction with the psychologist. On the long term it carries, as one in a series of statements, the process of developmental or therapeutic change. In his inaugural lecture, Dijkhuis (1965) contrasted the usual psychological description with this explorative statement and called it a psychologism, indicating that it neither has to be "true" nor "testable."

It is characteristic of the Reflecting Model that the psychologist perceives the individual as an equal who himself carries most of the responsibility for the content of the statement. This equivalence of psychologist and individual is reflected in the rule that the psychologist never bypasses the individual when giving information about him to the people in his surrounding. Because of the equivalent and the active contribution of the individual, the model implies a conception of man-as-responsible-for-his-actions (Hofstee, 1974).

For psychology as a profession it is important to note that the psychologist has little use of his scientific knowledge of the distribution of personality variables in the population. Evidently scientific knowledge concerning specific reinforcement techniques or specific feedback procedures is also of little value. Only very general conditions such as those formulated by Rogers concerning empathy, genuineness, and congruency (1957) seem to count. Thus, in the Reflecting Model, the psychologist cannot rely on his scientific education. In Figure 2, this is reflected in the separation of P from his science. Indeed, it is well known that psychotherapeutic effect has no systematic relationship with the therapeutic experience of the professional or his scientific training. In the area of mental health, this is expressed in the fading boundaries dividing academic and semiacademic disciplines in the production of psychotherapists, trainers, facilitators, and the like.

With this background, one may critically question whether the assistance to men as unique beings should be reserved for professional psychologists. It may be argued that the reflecting attitude of the psychologist has a positive, human quality. It is desirable that each person be trained to master this part of human communication, in the same way that it is good for each person to profit from this attitude found in other people. In fact, there has always been some ambivalence in the therapist's attitude. On one hand, he must be personally interested in the individual (c.f. Rogers's necessary and sufficient conditions!); on the other hand, he is being paid for it. Not long ago, one of my students compared visiting a psychotherapist with frequenting a prostitute. Disregarding the question which of the two professionals is injured by this judgment, it may be interesting to explore the possibility of doing away with the expensive psychologist and having two nonprofessionals interact through mutual disclosure and reflection. Such a situation is represented in the "Communicating Model" (Figure 3).

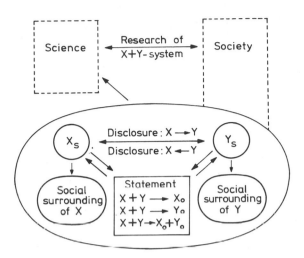

FIG. 3. The Communicating Model.

In this diagram the individuals are identified by the symbols X and Y. This notation is identical to the one used in the following section concerned with extreme rating. For the moment, and in order to finish the present discussion, it is sufficient to indicate the general symmetric aspects of Figure 3. As with the Reflecting Model, there is no direct connection between either of the interacting members, X or Y, and the science of psychology. The essential difference in the Reflecting Model is the complete symmetry in the social roles of the two interacting individuals. Each person discloses himself, and the statements, as the result of their interaction, pertain to each of them.

There are indications in the field of mental health that the Communicating Model is naturally taking over from the Reflecting Model. As was mentioned before, the boundaries between academic disciplines have faded with respect to the training of psychotherapists. Since 1960, in a parallel development, the reflecting interaction has spread from individual psychotherapy to group therapy, training groups, sensitivity training, and the like. In these groups the members disclose information about themselves to each other and communicate through psychologisms. The art of reflection also has become one mastered by professionals as diverse as managers and pastors. By now, it has pervaded the western educational system. It should be mentioned that this massive growth has been accompanied by the popularization of humanistic psychology. For large segments of society, humanistic psychology provides an articulated, ideal conception of man. The interaction pattern associated with the Reflecting Model, and especially the Communicating Model, seems perfectly fitted to reach out for this ideal. Each statement is a psychologism. It is meant as a vehicle of interpersonal communication and intrapersonal growth, rather than an objective, factual description.

These developments raise a new conception of the relationship between psychology and society. On one hand, the predictive power of psychological statements appears to be limited; on the other hand, the application of reflecting techniques is not reserved to professional psychologists. Professionals who have studied other disciplines and nonprofessionals can master these communicating skills equally well. Furthermore, statements emerging from the interaction of two communicating individuals are not primarily intended to represent any "outside" truth. They are meant to clarify, for each individual, a conception of his own being, the anticipation of his own future, and his experience with the other individual. If we welcome these developments, and I do welcome them, the question must be asked whether any task is left for the professional psychologist! My answer is: "Yes, but . . . " There remains enough work for the psychologist, provided that he is willing to exchange a great part of his activities in assisting individuals for scientific research!

For instance, as far as the psychologist is still practicing under the Predicting Model, he should make his statements brittle enough and his professional adminstration complete enough to be able to find out, in his own surroundings, whether his predictions are (usually) true, untrue, or untestable. Referring to the Reflecting Model, it seems necessary to continue research on the effects of so-called therapeutic interaction. In Figure 2, this is indicated by research of the P-and-I-system (in the ellipse), performed by the scientist who remains outside that system. As long as psychotherapists receive three to ten times as much as the average wage of factory workers it is morally imperative to find out about the effectiveness of psychotherapy. Psychotherapists, when asked about this issue, often refer to insurmountable operational problems in defining positive outcome. As an alternative, rather than compulsively continuing the "therapeutic ritual," one may contemplate simple "input research": comparing the amount of money and time involved with psychotherapy, as applied to people of different social classes and financial status by members of different schools (psychoanalitic, rogerian, behavioristic, gestalt, etc.) and of different disciplines (psychiatry, psychology, social work, etc.).

Theoretically more interesting is the development of more articulated communication techniques. In my opinion, these techniques must be designed in such a way that they also allow for empirical and scientific study of the communication process and its impact upon the partners. The techniques and research may be directed to the relationship between the professional and the individual client, as with Hermans's (1974) "confrontation technique." The focus may also be upon communication between two nonprofessional individuals. In the latter case, the two partners may profit from the psychologist's knowledge of these skills. As was indicated earlier, nonprofessionals are already using the reflecting attitude originally developed for professional and therapeutic intervention. One may wonder whether nonprofessionals could also profit from the accumulated knowledge on the subject of personality assessment.

In the first three-quarters of this century and starting with Binet's test of intelligence (Binet & Simon, 1905), an impressive amount of psychological knowledge and methodological know-how has been collected concerning personality assessment. I am not referring to the sophisticated statistical techniques in test construction or the intricate steps necessary for the calculation of test scores. At this moment I would especially like to draw attention to the representative sampling of behavior and opinions relevant to the construct that is being measured. The measuring of intelligence takes place through observation of reactions to a variety of intellectual problems; measuring an attitude, by registering the individual's reaction to a series of carefully selected and relevant issues.

The present suggestion is that systematic and representative sampling of relevant issues may improve the interpersonal communication between two individuals. Assessment techniques may perhaps be adapted to serve intrapersonal explorations and interpersonal understanding instead of the professional prediction of the individual's future behavior. One of the assessment techniques allowing for a transformation from predictive to communicating utilization is the Role Construct Repertory Test. Naturally, one can think of other tests that may serve the interpersonal interaction. However, at this symposium, dedicated to Kelly's psychology of personal constructs, it is appropriate to explore the communicative aspects of the test which was developed together with and as part of that theory. In the third section of this contribution, an account will be given of the adaption of the Role Construct Repertory Test as a technique in personal communication and interaction. However, the focus of the next section is on more theoretical research, research on the issue of extreme rating.

2. THE INTERACTION MODEL OF EXTREME RESPONDING: RESEARCH AND THEORY[3]

> . . . but I believe that part of the answer is that psychology must be practiced by nonpsychologists. [G. A. Miller, 1969]

The Maladjustment Proposition and the Meaning Proposition

Usually, the rating scale is employed as an instrument to study characteristics of the rated object (O), as in peer ratings; of the rater (J), as in self-ratings; or, sometimes, of C, the dimensional trait or contrast that defines the content of the scale. In our research, however, the characteristics of the instruments itself were studied. More specifically the question was: what makes people use the extreme positions upon the rating scale? Is it possible that the extremity of a rating (or "polarization") reflects formal conditions in the rating task? Put in this way the problem can be studied within the framework of the psychology of response style. The issue of response style or response set was raised originally by Cronbach (1946) as a problem of artifacts in the construction of psychological tests, especially of the so-called personality questionnaires. Thus it was a rather practical problem, connected with the practical purpose

---

3. The research discussed in this section is based on the author's doctoral dissertation (Bonarius, 1970b). The more recent literature concerning the general issue of response style is discussed in Bonarius (1975). A review of recent research in extreme responding is in preparation by Hesselink and Bonarius.

of constructing useful assessment tools. However, especially between 1955 and 1975, the study of response style became a relatively independent and fashionable topic of theoretical research.

According to Hamilton's (1968) review of extreme response style, there are consistent individual differences in the degree of extreme ratings. He tentatively proposes three theoretical explanations: (a) The tendency to respond in the extreme reflects a need to reduce ambiguity and to achieve certainty. (b) Extreme responses increase with heightened emotionality or drive, such as is presumably the case with highly anxious persons. (c) Extreme response style seems inversely related to developmental maturation. It seems that these three hypotheses may be subsumed by one that is less specific. All three hypotheses refer to differences between persons with respect to maladjusted or, at least, ineffective behavior. Their separate presentation might suggest an articulated empirical knowledge that, in fact, does not exist. At the present state of research it seems a better strategy to have one rough hypothesis to replace them. Let us call it the *Maladjustment Proposition:* The more maladjusted a person is, the more extreme his ratings will be.

O'Donovan (1965), concluding his review of research, proposes a two-factor theory. The first is J's pathology; for instance, neurotics tend to polarize. This pathology factor is comparable to the Maladjustment Proposition derived from Hamilton. O'Donovan's second factor is the meaningfulness of the rating task. This says that stimuli which appear to J as meaningful lead to extreme ratings, whereas "meaningless stimuli" lead to more reserved ratings, that is, less extreme ratings. This may be called the *Meaning Proposition*. Most of the research underlying the Meaning Proposition is stimulated by G. A. Kelly's *Psychology of Personal Constructs* (1955). Typically, in most of these studies each S gave self-ratings or ratings of personal acquaintances upon bipolar scales made up either of "extraneous contrasts" provided by the experimenter, the ECs, or of his own personal construct dimensions, the PCs. Polarization was compared, not between different groups of Js, but between PC-scales and EC-scales. The results of these investigations consistently support the Meaning Proposition in that ratings with PCs are always more extreme than with ECs (Bonarius, 1970b).

In Hamilton's (1968) review the stimulus variable is neglected in favor of the J variable; the discussion of the Meaning Proposition (O'Donovan, 1965) focused mainly on differences in meaningfulness of contrasts, thus on the C-variable. However, it is evident that in the rating task, the meaningfulness is codetermined by the kind of O to which C is applied. It may be argued that PCs are especially meaningful for a person when carrying out self-ratings or ratings of family members or close friends. According to Kelly's (1955) theory, the individual forms his personal constructs primarily in his contacts with these people. Let us call them the individual's "personal others" (POs), on the analogy of the individual's PCs. Superficial acquaintances, the "extraneous others" (EOs), may be outside the "focus of convenience" of the individual's PCs. This reasoning leads to the expectation that the difference in polarization between PCs and ECs is larger if calculated over POs than over EOs.

This expectation with respect to the C-variable and the O-variable can be tested together with the expectation derived from the Maladjustment Proposition with respect to the type of judge, that is, with respect to the "J-variable." This leads to a three-factor research model: the extremity of ratings can thus simultaneously be studied in relation to J, C, and O separately, and to all possible interactions between J, C, and O. The first multivariate experiment of this design was performed in 1967. This experiment was the fourth in the series of investigations which took place at the University of Groningen (Bonarius, 1970b). (For easy identification each in that series of experiments was numbered: EXP-1 indicates the first experiment, EXP-2 the second, EXP-3 the third, EXP-4 the fourth, and so forth. These identifications are maintained in the present summary of the research.) Since EXP-4 is the prototype of the other experiments in this section, it will receive a somewhat fuller description.

EXP-4: Meaningfulness or Maladjustment

The subjects of this first multivariate experiment were 125 male students who had previously filled in a standardized Dutch personality questionnaire, the ABV (Wilde, 1961), which gave each S a (percentile) score with regard to *Neuroticism*, to *Extraversion-Introversion*, and to *Test Attitude*. The purpose of the experiment, as told to the Ss, was to find out how persons judge other people. Therefore, S should ask himself in which terms he has been thinking of other people, and how he usually compared them; more specifically, which dimensions did he apply to them. He then wrote down two contrasts representing to him the two most important dimensions for describing people. Later in the experiment these two pairs of contrasts served as this S's two PCs. This procedure for obtaining PCs may be called the *Free Formulation procedure*. (This new procedure is different from the *Reptest Triad procedure*, sketched in part 3 of this article and used in all previous studies relating personal constructs and extreme rating). Each S then gave the names of five of his intimate acquaintances, such as his mother, father, brother, or sister. These names represented the S's "personal others" (POs). He then gave the names of five of his superficial acquaintances, the "extraneous others" (EOs): for example, an influential teacher, a successful person, or the teacher whose viewpoints he did not like.

Subsequently S rated his ten acquaintances with four scales, two made up of his own PCs and two of ECs. The two ECs were *objective–emotional* and *dependent–self-confident*. They were taken from EXP-3 (Bonarius, 1970b). The scales themselves, introduced as continuous, consisted in fact of 57 typed hyphens. The extremity of each rating was calculated by simply counting the number of hyphens between the rating and the middle of the scale. Within each $C \times O$ treatment the 10 distances (5 Os $\times$ 2 Cs) were added together to form one extremity score, EX. This resulted in four EX scores for each S. Now, at five increasing levels of Neuroticism (percentile level of 15, 30, 50, 70, and 90), groups of 5 Ss each were selected. The EX scores of these 25 Ss were analyzed by a $J \times C \times O$ analysis of variance, with factor J, factor C, and factor O fixed, and with repeated observations on the last two factors (Winer, 1962, p. 319).

Beforehand several predictions had been formulated. These are given together with the actual results:

1. A significant J-effect, such that the average EX score would increase from the least neurotic group to the most neurotic group. This prediction is in agreement with the Maladjustment Proposition derived from Hamilton (1968) and with O'Donovan's (1965) conclusion that neurotics tend to polarize. The prediction was not confirmed. The J-effect was not significant. Inspection of the data did not reveal any systematic trend in the EX scores under the different levels of neuroticism.

2. A significant C-effect, such that $EX_{PC} < EX_{EC}$. This prediction is in agreement with O'Donovan's Meaning Proposition. The prediction was confirmed. The C-effect appeared significant ($p < .01$); the average rating with PC is 16.3 hyphens from the midpoint of the scale and with EC it is 13.7 hyphens.

3. A significant $C \times O$-effect, such that the difference in polariza-

tion between PCs and ECs would be larger if calculated over POs
than over EOs. This prediction was based upon the theoretical argument that PCs are especially meaningful when applied to intimate
acquaintances. This prediction was also confirmed. The C × O-effect
was significant ($p < .05$) and the size of the differences was in
the predicted direction (see Figure 4).

Perhaps a significant O-effect and a significant interaction between
J and C or J and O might also have been predicted. At the time
the experiment was designed, no such predictions were made.
However, it is reasonable to assume that a person's intimate
acquaintances such as operationalized by the five POs are inherently
more meaningful to him than EOs and, therefore, should receive, as
such, more extreme ratings. The data did not show this effect. Nor
did they yield any significant J × C interaction or J × O interaction,
which would have supported O'Donovan's (1965) two-factor theory
of polarization.

Still, the results are quite encouraging, especially with Predictions
2 and 3. They gain even more weight because of the almost identical
results of a second and third analysis of variance. These differed from
the first in that, in the second analysis, the J factor was defined by
five levels of Extraversion and, in the third, by three levels of Test
Attitude. The Ss, 25 in the Extraversion analysis and 15 in the Test
Attitude analysis, were also selected from the complete pool of 125
Ss. With the second and third analysis of variance no specific

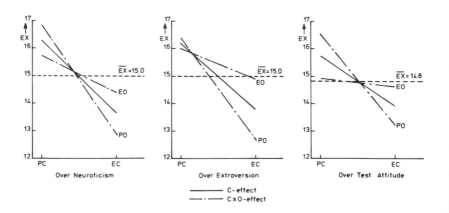

FIG. 4. Results of Experiment 4.

predictions with regard to J had been formulated, but Predictions 2 and 3 had been kept unchanged. In both analyses, again, only the C effect and the C $\times$ O-effect appeared significant and, again, in the predicted direction (see Figure 4).

Replications and Generalizations

Several other experiments were designed similar to EXP-4 to explore the reliability and generality of the significant results and to search for an underlying theoretical structure. The numerical results of these experiments are given in Table 1.

In *EXP-5* another sample of Ss from the same student population as in EXP-4 was tested. Since there were only 13 students available the J variable was not studied. Only the C-effect appeared significant in the predicted direction. In *EXP-6* the identical experimental task was repeated in Finland. Two C $\times$ O analyses were performed, one for a group of male Ss and another for a female group. Both groups yield a significant C-effect in the predicted direction. Only with the (more substantial) female group could the interaction effect of EXP-4 be reproduced ($p < .10$).

In *EXP-7* the list of role titles for obtaining the names of acquaintances was modified. As mentioned in the description of the results of EXP-4, it is reasonable to assume that a person's intimate acquaintances are in themselves more meaningful to the person than extraneous ones. However, in EXP-4 to EXP-6 this was not reflected in the extremity of the ratings of POs as compared with EOs (see O-effect, Table 1). Could it be that the specific role title list used in those experiments prevented more extremity of rating of PCs? In EXP-4 some EO roles seem rather "intimate"—for example, "an influential teacher," "a teacher whose viewpoints you did not like." In the adaptation of EXP-7 the (four) POs were father, mother, brother or sister, and best friend, and the EOs were physician or dentist, "person of own age, living in the neighbourhood but not well known," the "least known nextdoor neighbour," and the "best student at your grammar school." It was felt that if, essentially, ratings of POs are more extreme than of EOs, then this should become visible with this set of names.

The O-effect now appears significant in the predicted direction, whereas the results with respect to the C-effect and the C $\times$ O -effect tend to do the same. Another adjustment of the procedure consisted

Table 1

Summary Multivariate Research Concerning Personal Constructs and Extreme Responding

EXP	Subjects number	sex	type	Method of obtaining PC	Method of obtaining EC	Scale	C-effect $\overline{EX}_{PC}$	$\overline{EX}_{EC}$	p-value	O-effect $\overline{EX}_{PO}$	$\overline{EX}_{EO}$	p-value	C x O -effect $\overline{EX}_{PC}-\overline{EX}_{EC}$ over PO	EO	p-value	Remarks
4	25	M	stud.	FREE	Selected	cont.57--	16.3	13.7	+ .01	14.9	15.1	- F<1.00	3.9	1.3	+ .05	Neuroticism (1967)
	25	M	stud.	FREE	from	cont.57--	16.2	13.8	+ .01	14.5	15.5	- .25	3.7	1.1	+ .05	Extraversion (1967)
	15	M	stud.	FREE	EXP-3	cont.57--	15.7	13.9	+ .05	14.8	14.7	0 F<1.00	3.3	0.3	+ .06	Test Attitude
5	13	M	stud.	FREE	From EXP-3	7-point	1.83	1.69	+ .05	1.70	1.74	- F<1.00	0.05	0.10	- F<1.00	(1968)
6	7	M	stud.	FREE	Translated	cont.29--	8.18	6.76	+ .05	6.94	8.00	- .25	0.13	0.15	- F<1.00	Finland (1968)
	22	F	stud.	FREE	from EXP-3	cont.29--	7.88	7.13	+ .05	7.27	7.74	- .10	1.24	0.25	+ .10	Finland (1968)
7	20	M,F	Adol.	FREE	By psycho-logist	cont.57--	13.4	12.5	+ .25	14.7	11.3	+ .05	1.7	0.2	+ .25	Adolescents vs. Adults (1968)
8	16	M	Adults	PREF.+	PREF.-	cont.57--	11.5	11.9	- F<1.00	12.9	10.5	+ .005	-0.7	-0.0	- F<1.00	Managers (1968)
9	60	M,F	stud.	PREF.+	PREF.-	7-point	1.70	1.28	+ .001	1.62	1.36	+ .001	0.54	0.29	+ .001	Incompatibility(1968)
10	14	M	Adults	PREF.+	PREF.-	cont.57--	15.4	13.9	+ .05	15.0	14.4	+ F<1.00	1.8	1.3	+ F<1.00	Familiarity (1968)
11	22	M,F	Adol.	FREE/ /PREF.+	By psycho-logist	cont.59--	15.7	14.4	+ F=1.00	16.6	12.7	+ .005	1.6	1.5	+ F<1.00	Attractiveness
										15.4	14.8	+ .25	1.2	1.3	- F<1.00	Advertisement (1968)
12	64	M,F	stud.	PREF.+	Partner's PC	7-point	1.21	1.09	+ .05	1.19	1.12	+ F<1.00	0.07	0.07	+ F<1.00	Rorschach (1970)

in the selection of the subjects. Hamilton (1968) had found that in 9 of the 18 studies bearing on the issue, females rate more extremely than males and that children and adolescents rate more extremely than adults. In EXP-7, ten 14-year-old high-school students and 10 college-educated adults, equally divided over both sexes, served as subjects. Although average EX values are in the expected direction (female 13.2 and male 12.7; adolescents 13.2 and adults 12.7), the associated F values are smaller than 1.00.

In *EXP-8* a new procedure was used to operationalize PCs and ECs, the *Personal Preference Procedure*. This procedure is different from the *Reptest Triad Procedure* (EXP-1 to EXP-3) and the *Free Formulation Procedure* (EXP-4 to EXP-7): The subject is presented with a list of contrasts. He selects (by "picking" or "ranking") the descriptions he personally finds most useful for describing other people (the PCs) and those he finds least useful (the ECs). This preference procedure was used with 16 male managers of a large international company. The list of scales consisted of the six standard rating descriptions regularly used in the company's appraisal program. The subject rated eight colleagues. The four with whom he had relatively the most contact were the POs and the other four the EOs.

In EXP-8 the significant O-effect of the former experiment was repeated. However, contrary to expectation, the C- and the C $\times$ O -effect were not significant and the average EX values even pointed in the opposite direction. The explanation (post hoc) is that the ranking procedure to obtain PCs and ECs was a spurious part of this particular experiment, since each subject was trained to use all descriptions in the company's appraisal program!

Although the empirical results of EXP-4 to EXP-8 are not identical, they do suggest that it is the personal relevance of the objects and of the content of the scales that determines the meaningfulness of the stimulus components in the rating situation. In EXP-9 the question was raised whether other aspects of the stimulus could be systematically linked to extreme rating. There was the suggestion that "logical compatibility" of the poles of a rating dimension, such as with *objective–emotional* (used in EXP-4 to EXP-6) might make the subject give a compromise rating and, therefore, a less extreme rating than with a scale with incompatible poles.

In *EXP-9*, each S rated POs and EOs with each of 20 presented bipolar scales. After the rating task S ranked all 20 scales, by means of a two-stage procedure, from "most" incompatible poles to "least" and, similarly, from "personally most useful" to "least useful." Two analyses of variance were performed, one to study the effect of incompatibility, and the other to cross-validate the effect of personal meaningfulness. In neither analysis did "sex of judges" turn out to be a significant factor. Furthermore, incompatibility of the poles did not effect the extremity of rating! On the other hand, in this experiment the C-effect, the O-effect, and also the C $\times$ O effect are all in the predicted direction and of high statistical significance.

EXP-9 indicated the greater theoretical importance of personal meaningfulness as compared to incompatibility of the scales. This experiment also proved that the modifications (after EXP-6) of the role title list to elicit POs and EOs produce better operationalizations of the theoretical concept. Thus it was felt possible to change the research strategy somewhat and to explore what fundamental changes in the rating task are possible without causing the disappearance of the effect of personal relevance on the extremity of ratings. Thus the generality of the influence of personal meaningfulness on the extremity of ratings is studied.

For instance, in EXP-10 the question was posed whether the relatively greater extremity of ratings with PCs still would hold if the usual bipolar scale was replaced by a unipolar scale. Another question was which of two factors, familiarity or attractivity, contributed most to the personal meaningfulness of the object of rating. Interestingly, the data did not yield any statistically significant difference between unipolar and bipolar scales. Since the psychological width of scales did not itself fall within the scope of the present series of experiments, no attempt will be made to explore this interesting fact further. The C-effect appeared significant; that is, the relatively greater polarization with PCs is not changed if the comparison with ECs is made over unipolar scales instead of the usual bipolar scales. Although familiar persons receive more extreme ratings than unfamiliar ones, this effect does not reach significance. Since attractive persons much more than unattractive persons receive extreme ratings, the suggestion is that attractiveness is the more important of the two components of the personal relevance of acquaintances.

In the following experiments, the question was whether the same pattern of results would be obtained if the person is asked to rate nonhuman objects, rather than acquaintances. In EXP-11, the subjects rated advertisement slogans with PCs (obtained mostly by a Free Formulation Procedure) and ECs, formulated by the psychologist. In *EXP-12*, Rorschach Cards were rated. With the advertisements the POs and EOs were defined by selection of the most versus the least familiar slogans, and with the Rorschach, by selection of the most and the least attractive cards. The results in EXP-11 did not reach statistical significance. The Ss reported great difficulty in working with advertisement slogans. Still, with respect to the C and O variables the average EX values are in the expected direction. In the Rorschach experiment, subjects constructed "nonverbal" bipolar scales, each consisting of two cards (from a parallel set of Rorschach cards). In this experiment the C-effect did reach significance. Finally it is interesting to mention that in EXP-11 females tend to rate more extremely than males ($p < .10$) and in EXP-12 males tend to rate more extremely than females (again, $p < .10$)!

The Interaction Model: Theoretical Development and Empirical Test

Against the background of the Maladjustment Proposition derived from Hamilton's (1968) review of the literature it is surprising that in EXP-4 neuroticism was not related to extreme rating. As a matter of fact, in none of the eight analyses of variance which included a J factor could a significant J-effect ($p < .05$) be detected. Apparently, at least in the present data, there is no simple relation between, on the one side, extremity of rating and, on the other side, personality differences with respect to neuroticism, extraversion, test attitude, age, or sex. With respect to sex the last results reported in the last section (EXP-11 and EXP-12) are illustrative for the lack of consistency of extreme response style as a differential personality variable.

Compared with the miscellaneous results obtained with respect to the J factor, the empirical findings concerning the O factor allow for a more systematic conclusion, at least after in EXP-7 the role title list was adapted in order to have a better differentiation between intimate, personal and superficial, "extraneous" acquaintances. In all experiments performed after EXP-6 the ratings of POs are more extreme than of the EOs, and in four of the six analyses this difference was significant. These results suggest the formulation of an empirical law, the "Object Law": Ratings of stimuli which are personally relevant to the judge (the POs) are more extreme than ratings that are not so relevant and more extraneous to the judge (the EOs).

This Object Law receives support also from studies by other authors. Mogar (1960) has his subjects rate with the Semantic Differential six controversial concepts like *homosexual* and *murderer* and six noncontroversial concepts like *fisherman* and *dog*. The mean extremity scores of the controversial concepts were very significantly larger. In Cromwell and Caldwell's classical study (1962) there is a (not significant) tendency for old acquaintances to receive more extreme ratings than recent acquaintances. Koltuv (1962) reports a greater variance of ratings of familiar acquaintances than of unfamiliar ones. The study by Isaacson and Landfield (1965) may also be cited in support of the Object Law: They had their subjects sort PCs (as objects) and standard self-descriptive traits (also as objects) on a 9-point scale from "least like me" to "most like me." On the "most like me" side, the PCs received significantly more extreme positions. Finally, Bender (1969) reports more use of a "non-applicable" category when emotionally neutral and disliked acquaintances are rated than when liked acquaintances and the self are rated.

The results of the experiments described in the present series are even more consistent with respect to the C variable of the rating task. With the exception of EXP-8 all studies resulted in greater polarization with PCs than with ECs, and 9 out of 12 statistical analyses appeared significant (see Table 1). The exceptional result of EXP-8 has already been explained; it is doubtful whether the theoretical difference between PCs and ECs was operationally correctly realized. Greater polarization with PCs as compared to ECs was, at varying levels of statistical significance, also established in EXP-1, EXP-2, and EXP-3 (Bonarius, 1970b) and in studies reported by other authors: Mitsos (1961) at a chance level of .01; Koltuv (1962) at .01; Cromwell and Caldwell (1962) at .005; Landfield (1965) (no chance level reported); Isaacson (1966) at .001; Bender (1968) at .01 and Bender (1969) at .01 (see also the contribution in this volume by A. W. Landfield).

The collected evidence overwhelmingly conforms to what has been called the (first) empirical law in the psychology of personal constructs (Bonarius, 1967b). This "Construct Law" says that ratings with PC scales are more extreme than ratings with EC scales.

This law seems very "robust" (see Table 1): It is valid for 7-point scales, 11-point scales, and "continuous" scales consisting of 29 and 57 hyphens. It is valid for at least three different forms of operationalization of personal constructs: with the Reptest Triad Procedure, the Free Formulation Procedure and the Personal Preference Procedure. Its validity was not diminished when unipolar scales were used instead of the usual bipolar scales, nor when the rating of personal acquaintances was replaced by the rating of Rorschach Cards and the usual verbal form of the contrast by a nonverbal form. Finally, it appears valid with a wide range of different raters: British, Dutch, Finnish, and Americans; adolescents, students, and teachers; people covering the whole range of Neuroticism, Extraversion, and Test Attitude; males and females.

With respect to this C factor it seems difficult to think of aspects other than personal relevance that may influence the degree of extreme ratings in an important way. One such aspect was studied (EXP-9): the incompatibility of the poles of bipolar scales. However, the empirical evidence did not support the expectation that incompatibility is an important factor.

The Construct Law says: ratings with PCs are more extreme than with ECs; the Object Law says: ratings of POs are more extreme than ratings of EOs. The "personal relevance" plays a central role in both laws. It may be argued that the essential aspect of a PC is its "proper relation" to the judge, in contrast to the "extraneous relation" between the EC and the judge. Again, the essential aspect of a PO is its "proper relation" to the judge, in contrast to the "extraneous relation" between the EC and the judge. In diagram *a* (see Figure 5) the proper relations are represented by the solid lines and the extraneous relations by the dotted lines. It is also possible to think of a proper relation between the C and the O components. For instance, one may postulate a proper relation between PC and PO. They "belong together," because both are positively related to the judge. In diagram *b* this is indicated by the solid line between PC and PO. Empirically this proper relation is reflected in the rather consistent C $\times$ O-effect (see Table 1) in that ratings with PCs are more extreme than of ECs, especially if measured over POs rather than EOs. In EXP-4 such an interaction was repeated in three separate sets of data. The results with EXP-9 are statistically even "more significant." Nonsignificant trends in the expected direction come from EXP-6,

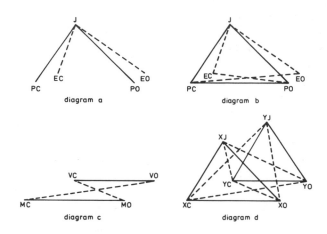

FIG. 5. The development of the theory of extreme ratings.

EXP-7, EXP-10, and EXP-12. Of the 12 sets of data, only 4 yield trends contrary to expectation, and the associated F values are all smaller than 1.00.

By introducing the terms "proper relation" and "extraneous relation" between the components of the rating situation, it becomes possible to discard the special notations and connotations from the psychology of personal constructs that up until now had guided the presented research. In the psychology of personal constructs, the extraneous components were operationally defined only in a negative way: an EC is a contrast *not relevant to J*; an EO is an object *not relevant to J*. But one may also think of the proper relation between, say, contrasts in the area of visual art (VCs) and visual art objects (VO). The expectation is that ratings of VOs with VCs will be more extreme than with other contrasts, let us say, in the area of music (MCs). However, although MCs are defined negatively with respect to paintings (there is an extraneous relation between MC and VO (see Figure 5, diagram *c*), they are positively defined with respect to music objects (MO). Consequently the ratings of MOs with MCs will be more extreme than the ratings of MOs with VCs. This is the same as saying that the extremity of ratings depends on the "proper interaction" between the C variable and the O variable.

The idea of "proper interaction" was tested empirically in *EXP-13*, which was focused on the example of music and paintings. The two MCs and the VCs were carefully selected by a pilot study (Bonarius, 1970b); they were VC: photographic-psychological and realistic-simplified, and MC: major-minor and rhythmic-smooth. The MOs were six fragments of classical music of 20 to 30 seconds' duration. Similarly there were six VOs, slides of paintings by Chagall, Goya, Michelangelo, Picasso, van Gogh and W. Vandevelde. Ss in EXP-13 were first-year psychology students. Each S rated the MOs and the VOs with four 7-point scales: two made up of the two MCs and the other two of the two VCs. The objects were presented to all Ss by means of an amplifier system (MOs) and a slide projector (VOs). The sequence of the object was properly balanced.

The results of this experiment dramatically illustrate the theoretical argument: the MOs receive more extreme ratings with MCs (average EX $= 1.88$) than with VCs (EX $= 0.94$) and the VOs receive more extreme ratings with VCs (EX $= 2.14$) than with MCs (1.34). This significant statistical interaction ($p < .0005$) is a reflection of the theoretical "proper interaction" between C and O. This is also evident from the subjective ranking of the contrasts after the rating task. From the total of 143 Ss, 130 ranked the MCs as more useful than VCs for describing MOs, whereas 123 ranked the VCs as more useful than MCs for describing VOs.

A comparison in Figure 5 of diagram *c* with diagram *b* leads to the question what it would mean in theoretical and empirical terms if on top of each of the two lines, MC-MO and VC-VO, a triangle of solid lines were constructed similar to the one triangle of solid lines J-PC-PO. Obviously, the music triangle would be headed by an MJ (who may be a musician, a composer, or perhaps a music critic). The other, the painting triangle, would be headed by a VJ (who may be an active painter, a collector, or, again, a critic, but this time of visual art). The importance of this game of imagination is its suggestion of a more complete model of polarization.

Such a complete model is indicated by diagram *d*. The two triangles consisting of solid lines are labeled X system and Y system rather than the less abstract "area of music" and "area of painting" suggested in the last paragraph. However, in the following argument, the reader is of course free to think in terms of music and paintings or, perhaps, in terms of the personal construct systems of two individual persons, X and Y, or in terms of any other pair of mutually independent systems. More essential than the labels are the definitions connected with the model.

Each system consists of three components, J, C, and O, and is characterized by proper relations between these three components. Thus, the X system is characterized by proper relations between XJ and XC, between XJ and XO, and between XC and XO (see the three solid lines of X system in diagram *d*) and among XJ, XC, and XO together (the triangle enclosed by the three solid lines). Similarly, the Y system is defined by proper relations between YJ and YC, between YJ and YO, and between YC and YO (see the three solid lines of Y system in diagram *d*) and among YJ, YC, and YO together (the triangle enclosed by the three solid lines). Extraneous relations exist when one of the two or three components belongs to the other system. In diagram *d* extraneous relations are represented by dotted lines and by triangles enclosed by one solid and two dotted lines.

The general expectation is that ratings resulting from a proper relation are more extreme than ratings resulting from the corresponding extraneous relations. That is to say, the extremity of rating depends on the proper interaction between two of the three, or between all three, fundamental variables of the rating situation. Therefore this model is called the *Interaction Model* of extreme ratings.

The abstract simplicity of diagram *d* does not by itself guarantee that the Interaction Model of extreme ratings is a good one. The relevance of the model should be checked against its capacity to represent the "real world" of extreme ratings. Can the model subsume the existing empirical knowledge of extreme ratings? Is it possible to derive from the model new expectations concerning extreme ratings and will these new expectations be verified in subsequent empirical research?

The existing empirical knowledge with respect to the C factor, the O factor and the C $\times$ O interaction is obviously very adequately represented by the model. The sequential construction of diagrams *a*, *b*, and *c*, was in fact based on this knowledge; and the essentials of each of these three preceding diagrams are completely represented in diagram *d*. On the other hand, the results of the empirical research in which the J variable was systematically studied in no way contributed to the construction of any of the four diagrams. The reasons are obvious: the existing empirical knowledge concerning the J variable is not sufficiently consistent to justify a modification of the Interaction Model.

The scientific value of the Interaction Model would substantially increase if the model as a whole could be subjected to empirical test. Material for such a test should be collected according to the experimental design presented here.

	XC		YC	
	XO	YO	XO	YO
XJ				
YJ				

That is to say, XJs and YJs rate XOs and YOs with both types of contrasts, XCs and YCs. The expectations connected with such an investigation are represented in Figure 6.

There is no reason to expect the extremity of ratings with XCs, as measured over both types of judges and over both types of objects, to be different from those with YCs, again as measured over both types of judges and objects. Thus, there will not be a main C-effect (see Figure 6a, solid line). Similarly there will not be a main O-effect and a main J-effect. However, there will be a significant C × O-effect, because the extremity of rating depends on the proper interaction between C and O (see Figure 6a). Similarly there will be a significant J × C-effect (in Figure 6 this is reflected in the downward slope of the solid line in *b* and in the upward slope in *c*) and a significant J × O-effect (in Figure 6 this is reflected in a higher midpoint of the dotted XO line in *b* than in *a* and a lower midpoint of the dotted YO line in *b* than in *a* and also in the higher midpoint of the dotted YO line in *c* than in *a* and a lower midpoint of the dotted XO line in *c* than in *a*). Theoretically, the expected C × O interaction is identical to the interaction in EXP-13 with respect to the ratings of music and paintings, the expected J × O interaction is identical with the Construct Law, and the expected J × O interaction is identical with the Object Law.

Finally, a J × C × O -effect is to be expected in that the ratings in the specific XJ-XC-XO combination will be more extreme than the ratings in the other three combinations involving XJ (in Figure 6 this is reflected in the steeper slope of the XO line in *b* than in *a*) and in that the same will be true comparing the YJ-YC-YO combination with the other three combinations involving YJ (compare the steeper slope of the YO line in *c* than in *a*). Theoretically this expected second-order effect is identical with the C × O-effects as established in EXP-4, EXP-6, EXP-7, EXP-9, EXP-10, and EXP-12.

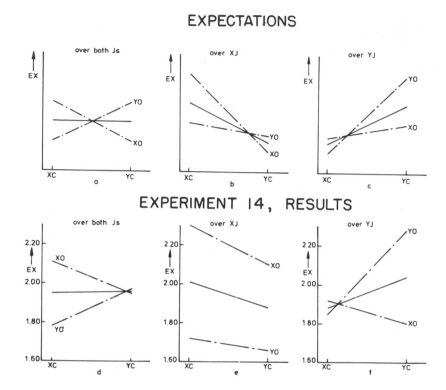

FIG. 6. The Interaction Model of extreme ratings.

Of Persons and Paintings: A Test of Interaction

In the series of experiments performed in Groningen, the last experiment, EXP-14, was planned to test the expectations derived from the Interaction Model as a whole. It was realized that the set of expectations is based on the assumption of the mutual independence of the X system and the Y system. Thus, it is necessary to find or to create two separate systems, X and Y. Nevertheless, the XJs should have some knowledge of the YOs and the YCs, and the XJs of the XOs and the XCs. Otherwise, it would be an unrealistic and meaningless task for S to rate the objects and to use the contrasts from the other system. This complicated precondition could be fulfilled in the area of paintings.

The material was collected from first-year students in psychology during one of the first introductory classes. The Ss were divided at random in pairs, each pair consisting of an XJ and a YJ. Slides of ten paintings were presented to the whole class. Each S was asked to produce personally two contrasts meaningful for the description and comparison of paintings. This Free Formulation Procedure was explained by the contrast *beautiful-ugly*. The Ss were told not to use this example. After another presentation of the series of slides S wrote down which of the paintings most moved him personally. In this way two PCs and one PO of each S were available. In terms of the Interaction Model the PCs and the PO of XJ are the XCs and the XO and the PCs and the PO of YJ are the YCs and the YO. The partners in each pair of Ss exchanged the own two contrasts and the own object for those of the other. Then each S rated his own painting with four 7-point scales, two made up of his own contrasts and two by those of his partner. The same was done with the painting of the partner.

After the rating procedure each S expressed his opinion concerning his partner's painting by indicating whether he too found that painting impressive. Finally, the four employed contrasts were rank ordered from "most useful" for describing paintings to "least useful." The purpose of these last steps was to check the independence of the X system and the Y system of each pair with respect to the O component and the C component.

For several reasons the data of 84 students from the original pool of 164 were eliminated: Nine pairs of Ss were eliminated because one of the partners or both had not understood the instructions properly. Twenty-six of the remaining pairs of Ss were eliminated because within each pair the XO was identical to the YO or one of the partners or both found the painting chosen by the other "very moving." These eliminations increase the probability that within each of the remaining pairs of Ss the O component in the X system is really independent of the O component in the Y system. For a similar reason but with respect to the C-component the data of another 14 Ss were removed. These subjects had indicated with the ranking procedure that the contrasts of their partner were more useful than their own contrasts.

The data of the remaining 80 Ss were subjected to a J $\times$ C $\times$ O analysis of variance. All three factors consisted of two (fixed) levels: factor J of XJ versus YJ (in each condition 40 Ss), factor C of XC versus YC and factor O of XO versus YO. The sex variable had not been controlled and thus was not entered as a separate factor. Per S the EX score was defined as the sum of the two distances in each of the four C $\times$ O combinations.

The predictions for the experiment were identical to the statistical and the graphical expectations formulated and explained above. In brief, there is no reason to expect significant main effects, but all three first-order interactions and the second-order interaction will be significant and of the character expressed in Figure 6.

The results are almost without exception as predicted. The C $\times$ O-effect was significant at $p < .01$, the J $\times$ C -effect at $p < .05$, the J $\times$ O-effect at $p < .0005$, and the J $\times$ C $\times$ O-effect approached the usual significance level ($p < .10$). All these significant differences are of the predicted character (see Figure 6, d, e, and f, in comparison with a, b, and c). Not predicted was the difference between XOs and YOs. XOs received more extreme ratings than YOs (average EX values respectively 2.03 and 1.88; $p < .05$). It has not been possible to find an explanation for this unexpected main effect which makes the XO line in Figure 6d higher than the YO line. The main C-effect and the main J-effect were not significant and, indeed, hardly yield differences in the average EX values (see solid lines in Figure 6, d, e, and f).

The results of this last experiment strongly support the Interaction Model of extreme ratings. The complex set of predictions derived from this model is completely confirmed and the results are statistically significant.

That is to say, the research has led to a clarification of the complexities connected with the problem of extreme rating. Differential psychological explanations, such as proposed by Hamilton (1968), should be replaced by general psychological explanations, derived from personal construct psychology. It appears from a recent literature study (Hesselink & Bonarius, manuscript in preparation) that this conclusion is not contradicted by the research performed by other authors after Hamilton's review (1968) was published.

3. THE INTERACTION MODEL OF COMMUNICATION: REPTEST INTERACTION TECHNIQUE

The people at large will have to be their own psychologists, and make their own applications of the principles that we establish. [G. A. Miller, 1969]

The Interaction Model is the final product of a series of investigations concerning the extremity of ratings. The question should be asked, What is the psychological importance of this research? The differences in extremity are small. One should not expect practical application, such as the construction of a personality test or a weighing formula correcting factual ratings for extreme response bias. However, if the rating task is seen as a paradigm of other situations of more human importance, then the Interaction Model may lead to interesting new questions, stimulate research in more relevant areas, and, perhaps, guide the psychologist's course of action in his daily work. On another occasion, an attempt was made, at a speculative level, to pursue the implications of the Interaction Model with respect to meaningfulness and maladjustment (Bonarius, 1970b). At present, the implications of the Interaction Model will be explored with respect to (interpersonal) communication.

Suppose that in diagram d (Fig. 5) of the Interaction Model, the X system represents a 45-year-old father and the Y system, his son of 20 years. Such a separated father-son combination is not unusual. In the middle-class culture of our time, the father may be absorbed in his career, concerned with secretarial duties in the local branch of a political party and the stimulation of family members to enjoy the social life in the town. The son, however, is involved in the challenge of sex, the use and the misuse of economic power, and hypocrisy in the church. The father may prefer, in his language, construct dimensions such as *hard working–laissez faire, contributing to–taking advantage of* and *loyalty–obstruction*, whereas the son may think of terms of *personal–economic development, love–agression* and *creating–consuming*. If it were possible to have the father and the son rate their own objects of interest and those of the other, with scales made up of their own dimensions and those of the partner, the expectations as regards extreme ratings would be identical to those formulated with the description of the Interaction Model and as established empirically in EXP-14. However, more relevant than such a replication is the question of the interpersonal relation between this father and his son.

Similarly important questions may be asked with respect to other dyads of persons or groups of persons. What is the relationship between husband and wife, patient and therapist, policeman and junky, Maoist and capitalist? These examples suggest the existence of pairs of X and Y systems, psychologically independent with respect to the involved J, C, and O-components, but which are nevertheless physically facing one another, uncertain of the other's intention. Unless one believes that one of the two systems can monopolize the truth and, therefore, reign over the other system, it is evident that communication between the two systems is necessary for settling conflicts. It may well be that the Interaction Model can help in providing criteria regarding the presence or absence of communication and in suggesting techniques for improving communication.

According to the Interaction Model, perfect communication exists between two systems, X and Y, provided that the X triangle coincides completely with the Y triangle. In terms of empirical observations, one would expect that in this case the extremity of ratings resulting from relations within either the X system or the Y system would not be different from those resulting from intersystem relations. That is to say, extraneous relations are absent, all relations are meaningful, thus communication is perfect. Departures from perfect communication between the two systems would occur if only the J-O lines coincide (XJ and YJ have both a meaningful relation with the same kind of objects, but they "talk" about them in different ways), if only the J-C lines coincide (XJ and YJ both "talk" in the same terms but about different things) and if only the C-O lines coincide (certain things can best be "talked about" in specific terms; however, it is not sure whether XJ or YJ or both will be concerned with this C-O area). Finally, imperfect communication exists if the two triangles are not directly connected and thus are mutually independent, as depicted in diagram *d*.

This Interaction Model of communication, speculative as it is, contains some promising suggestions. For instance, the Interaction Model provides a scheme for a systematic inventory of techniques that may facilitate improvement of communication. These faciliating techniques may focus on a rapprochement of the J-O lines of both systems, of the J-C lines, the C-O lines, or even of the completed J-C-O triangles. The largest part of this section is reserved for a description of one of these techniques, the Reptest Interaction Technique. This technique focuses on a rapprochement of the completed J-C-O triangles. Beforehand some of the other techniques will briefly be indicated to illustrate the more general relevance of the Interaction Model for the problem of communication.

One of the most logical ways of improving communication between people is the educational system. Viewed from the Interaction Model, the school is shown to work mainly in bringing about meaningful C-O relations between several kinds of objects and the specific terminology associated with each of them. People who share an education in, say, music have at least one area in which they can communicate, and this communication may continue on into other areas. Imagine our 45-year-old father attending an evening course in political science and discovering his son among the group of younger students.

A rapprochement initiated from the J-O line may be realized when the persons in both systems are brought together and become involved in a joint project. This approach is present in therapeutic techniques relying on arts and crafts, but also in marital situations where the estranged partners rediscover one another in the care of their child. The father and son in our example might improve their communication after having taken part together in a community program for teenagers, even if their initial motives might be different.

A third group of communicating-facilitating techniques is directed at the J-C line. Typical of these approaches is that one (or both) of the partners explicitly studies the other's way of thinking. The Rogerian therapist, for instance, is focusing on the client's "personal language"; his client's experiencing is more important to him than the facts or events in the experience. Indeed, it is not unlikely that a "good listener" is not simply a person who listens to *what* another has gone through, but can share *the way in which* this has been experienced. Modern Gestalt techniques are also located at the J-C line, although in Gestalt the way of experiencing does not necessarily imply verbalization.

The last group of techniques attempt to bring together the completed J-C-O triangles. Here belong many forms of role playing. Imagine, for instance, if in the bargaining process between representatives of union and industry, between the diplomats of different countries, or between government officials and the people's representatives, the negotiators were to shift positions and play the opponent's role. The impact of this type of role playing might be very strong. Or imagine the father and the son in our example watching one another as protagonists in a series of psychodrama sessions. Or, have the father and son both play the role of a third person, as in Kelly's Fixed Role Therapy (1955, chap. 8; Bonarius, 1967a, 1970a).

This is not the place to explore the numerous possibilities of role-playing. As started previously, the remaining part of this section will be spent on the Reptest Interaction Technique (RIT). The RIT is an adaptation of Kelly's Role Construct Repertory Test (Reptest), which Kelly introduced as part of his theory of personal constructs (1955, chap. 5 and 6). At that time, the Reptest was welcomed as an important contribution to the existing battery of personality tests. In fact, until 1970 the Reptest received more attention than the theory of personal constructs of which it is an integral part.[4]

In 1955, the Reptest was indeed a progressive technique. In its original form, it provides the professional a means of sampling the important constructs which the individual uses in his relations with other people. The directions with the test are such that the sampling is relevant and representative of the individual's personal construct system, of his personal system of experiences (Bonarius, 1965). Compared with personality inventories such as the MMPI and the California Psychological Inventory, the Reptest allows the subject to tell about his experiences in his own language. Compared with projective techniques such as the TAT or Van Lennep's Four Picture Test (1951), it is more direct in the assessment of the individual's experience of significant other persons. Furthermore, Kelly already described an objective, nonparametric procedure for analyzing Reptest data (Kelly, 1955, chap. 6) seven years before Shepard's articles in *Psychometrika* (1962a, 1962b) started a whole new era of multidimensional scaling and well ahead of the recent developments in cluster analysis (Everitt, 1974; see especially the contribution in this volume by Seymour Rosenberg).

Although the Reptest opened up completely new ways of personality testing, there is no doubt that it was introduced within the classical tradition of personality assessment. As such, it belongs under the Predicting Model (see part 1). I believe, however, that Kelly would welcome alternative use of the Reptest. It can be argued that utilization of the Reptest under the Communicating Model may in fact lift up the individual to the position of the psychologist's fellow scientist. And it is this conception of man, of man-the-scientist, which has been the metaphor of the whole psychology of

4. The first reviews on personal construct psychology were published by Bonarius (1965) and by Bannister and Mair (1968). They contain mainly empirical research of the Reptest or theoretical issues studied by means of this test.

personal constructs (Kelly, 1955, p. 4; see especially the contributions in this volume by Miller Mair and by Alvin W. Landfield).

Given the Communicating Model of professional practice, developed in part 1, and given the Interaction Model of extreme responding, developed in part 2, the transformation of the *Role Construct Repertory Test* into a *Reptest Interaction Technique* (RIT) appears to be amazingly simple. As a matter of fact, it seems as if the Reptest is much better suited for interpersonal communication than for diagnostic prediction. Of course, in order to receive a clear impression of the interaction possibilities of the RIT, it is necessary to know the essential features of the original test. These important aspects will, therefore, first be summarized before we turn to a description of the RIT.

In the Reptest, the subject is presented with a role title list containing 20 to 30 different roles, for example, father, mother, friend, a person you dislike, your boss. He is asked to write down the names of the persons in his environment who fit each role. These names are called "figures." The experimenter then presents three of the figures and asks which two are alike in an important aspect and, at the same time, different from the third. This aspect or *construct-dimension* is written down in bipolar form. The pole applying to the two similar figures is called the construct; the other pole, the contrast. Several construct-dimensions are elicited by repeating this procedure a number of times, usually 20 to 30. All the roles are used approximately the same in the triads, so as not to bias the sampling. This form of the test may be called the *listform*.

Kelly also presented the *gridform* of the Reptest. Here the individual writes down all the figures at the top of a rectangle. Then, after having formed the construct-dimension on the first triad of figures he puts a mark (e.g., a V-mark) under each of the other figures to whom the construct can be applied. If not the construct, but the contrast applies, he puts a Λ-mark at the cross section of the construct-dimension and that figure. The end product is a grid with the figures placed on the top row, the list of constructs at the righthand column, and V- and Λ-marks scattered inside the rectangle.

From the content of the responses, the psychologist can derive hypotheses and predictions about the way in which the individual copes with his world. These hypotheses are derived as those from the projective test. However, in contrast with the projective test, the Reptest is directly connected with a specific personality theory, the theory of personal constructs. In his original presentation, Kelly (1955, chap. 5) gave some examples. With the gridform of the Reptest, it is possible to reduce the data to a few basic dimensions. The philosophy, of course, is that the psychologist can then better manage the given information. As noted, Kelly himself developed a "nonparametric factor analysis." Other analyzation techniques have been developed by Slater (1964), Bannister and Mair (1968), and Landfield (1971). There have been several reports written on the application of these techniques for theoretical and practical purposes (Bonarius, 1965; Bannister & Mair, 1968; Fransella, 1976; Landfield, 1971; Pigeaud, 1976; Van Rossum, 1975). No further attention will be given to these applications since they were made from the Predicting Model.

A simple but rather superficial definition of the RIT is the administration of a Reptest by two people to each other. This description is not very accurate. First, the test instructions of the Reptest were adjusted because it appeared from professional experience that they were not always easily understood. A very important difference with the Reptest is the symmetrical position in the RIT of the two participants. Less visible, but perhaps most essential, is that, in contrast with the Reptest, the purpose of the RIT is to structure the process of personal clarification and interpersonal understanding of the two partners: the RIT is used under the Communicating Model, whereas the Reptest is administered under the Predicting Model.

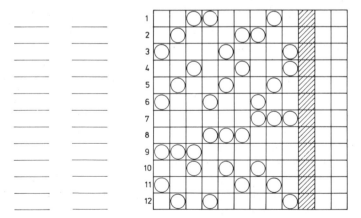

RIT GRID

FIG. 7. Example of recording form worksheet, Reptest Interaction Technique.

Following the notations of the Communicating Model, developed in part 1, we may designate one of the partners in the RIT as X and the other as Y. Following the Interaction Model, developed in part 2, we may be even more specific: the other people in X's personal world may be designated XOs (in terms of the Reptest, the XOs are the figures elicited from X) and X's personal constructs may be designated XCs. Similarly, one may talk of YOs and YCs. It may even be more appropriate to use the symbols XJ and YJ whenever either person is explicitly differentiating, verbally or behaviorally, between people by means of his owns constructs or by means of other dimensions. The application of these notations makes it possible to rely on the Interaction Model for future research. These notations allow for economical identification of each of the two partners engaged in the RIT, their separate systems of constructs and objects, and the effect of specific combinations from these systems. However, it is hardly necessary to use these notations in the rest of this paper. In these pages, the RIT and the experience with the RIT are only discussed in descriptive terms, without reference to quantitative, empirical research.

The RIT was created in order to make professional techniques available to nonprofessional people. In the area of personality assessment, the instruction of the examinee is often complex. In this respect the Reptest is no exception. What kind of adjustment would make it possible for two individuals without training to understand the intricacies of the RIT? It was thought that this problem might be solved by presenting the RIT in the form of a game. Most people find it quite natural, when learning to play a parlor game such as Monopoly or Scrabble, to work with a set of rules. There is little reason that they would not be willing to read the rules that go with the RIT, provided, of course, that they would subscribe to its purpose (Bonarius, 1976).

In its present, still provisional form, the descripton of the RIT begins with a short indication of its purpose: "to help two persons make clear to one another what they feel about other people, each other, and themselves." This announcement is followed by a short explanation, in nonprofessional language, of the main ideas of the psychology of personal constructs: the point is stressed that when I find John *shy* or *brooding*, I am the one who is applying these characteristics to John. He is not in himself *shy* or *brooding*; a third person might instead call him *quiet* or perhaps *independent*. That is to say, in calling him *shy*, I am revealing as much about my expectations of other people as about the way John himself is. It is further explained that my way of seeing John does affect the way in which we relate. However, because the characteristics *shy* and *brooding* are not "in" John but attributed to him, an open communication with John may bring me to approach him from other perspectives. Similarly, as John is now informed of how I think of him, he may become more aware of my expectations and, therefore, may feel more free towards me.

The technical rules are explained for each of the four phases of the RIT separately.

In the first phase, the names of *personal others* are exchanged. Each partner writes down at least 9 persons in his environment fitting the roles on a role title list. This list is adapted from the Reptest. It contains 14 roles, guaranteeing that each individual can come up with the required nine names. The participants take turns and work aloud. It sometimes happens that they write down the same person's name because the circles of friends overlap. This is allowed. However, the partner's name may not be used in this phase of the RIT for reasons that will soon become clear. The participants are stimulated to discuss the persons and to get acquainted with the people living in the partner's "personal world." In terms of the Interaction Model: XJ is getting to know the relationship between YJ and the YOs and YJ is getting to know the relationship between XJ and the XOs.

In the second phase, the *personal constructs* are elicited. This is done with the help of the triads indicated on the RIT grid (see Figure 7). Each individual fits a sheet with the names of the nine "personal others" above the first nine columns of his grid. One of the participants begins. Talking aloud and using the three people whose names are above the three circles in the first row, he tries to formulate a personal construct. His partner is stimulated to ask questions and help him to clarify his construct dimension. It is assumed that in this discussion the "real meaning" of the underlying personal construct will be communicated fairly well. The final formulation written at the left of the grid must be a short and simplified indication of this construct, and is understood as such by both participants. Hereafter, the partner formulates his first construct in the same way and writes it down at the left of his own grid. The participants continue to alternate, using the different triads indicated in the rows of their grids, until each has 12 personal constructs recorded at the left of his grid. In terms of the Interaction Model: in this phase XJ is getting to know the relationship between YJ and the YCs and YJ is getting to know the relationship between XJ and the XCs.

In the third phase, the *personal constructs are applied to the personal others*. The first participant considers his construct dimension at the first row and decides which other people in his grid the construct pole is applicable to and to which the contrast applies. Sometimes a problem arises when the construct dimension is too specific and depends on the original triad. In such a case, it is permissible to modify the construct slightly. The applications are discussed with the partner. This helps one to clarify and to communicate how in one's system the people are located with respect to the constructs, and how the constructs are more precisely defined by people. The application of constructs and contrasts is similarly recorded, as in the Reptest. Then the partner applies his first construct dimension to people in his grid, after which it is again the first participant's turn, and so on. In terms of the Interaction Model: in this phase, XJ is getting to know the relationship between YOs and YCs, and YJ is getting to know the relationship between XOs and XCs.

Both partners are now aware of an important and representative part of the other participant's personal system of people and constructs. They not only know what words the other is using, but also the underlying construct dimensions as discussed in their interaction, and as expressed by its appplication in the grid. One may say that each participant now has a map available of the other person's private life, where the constructs are the roads, and where the people are located at the intersections. The question remains, Where on this map is the person himself located, and where his partner? The answer to this question may be found in the fourth phase of the RIT.

In the fourth and final phase, a *personal encounter* takes place. Above one of the last two columns on the grid the participant writes his own first name and, above the other column, the first name of the other. In turn, each person, beginning with his first construct, makes explicit his view of himself and, at the same time, how he compares to his partner. The applications of the construct dimension to self and partner may be recorded on the grid by the usual Reptest marking. The experience with the RIT thus far indicates that in this phase some individuals have a great deal of trouble categorizing one another by what is felt to be impersonal checkmarking. The advice is to try it anyway, in order to have a complete record of the present relationship between the two partners. However, if this specific task appears too artificial, it will suffice to discuss how one feels about himself in comparison with the partner, how one would like to be, and so forth. Indeed, the most important thing is to take ample time to listen to one another's feelings and evaluations and, perhaps, to change one's construction of self or partner. In terms of the Interaction Model: it is in this final phase that existential communication and constructive confrontation is possible between the complete XJ-XC-XO triangle and the complete YJ-YC-YO triangle.

It is clear from the description of these *technical rules* that people who play the RIT work towards an intensive personal acquaintance. The intrinsic power of the RIT is such that the participants will have a knowledge of the other at least as intimate as the psychologist's knowledge of his client who has been tested with the Reptest. Under the Predicting Model, the client's privacy is protected by the professional ethics subscribed to by the practicing psychologist. It seems necessary to transform part of the professional ethics into *rules of conduct*. Under the Communicating Model, these rules may guide the participants engaged with the RIT. In the provisional manual of the RIT, the technical rules are preceded by the following rules of conduct:

1. The RIT is a confidential game. The partners are not supposed to discuss the specifics of the mutual disclosure with other people.

2. The RIT may never be forced on one partner by the other. Even after a start has been made, it may be that one of the particpants does not wish to continue. Then he should propose a pause or even an early termination of the procedures.

3. The RIT offers the opportunity for an exchange of personal viewpoints. This means that the "truth" of the statements must never be questioned. Participants may ask for further clarification. Helpful are remarks such as: "What do you mean by this?", "You just said one thing and now you say another; how can they be compatible?", and "Can you tell me more?"

The importance of these general rules of conduct is self-evident. It follows from the Communicating Model that particpants in the RIT are themselves responsible for keeping these rules. There is no outside agency, such as a psychologist, present to enforce the rules.

The participants are treated as mature individuals who will respect the intimacy and the privacy of another person as psychologists do in professional practice. The RIT itself may have intrinsic qualities which invite this responsibilty in partners in a natural way. Some of these qualities should be briefly indicated.

In the description in part 1 of the Reflecting Model, it was mentioned that the individual's self-disclosure might enhance personal growth, provided that the other person shows empathy, genuineness, and positive regard. To increase the possibility that these conditions are also fulfilled by the RIT, it is said in the provisional manual that the technique is especially suited for people who already feel sympathetic towards one another. The technique is not recommended when there is little mutual affection or as a means of solving great interpersonal problems.

Another aspect pertains to the reciprocity of self-disclosure. Cozby (1973) has recently reviewed the evidence that the intimacy and the amount of disclosure an individual is willing to show to another person is highly correlated with the intimacy and the amount of disclosure this person is giving him. This has been a reason for making the RIT an alternating technique. It is assumed that mutual trust is building up when the personal information from one individual is immediately followed by information of the same degree of intimacy from the other.

As an interaction technique, the RIT is not intended to produce a quick and vehement confrontation between two persons. The two participants start simply to tell one another about their personal friends. Gradually and carefully this is followed by a discussion of how they see other people, with the explicit exclusion of self and partner. Thus they have already clarified their own system of thinking before they are directly addressing one another. This procedure will diminish the occurrence of interpersonal misunderstanding: when my partner finds me *serious*, I already know from his description of other people to what extent he regards this a positive value. Indeed, the RIT implies a *contextual approach* to dyadic communication (see the contribution in this volume by James C. Mancuso) preventing unnecessary threat. Therefore, this form of communication will often be less dramatic than that of modern psychological techniques such as sensitivity training and Gestalt therapy.

At the end of part 1, it was suggested that scientific psychology should address itself to the development of more articulated communication techniques. The special requirement was that these techniques be designed in such a way that their impact could be evaluated empirically. At this moment, it is not clear whether the RIT can fulfill this requirement. However, compared with the communication procedures in modern educational and therapeutic psychology, the communication processes within the RIT are systematically and continually recorded on the participants' grids. Admittedly, these records are far from complete. In fact, only the conclusions of the conversations are registered. The most sensitive and beautiful moments probably escape recording. One should realize, however, that some objectivation of the richness of the actual communication must take place. In the case of the RIT, this reduction is done by the partners themselves. In comparison with the usual empirical procedures, their personal influence is thus maximized. If the participants want, they can provide the research psychologist with the representation of their interaction, economically stored in two RIT grids. From experience with the Reptest it is evident that this format of data is open for numerical analysis (Bannister & Mair, 1968; Bonarius, 1965; Slater, 1964; Fransella, 1976; Van Rossum, 1975).[5]

At this moment, it must suffice to indicate this perspective for scientific study. As yet, no quantitative research on the RIT has been performed.[6] However, the possibilities of the technique have been explored by a number of people, mostly, but not exclusively, psychology students. These students participated in the project in which the RIT was developed. What are their experiences? The general reaction to the RIT is positive. For instance, one of them remarked with respect to the personal encounter in the fourth phase: "The atmosphere was relaxed and familiar. This was not different from other talks we sometimes have. We rapidly came to say very personal things which we would otherwise not have touched so quickly, or even not at all. The constructs served as starting points." This student did not want to write on the grid the applications to one

5. In Hermans's Confrontation Technique, a similar recording of the communication process is obtained. However, some of the verbalizations are made by the psychologist who is administering the test.

6. In collaboration with Dr. Franz Epting, University of Florida, a research project is planned relating the RIT with Jourard's concept of self-disclosure.

another of the construct dimensions, commenting that "a personal talk cannot be represented in scores."[7]

The most negative reaction was that the RIT would not contribute to the already existing mutual understanding. This particular student reports: "As soon as we thought about the first construct, there arose a tense atmosphere more task-oriented. Although we see one another quite often, the strain remained. Indeed, this immediately disappeared after the last mark was put down." She also commented on the procedures: "It struck us that in some triads one intuitively sorts the people and only afterwards searches for a fitting construct. . . . In that way, the construct formation is tremendously curtailed and artificial. The possibility is then excluded of other sortings and other constructs that may even be more important." Concerning the effects, she said: "Meanwhile, we did not notice any more understanding of one another . . . , even when we focused on ourselves and one another with respect to the own constructs and to those of the other. Unfortunately, this also yielded nothing. We completely agreed with one another."

Concluding this part, a more extensive report of one other student will be described. Like all other students who took part in the project, she had tried out a preliminary form of the RIT with one of the members of the group. In that form the "personal others" were replaced by the names of the other students. This modification was used with the purpose that the students might become more personally acquainted. This one student described it as a very good way to get to know the other member: "The technique stimulates the exchange of concrete, very explicit and relevant information which, furthermore, is neatly ordered. . . . The procedure may at first appear as a very artificial and indirect form of communication, but my partner and I felt the opposite. . . . Usually, in beginning acquaintanceship, the conversation is confined to vague remarks; more extreme statements are quickly put back to relative proportions. Guided by this technique, however, one moves straight ahead to topics which induce deep and personal contact. The natural embarrassment when discussing one another is here absent because it is felt that it is the test that is bringing up these issues. If for some reason or another one still does not want to respond, then this must be made explicit, whereas in ordinary

7. This quotation and those following have been translated by the author from the original Dutch reports.

conversation the whole topic is avoided." This student and her partner did feel some embarrassment when they had to speak out how they construed one another, because "the application of the construct pole or the contrast pole was not only a representation of what one is thinking, but might also have a very clear and direct impact on the relationship. This scoring of yourself or the other creates the possibility that the other sticks to a statement which in such an early stage of a relationship cannot be considered as permanent and hardly as articulate."

This girl played the RIT with a male friend whom she had already known for several years. At the beginning she was very sceptical, "because I had found it a very useful means in learning to know a person and could not imagine how it could be helpful with someone whom I assumed to already know very well. I also thought that the RIT would put things under such a special light that only a 'black-and-white picture' would remain of the topics that we had earlier discussed intensively. In lacking articulation [in the application of the constructs], it might diminish clarification rather than stimulating it. However, because of the good experience in becoming acquainted with the other group member, I wanted to give the RIT with my friend at least a good try."

She continued: "My friend and I share several acquaintances. After some discussion, we decided that we would choose from them six common figures about whom we both feel strong emotions. Towards three of these people we have opposite feelings, one of us positive ones and the other negative ones. The purpose of this choice was to move directly to straight communication of new issues or to further clarification of old ones; these common figures would make us speak out about things that had always been lying around as either too important or too difficult."

In defining her own way of doing this, the student's anticipation of a positive outcome was much greater. While playing the RIT it struck her that, contrary to expectations, "it did lead to better articulation, just because of the fact that we already knew one another so well. This came from the very precise way of formulating the construct dimensions, in which we helped one another very much, and which took a very long time. We gave ourselves the task of avoiding constructs with moderators such as 'sometimes,' 'often,' and 'not so much' in order to derive the optimum benefit from the formulations of the dimensions." This student apparently discovered some of rich opportunities available in the RIT. She also became aware of its essential purpose when she wrote: "During the test-taking, I slowly began to see it from a different perspective. At first I had seen it as a task: the grid had to be filled out and, after the results came in, it could be evaluated. Later on I saw the test as a means by which the figures could stimulate me to an explicit, clear, and articulated formulation of how I viewed them within my own construct system. In other words, the goal shifted from clarifying to my friend how I thought of the specific figures towards a further communication to him, and a deeper clarification of my own construct system and its application."

CONCLUDING REMARKS

At the end of this contribution some conclusions may be drawn. In the opinion of the author, they may also be considered as major propositions. They require further development and should be subjected to empirical testing by professional practice and scientific research.

1. Personality tests and other assessment techniques with only limited predictive validity may still be of importance for individuals, provided that relevant behavior is sampled. Such a test must be described in simple and transparent terms and stripped of unnecessary "scientific" ritual. In this form, it may be transferred from its predictive function to a communicative one; that is, the test can serve as vehicle to the ongoing communication between ordinary, nonprofessional persons. This proposition is summarized in the Communicating Model (part 1). This model has guided explorations in the communicating utilization of Kelly's Role Construct Repertory Test and has led to the Reptest Interaction Technique (or RIT) discussed in part 3.

2. Experimental research of issues in psychology with very little direct relevance for human well-being may still be of importance for individuals, providing that it leads to systematic models. Such a model must be simple and transparent, and must fit the data without unnecessary numerical transformations. The abstract model itself may then be transferred to another, more important area of human behavior, and stimulate new approaches in that field. Experimental

research on extreme rating did in fact lead to such a simple conceptual scheme, the Interaction Model (part 2). This model has guided explorations in the communication between two individuals concerning their systems of personal constructs (part 3).

3. The theory of personal constructs is an individual psychology in that it studies the personal system of thoughts and experiences. Kelly acknowledges that each person is a social being living amidst other people. However the *Commonality Corollary* and the *Sociality Corollary*, which pertain to this issue, occupy the last position in his basic theory (Kelly, 1955, chap. 2). In fact, there are no specific indications as to how the personal constructs of one person may influence those of the other. An explicit focal point of the present contribution has been that a person's construction does indeed affect what is to happen. This leads to the imperative of personal clarification and interpersonal communication. The RIT partly serves the fulfillment of this requirement. This is made possible because of the fact that the RIT was developed under the Interaction Model which, apparently, superordinates the individual construct systems of the two participants. It may thus be argued that the Interaction Model transfers the theory of personal constructs from the area of individual psychology into the field of social psychology.

REFERENCES

Bannister, D., & Mair, J. M. M. *The evaluation of personal constructs.* New York: Academic Press, 1968.

Bender, M. P. Friendship formation, stability and communication amongst students. Unpublished master's thesis, Edinburgh University, 1968.

Bender, M. P. To smile at or avert the eyes from: The formation of relationship among students. *Research in Education* No. 2 (Manchester University Press), 1969, 32–51.

Binet, A., & Simon, T. A. Méthodes nouvelles pour le diagnostic du niveau intellectuel des anormaux. *l'Année Psychologique*, 1905, **11**, 191–336.

Bonarius, J. C. J. Research in the personal construct theory of George A. Kelly. In Brendan A. Maher (Ed.), *Progress in experimental personality research* (Vol. 2). New York: Academic Press, 1965. Pp. 1–46.

Bonarius. J. C. J. De fixed role therapy van George A. Kelly. *Nederlands Tijdschrift voor de Psychologie*, 1967, **22**, 482–520. (a)

Bonarius, J. C. J. Extreme beoordelingen en persoonlijke constructen: Een vergelijking van verschillende indices van extremiteit. *Hypothese*, 1967–1968, **12**, 46–57. (b)

Bonarius, J. C. J. fixed role therapy: A double paradox. *British Journal of Medical Psychology*, 1970, **43**, 213–219. (a)

Bonarius, J. C. J. Personal construct psychology and extreme response style. Doctoral dissertation, University of Groningen, Netherlands, 1970. (b)

Bonarius, J. C. J. Response style psychology: The rise and the fall of a fashion. Utrecht: Psychologische Geschriften, PG–75–42–EX, 1975.

Bonarius, J. C. J. Reptest interaction technique: Manual. Utrecht: Psychologische Geschriften, PG–76–13–EX, 1976. (Dutch version in Psychologische Geschriften, PG–76–12–EX, 1976.)

Buytendijk, F. J. J. *Algemene theorie der menselijke houding en beweging*. Utrecht: Spectrum, 1957.

Cozby, P. C. Self-disclosure: A literature review. *Psychological Bulletin*, 1973, **79**, 73–91.

Cromwell, R. L., & Caldwell, D. R. A comparison of ratings based on personal constructs of self and others. *Journal of Clinical Psychology*, 1962, **18**, 43–46.

Cronbach, L. J., Response sets and test validity. *Educational Psychological Measurement*, 1946, **6**, 475–494.

De Groot, A. D. *Een minimale methodologie op sociaal wetenschappelijke basis*. The Hague, Netherlands: Mouton, 1971.

Dijkhuis, J. H. *Klinische benadering en klinische psychologie*. Utrecht: Bijleveld, 1965.

Dilthey, W. *Einleitung in die Geisteswissenschaften* (Gesammelte Schriften, Vol. 1). Stuttgart: Teubner, 1959. (Originally published, 1883.)

Everitt, B. *Cluster analysis*. London: Heineman, 1974.

Fransella, F. The theory and measurement of personal constructs. In K. Granvill-Grossman (Ed.), *Recent advances in clinical psychiatry*. Edinburgh: Churchill Livingstone, 1976. Pp. 81–113.

Hall, C. S., & Lindzey, G. *Theories of personality*. New York: Wiley, 1957.

Hamilton, D. L. Personality attributes associated with extreme response style. *Psychological Bulletin*, 1968, **69**, 192–203.

Hermans, H. J. M. *Waardegebieden en hun ontwikkeling: Theorie en methode van zelf-confrontatie*. Amsterdam: Swets & Zeitlinger, 1974.

Hofstee, W. K. B. *Psychologische uitspraken over personen*. Deventer, Netherlands: Van Loghum Slaterus, 1974.

Husserl, E. *Logische Untersuchungen.* Halle, E. Germany, 1900.

Isaacson, G. S. A comparative study of the meaningfulness of personal and common constructs. Unpublished doctoral dissertation, University of Missouri, 1966.

Isaacson, G. S., & Landfield, A. W. Meaningfulness of personal versus common constructs. *Journal of Individual Psychology,* 1965, **21,** 160–166.

Kaplan, A. *The conduct of inquiry.* San Francisco: Chandler, 1964.

Kelly, G. A. *The psychology of personal constructs.* New York: Norton, 1955.

Koltuv, B. B. Some characteristics of intrajudge trait intercorrelations. *Psychological Monographs,* 1962, **76,** (33, Whole No. 552).

Kouwer, B. J. *Existentiele psychologie: Grondslagen van het psychologische gesprek.* Meppel, Netherlands: Boom, 1973.

Landfield, A. W. Meaningfulness of self, ideal and other as related to own versus therapist's personal construct dimensions. *Psychological Reports,* 1965, **16,** 605–608.

Landfield, A. W. *Personal construct systems in psychotherapy.* Chicago: Rand McNally, 1971.

Linschoten, J., & Van den Berg, J. H. *Persoon en wereld.* Utrecht: Bijleveld, 1953.

Miller, G. A. Psychology as a means of promoting human welfare. *American Psychologist,* 1969, **24,** 1063–1075.

Mischel, W. *Introduction to personality.* New York: Holt, 1971.

Mitsos, S. B. Personal constructs and the semantic differential. *Journal of Abnormal and Social Psychology,* 1961, **62,** 433–434.

Mogar, R. E. Three versions of the F scale and performance on the semantic differential. *Journal of Abnormal and Social Psychology,* 1960, **60,** 262–265.

O'Donovan, D. Rating extremity: Pathology or meaningfulness? *Psychological Review,* 1965, **72,** 358–372.

Pigeaud, R. Waarnemingen van overeenkomsten tussen zelf en anderen. Utrecht: Psychologische Geschriften, PG-76-01-IN, 1976.

Rogers, C. R. *Counseling and psychotherapy.* Boston: Houghton Mifflin, 1942.

Rogers, C. R. *Client-centered therapy.* Boston: Houghton Mifflin, 1951.

Rogers, C. R. The necessary and sufficient conditions of therapeutic personality change. *Journal of Consulting Psychology,* 1957, **21,** 95–103.

Shepard, R. N. The analysis of proximities: Multidimensional scaling with an unknown distance function. I. *Psychometrika,* 1962, **27,** 125–139. (a)

Shepard, R. N. The analysis of proximities: Multidimensional scaling with an unknown distance function. II. *Psychometrika*, 1962, **27**, 219–246. (b)

Slater, P. *The principal components of a repertory grid.* London: Vincent Andrew, 1964.

Spranger, E. *Lebensformen, Geisteswissenschaftliche Psychologie und Ethik der Persönlichkeit.* Tübingen, W. Germany: Neomarius, 1950.

Van den Berg, J. H. *The phenomenological approach to psychiatry.* Springfield, Ill: Charles C. Thomas, 1955.

Van Lennep, D. J. The four-picture test. In H. H. Anderson & G. L. Anderson (Eds.), *An introduction to projective techniques.* Englewood Cliffs, N.J.: Prentice-Hall, 1951.

Van Rossum, G. Effect-evaluatie in de casuistiek met de repertory-grid techniek. *De psycholoog*, 1975, **10**, 490–501.

Wilde, G. J. S. *Neurotische labiliteit, gemeten volgens de vragenlijstmethode.* Amsterdam: Van Rossem, 1961.

Winer, B. J. *Statistical principles in experimental design.* New York: McGraw-Hill, 1962.

Addendum

*T*he format of the Nebraska Symposium was modified this year to accommodate visitors from other states and foreign countries and to maximize the impact of the symposium on both the speaker and his audience. The symposium was held for one week rather than in two separate shorter sessions and speakers were asked to attend the entire symposium. In addition to the speakers, a number of psychologists, all members of the Clearing House for Personal Construct Research, were invited and led small discussion groups which formed after each lecture. One-third of these sessions were tape-recorded. Participants also were asked to state their views about the issues and themes which they encountered in the small groups.

Since the format for the small groups was unstructured and discussion leaders were asked not to restrict conversation to the previous lecture, there was considerable variation of discussion within and between groups. Max Lewis, who assisted in recording small group discussions, noted that several major themes emerged in the sessions. Sarbin's presentation set the stage with the contextual theme. Much of the discussion centered on whether individual construct systems are usefully analyzed in isolation, and whether or not Kelly's Sociality Corollary had been overlooked to some extent in the symposium presentation. A second major theme Lewis heard was the relationship of personal construct theory to the rest of psychology. Participants seemed confident that the theory has a secure place in psychology as a whole. Lewis observed that the body of construct research is becoming more cohesive; people in other areas of psychology are accepting an interest in construct theory and methodology as valid; and both "insiders" and "outsiders" are attempting to relate personal construct theory to other research areas.

Some of the discussion seemed congruent with placing greater emphasis on the Sociality Corollary. The idea was expressed that psychologists should give their subjects more opportunity to talk with them and to talk back to them. However, one participant expressed the feeling that he might have some difficulty obtaining grant support if he too seriously considered unorthodox research designs. Another participant thought that the personal construct investigator should study communication processes between individuals, a point emphasized later by Dr. Bonarius. Dr. Laurie Thomas, director of the Learning Center, Brunel University, London, shared his ideas about "learning conversations" and his paradigm for conversational research which considers the "inner person" of the learner.

What is the Purpose of Theory?

Another theme evident in several groups can be stated as a question: What is the purpose of a theory? Arlene Lewis stated that one can do the most service for personal construct theory and Kelly's conception of man by elaborating it rather than by trying to prove it. Dr. Rosenberg commented that what was underrepresented in the discussions was Kelly's programmatic ideas for further research, particularly in the light of current work on methods. He then stated, "I think the best way of keeping Kelly's contributions alive, anyone's for that matter, is by elaborating it. It is not the purist who promotes behaviorism, psychoanalysis, etc. Look what Titchener did to structuralism—we still don't know whether there was anything worthwhile there as a consequence."

As to what Kelly was trying to do with his theory, participants felt that he challenged psychologists to consider new possibilities. However, he did not want psychologists to trade one set of fixed ideas for another. Kelly's theory was designed to encourage the psychologist's continuing elaboration and exploration of ideas and his willingness to play about with the answers. Even as the psychologist tests and supports his ideas within research frameworks, he will understand that they are temporal and context-bound and will recognize the inevitability of their reconstruction. He hopes that his efforts to talk clearly about his ideas may encourage others to use them as springboards to more useful or more profound conceptions.

Particularly relevant in this regard were some of Mrs. Kelly's recollections of their world tour. Not only was Dr. Kelly able to envision and plan out the trip at the most abstract and most concrete levels, but he seemed to have in mind a certain approach to data gathering and theory construction. Here the importance of avoiding fixed ideas is clearly seen in Kelly's actual behavior. He devised ten questions which he asked individuals at each step of his tour. Kelly's concern appeared to be in gathering such cross-cultural information, not to synthesize a set of answers but rather to elaborate his understanding by continuing to ask questions.

Ecology of Personal Construct Theory

The ecology of personal construct theory also was discussed at some length by group participants. Although Dr. Sarbin presented the broader academic context of the theory, there was much agreement that more personal factors also contributed to its development. Mrs. Kelly, who attended the symposium for two days, expressed the opinion that where the author lived contributed importantly. In the discussion of Dr. Kelly's life on a farm in Kansas, Dr. Bannister stated that he recently visited the area and was uncertain whether he could locate the place again. He noted the featurelessness of the Kansas farmland and that a person would have to impose structure on it. In reply to a question about the most persistent professional activity in which Dr. Kelly engaged, Mrs. Kelly commented that he always worked with at least one psychotherapy client and he never charged a fee. He perceived this activity as a continuing, personal contribution to society.

John Hoad, of Princeton University submitted the following statement of his views of the ecology of personal construct theory:

> The assiduous detective can find numerous references in *The Psychology of Personal Constructs* to people who influenced Kelly, positively or negatively. Four main tributaries of ideas are important to the philosophical position that he developed, whether by direct borrowing on his part or by crystallization out of the more general thought world of the 20th century.
>
> 1. Kelly was an admitted pragmatist, in the sense of Dewey and James. He took the notion of "anticipation" from Dewey

and he referred to Dewey more generally as one "whose philosophy and psychology can be read between many of the lines of the psychology of personal constructs" (p. 154). The notion that "truth is made" is strong in James, though Kelly was (by comparison with James) more guarded and less solipsistic in his presentation of reality out there and reality as we construct it. Bertrand Russell's critiques of James (in essays of 1908 and 1909) are worth reading as challenges and correctives to some of the things pragmatism could lead to.

2. Kelly was a process philosopher. Strangely, there are no references to Whitehead. But the thought of life as event, as flux, as process, is there, perhaps also stimulated by Dewey. Here too we can enlarge our appreciation of Kelly by enlarging our understanding of process thought and the critique of it. There are continuities ("replications of past events") that provide us identity, and there are experimentations that lead to new growth. Kelly leaves us to wrestle with the balance of these two. The wider philosophical debate may throw light on the issues.

3. Kelly planted himself in the stream of modern science. His model of "man as scientist" is subject to change and enlargement with our understanding of what science is and how it works. Einstein's relativity theory, that ushered in the 20th century, is a close forebear of Kelly's "constructive alternativism." Also, understanding the "range of convenience" of science as a perspective is important to what we can make of the model. Kelly had two main notions of scientific behavior: (a) to predict and control, and (b) to experiment with the unknown. The first lends itself to the data computation approach of Seymour Rosenberg and the second to the metaphorical openness of Miller Mair. A Bannister-Rosenberg debate in one group seemed to spin off from each taking a stand in one of these positions.

4. Kelly was influenced by biblical thought. His father was a Presbyterian minister. There is not much explicit reference to biblical ideas in *The Psychology of Personal Constructs*, but Don Bannister thinks it is an important element and reported in one group how Kelly once told a seminar that "Jesus was the greatest personal construct theorist." We may note that Kelly referred to Jesus' teachings about repentance as a rethinking

process and rebirth as a creative embracing of the future, as a preformulation of his own thought (p. 381). We may elaborate by adding that faith, for Jesus, is an anticipatory construct. It is eschatological, that is, it acts in the present with an eye open to the future. Faith is creative too. Kelly's statement that "no man need paint himself into a corner" is a correlate of Jesus' statement that "faith moves mountains." The British religious philosopher John Hick has developed the concept of faith as an "as if" perspective. Kelly would have been interested in that, for he was more concerned than most psychotherapists with the superordinate philosophical presuppositions that influence therapeutic considerations. Extending Kelly's thought, we may say that each person's "God" is definable as his ultimately superordinate construct. The superordinate eventually filters down into the subordinates. A further point: many of Jesus' parables read like a role repertory exercise in dichotomous constructs: "A man had three servants, two acted thus, but the third acted this way . . .".

Study of possible influences and the thought milieu out of which Kelly's work came serves to enlarge our conception of what he was on to, but it also underscores the originality and power of his own unique contribution. These four horses that pulled his chariot became a team and took new direction under the impress of his unique creativity.

In one group, the statement was made that Kelly was more interested in "text than context." Moreover, he seemed most studious and purposeful in avoiding a definite relationship between his theory and other formulations. Perhaps, from Kelly's own view, his theory was significantly new. Also, he may have been concerned about the possibility that his system would be lost if he used terminology which overlapped with the terminology of other theorists. It would have been too easy for psychologists to say that construct theory was "nothing but this or that other theory." Those who have worked with Dr. Kelly know that he tried to avoid statements which include "nothing but." He preferred propositional construction and stated that much of his theory is couched in propositional terms. In this context, it then seems reasonable to assume that Kelly wanted to make it difficult for others to perceive his theory in simplistic ways. However, psychologists, being facile construers, sometimes have taken the "nothing but" attitude toward the theory. One of the most delightful examples of how an author may fix personal construct theory was provided by Dr. Bannister: recently, a British author of strong Marxist convictions stated that Kelly was the last bastion of capitalism with its rugged individualism. The most obvious example of how psychologists may fix the theory is the tendency for "real" scientists to dismiss the theory because Kelly's "man-the-scientist" is not really a scientist but a "metaphor." (The term was frequently used in the discussion groups.) These "real" scientists may fail to appreciate the central importance of metaphor in all science and in daily living.

Constructs More Than Words

Another apparent theme was the observation that constructs are not just sets of words. They are discriminations. In the context of this theme, there was much discussion of preverbal anticipations and the communication of constructs in ways not directly dependent on a conventional Rep Test. Dr. Bannister suggested that "we discuss the discussable in a verbal culture." Implied in this statement is the possibility that verbal cultures may actively avoid that which is difficult to verbalize. The personal construct psychologist must attend more to nonverbal communication. Related to this discussion of nonverbal construction, comments were made that some people confuse cognitions with constructs and then reason that constructs are devoid of emotion. Regarding emotionality, two comments are of particular interest: (a) "We may not be able to say what it is, but we often seem to be clear about what it is not," and (b) "It is difficult to separate emotions from cognitions. To say that a construct is just cognitive or just emotional may not make much sense." It became obvious from this line of discussion that the second- or third-generation construct researchers will not avoid emotional construction or nonverbal communication as areas of study.

This section on nonverbal construction is well summarized by a quotation from a student at the University of Florida, Robert A. Neimeyer.

"Construing," warns Kelly, "is not to be confounded with verbal formulation. A person's behavior may be based upon many interlocking equivalence-difference patterns which are never communicated in symbolic speech" (1955, p. 51). Despite this caveat, researchers have consistently operationalized "constructs" as the verbal responses elicited by the Rep Test and derivative procedures, thereby systematically neglecting what is, perhaps, the greater part of the person's system. This is not to gainsay the importance of verbal constructions or the relevance of researching them, for linguistic articulation of personal meaning provides the vehicle for the sharing of human significances, and the importance of such sharing can hardly be exaggerated. Rather, the objection is to the *exclusiveness* with which we study verbal dimensions of meaning. Such explicit constructs represent an intermediate rung on the ladder of abstraction. Their focus of convenience is human action in the world; they leave shrouded in preverbal mystery both the ultimately personal and the ultimately impersonal aspects of the self. No explicit constructs verbalize the core of the person's unique identity, nor do they adequately "voice" the dynamics of acquiring a seemingly autonomous habit or skill. This is not, however, tantamount to saying that these facets of the person are devoid of bipolar structuring. Thomas, Bonarius, and others have demonstrated that a durable system for ordering undifferentiated experience embraces both tacit and explicit constructions.

Because of its unobtrusiveness, it is easy to overlook the pervasiveness of tacit construing. Upon our first encounter with the unfamiliar object or event, it is at first only sketchily outlined in consciousness; we may have gleaned from it only an ambiguous aura of its "style" or significance. These first tentative constructions of the new experience are tacit, and constitute the fundament of later, more articulate understandings.

Nearly all construct theory research to date suffers from a sampling bias, taking as its data only dimensions of meaning that are easily verbalized. Perhaps now, twenty years after Kelly's cornerstone work, it is time we accept the challenge to broaden our methodology and expand our investigative efforts in order to plumb the full depths of human construing. The subject matter for such enlarged study would encompass the panorama of human activity; for any patterned expression is evidence of implicit construction.

Man knows more than he can tell, and if personal construct psychology is to claim to offer any comprehension of man, it must elaborate its working definition of "construct" to encompass not only man's verbal formulations of his experience, but his preverbal understandings as well.

Anticipation

The subject of anticipation was certain to arise in discussions of personal construct theory. One participant asked, "Why can't we begin with a person's anticipations and order their implications for fixity and change? Why does one have to go back to biology to have a psychology? For that matter, why does one always have to consider early life experience as if our constructions of those experiences *now* were the constructions *then*?" In reply to these questions, the comment was made that some people need those kinds of constructs in order to go about their lives into the future. They need to erect some sort of solid base in biology or early life experience. It isn't necessary to reject how people go about their individual lives. Personal construct theory allows us to encompass all manner of life constructions, even those that are very different from our own.

John Hoad was concerned about misinterpretations of Kelly's view of anticipation. He stated that Kelly did not mean to "rob the person of his life right now." Anticipations can be of the *now* variety: for example, "This is the best way of handling a situation right now as I project things into the future." Hoad further states that one may speak of global versus detailed kinds of anticipations. An example of the global anticipation might be an "anticipatory conviction" about being adequate for whatever happens in the future, perhaps even one's eventual confrontation with death. Statements such as "I can ride with the punches" link longer-term, global predictions with anticipations of the "right now."

Validation versus Reinforccement

The concept of reinforcement received some attention following Dr. Mancuso's description of the effective parent as a "novelty moderator." The "novelty moderator" allows and encourages the child to see the world in his own way—to explore the world. The child needs to understand the constructs of others—the socialization process is necessary—if he is to communicate and to live in the world without undue stress and strain. The parent, as the novelty moderator, helps the child relate to the world without threatening or impeding the development of the child's sense of importance and individuality. The child learns to understand and appreciate the world about him in ways that do not deny his right to make some decisions or to have contrasting thoughts, even as he may not act on them.

When a parent "reinforces" a child within the model of behaviorism, the parent does not have to be concerned about how the child is construing his world. One does not have to concern himself with the feelings, thoughts, and constructs of the child. The parent need not employ constructions related to the Kellian Sociality Corollary, which states that one plays a social role only when one's behavior toward another shows some effort to understand the other person from his viewpoint. In other words, what you do as a parent does not have to reflect some attempt to understand the child as a person. Within personal construct theory, an essential aspect of being a person or treating others as persons is to admit the importance of feelings, emotions, and values in relationship to behavior. Most of us, even behaviorists, treat ourselves as persons and want to be treated as persons. It is the others whom we do not treat as persons. When the parent interacts with the child as a person, the parent may moderate his expectations of the child; may deepen his appreciation of his own values and the problems one encounters in communicating with them; and may, on occasion, begin to question certain positions he has taken. The parent, in the context of viewing the child as a person, is relating to the child, not merely trying to control him. The struggles of childhood too often are struggles against coercion—something superimposed on them as contrasted with something related to them.

Individuality, Commonality, Sociality

An unresolved theoretical and methodological issue which seemed implicit or explicit in many discussion groups was reflected in questions about whether some methods are too abstract; emphasize "in-common" man to the exclusion of the person; confuse "in-common" man with the "whole man"; or emphasize the individual to the exclusion of the "person-in-society." In other words, there was concern about how one might best integrate Kelly's Individuality, Commonality, and Sociality corollaries.

Related to the debate over individuality, commonality, and sociality was a discomfort felt by some participants about content postcoding of personal constructs which investigators such as Rosenberg and Landfield have found useful. Those who questioned the adequacy of current postcoding procedures employed the following arguments: (a) Content postcoding may be done in ways which fragment the individual, that is, by judging the meanings of individual construct poles out of the context of how the person organizes his system and what he emphasizes as most important, most organizing, or most superordinate. (b) Content postcoding may remove the construct from the context—that is, people, situations—in which it was first elicited. (c) The concreteness of content coding may encourage reification of the codings. (d) A superficial coding of a construct pole might lead to the misinterpretation of descriptions, for example, a description such as "fun." The term "fun" might simply point to positive and negative feelings used by a person who is limited in vocabulary but possibly not as limited in construction. One must be careful not to confuse words with constructions. (e) Finally, content coding of single descriptions may more easily lead to projections of the value systems of the investigators.

Although these remarks are meaningful and can be appreciated, some participants contended that such arguments, if carried too far, might constrict the investigator's explorations and elaborations of personal construct theory. As one person stated, "Anything which leads to interesting elaborations of ideas, either within the individual's meaning system or within the theory, can be useful." The feeling was also expressed that one should not confuse the particular postcoding procedure being used at a moment of time with a conception of the investigator himself. Granted, the investigator's values are represented in whatever he does, but the investigator should be credited with being more than just a particular set of research postcodings. It is the way in which one uses his postcodings that may be most important. Obviously, he could reify them and (paraphrasing Dr. Mair) become a willing victim of his metaphors.

But ideally, the investigator will not reify his content codings nor eschew empathetic understandings of how individuals think, and will be concerned about how to integrate individuality with commonality, keeping in mind that contents are embedded within organizational structures and processes.

Greg Friedman commented that although a number of reasonable and well-formed criticisms of postcoding techniques were given, some of the responses to these criticisms sounded a bit apologetic.

> Is it not possible that the effort put into developing such schemes may contribute to reconstruction rather than reification? Like the many Eskimo words for "snow," the elaboration of an area of interpersonal relations may aid definition and redefinition. True, we must be careful not to endow postcoding categories with some quality of unalterable reality. Perhaps the Choice Corollary is relevant here. It would seem that one point of this corollary is the active role of the person in extending meaning. Postcoding may contribute to extension and definition when viewed in this light.

Mary Ann Barr contributed a postscript to the discussion of content postcoding.

> We (researchers) are scientists (people) too—trying to understand and anticipate others in our research. A postcoding system can be thought of as a way of subsuming others' constructs in a more abstract way, one which may be permeable enough to subsume more than one set of others' constructs. As long as we (the scientists) realize this is our construction of their constructions and not their constructions, we may remain open to the inadequacies of our particular methods and try to improve them, always recognizing, of course, that there may be other ways of construing the content of constructs.

Man-the-Scientist Metaphor

All too often people assume that Kelly's theory can be disproven if it can be shown that scientists in the real world do not function as Kelly suggested people-scientists do. Greg Friedman comments,

My point on this, out of some personal conviction, is that Kelly was not interested in the accounts of scientists' processes but in the processes of their accounts! It is not that Skinner says he does or does not behave according to Hull's hypothetico-deductive method that is important. Rather, the question is, can we understand how Skinner comes to say whatever he does? He is free to construe himself and the world as he will, but that he does construe these things and then chooses to elaborate some aspects of his system over others is the personal construct theorist's point of interest. In other words, can we not understand by subsuming in our construct system the thoughts and feelings of those who would invalidate the study of thoughts and feelings?

Another participant commented that Kelly's man-the-scientist is not necessarily the idealized scientist or *the* scientist as a particular psychologist views him. Kelly tried to encompass the varied observational, interpretative, emotional, verbal, nonverbal, social, and anticipatory natures of persons. It is a good bet that Kelly used the scientist metaphor as a strategy for talking to psychologists, in a language they might understand, about their paradoxical application of one set of constructs to themselves and a different set to their subjects.

That Kelly could try out other metaphors is built into the theory at the level of constructive alternativism. In this regard, Dr. Thomas Karst commented that Kelly built a "self-destruct" mechanism into his theory. If Kelly's scientist is viewed as a metaphor, an "as if" statement, one then explores with it. One doesn't "buy it."

Contextualism

Drs. Sarbin and Mancuso placed Kelly's theory within the contextualist philosophy. However, Sarbin expressed the view that the contextualist "actor" is a broader conception than Kelly's "man-the-scientist." Debates on this point seemed to reflect the different personal definitions of *scientist* and *actor*. The scientist may be construed as most rational and cognitive, whereas the actor may play multiple roles in the context of an infinite array of dramas. The actor may also be construed as one who either is restricted by his role or is not committed to his role, whereas the scientist, defined by his processes, can be seen as committed, emotional, and exploratory. However, when the scientist is construed within the confining framework of his carefully articulated experiments, he might be understood as a rather boring, unemotional, and unsocialized fellow.

Some participants perceived the role of scientist as most permeable, encompassing all possible roles of the human drama. Other participants thought that Kelly had not sufficiently elaborated his "scientist" in the direction of social interaction and broader social contexts. Whether or not Kelly's scientist metaphor is a broader or narrower conception than the actor metaphor, there was agreement that Kelly's science is more encompassing than the stereotypic conception of idealized science as described in textbooks.

In the following quotation, Steve Skulsky presents his position on contextualist "instantiating" and Kellian "construing."

Sarbin begins by citing Stephan Pepper's root metaphor concepts. We are told that there are six categories of world hypotheses: animalism, mysticism, formism, mechanism, contextualism, and organism. Each of these root metaphors is a way of instantiating, making sense of the chaos of the world by using a metaphorical framework. Contextualism is that world hypothesis that uses the historic event as root metaphor. Sarbin acknowledges that this places the focus of contextualism on a pragmatic evaluation of continual process and change. However, he claims that Kelly, by utilizing the metaphor of "man-the-scientist," creates a purely cognitive theory that preserves the mechanistic notions of causality and prediction. Sarbin would have us accept the dramaturgical perspective of "man the actor" (à la G. H. Mead and Sarbin himself). He proposes the notion that an "as if" role theoretical analyis, that is, implotment, is necessary to include the social context of construing. In other words, he claims that Kelly's personal construct theory is not contextual enough.

Now, I am not a personal construct theorist; however, it appears to me that Sarbin has not given Kelly a fair shake. Sarbin would have us believe that his concept that thought is hypothetical instantiation is not "just" a cognitive theory, but that Kelly's concept of "scientific" construal is "just" a cognitive theory. It appears that we would need to examine, in turn, what the process of instantiating and the process of construing involve.

Instantiating involves not only conceptual thought, but bodily attitudes, feelings, perceptions, etc. This occurs because the "actor" metaphor implies taking a role that involves human action in a social situation. Or, in other words, imagined actions, thoughts, perceptions, and sensations occur because of a specific, "totalistic," interhuman interaction. Now, the only way Sarbin could claim that construing involves only conceptual principles is by translating Kelly's "man the scientist" idea into a view of science as a purely rational endeavor. Neither Kelly nor I believe in this limited a view of science. At least since Carl Rogers's view of science as consensual validation by a specific reference group, almost all psychologists have recognized the shared interhuman essence of science. Polanyi's concept of "tacit knowing" processes that are taught by apprenticeship, Koch's concept of shared language communities that use words to "tag" discriminations made by at least two people together, and Gendlin's ideas of explicating felt meanings have all placed science in its person-person-situation model. That is, science is not "just" rational. It is much more—shared human interaction with a multitude of feelings and thoughts. When science is conceptualized in this manner, "man-the-scientist" can no longer be set up as a "straw man," purely cognitive view. Instantiating and construing are equivalent when we realize that both are based on a view of man that incorporates "bodily lived," interhuman experience.

Possibly, to prevent some confusions, utilizing an example of actual human action will help. Sartre's famous picture of a waiter in a cafe will do nicely. Sartre describes the waiter as not quite being able to look "as if" he is "naturally" a waiter. All of his movements are a bit overdone: "he is playing at being a waiter in a cafe." This type of "as if" performance is not equivalent to a full-blooded construct. Constructs are "metaphors that are meant," that is, lived with commitment. When personal construct theorists speak of cognitive complexity they signify much more than purely intellectual concepts of roles to play. Constructs involve "totalistic" interpersonal interactions. Flexibility in living is not purely rational, it involves complex, nonverbal components. I, for one, would choose to be a waiter, not "play" at being one.

Perhaps the most constructive outcome of the debates over instantiation versus construction and actor versus scientist was an awareness shared by the construct researchers that they must more actively explore the implications of personal construct psychology in more meaningful social contexts. Mancuso's "novelty moderator," Thomas's "learning conversations," Bonarius's "interaction model," and Landfield's application of the Sociality Corollary within the "Interpersonal Transaction group" are attempts to elaborate construct theory in the direction of the social context. However, as investigators expand into broader social contexts, they should keep in mind that even those contexts are constructions of men—not "just" environmental facts.

FINIS

It may be inappropriate, if not impossible, to attempt a definitive summary of the exchanges and explorations that took place in the discussions at the symposium. One participant, Professor Herbert Howe, noted a parallel between the process of the symposium and personal construct theory itself, in that the sessions encouraged the kind of questioning and reconsideration which is central to Kelly's work. The following quotation (1970, p. 1) provides both a fitting conclusion and an invitation to further questioning:

> Like other theories, the psychology of personal constructs is the implementation of a philosophical assumption. In this case the assumption is that whatever nature may be, or howsoever the quest for truth will turn out in the end, the events we face today are subject to as great a variety of constructions as our wits will enable us to contrive. This is not to say that one construction is as good as any other, nor is it to deny that at some infinite point in time human vision will behold reality out to the utmost reaches of existence. But it does remind us that all our present perceptions are open to question and reconsideration, and it does broadly suggest that even the most obvious occurrences of everyday life might appear utterly transformed if we were inventive enough to construe them differently.

Subject Index

Author Index